HITLER'S
WARRIORS

HITLER'S
WARRIORS

GUIDO KNOPP

Translated by Angus McGeoch

SUTTON PUBLISHING

First published in 1998 by C. Bertelsmann Verlag GmbH, Munich,
under the title *Hitlers Krieger*.
This English translation first published in 2005 by
Sutton Publishing Limited · Phoenix Mill
Thrupp · Stroud · Gloucestershire · GL5 2BU

In collaboration with Christian Deick, Friederike Dreykluft, Rudolf Gültner,
Henry Köhler, Jörg Müllner

Research: Christine Kisler, Silke Schläfer, Heike Rossel
Translation: Angus McGeoch

British Library Cataloguing in Publication Data
A catalogue record for this book is available from the British Library.

ISBN 0-7509-2601-5

Typeset in 11.5/15pt Photina.
Typesetting and origination by
Sutton Publishing Limited.
Printed and bound in England by
J.H. Haynes & Co. Ltd, Sparkford.

Contents

Picture Credits

List of Illustrations

Introduction

'I believed – and I was mistaken.' This belated show of remorse by Hitler's field-marshal, Wilhelm Keitel, before the Nuremberg war crimes tribunal, remains an isolated attempt by a senior Nazi officer to face up to his past. Most of the top echelons who abetted the dictator in his war of aggression pleaded their military obligation to obey orders and denied any personal guilt. In a postwar Germany, which placed suppression of the truth above honest enquiry, they worked assiduously to create the legend of a Wehrmacht with clean hands, a Wehrmacht that was neither involved in nor even aware of the mass murders perpetrated by the regime.

From the very earliest days of Hitler's dictatorship many senior officers closed their eyes to the growing Nazi terror. From the beginning of the war, the Wehrmacht, led by its General Staff, was a dependable tool of tyranny. In the heady days of the first victories, many officers hoped for fame, recognition, promotion and reward. Only a few were willing to heed General Beck's words of warning, that 'a soldier's obedience has a limit, where his knowledge, his conscience and his responsibility' forbid the execution of an order. Still fewer summoned up the courage to offer active resistance against the criminals who were running their country. With an eye to their careers, the majority of senior military withdrew to their own sphere of duty and to the soldier's traditional obedience to orders. As the theologian Dietrich Bonhoeffer predicted: 'The man who is driven by duty will in the end by forced to discharge this duty towards the Devil himself.' His prophecy was to be horrifyingly fulfilled by the military elite of Nazi Germany.

Even when faced with monstrous crimes, resistance by those generals who were sceptical towards Nazi ideology remained restricted to a small circle. Not a single field-marshal on active service supported the men who almost succeeded in killing Hitler on 20 July 1944. Erich von Manstein was one who rebuffed the conspirators with the categorical statement: 'Prussian field-marshals do not mutiny.' It was a fatal vacillation: only the military leadership would have been powerful enough to topple Hitler's Reich from within. Moralistically, they described the only legitimate way out of catastrophe as 'high treason'.

At the end of the war, only a few of those to whom Beck addressed his appeal to their sense of responsibility were called to account. By contrast, General Beck held firm to his convictions and had to pay for them with his life. The two different sets of circumstances show at least that there is no such thing as 'the generals' any more than there is 'the Wehrmacht'.

Rommel, Keitel, Manstein, Paulus, Udet and Canaris – these six careers are very different, but all were caught in the conflict between obedience and conscience, between self-censorship and protest. The six men could not be more dissimilar. This selection of German generals (and an admiral) under Hitler is not wholly representative, yet in their totality these six revealing careers certainly help us to answer the question as to how 'it' could have happened. What made those officers place their skill at the service of a murdering warlord? What did they know about the crimes of the regime? How deeply were they implicated? To what limits did their obedience extend?

'Hitler trusts me, and that's all I want', *Erwin Rommel* once said. The Nazi propaganda machine turned him into a myth that outlived the Reich, which throughout his life he believed he was serving. To this day the legendary 'Desert Fox', the brilliant commander in the North African campaign, has his champions on both sides. At the pinnacle of his success, it seemed that his reputation alone was worth whole divisions. In gratitude Hitler promoted him to be the youngest field-marshal in the Wehrmacht. As an officer he had reached his goal.

But as a fighting soldier this was when his downfall began. From then on there were only defeats.

Yet unlike most generals in the Wehrmacht, Rommel had the courage to challenge Hitler openly about the errors in his 'leadership'. On 15 July 1944 he demanded that the war leader give up his supreme command of the Wehrmacht. The conspirators of 20 July knew of Rommel's critical stance and planned, following a successful coup, to appoint him as the new Supreme Commander – admittedly without informing their chosen candidate, for Rommel would never have given his approval to tyrannicide. Until the attempt was made on Hitler's life, he nurtured the deluded hope that he could persuade the Führer to make a separate peace with the Western Allies. The men of the resistance tried several times to open discussions with the field-marshal, but every time they failed, because of Rommel's unresolved conflict of conscience between his oath as a soldier and the loyal discharge of his duties on one hand, and his insight into military realities on the other.

Nevertheless, after 20 July, he was targeted in the 'clean-up'. The man pulling the strings behind the scenes was his long-time personal enemy, Martin Bormann, to whom 'the Führer's favourite general' had been a considerable irritant. On 14 October 1944 Hitler despatched two generals to Rommel's home. They presented him with a stark choice: suicide, followed by a state funeral, or a trial before the People's Court and reprisals against his family. Rommel decided to take his own life.

This honourable soldier never learned the full extent of Nazi genocide. He exemplified military virtues in their most pronounced form. As he saw it, he was serving his Fatherland; as history knows, he was serving a criminal. Like many Germans, he was taken in for far too long by the propaganda that mendaciously claimed Hitler's aims to be identical with German interests. When he finally saw through this deception, it was the beginning of a conversion, which perforce remained uncompleted. 'Minor virtues, such as obedience, discipline and bravery are marvellous', his son Manfred Rommel says today, 'provided they serve a major virtue: love of humanity or of the truth.' With Erwin Rommel this was not the case, and therein lies his tragedy.

With *Wilhelm Keitel* it was different. He was the archetype of the compliant soldier in the service of the dictator. His obedience knew no bounds. As Keitel stated after the war: 'If an order had been given, then I did what I considered to be my duty, without letting myself be distracted by the possible, though not always ascertainable, consequences.' His devoted attitude to Hitler earned him the mocking nickname *Lackeitel* (in German '*Lackei*' means 'lackey'). Like a broody hen he shielded Hitler from those few who had the courage to confront him.

Yet the field-marshal was more than just a bemedalled marionette: in the early 1930s he played a central role in the secret rearmament of the Reichswehr, which later made possible Hitler's wars of aggression. As chief of the Wehrmacht Supreme Command he was a key figure in the involvement of the army in the bloodthirsty activities of the regime. The terror orders that he signed – especially those for the invasion of the Soviet Union – paved the way for innumerable war crimes. The notorious 'Commissar Order' bore Keitel's signature, as did the instruction to transfer over 100,000 regular soldiers to the SD (Himmler's 'Security Service') as reinforcements in the perpetration of mass murder. The death through starvation and disease of over 3 million Soviet prisoners-of-war was accepted approvingly by him, with the comment that nothing less than 'a conflict of ideologies' was being fought out. In the closing weeks of the war, his orders that German troops should 'dispose of' deserters without trial, cost thousands of – mostly young – lives. The fact that Keitel, of all people, was forced to sign the unconditional surrender of Hitler's Germany, for the benefit of the Russians, in Berlin, is seen as one of the great ironies of history. Even then, with his monocle and field-marshal's baton, he affected the bearing of a Prussian officer, who had lived only for the 'performance of his duty'.

Yet with his submissiveness and his unbounded obedience Keitel was not merely a product of the system; he fulfilled the most important condition for the smooth functioning of that system: the suppression of scruples and reservations in favour of the unquestioning execution of the Führer's will.

Keitel's remorse in front of the judges at Nuremberg, his confession to having 'believed' and been 'mistaken', came too late, and in view of such monstrous wrongs appeared as naive as it was cynical. His last wish, to be shot as befitted a soldier, was refused by the judges. He was hanged on 16 October 1946.

Erich von Manstein survived the war. To Hitler he was the 'best brain' among his generals; to the Allies their 'most dangerous opponent'. His life exemplifies the majority of those conservative Prussian generals who disliked Nazism and distanced themselves from it – and yet waged a pitiless war as willing tools of Hitler. In 1940 Erich von Manstein worked up the operational plan for the invasion of France, thereby establishing his reputation as a 'military genius'. Senior generals had spoken out against Manstein's high-risk concept. Only Hitler consistently backed the 'sickle-cut' plan, which led to the greatest military triumph of his career – the victory over France. Following the invasion of the Soviet Union in 1941, Manstein and the Eleventh Army conquered the Crimea, capturing Stalin's strongest fortress, Sevastopol. By now promoted to field-marshal, he nonetheless failed to breach the Soviet encirclement of the Sixth Army. He urged Hitler to order a break-out, but the Führer refused, thereby sealing the fate of more than 250,000 German troops caught in the Stalingrad pocket. After the surrender of Stalingrad, Manstein hoped to declare an honourable military 'draw', but for Hitler that was unthinkable. After violent disagreements over the conduct of the war in the east, Hitler dismissed Manstein as commander of Army Group South. The great strategist was never given another post.

The attempts by the military resistance to win Manstein over to their cause were dismissed by the field-marshal. Deeply rooted in the Prussian tradition, to the end he felt committed to his oath of obedience. He contradicted Hitler on military matters, but assassination remained a taboo for him. He always regarded himself as a 'non-political soldier' who did what he was best at: waging war – without acknowledging the criminal nature of the goals Hitler was pursuing. In the end came catastrophe and his own recognition that 'in my upbringing and education I was unprepared for the challenge of Hitler's dictatorship'. In 1949 a British military court in Hamburg sentenced Manstein to eighteen years' imprisonment. But he served only part of his term. In May 1953, following protests by Churchill and Montgomery, he was released on grounds of ill-health. He then offered his services as a welcome and knowledgeable adviser on building up the Bundeswehr, the army of the Federal Republic.

Manstein was a skilful card-player but an innocent when it came to political strategy. He failed to recognise Hitler's nature and true goals; he placed his abilities at the service of a criminal in the belief that he was serving the Fatherland. That was Manstein's contribution to the downfall of the Germany that he, as a military commander, believed he could preserve. He was nothing less than a brilliant soldier, but nothing more either.

This was equally true of *Friedrich Paulus*. His name is inseparably linked with Germany's devastating defeat at Stalingrad. As commander of the Sixth Army trapped in the city on the Volga, he stood no chance against the overwhelming superiority of the Red Army. Day by day the encircled troops saw their supplies dwindling; and day by day the distance from the German front line grew greater. Nevertheless, for weeks on end, the battle-weary units succeeded in holding down a total of eight Soviet armies and a sizeable part of its air force. In doing so they made it possible for Germany's Army Group A to withdraw from its operations in the Caucasus.

But the situation for more than 250,000 Wehrmacht soldiers was hopeless. All attempts to extract an order from Hitler finally to evacuate the pocket, by breaking out to the west, ended in failure. The dictator had made up his mind that he would rather sacrifice the Sixth Army than voluntarily abandon Stalingrad, the city that bore the name of his most important adversary. He radioed his cynical message of thanks to the besieged troops for their 'contribution to saving western civilisation'. Paulus knew that his promotion to field-marshal shortly before the end of the siege was an order to take his own life. Yet he did not give his warlord that satisfaction: Paulus chose captivity. Not until the hour of his defeat did he refuse to obey orders – preferring to share the fate of his troops. On 31 January 1943 he became the first field-marshal in German military history to be taken prisoner by the enemy. The events of Stalingrad have been dealt with in countless books and films, yet the story of Friedrich Paulus' life before and after Stalingrad has remained largely unexplored. It was he who developed the plans for invading the Soviet Union. Later, as the figurehead of the 'National Committee for Free Germany', he urged his erstwhile comrades-in-arms to change sides. As a prosecution witness at Nuremberg he gave evidence against his former superiors. Yet until 1953 he remained a prisoner-of-war in the Soviet Union, as Stalin's most important trophy of war. During the Cold War, his decision to remain in Communist East Germany provided ample material to both German states for their propaganda battle. Thus Paulus, who always wanted to remain a non-political army staff officer, became for the second time an unwilling object of public scrutiny. It broke him. Four years after his release he died in Dresden – on 1 February 1957, the 14th anniversary of the surrender of Stalingrad.

Ernst Udet did not even live long enough to see that surrender. He said of himself: 'For the sake of flying, you sometimes have to make a pact with the Devil. Only you must not let yourself be devoured by him.' As the model for 'Harras', the hero of Carl Zuckmayer's play, *The Devil's General*, his fate was not forgotten in postwar Germany. Yet the authorial liberties taken by Zuckmayer have distorted our view of the 'real' Udet. The Nazi regime found that his fame as a First World War flying ace and as an actor in adventure films provided welcome propaganda material for building up the Luftwaffe. Hermann Göring himself promoted Udet from cockpit to office desk, as 'Air Armourer-General', where he helped to co-ordinate the rearmament for Hitler's planned aggression. The successes of the Luftwaffe during the *Blitzkrieg* campaigns persuaded even Udet to believe in the invincibility of German bombers and fighters. Yet, in Göring's Ministry of Aviation he was the wrong man in the wrong place. The gifted pilot turned out to be a poor administrator. As his rival Erhard Milch put it: 'Hitler rightly regarded Udet as one of Germany's greatest pilots; and wrongly as one of its best aviation technologists.' Out of his depth in a continuously expanding area of responsibility, worn down by quarrels with his staff and superiors, exhausted by unachievable targets, he was left alone to make decisions which were to prove fatal for him.

He spent less time in his office than on living it up and chasing skirt in the bars of Berlin. At parties and Nazi gatherings he was always the centre of attention, famous for his numerous affaires and alcoholic binges. Berlin socialites loved the talented cartoonist and entertaining raconteur. And he enjoyed his popularity to the full.

The Luftwaffe's poor showing against Britain's Royal Air Force destroyed the illusion of the indestructibility of the German pilots and exposed disastrous foul-ups in planning. Göring, the Luftwaffe chief, branded the 'Air Armourer-General' as the scapegoat and dropped him like a hot potato. On 17 November 1941 Ernst Udet took his own life. On the wall of his bedroom he had left a farewell message, full of bitter accusations against his rivals in the Ministry of Aviation. The last sentence was directed at Hermann Göring: 'Ironsides, you betrayed me.' The regime hushed up the suicide, announced that Udet had crashed during a test-flight, and staged a grandiose state funeral. His voice breaking, Göring hypocritically mourned the loss of his 'best friend'.

Unlike the pilot 'Harras' in Zuckmayer's play, Udet had no part in anti-Nazi resistance. His suicide was not the result of any insight into the criminal nature of the regime. His opposition to it went no further than making corny jokes in the officers' mess. Years of heavy drinking and drug-abuse had made him an easy target for his rivals to intrigue against. Of the heroic airman of Nazi propaganda, nothing remained but the handsome exterior.

Whether or not Udet saw which way the regime was heading, he certainly gave no indication of it to those around him. He may have had doubts, but what is certain is that he hid the failures in his professional and personal life behind the mask of a happy-go-lucky boozer, until he was such a physical and mental wreck that he could see no way out, other than the theatrical exit he himself chose.

Wilhelm Canaris did not have the opportunity to commit suicide; he was executed by the regime he had served. His espionage network was talked of as Hitler's 'miracle weapon' on the invisible battleground of the secret services. Because of his contacts with the men who attempted to assassinate Hitler, and because he was murdered in a concentration camp, Canaris became a legend of the military resistance: the head of the Abwehr, German military intelligence, was a master of disguise and of the double game. Discreetly and efficiently his spies paved the way for Hitler's wars of aggression, while Canaris himself worked for the removal of the dictator. He urged his staff to co-operate closely with the Gestapo, Germany's much-feared secret police, while he himself, under the guise of secret service operations, was organising the escape of victims of political and racial persecution.

The admiral's high-risk game is typified by his love–hate relationship with the head of the SS Security Service, Reinhard Heydrich: while Abwehr agents and their rivals from Heydrich's Central Office of Reich Security fought a bitter turf-war behind the scenes, the two bosses maintained a private 'friendship' for many years, with musical evenings and morning rides together.

How necessary was it for a man to be Hitler's accomplice, in order to be able to remain his adversary? As chief of the Secret Field Police Canaris was responsible for the part it played in the atrocities committed behind the Polish and Russian fronts. Yet at the same time he acted as 'guardian angel' to resisters on his staff, like Hans Oster and Hans von Dohnanyi, whose plans to overthrow Hitler he actively encouraged.

At the beginning of 1944 blunders in the Abwehr's espionage operations provided a pretext for sidelining Canaris, already under suspicion, and placing him in an unimportant job. After the attempt on Hitler's life on 20 July 1944, the admiral was arrested and finally imprisoned in Flossenbürg concentration camp. Only a few days before the war ended, he was murdered by an SS death squad.

Not until the very last moment did Canaris, under interrogation, confess to any involvement with the resistance. Since being appointed secret service chief he had tried to play both ends against the middle and had become hopelessly trapped between obedience and morality. Without his help many people would not have been rescued; under his orders far too many died. Like many conservatives from the Kaiser's era he considered he was serving the Fatherland, rather than aiding Hitler. To the very end he clung to this mistaken belief.

I would like to thank all those who helped in the writing of this book: the authors Christian Deick, Friederike Dreykluft, Rudolf Gültner, Henry Köhler and Jörg Müllner, the researchers Silke Schläfer, Christine Kisler and Heike Rossel; and my specialist advisers Ralf Georg Reuth, Winfried Meyer, Sönke Neitzel, Torsten Dietrich and Armand von Ishoven. Above all I would like to thank my editor Johannes Jacob, without whose sensitivity and skill this book would not have been possible.

CHAPTER ONE

The Idol – Erwin Rommel

Give your sweat freely – but not your blood

Courage is the conquest of fear

The German Wehrmacht is the sword of the new German ideology

The Führer knows exactly what is right for us

Hitler trusts me, and that's all I want

That pathological liar has now gone completely insane; he has inflicted his pure sadism on the men of 20 July, and we have not seen the end of it!

The war is as good as lost!

Hitler dead is more dangerous than Hitler alive

I have no feelings of guilt. I was involved in no crime. All my life, I have only served my Fatherland

Erwin Rommel

———————— * ————————

Rommel, Rommel, Rommel, Rommel! What else matters but beating him?

Winston Churchill

Germany has produced many ruthlessly able generals. Rommel was of a different calibre. He stood head and shoulders above them.

Sir Claude Auchinleck, C-in-C of British forces in the Middle East

The German people, placing its faithful trust in your qualities of leadership and in the bravery of the German and Italian troops under your command, will pursue with me the heroic struggle to defend Italy.

Adolf Hitler

I myself thought Rommel a very conceited man, who adored having himself photographed from morn till night. However, experience shows that vain people are never the most capable, because a really able man does not find it necessary to thrust himself continually in front of the cameras.

Martin Bormann, Hitler's 'secretary'

My father was actually a very warm-hearted person. It was just that he hid it all under a hard shell. It affected him deeply when men he knew were killed or wounded.

Manfred Rommel

In retrospect, Rommel was one of the most arrogant military figures I ever met. This showed itself particularly in his behaviour towards his inferiors.

Baldur von Schirach

Rommel's a wolf-cub; he's no fox.

Gerd von Runstedt, C-in-C of German forces in the West

My husband is the greatest optimist. When he sees a bright light anywhere, he makes for it. But if he doesn't see one, and makes a judgement, his judgement is still the right one.

Lucie Rommel

Any man who fell under his spell became a soldier. Despite the immense pressures on him, he possessed apparently inexhaustible strength and vitality, the ability to get into the mind of his opponent and to anticipate his probable reaction. His planning was full of surprises, intuitive, spontaneous and not always easy to interpret.

Theodor Werner, latterly Rommel's ordnance-officer

Rommel's character defects single him out as a particularly disagreeable phenomenon, but someone with whom no one wants to pick a quarrel, because of his brutal methods and of the support he gets from the very top.

Franz Halder, Chief of the Army General Staff

Maybe Rommel wasn't a great strategist. But he was definitely the best man in the whole German army for the desert war.

General Fritz Bayerlein

There is no doubt that Rommel placed great hopes in Hitler and then saw these hopes shamefully dashed. Equally I have no doubt that Hitler placed great hopes in Rommel and was also disappointed in the end.

Meinhard Glanz, retired general in the German Afrika Korps

Rommel is a difficult man to deal with, because he does not like being subordinate. In Africa he was very independent.

Wilhelm Keitel, Chief of Staff of the Combined Services High Command

Rommel's resistance to Hitler's tyranny, which cost him his life, I consider a further credit to him.

Winston Churchill

The Führer did not wish to humiliate him before the German people, and therefore gave him the opportunity to take his own life by means of a poison pill, given to him by the two generals as they drove along. Death would have occurred within three seconds. Had he refused, he was to be arrested immediately and taken before the People's Court in Berlin. My father chose to take his own life.

Manfred Rommel

I would like to make it clear once again that my husband had nothing to do with the preparation or carrying out of the [assassination plot of] 20 July, and that, as a soldier, he refused to go down that path. Throughout his career he was always a soldier, never a politician.

Lucie Rommel

———————————————   *   ———————————————

The decor in the Ministry of Propaganda in Berlin was far from the usual Nazi bombast. In the place of white marble there was only a whitewashed wall. The emblems of the Third Reich were conspicuously absent. No banners, no torch-bearers, no cathedral of light, just a spotlight in which the leading actor cast an outsize shadow.

The man looked like the archetypal German soldier: blond and blue-eyed, matching the ideal of the period, with striking features; it seemed as though the Führer's favourite sculptor, Arno Breker, had carved them in stone. But it was not for this reason that he had been promoted to be the Wehrmacht's most-filmed general. The victorious army commander, who was now projecting his whole charisma as the cameras rolled, fitted perfectly with the clichés of Dr Goebbels' propaganda: an officer who saw front-line action in the First World War, who was one of the few army commanders to have been awarded imperial Germany's highest decoration, the *Pour le Mérite* – he was a daredevil, who had made the impossible happen. There stood the man Hitler had praised as 'one of Germany's best army commanders' – and he was saying what the top Nazis loved to hear:

he talked of 'victory against superior odds', and of how 'despite great difficulties, the task will be completed'. According to his creed: 'What matters is the will to victory', and in this there was no one to surpass him.

Goebbels had selected him for a completely new project: it was necessary to preserve for posterity the success of the German Wehrmacht which, under its supreme commander Adlof Hitler, was now master of the European continent from North Cape to North Africa, and from the Atlantic to the Volga. As Hitler's mouthpiece, Goebbels had commissioned a series of portraits of the victorious generals; Hitler's heroes were to display to the German nation the achievements of National Socialism at war. And the man with whom the filming had begun in the spring of 1943 appeared particularly suited to the role: Erwin Rommel, the victor of Tobruk, the hero of North Africa, the 'Desert Fox'. At that moment, no other army commander enjoyed such a high reputation. Hitler had promoted his 'favourite general' and now wanted, for his part, to profit from Rommel's successes. Goebbels' propaganda machine had turned Rommel into an idol through the reports of the weekly German newsreels. The Nazis were now exploiting their hero, and the hero let himself be exploited. In politics, Rommel was an innocent. For him, politics meant serving the Fatherland. And since the leader of this Fatherland was called Hitler, to Rommel '*Führer, Volk und Vaterland*' were one and the same.

And yet this scenario also clearly shows up the personal dilemma of *Feldmarschall* Erwin Rommel: despite all his experience in front of the cameras he looked unsure of himself, and spoke like a drama student who knew his words well enough, but had no idea what his teacher expected of him. Anxious for approval, he seemed to be looking behind the camera for his unseen mentor, asking, 'Was that all right?' But this was a general speaking, a man convinced of the military necessity of his actions – and who gave no thought to the consequences of his victory. If asked, 'Did you serve?', he would have replied innocently: 'Yes, I served and I am still serving.' To whom this deeply and spiritually convinced soldier was of service, he omitted to mention. In the epilogue to his book, *Infanterie greift an*

(Infantry Attacks) Rommel wrote: 'In the west, east and south lie German riflemen, who followed to the bitter end the road of supreme duty to nation and homeland. We are constantly charged by those who survived and by coming generations, to do no less than those men did, when called on to make a sacrifice for Germany.' A sense of duty and self-sacrifice, courage and patriotism – those were the guiding principles that governed his actions. Those words are the key to understanding why he acted as he did – words that can explain the triumph and the tragedy of an outstanding figure in German military history.

The boy who first saw the light of day on 15 November 1891 in the south German town of Heidenheim was the son of a schoolmaster, and thus not born to a military career. There was no notable family tradition of service in the armed forces. Since the officer corps was a snobbish world, it did not greatly help your path to the top if you came from the intellectual middle class of provincial Swabia. Even his physical characteristics hardly singled Erwin Rommel out for a life of soldiering. As a child he was small and pale. His scholarly achievements at the local secondary school were average, and while he showed a particular aptitude for mathematics, the fine arts interested him but little. His ambition was to be an aeronautical engineer, and he was keen to get a job at the Zeppelin factory in nearby Friedrichshafen, on Lake Constance. But his father had other ideas for the future of his eldest son: he was to become an army officer. Erwin complied obediently. However, both the artillery and the pioneers turned down this rather weedy young man. With as much obstinacy as obedience Erwin Rommel applied for a third time – and was finally successful. On 19 July 1910 he joined the army of Württemberg* as an ensign in the 124th King Wilhelm I Regiment of infantry. The following year, during a course in warfare at the Royal Cadet School in Danzig, he met Lucie-Maria Mollin, a headmaster's daughter, whom he married five years later.

---

* At that time, Württemberg, like Bavaria and Saxony, was a semi-independent monarchy within the Prussian-dominated German Empire.

Erwin's military career had a promising start. In 1912 he was promoted to *Leutnant* and returned to his home regiment, stationed in Weingarten, where he trained recruits. For a short time he was seconded to the 49th Field Artillery Regiment in Ulm. When war broke out in 1914 Rommel, even as a professional soldier, succumbed to the general jubilation, and wrote to his bride: 'So it's happened at last.' It was in Belgium and northern France that the young officer first saw action at the front. After only a month of fighting he was awarded the Iron Cross (Second Class), and then in January 1915 he was the first soldier in his division to win the Iron Cross (First Class), and was promoted to *Oberleutnant*. At the age of 25, now a company commander in the Württemberg Mountain Battalion, he had his first experience of leading a unit. The imperial army sent its keen young officer to the Balkans. In France Rommel had seen the reality of the trenches; now, fighting the Russians on the Romanian front, he gained his first experience of mobile warfare. In 1917 he found himself on the Isonzo front, between Austria and Italy, and took part in the battle for Monte Matajur, considered an impregnable Italian stronghold. It became increasingly apparent that this young officer had a talent for motivating his men, and was brilliant in adapting his tactics to changing circumstances.

For the first time Rommel was fighting a war on his own initiative; if the situation demanded it, he would ignore his original orders and do what he considered militarily necessary. His success proved him right. However, in the storming of Monte Kuk, he was denied the decoration he deserved – because, due to an erroneous report, the medal was awarded to one *Leutnant* Ferdinand Schörner who, like Rommel, would also become a field-marshal in the Second World War. Nonetheless at the end of December 1917 Rommel did receive the coveted *Pour le Mérite* for capturing Monte Matajur. He was aware of the special significance of the medal known as the 'Blue Max'. As he noted later: 'At that time it was an unprecedented decoration for a battalion like ours.'

As Rommel told his son Manfred many years later, he himself felt the honour was entirely justified, since false modesty was not his style: 'Even as a young man, I knew how to command an army.' The ambitious officer was brimming with self-confidence, and with every reason. In the fighting on the various fronts in the First World War, Rommel had already shown the characteristics that would later distinguish him: doggedness, tactical cunning, ambition, initiative and the confidence to ignore orders from superior officers. In January 1918 he was transferred from front-line duties to the general staff of No. 64 Command. In October of that year, just before the war ended, came his promotion to *Hauptmann* (captain).

> . . . thrifty, dependable and skilled in gymnastics.
> *Rommel's father, commending his son to the Württemberg army in 1910*
>
> My father spoke in the Swabian dialect, though with aspirations to High German. At home, or when he was annoyed, which happened frequently, he lapsed back into *Schwäbisch*. But normally he made an effort to speak *Hochdeutsch*.
> *Manfred Rommel*
>
> Back in the First World War, when I saw him for the first time, he was slim, almost schoolboyish. But he was imbued with a burning eagerness, always on the look-out for action, and fascinated by it.
> *Theodor Werner, latterly Rommel's ordnance officer*

With the surrender of imperial Germany, Rommel, like other soldiers returning home from the war, had difficulty in making sense of things. The former authorities no longer existed; the Kaiser had abdicated, and the old ruling class had vanished for ever. The unity of Germany was threatened internally by separatist movements, and externally by the policies of the victorious nations. Like most Germans in the years that followed defeat, Rommel had no more intense desire than that the fetters of the Treaty of Versailles should be removed 'no matter by whom'. With the old order, calm and internal security had also disappeared. Chaos and revolution prevailed. Hunger and cold threatened the lives of people who up to now had scarcely given a thought to power politics.

But fortune did not desert Erwin Rommel. The seasoned soldier was one of just 100,000 men in the armed forces that the victorious powers allowed the new German republic to maintain. Young *Hauptmann* Rommel, who had earned a reputation as a 'close-combat expert' in action at the front, found a billet in the drastically diminished Reichswehr of the Weimar republic. In 1921 he became a company commander in the 13th Infantry Regiment, based at Ludwigsburg, near Stuttgart. But in the years that followed, his career came to a standstill. For eight long years, whether he liked it or not, he had to follow the old infantryman's maxim: dig in and lie low. Then began a period in which the specialist in mobile warfare had to prove his capacity for mobility in peacetime too, and away from the battlefield. In October 1929 he was appointed as an instructor at the School of Infantry in Dresden. This training establishment had earlier been moved from Munich to the city on the Elbe, for a compelling reason. In November 1923, the young graduates of the school had shown undisguised sympathy for the man who, by leading a march on the Feldherrnhalle military memorial, tried to seize power in the Bavarian capital and ultimately the whole of Germany. His name was Adolf Hitler.

Rommel took no interest in the political notions propagated by the Austrian corporal. He saw himself as a soldier, not a politician. Consequently, he had anxieties about any future war, mused on the causes of military defeats and came to the conclusion that the army in its old structure, dominated by the aristocracy, did not meet the demands of modern warfare. The lectures he gave on military strategy and tactics were rooted in his personal experiences of war. Simultaneously he was working on a book in which he encapsulated his thinking on contemporary warfare. He had ample leisure for writing, since his career as a soldier was marking time.

In the First World War he had repeatedly come up against the limits imposed by military tradition. True, he had got as far as company commander and his outstanding achievements had added lustre to his service on the front line. But as soon as more senior assignments were being handed out, or higher-ranking officers were available, he had to take a back seat. Performance alone was not enough in the imperial army; family background and seniority took precedence.

Even under the Weimar Republic Rommel felt at a disadvantage. Despite several attempts, he was not permitted to take the staff course. The officers on the general staff, usually aristocrats, were none too keen on successful upstarts and competitors. The Rommel family could point to no illustrious forebears who might have fought great battles at the side of their feudal lord.

On the other hand, Rommel's superiors did not fail to recognise his achievements. They credited him with 'crystal clarity of character', describing him as 'unselfish, unassuming and modest, popular with his colleagues, and greatly admired by the men under him'. The CO of the School of Infantry, Wilhelm List, who was promoted to field-marshal in 1940, was one of many who praised Rommel as a 'first-rate soldier'. But in two decades as a professional army officer, Rommel had only had four promotions, taking him from the equivalent of 2nd Lieutenant to Major. So far, the great career he had dreamed of had been denied him. And no doubt it would have continued to elude him, had it not been for dramatic changes in Germany.

> Hitler had read my father's book on the First World War.
> *Manfred Rommel*
>
> In our family no one belonged to the National Socialist Party.
> *Manfred Rommel*
>
> He never asked anything of a soldier that he would not have asked of himself.
> *Wilfried Armbruster, one of Rommel's interpreters*

In October 1933 Rommel took up his new posting as officer commanding III Battalion, 17th Infantry Regiment, based in Goslar, in the Harz mountains of Lower Saxony. It was a regiment with a glorious past, which had taken part in the Seven Years War and fought against Napoleon at Waterloo. It was in his new function that Rommel first made the acquaintance of the man who by now had risen to the position of 'Führer and Reich Chancellor'. In September 1934 Hitler attended the Reich Farmers' Conference in Goslar. As usual, an SS unit acted as the Führer's personal escort and also provided a 'guard of honour'. Rommel protested, and insisted that his soldiers should form the honour-guard company. If his men could not be trusted with the Führer's protection, he said, he would stand them down. Rommel had his way, visually at least. When Hitler inspected the units on parade, Rommel's soldiers stood in front of the SS formation. What is more, Rommel marched second in line, just a few yards behind Hitler. But their relationship became closer than that.

The non-political soldier never joined the Nazi Party or any of its offshoots. In the first years of Nazi rule, when Hitler was consolidating his power and had to take the old elites into his calculations, especially in the military hierarchy, Rommel regarded this predominantly as something positive. Like many others, he welcomed the fact that Germany now had a regime which appeared to value military virtues like obedience, discipline and order. If there was to be an end to Germany's international ostracism – what patriot would gainsay this demand, repeated by Hitler like a mantra? If the army was to be modernised and strengthened – what objection could a professional soldier like Rommel have to that? When, on 'Potsdam Day' at the Garrison Church in the presence of the grizzled President Hindenburg, the new Reich Chancellor declared his reverence for Prussian tradition, who present would not have felt that the Führer was speaking to him from the soul – even to a Swabian like Rommel? In June 1934, Hitler liquidated the leadership of the SA storm-troopers, including his oldest friend Ernst Röhm, and decided instead to back the Wehrmacht. At that moment, if not before, there seemed to be a complete identity of interests between the new Reich Chancellor and the military. They had common goals, and now they had to achieve them together.

In fact, this was a deliberate subterfuge – but how many were aware of this, or even suspected it at the time? Rommel was one of those who allowed himself to be deceived: he believed Hitler's promises and failed to see that they were the opening gambit in a completely different game: a game in which a very special role would be assigned to Rommel.

In September 1935, only two years after his advancement to major, he was promoted to *Oberstleutnant* (lieutenant-colonel) and made head of the School of Infantry in Potsdam. The Reich Ministry of War believed that, in him, they had found someone who could improve the relationship between the Wehrmacht and the leaders of the Hitler Youth. Yet Rommel's mission ended with little success. His brusque military manner, and his constant appeals for toughness, got on the nerves of the 'aesthetic' Baldur von Schirach, the part-American leader of the *Hitlerjugend*. Rommel met with greater success as an author; 1937 saw the publication of his book *Infanterie greift an*, based on his lectures at the Dresden School of Infantry. In the next few years it became a best-seller, with sales of nearly half a million copies. His most eminent reader was none other than Adolf Hitler. A former pupil of Rommel in his Dresden days, Nikolaus von Below, was now Hitler's Luftwaffe adjutant and had drawn the Führer's attention to the book. Hitler's verdict was that it reminded him of the 'happiest' time of his life. Many of its descriptive passages corresponded to his own experiences in the First World War.

Two years later Rommel was promoted once again. At the beginning of October 1938 the newly appointed colonel succeeded in approaching Hitler's immediate entourage, though for the moment only briefly. He was appointed to the command of the Führer's escort battalion. In this capacity he saw at first hand the enthusiasm of the German-speaking population of the Sudetenland, who cheered the invader of Czechoslovakia like a Messiah and turned the Führer's journey into a triumphal progress. Rommel, too, fell increasingly under Hitler's spell. He 'radiates a magnetic, even hypnotic power', Rommel wrote admiringly to his wife. He heaped paeans of praise on the dictator of Germany: 'Summoned by God or

Providence to lead the German people upward to the sun', he wrote of the man who henceforth would determine *his* destiny too.

This assessment was based on mutual benefit. When Hitler needed to appoint someone to command the new war-school in the Austrian town of Wiener Neustadt, he remembered the author of *Infanterie greift an*. In order to refine his plans for a future war, it was very important for Hitler to instil into the rising generation of officers the modern ideas of a flexible and above all rapid and mobile form of warfare. Rommel was put in charge of the Wiener Neustadt school in November 1938. With his customary energy and ambitious goals, Rommel set about building up the most modern war-school in Europe, faithful to Hitler's brief. However, he had to break off from his work whenever Hitler had special assignments for him. Remembering his triumphant progress through the Sudetenland, Hitler would need Rommel again, once 'the rump of Czechoslovakia had been dealt with', when he entered Prague as its conqueror. Rommel was again to provide an escort to guarantee his security. But on Rommel's advice, Hitler did not wait for a large escort squad, but drove directly to the seat of the Czech government in Prague Castle. Whereas in Goslar Rommel had walked several paces behind the Führer, the German newsreels now showed Rommel at Hitler's side as they drove up the steep hill to the Hradčany citadel.

However, it was the invasion of Poland that gave the decisive boost to Rommel's career. On the outbreak of war, he was appointed commanding officer of the Führer's headquarters and retrospectively promoted to *Generalmajor* (major-general). He wrote to his wife: 'I've been told I have the Führer to thank for my latest promotion. You can imagine my delight about it. To have his appreciation of my activities is the summit of all I could wish for.'

In his new function he was in Hitler's immediate field of vision, was allowed to attend situation conferences, and – the acme of recognition – occasionally to add his own contribution to the discussion. What he admired in Hitler was that he 'can immediately grasp the essential points and draw a solution from them'. Rommel was more and more in thrall to Hitler. He genuinely believed that everything this man did was in the best interests of Germany. In

August 1940 Rommel noted in his diary: 'Where on earth would we be without Hitler? I don't know if there could ever be a German who has such a brilliant mastery both of military and political leadership.'

Rommel had become, once and for all, Hitler's loyal warrior – or so it seemed. Even in his private correspondence he now frequently signed off with the words *Heil Hitler!* In the spate of letters Rommel wrote to his wife, his growing admiration of the dictator, close to idolatry, is clear to see. 'I'm spending a lot of time with the Führer. This trust he has in me gives me the greatest delight, more even than my general's star. The Führer will certainly make the right decision. The Führer knows exactly what is right for us.' To stand high in Hitler's estimation meant everything to Rommel. He seemed to be literally thirsting for further signs of Hitler's favour, and proudly retailed each friendly remark in letters to his wife. 'Yesterday I was allowed to sit next to him.' He noted with satisfaction every little attention paid him by his adored Führer ('He is exceptionally friendly to me' and 'I was occasionally permitted to put in a word').

However, in the last analysis, Rommel was a soldier by nature and did not want to be bothered with matters of etiquette. He asked to be given a front-line command. The army personnel office initially responded with scepticism to Rommel's request to be given command of a panzer (armoured) division, and enquired whether an infantry officer had any knowledge of how armour should be deployed. Evidently Rommel was unable to dispel these doubts. It is probable that Hitler intervened personally on Rommel's behalf in February 1940 and got him put in command of the 7th Panzer Division, stationed in the Rhineland. On his departure from the Führer's headquarters, the new panzer general was given a copy of *Mein Kampf*, with a personal dedication from the author: 'To *Herr General* Rommel, in cordial remembrance.'

Wherever Rommel is, you'll find the front.

Army saying

> For those old gentlemen used to trench-warfare in France, the
> way Rommel and his 7th Panzer Division broke through . . . was
> an incredible new way of waging war. And everyone knew that
> Hitler had made it happen.
>
> *Winrich Behr, Afrika Korps*

For Erwin Rommel as a commander on active service, the war
began on 10 May 1940, in the Eifel mountains, close to the French
frontier. For the first time he was in command of a panzer formation,
which was organised on lines conceived by Heinz Guderian* and now
in the western campaign was to form the spearhead of the Fourth
Army. The 'Father of Armoured Warfare' agreed with Rommel's
views on modern warfare: 'rapid' and 'mobile' were the key-words.
What Rommel had written in his book on infantry warfare appeared
in a similar form in Guderian's book, *Achtung, Panzer!*

Commanding the 7th Panzer Division was very much to Rommel's
taste. Here he had a force with which he could put his ideas on
warfare into practice: rapid advances, taking the enemy by surprise,
with a high degree of independent initiative and discretion in
decision-making by the commanding officer. The period between his
appointment and first going into action was just long enough for his
troops to get to know him.

In contrast to the usual practice among commanders of large
formations, Rommel did not lead his troops from a map-table in a
rearward command post. He was to be found in the very front line,
gaining a first-hand picture of the opportunities and imperatives of
the battle – and this proved successful. 'Tight control of the fighting',
he wrote later, had made it possible to cross the Meuse with such
surprising speed. The prerequisite for this had been that Rommel
himself had been able to find out about the military situation on the
spot and give appropriate orders in person to the regimental

---

* Heinz Guderian (1888–1954) was a pioneer in the use of armour. In 1938 he was appointed
General of Armoured Troops and in September 1939 led the XIX Army Corps into Poland.

commanders. Rommel spearheading an assault – such was the image of this rising star in the military firmament. In the first five days of the advance, Rommel was twice decorated for his military successes. Six days after the start of the invasion his tanks had crossed Belgium and were on French soil.

His troops quickly became known as the 'phantom division'. A French general, in a subsequent conversation with the young army commander, gave the reason for Rommel's success: 'You're too fast for us, much too fast!' Risk-taking and elaborate bluffing, intuitive grasp of the situation and a tactical sense, a new reporting procedure that would later be introduced throughout the army, and the flawless deployment of a modern armoured force – these were what guaranteed his triumph. Nevertheless, given the enormous speed of advance, this style of warfare was not without its critical moments. Thus Rommel did not halt, as originally planned, in order to let his own troops catch up, but, riding in the leading vehicle, continued to thrust further and further into France. Protection of his flank, providing cover for his advance units as they raced ahead – these traditional principles of military tactics were challenged by Rommel with his new offensive strategy. Had the opposition been given the time to attack the over-extended German columns, Rommel would not have been in a position to lead his own units in such a way that a counter-attack could have been perceived and repelled. If the opposing French and British armies had had the time and strength to mount an offensive the consequences for Rommel's troops would have been fatal, not least because contact between the commander and his own divisional staff was by no means always maintained.

Within scarcely a week Rommel's tanks had crossed the Meuse and penetrated nearly 180 miles into enemy territory. With very low casualties on their own side, the Germans had taken several thousand French prisoners. The first serious test occurred when strong British forces pierced the German flank, but even this Rommel overcame with bravura. On 26 May, after the British had been forced to withdraw their Expeditionary Force, Hitler personally added a higher honour, the Knight's Cross, to Rommel's Iron Cross. The general was fêted as a hero in his homeland. A full-length film, partly reconstructed, called *Victory in the West*, made Rommel a screen star in Germany. A myth was born and from then on was carefully cultivated.

This acclaim did, however, have its disadvantages. As one of Hitler's 'favourites', Rommel was not particularly respected among the top echelons of the military. In the course of his successful thrust into France, Rommel had repeatedly made independent decisions, broken the rules when he thought it necessary, and despite all his success had once again provoked the disapproval of his superiors. No matter how much his soldiers revered him, opposition to his conduct was stirring. It was a Major Heidkämper, one of his divisional staff officers, who committed to paper these objections to the successful commander's leadership style. Thus opinions about Rommel among the most senior Wehrmacht generals remained divided. On one hand, General Hoth allowed that his subordinate had 'taken the command of panzer divisions along new paths'; but at the same time the Chief of the General Staff, Franz Halder, considered him 'a general gone mad', who frequently disregarded the orders of his superior officers.

Yet nothing succeeds like success. And Hitler set great store by the success that Rommel had brought him. Which meant that he also valued Rommel. The dictator knew that Rommel had made a considerable contribution to the victory over France. And Rommel knew full well to whom he owed this opportunity to prove his military skill.

As an army commander, Rommel's star was in the ascendant. In December 1940 Hitler wrote to him saying he could be proud of 'what you have achieved'. But the greatest victory was still to come.

> However, from the close of the western campaign onward, Rommel became increasingly concerned about the ideology of the Nazi regime and its conduct of the war. His anxieties were to be confirmed by bitter experience.
>
> *General Hans Speidel, retired*

> Rommel was a general who led from the front, who dashed ahead of his troops. To us young men he was the epitome of a military leader.
>
> *General Meinhard Glanz (retired), Afrika Korps*

In September 1940 Mussolini had proposed the invasion of Egypt. He did not want to be seen lagging behind Germany, which had just dealt a devastating blow to its 'traditional enemy', France. But the Italian offensive soon ground to a halt in front of the defensive positions of the British and their Commonwealth allies. When these troops launched their counter-attack the Italians lost eight divisions. At the start of his African adventure Mussolini had boasted that he wanted to wage his own war in the south, 'not with Germany, not for Germany, but for Italy at Germany's side'. Within a few weeks of the unsuccessful Italian assault, the fascist colonial empire of *Il Duce* was on the point of breaking up. He was now forced to go cap in hand to his German ally and ask for assistance, if he was to avoid complete defeat.

Hitler promised his help, less from a feeling of solidarity than from clear German self-interest: by supporting the Italian forces in North Africa he could prevent the imminent surrender of his ally and the unwelcome consequences that this would bring; what is more, he could tie down enemy troops and, most important of all, obstruct Britain's vulnerable supply-routes in the Mediterranean. It was a decision of strategic importance, reached at a secret conference on 3 February 1941, under the code-name *Sonnenblume* ('Sunflower'). Nor was it surprising that Hitler did not despatch to North Africa the first candidate that came to hand, but rather 'the most audacious general of armoured forces we have in the German army'. Erwin Rommel was the man who would extricate Mussolini's forces from the mess they had got themselves into in North Africa. Originally the Army High Command had earmarked other generals for this mission. The first choice to lead the operation was Erich von Manstein, the intellectual progenitor of the battle-plan that defeated

France; then General Baron von Funck was proposed. But Hitler opted for a man who had been deprived of general staff training under the Weimar Republic. He now promoted Rommel to *Generalleutnant* (Lieutenant-General) and personally briefed him on his new assignment.

Rommel felt under an obligation to justify Hitler's decision as swiftly as possible. When he first set foot on African soil, on 12 February, he immediately earned respect with a deceptive ploy: in Tripoli he ordered the few tanks he had brought with him to drive round and round the block, thus giving gullible observers the impression of a strength that he certainly did not possess. 'General Bluff' had pulled off another trick. An agent promptly reported to London that more than 1,000 German tanks had been landed in North Africa. It was an early example of the ingenuity of this unconventional military leader, who would summon up many a will-o'-the-wisp in the future. The new commander knew how to use the shimmering desert heat to give distant observers the impression that a massive army of tanks was advancing on them – even though they were nothing but improvised wooden bodywork built on Volkswagen wheel-bases. Seen close to, these 'Rommel-tanks' would scarcely have scared a child – but at a distance they could impress the opposition.

Yet the success Rommel achieved with his first offensive in late March 1941 could not be explained by these conjuring tricks alone. The military position of the Italian formations in North Africa was disastrous. The British thought little of their fighting ability: 'Sand in the carburettor is a far more serious problem than the Italians', was a widespread verdict. Around 150,000 Italian soldiers had been taken prisoner, the supply-stores of their German allies were in enemy hands, and the morale of the troops appeared broken. Tobruk, El Agheila and the whole of Cyrenaica had been captured by the British, and they now threatened Tripoli.

The inventory that Rommel took at the outset gave little cause for optimism: the Italian units, the Ariete armoured division and the motorised Trento division, were still not fully equipped. Even so, they were numerically far superior to the German formations, since the assembling of the Afrika Korps was only just beginning. True, the commanding officer was already at the front, but for the time being he could only rely on elements of the 4th Light Division under General Streich. The 5th Panzer Regiment, which was part of this division, only consisted of about 120 tanks. The Germans were still inadequately equipped for desert warfare. They lacked sand-filters for their carburettors – essential for survival in the desert war – as well as wide-tread tyres, which did not immediately sink into the sand. The German troops were not prepared for fighting in the desert. They were neither accustomed to the climate, nor was their equipment up to the challenges of heat, sand and wind. Many of them had a mistaken impression of the war that awaited them in the desert, and not least their commander. When he heard about his new posting, he told his wife in a letter that at last he had a chance to do something about his rheumatism in the hot desert climate. He had not reckoned with the cold desert nights.

On 19 February 1941 Rommel's army corps was given the official designation under which it would storm to fame: the Deutsches Afrika Korps. But it would be May before the 15th Panzer Division arrived in North Africa, bringing its forces up to combat strength. The supply-lines of the Axis powers by both sea and air were under constant threat from Britain's Royal Air Force and Royal Navy stationed in Malta. Another problem was the confusion over responsibilities. Even though, in the course of the North African campaign, Rommel made his career, being promoted from commander of the Afrika Korps to commander-in-chief of an armoured group and finally rising to command an army, he remained formally subordinate to the Italian supreme command. Not only did every operation have to be approved by the *Supremo Commando*, but the German OKH (Army High Command), which counselled caution on Rommel's part, wanted, before the main assault, to see a plan of how Rommel proposed to recapture Cyrenaica. And the OKW (Combined Forces Supreme Command), and thus Hitler himself, also let it initially be known that: 'General Rommel is ordered not to run any risks, and especially not to jeopardise his flank, by extending his column towards Benghazi.'

From 24 March onward Rommel put his opponent's strength to the test with small, and still rather cautious probes, in the course of which, at the end of March, his troops were able to drive the British out of their forward positions in El Agheila. A week later, on 31 March, Rommel's troops launched their first big offensive. Their objective was to retake Cyrenaica. The effect of surprise, combined with Rommel's strategic skill, made possible the first victories over superior British forces, which – by happy chance – were just undergoing a reorganisation. The new commander in Cyrenaica, General Neame, had just as little desert experience as his German adversary, while the British High Command, under General Wavell, was sitting safely on the Nile, far removed from the battlefield. Unlike his British opposite number, Rommel had made use of the previous weeks to get a first-hand picture of the situation and the requirements for an attack. Flying in a small Fieseler Storch, he had personally reconnoitred the terrain and noticed that the British were far from ready with the construction of their positions. What impressed him not least were the enormous distances that any assault would have to cover. Despite the warnings and even an express order from the OKW not to push forward beyond Agedabia, Rommel risked a further advance when he saw that the situation was favourable. Al Agheila, Agedabia, Benghazi, Derna, Mechili – these were the names Rommel notched up on his first advance towards Egypt. Within ten days he had pushed the British front line back almost as far as the Egyptian frontier. Everything the British forces under Wavell had taken in two months' fighting, the German general and his Afrika Korps won back in barely two weeks against vastly superior odds. A German newsreel showed a German soldier crossing out the words 'Wavell's Way' on British signposts and replacing them with 'Rommels Weg' – a visible sign that North Africa had a new master. The success of 'Operation Sunflower' was huge, and it created a legend that fed on itself.

He was considered a capable, courageous and dependable general, who led his campaigns brilliantly but with prudence, who did not fight battles for his own greater glory, but simply to win them. He was the enemy of the British, and of course it was the hope of the Egyptians that he would bring their occupation to an end.

Mahmoud Anis Fathy, military historian, Cairo

After his success in leading troops in France and now in Africa, Rommel had earned a reputation as a general who knew how to spur on his men. Even in the First World War he had demonstrated the ability to lead and motivate the soldiers under his command. His men soon discovered that he would not ask anything of them that he was not prepared to do himself. 'He wasn't the didactic, know-all type, who could do everything better than you', Meinhard Glanz, a North Africa campaigner, remembers. Rommel had a new style: 'Being a leader means taking care of your soldiers, sharing whatever they come up against. That's what Rommel did; and he succeeded along with his men.' It is here that we find the root of how he transformed the desert war. Sweat holds people together – in the North African desert this motto was no empty cliché. 'Rommel was a father to us, and he was more than that. He meant so much to us that even today an invisible bond of community holds us old North Africa hands together. It grew spontaneously from our shared experience of the desert battlefields.' That is how, moist-eyed, an old Afrika Korps fighter describes the Rommel myth.

The commander-in-chief did not avoid danger zones, even when his own life was at risk: 'Wherever Rommel is, you'll find the front', was a common saying. And the front was everywhere. So Rommel turned up everywhere to urge his troops forward. He was not the kind of general to sit safely in the rear command-post, making decisions at a green baize table, and demanding the impossible from the troops at the front, with no first-hand experience of conditions there. Someone who fought with him in the early days, Karl Zimmermann, can still remember today the special qualities of General Rommel: 'He wasn't the sort of general who stays well to the rear and gives orders from there. He was always in forward positions, alongside the ordinary soldiers.' Gerd Schmückle, later a general with NATO, describes the great respect that Rommel showed to despatch-riders, whose valuable service he could appreciate. Rommel was a general with the common touch, but also someone who drove his men to the limits of their endurance. When he saw a motorised unit halt during an attack, he flew over the resting soldiers in his Storch and threw a note out to them. 'If you don't drive on immediately, I'm coming right down! Rommel.' The story was soon making the rounds among the troops. It may raise a smile now, but we should remember this: if Rommel was hard on his troops (and equally hard on himself), if he drove them tirelessly time after time, then, as the former youth training officer, he was also putting into practice the ideal that his supreme commander imposed on the youth of Germany: to be as hard as Krupp steel, as tough as leather, as fleet as a greyhound.

Much of Rommel's success was only due to the coincidence of many separate factors, which no planning could have taken into account. It is our hindsight that transforms this into brilliant strategy. In fact, Rommel was not someone who developed elaborate plans, but rather he was a gifted tactician who recognised the advantage of the moment and knew how to exploit it. 'No plan survives the first contact with the enemy', was his favourite saying. He relied on improvisation, a rapid grasp of the situation and, above all, swift reaction. Despite his successes in North Africa, Rommel occasionally admitted afterwards that there were times when he had only a vague idea of where his units were located at a given moment. In the nature of desert warfare, the opposing forces at times became so thoroughly wedged together that it was not always possible to make out where the front actually ran. On more than one occasion Rommel nearly landed in the middle of an enemy unit, because wind and sand obscured visibility and he became disorientated. Halder, chief of the general staff, noted with irritation in his diary that this unpopular upstart Rommel was 'in no way fit for his command. He spends all day racing around his widely scattered troops, launches reconnaissance probes, and spreads his forces too thinly. No-one has a full picture of the distribution of his troops and of their fighting strength.'

Nevertheless, in 'Operation Sunflower' he had the fortune that favours the bold. Encouraged by his success, Rommel chose Tobruk as the target of his next assault. But his two offensives against this strategically important port, on 14 and 30 April 1941, both failed and for the first time Rommel faced major problems. To Rommel's bad luck was added the further embarrassment that on 27 April the General Staff had despatched General Paulus* to North Africa to report on progress. Paulus later described Rommel as an 'energetic leader of his troops', yet he too saw how the general repeatedly drove his troops forward, despite Italian anxieties that he was over-extending his supply-lines. He was a 'gambler' who forged ahead without the necessary preparation – such was the unflattering verdict of the top military brass in Germany. The chief-of-staff, Franz Halder, wrote in his diary on 6 July 1941: 'Personal relationships are clouded by General Rommel's aberrant nature and unhealthy ambition. His character defects single him out as a particularly disagreeable phenomenon, but someone with whom no one wants to pick a quarrel on account of . . . the support he gets from the very top.'

For there was one person who remained loyal to the man he called his 'favourite general', and that was Hitler. And Rommel justified the hope placed in him. After the failure of the German spring offensive on Tobruk, the British, Australian and Indian defenders of the stronghold launched their counter-attack, 'Operation Battleaxe'. But in the tank battle of Sollum Rommel and his troops passed the test with flying colours. The British and their allies had arrived on the Libyan–Egyptian border with about 200 tanks, with the aim of depriving the Germans of the territory they had gained. The attack began in the early hours of 15 June. After three days of bitter fighting, the British were forced to retreat. Despite greatly superior equipment, and despite support from the Royal Air Force, which had control of the air over the battlefield, Rommel's small army succeeded

---

* General Friedrich Paulus later achieved notoriety when he surrendered Stalingrad in January 1943 and became a prisoner-of-war of the Russians (see Chapter 4).

in repelling the assault. The British saw half their tanks destroyed, while the Germans lost only one in ten of theirs. The psychological consequences were enormous. These successes put Hitler in 'the very best of moods'. He congratulated his general, heaped him with tokens of his favour, and promoted him once more. Rommel's rivals in the General Staff were foaming at the mouth with rage. Erwin Rommel had now risen to 'General of Panzer Forces' and commanded no less than ten German and Italian divisions.

> The British newspapers are paying the highest tribute to General Rommel. This is a sign that the British are feeling uncomfortable, for they only praise their adversaries when they are being beaten, since that gives a better justification for their defeat.
>
> *Joseph Goebbels, diary, 20 December 1941*
>
> Only if he surpasses the normal stature, only if he is hewn from a special timber, does a commander of the opposing side gain such a reputation.
>
> *General Sir Claude Auchinleck, Rommel's opponent in North Africa.*

Nothing happened to alter the great admiration that Hitler had for 'his' Rommel at this time, even when his troops had to withdraw, as the new British commander-in-chief, Sir Claude Auchinleck, began his counter-offensive, code-named 'Crusader', on 18 November 1941. There was remarkable unanimity between Hitler and the officers on Rommel's staff in their assessment of the general. In the memoirs of Fritz Bayerlein, Chief-of-Staff of the Afrika Korps, we read: 'A commanding officer must be distinguished by toughness, dedication to his troops, instinctive judgement of terrain and enemy intentions, speed of reaction and robustness of temperament. All these qualities are embodied to a rare degree in General Rommel.' This judgement, from someone who worked closely with Rommel, was matched in a personal New Year message sent by Hitler from his 'Wolf's Lair' headquarters in distant East Prussia: 'I know that in the New Year I can rely on my Panzer Group.'

Indeed, 1942 was the year of greatest triumph for Rommel's forces – and of their bitterest defeat. First came the triumph: 'The fortress of Tobruk has surrendered. All units are regrouping and preparing to continue their advance', announced Rommel on 21 June in a radio message to all elements of the Afrika Korps. Once again the general had led the assault at the head of his units. As the minutes of Rommel's staff noted: 'After enemy push with rapid armour, CO personally launches counter-thrust, whereupon enemy tanks retreat.' The attack was a successful mixture of bluff, tactical skill, combat strength, speed and courage. By a cunning feint, Rommel gave his enemy the impression that his troops were preparing to advance on Alexandria. At the same time, the Luftwaffe deployed all the aircraft they could muster in a concentrated bombing attack on the fortifications of Tobruk – then the panzers arrived. They succeeded in driving a wedge between the British troops commanded by General Ritchie and in breaking through the ring of defensive positions. More than 30,000 British and Commonwealth troops were taken prisoner.

Rommel had now climbed to the summit of his military career. He had only recently been promoted to full general – the youngest in the Wehrmacht – and now Hitler appointed him *Generalfeldmarschall* and decorated him with the sword and oak-leaves of the Knight's Cross. When he received the news that Hitler would be sending him his field-marshal's baton, he is reported to have replied: 'I'd rather he sent me a division.' However, other accounts focus on the almost childish delight that Rommel showed when he heard of his promotion: the fifth in the space of three years. The new field-marshal was sufficiently vain to take a pride in these honours. The first letter he wrote home was signed, not with his name but with the words 'Your Field-Marshal'.

Most of all, stay healthy for us two 'men' and continue to bear with courage your lot as a soldier's wife.

Rommel, in a letter to his wife, 20 May 1942

> In all departments do your duty and be disciplined. That is your main task in wartime. I'm particularly glad that you're enjoying your service in the Hitler Youth. It will be of great value to you in later life.
>
> *Rommel, in a letter to his son Manfred, 16 May 1942*

'Forward to victory for Führer, *Volk* and Reich': it was with these rather hackneyed words that Rommel replied to Hitler's telegram of congratulations. But to him, 'Forward' was far from being an empty slogan. He intended to seize the advantage of the moment, defeat the demoralised British and their Commonwealth auxiliaries, then push on to the strategically important Suez Canal. Yet Rommel's thoughts were already taking him still further eastwards. As Wilfried Armbruster, Rommel's interpreter in North Africa, puts it: 'At the rate we were going, we might have got right through to Palestine.' For at that time there was still the 'Big Plan': the troops of Army Group South, operating in southern Russia, were to fight through the Caucasus, and then, after invading Iran and Iraq, they would link up with Rommel's panzers somewhere in the Middle East. Some of the ordinary soldiers actually knew where: in the chorus of the song about the 'little bird in the forest', the words changed for a few weeks in 1942, so that friends would meet again, not 'back home' but 'at the station in Jerusalem'.

At first, neither the Italian dictator and his *Supremo Commando*, nor even the high command of the German army, would countenance these far-fetched plans. Instead, they urged the long-planned occupation of Malta, situated in the narrowest part of the Mediterranean, between Sicily and North Africa, in order to secure permanently the Axis supply-routes to North Africa. Hitler, who had rejoiced at the fall of Tobruk as 'a stroke of destiny for the German people', advised Mussolini, the nominal commander-in-chief of Axis forces in North Africa, on 23 June 1942, to pursue the British 8th Army 'to the very last trace of a single man', since 'the goddess of fortune in battle only ever brushes once the face of an army commander. He who fails to grasp her at such a moment, is unlikely ever to catch up with her again.' Rommel did not succeed in grasping her. The decision, taken over-hastily in the euphoria of victory, to press on with the advance into Egypt, would return to haunt him. After only a few weeks, the progress of the few serviceable tanks that Rommel still had ground to a halt in the narrow strip of land between the Quattara depression and the Mediterranean – at a god-forsaken desert village called El Alamein.

Around this time Goebbels' propaganda machine was running in top gear. 'Special bulletins' came thick and fast. 'Rommel's magnificent victory' or 'Rommel's body-blow leaves the British winded' were the kind of headlines that were seen in the Nazi-controlled press. Rommel's success was intended to give the 'national compatriots' back home the confidence in victory that they had lost on the battlefields of the eastern front. As early as the winter of 1941/2 his advance through the desert heat had been intended as a diversion from the icy disasters on the eastern front – even though North Africa was only a minor theatre of war, in which just three German divisions were engaged, while in the east over 150 Wehrmacht divisions were battling with the Red Army. After the triumph at Tobruk, Goebbels had one of Rommel's front-line reporters specially flown to Berlin so that he could give a personal picture of the situation and of the propaganda opportunities offered by the North African victory. 'Shaking hands on certain victory', ran the headline on the front of the *Hamburger Illustrierte* of 10 October 1942. The Führer was offering his hand to the highly decorated field-marshal. In the third year of the war, cinema-goers could watch a newsreel of the beaming hero: Rommel in a clean, dapper uniform, Rommel triumphing over the British, Rommel the brilliant field commander, giving orders to his victorious divisions with an expansive gesture of the hand. These images placed little importance on historical accuracy. For the benefit of Goebbels' cameras Rommel issued instructions to units that simply did not exist. The honorary title of 'Phantom Division', as his 7th Panzer Division was dubbed by the opposition in the French campaign, took on a new meaning here in the desert.

Joseph Goebbels recognised the potential that Rommel's victory offered to Nazi propaganda. The home front needed heroes, in this third year of conflict the war-weary Germans had to have prototypical winners. And Rommel was predestined for this role – a role he was all too willing to play. Goebbels saw that 'no general was more imbued than Rommel with the importance of propaganda for the war effort'. This was not something that could be counted on in the German general staff, which on their own initiative and not infrequently on Hitler's instructions, shunned publicity and contact with the Nazi-controlled press. Heinz Guderian, no less gifted a tank strategist than Rommel or Manstein, wrote to his wife in defiant expectation of victory in Russia: 'On no account do I want propaganda à la Rommel focused on me personally.' The brand-new field-marshal had fewer scruples in this regard. Rommel was nothing if not a modern general.

Even during the fighting in France, two staffers from the Ministry of Propaganda, Karl Hanke and Karl Holz, sought direct contact with the commander of the 7th Panzers. Rommel's successes in the field were the stuff of popular legend. Hans Albers' lyrics to a popular song, *Auf der Reeperbahn nachts um halb eins* ('Half past midnight on the Reeperbahn') were amended in the field-marshal's honour:

> *Auf der Rommelbahn nachts um halb drei*
> *Jagen Geister mit achtzig vorbei*
> *Rommel selbst voran, jeder hält sich dran,*
> *Auf der Rommelbahn nachts um halb drei*
> (Half past midnight on the Rommel Highway
> Phantoms zoom past at eighty
> Rommel himself is in front, everyone else keeps up)

Even in 1940, Rommel's victories were being turned into popular hits.

The Permanent Secretary at the Ministry of Propaganda, Alfred-Ingemar Berndt, became an ordnance officer in North Africa and thus set up a direct line between the 'Desert Fox' and the propaganda boss. The hero-worship sometimes slid into downright *kitsch*. A painted portrait published as a postcard showed a determined Rommel with strikingly stylised features. The propaganda portrayed the ideal German general and bent the facts in a way apparently necessary for a 'German' military leader: a 1941 article in the weekly magazine *Das Reich* misleadingly described Rommel as the son of a working man. That was not the only mistake: it claimed that Rommel left the army after the First World War and studied at the university of Tübingen. And the statement that as an officer in the SA he had Nazi ideology personally explained to him by Hitler belongs to the realm of pure fantasy. That is how Goebbels' and his fairytale-spinners would have liked their ideal German general to have been. Yet Rommel was never a member of the SA storm-troopers, nor did he join the Nazi Party, either before or after 1933.

Much as Rommel enjoyed being characterised as the 'Master of the Desert War', he was irritated at the way he was totally taken over by the Nazi propaganda machine. He made a complaint to Berlin, but it was ignored. Rommel may have simply accepted the fact that people were saying he spoke perfect Arabic. This would explain his popularity with the Arabs, who hated the British, seeing them as occupiers, and who greeted Rommel's troops as liberators. In fact Rommel knew barely fifty words of Arabic – but what did Goebbels care? He preferred to paint a romanticised picture of Rommel's Afrika Korps. And since sandstorms and plagues of flies gave as unpleasant an image as did the dirt-caked, thirsty and hungry soldiers, he had to reinvent the desert war. The public were shown cheerful, well-fed infantrymen having a pleasant rest in the desert sand, frying eggs on the hot bonnet of a truck; or idyllic scenes in an oasis with donkeys, date-palms and Bedouin children at play. War became a children's game, no word of hardships, supply problems, misery or death.

By now even the British seemed to have succumbed to the fascination of the man who had beaten their troops. Having been driven out of Tobruk, the Allies were faced with a military and a psychological problem: according to an opinion survey in the United States, Rommel was the most famous German after Hitler. In the British House of Commons Churchill presented the German general as a man whose abilities were touched with genius. The men of the British Eighth Army admired Rommel, because he had beaten them.

And here lay the problem for the Allies: Rommel's name alone had become a potent weapon in psychological warfare. Douglas Walter, a soldier in the Eighth Army, describes the feelings evoked by the name of Rommel, whom the Allies, like the Germans, had christened the 'Desert Fox': 'The people in our headquarters kept on stressing: he's not unbeatable. But we didn't believe them.'

In order to combat their own lack of courage, the British High Command was compelled to take counter-measures. Even if their own soldiers paid homage to the ability of their opponent, there had to be a limit. The British commander-in-chief, General Auchinleck, issued the appropriate order to his officers: 'There exists a danger that our friend Rommel is becoming a kind of magician or bogeyman to our troops, who are talking far too much about him. He is by no means a superman, although he is undoubtedly very energetic and able. The important thing now is to see to it that we do not always talk of Rommel when we mean the enemy in Libya. We must refer to "the Germans" or "the enemy" and not always keep harping on Rommel.'

Nowhere is the acknowledgement of their adversary's success and achievement more clearly expressed than in the postscript that Auchinleck added to his orders: 'I am not jealous of Rommel.'

Auchinleck would have no further chance personally to break the spell cast by his German counterpart. Rommel had made failures of two British commanders-in-chief in succession. The third man to head up the British forces in North Africa was General Montgomery. The task of his Eighth Army was to drive back the German heroes from El Alamein, just 50 miles west of Alexandria and the Nile delta. Despite all the previous German successes, the prospects were favourable. Faced with Allied control of the air and their overwhelming numerical superiority on the ground, Rommel's forces could offer little resistance to the third British offensive, which began on 23 October. Furthermore, the German commander-in-chief was not with his troops. Struck down with illness, he was spending time at home. But even a commander of his stature would have had nothing to put up against the superior British forces – except his legendary reputation. Yet what use was the myth of invincibility against the 1,110 and more tanks that Montgomery threw into the battle? The combined German and Italian formations could not even muster half that number. The Axis positions were simply overrun. 'You can't stop a steamroller with a Volkswagen', declared Douglas Walter, retrospectively comparing the Allied superiority with the earlier successes of 'General Bluff'. All that remained was to stage an orderly retreat. And this is what Rommel requested from his supreme commander, Hitler, as soon as he returned to the North African battle-front.

On 3 November he received a reply by telegram, which shattered his boundless trust in the ability of 'the greatest military commander of all time'. It read: 'Given the situation you find yourself in, there can be no other thought than to hold out, not to give an inch, and to throw every weapon and every fighting man into the battle. You can show your troops no way but the one that leads to victory or to death.'

It was one of Hitler's typical no-surrender orders, which faced the fighting forces with impossible tasks, and stubbornly ignored military necessity and inevitability. Reluctantly, yet obediently, Rommel ordered a halt to the retreat that had already begun, 'because', as he wrote, 'I myself had repeatedly demanded unquestioning obedience and consequently wished to subordinate myself personally to this principle.'

Yet Rommel soon realised what consequences his obedience would entail – and now decided to act on his own initiative. In direct defiance of the unambiguous instructions from his supreme commander, the field-marshal ordered a retreat, in order to save what there was to be saved. A day later, Hitler did after all give Rommel the permission he had requested, to retreat to the headquarters position. The remnants of Rommel's Afrika Korps were driven back beyond Benghazi by Montgomery's superior forces. The Battle of Alamein had been lost. And worse was to come: on 7 and 8 November 1942 British and American forces landed on the coasts of Morocco and Algeria, in Rommel's rear. The Axis powers now found themselves facing every army's nightmare: they had to wage war on two fronts. The Allies had massive numerical superiority over the Germans and their Italian partners. While the opposition's logistics functioned superbly, Rommel was labouring under enormous supply problems. The relative strengths of the two sides shifted ever more rapidly to the disadvantage of Germany's desert army. Even for someone of Rommel's ability it was now simply a question of delaying the defeat he could no longer prevent. His panzer forces had to withdraw.

On 26 November the field-marshal decided to make a desperate bid to save the situation. He would go and put his case in person to Hitler; he would make it clear to him that, in view of the supply situation, Allied air superiority and the deadly pincer movement of Eisenhower's and Montgomery's armies, there was only one possibility: to withdraw from North Africa, salvage valuable equipment and preserve combat-fit units for the conflict in Europe. Rommel turned up unannounced at Hitler's eastern headquarters in Rastenburg. He did not pull his punches: 'The situation in Africa demands that I spell it out to you in person and present my thoughts on how it will develop from now on', he told Hitler, and then watched as the Führer completely lost control of himself. Rommel was now subjected to what other senior officers had already experienced, and that would still face others with high military responsibility. In the presence of others Hitler gave his favourite general an almighty roasting and bawled at him: 'Retreat is out of the question. We must hold on. Give up Africa? Impossible.' Then he showed the completely flabbergasted field-marshal the door. What then ensued may sound grotesque, yet it is similar to the experience of many others who had dealings with Hitler. Manfred Rommel tells how his father described the scene: 'Hitler threw my father out, then hurried after him and called him back. Then he asked my father: "How many rifles have you got?" and my father said: "We haven't counted them."' This apparently annoyed Hitler so much that he heaped more and more abuse on Rommel, until the latter blurted out: 'You'd better go to Africa yourself, *Mein Führer*, and show my men how to defend themselves with rifles against British tanks.' We may blame Rommel for the admiration he had fostered for Hitler. But we must acknowledge the fact that at this moment he did not keep his views to himself – and in this he was untypical of Wehrmacht generals.

A number of biographers of Rommel see this episode as an early cause of his gradual change of attitude towards Hitler. The lack of self-control, the lack of insight – these were not appropriate to the kind of responsible statesman that Rommel wanted to see leading Germany. 'They don't see the danger, and they don't even want to see it', he told his wife dejectedly. But Rommel was a soldier; principles, like orders and obedience, were part of his nature. So he obeyed, contrary to his own conviction.

What followed had been inevitable all along: a gradual but steady retreat. For two months Army Group Africa kept up its resistance – without its great commander. True, Hitler had given his approval to the withdrawal, yet 'the greatest military commander of all time' was increasingly irritated by the way his erstwhile favourite did things 'off his own bat'. On 9 March 1943 Rommel was recalled from Tunisia. There has been much speculation over the reason for this. Perhaps Rommel had been so weakened by the illness which had already necessitated his absence on home leave from the front during the critical phase of the British offensive, that he was no longer in a position to carry on the fight. Was Rommel's recall a punishment for his failure in the field or a reaction to his contradiction of the Führer? Conversely, did Hitler want to spare his former favourite the disgrace of surrender? Or did he fear losing another field-marshal to the opposition, only weeks after Paulus had capitulated at Stalingrad and become a prisoner-of-war of the Russians?

Yet even though Rommel did not see the situation in North Africa in as rosy a light as Hitler had demanded, and even though the 'Desert Fox' was unable to avert the impending defeat, the dictator of Germany had not withdrawn his favour from his favourite general. The award of a bar to Rommel's Knight's Cross was announced after a delay of two months, and the name of the victor of Tobruk was kept out of the news of the bitter end to the fighting in North Africa. His legendary reputation was not to be besmirched with defeats; his aura of victory was to be preserved. The myth of the great idol had enormous propaganda value on the home front. Before the final collapse of the German front in Tunisia, Rommel was recalled, because 'it would be very detrimental to his name' if he were to remain in North Africa. On 12 and 13 May Rommel's successor was forced to capitulate. The war in the desert was at an end.

The field-marshal was put on display as the undefeated hero. It was a role that the army commander and man of action did not feel comfortable in: 'While the war is on, a field-marshal is a prisoner in his own country', he told his wife in a mood of profound depression. But the dedicated soldier was not a mere prisoner on the home front; he allowed himself to be shown off and led around like a performing animal.

Not even the defeat of the Afrika Korps made any difference to the adulation for the recalled field-marshal. On Goebbels' instructions a new propaganda campaign was launched with Rommel as its figurehead. It may be considered justifiable to rank his military achievements, as Nazi propaganda did, on a par with those of Moltke, Hindenburg, Blücher and Gneisenau. Yet the general was then elevated to the status of superman; the presentation of Rommel was so grotesquely exaggerated as to become ridiculous. He was lauded as 'a comet in a great orbit', described as being 'transfused with sacred zeal', his personality was raised to the realm of myth. The propagandist Alfred-Ingemar Berndt even tried to sell his defeat as a victory. 'Twenty-seven months of fighting in Africa' was the title of a radio talk, in which Berndt glorified Rommel's heroic struggle against a superior adversary. And Rommel acted out the part that had been assigned to him.

In the spring of 1943 he went in front of the cameras at the Ministry of Propaganda and described his experiences in the desert war. He paid tribute to the achievements of the 'German soldier', who had crushed the opposition with 'lightning strikes' and, dashing onward in 'relentless pursuit' of final victory, never resting, defying the forces of nature, be it sandstorm or a plague of flies, finally 'pushed the British into the sand'. He spoke of the heat, the hardships, the meagre rations and, again and again, of the enemy's superiority in men and equipment. In summing up, he always said what the Nazi leadership wanted to hear: 'The German soldier has come through this difficult period with flying colours.' Needless to say, there were ceaseless attacks by a strong opponent; of course those were 'tough weeks, which took us to the brink of destruction'. But even in the most hopeless situation, there was a happy outcome: 'And in spite of everything the German troops came through those difficult days.' Was Rommel – the Desert Fox – a fervent patriot, or a naive propaganda mouthpiece, a helpless puppet?

Rommel's correspondence is packed with eloquent praise for Hitler, with almost hymn-like eulogies to his revered Führer. As well as increasing admiration for the German dictator, his letters also contain assessments that fly in the face of reality. When the Germans marched into Warsaw, he wrote: 'The population is breathing a sigh of relief to see that we have come and rescued them.' Yet Rommel was not the blindly enthusiastic admirer of Hitler that he appears to be in his letters. When examining his correspondence as source material, it is necessary to remember that the Third Reich was reliant on informers and surveillance; everyone had to assume that anything said or written at any time might be passed on to the Gestapo or some other organ of the Nazi regime. Confidentiality of the mail did not exist. Many letters were opened by the censors. If Rommel had committed his criticisms to paper he would have put himself and his family at risk. Every incriminating letter meant danger for the cause with which it was concerned, for the sender and not least for the recipient.

If a high degree of evidential value is ascribed to Rommel's correspondence, then it must be pointed out that, in letters to his wife, he very rarely discusses politics. This was more a matter of the great strategist's naivety than his lack of interest. If he did not agree with decisions made by the regime, Rommel blamed others, but not Hitler. 'Unfortunately the Führer is surrounded by a gang of scoundrels. But most of these party heavies are leftovers from the old days, from the street-fighting era of the Movement.' Rommel appears to have believed that with time this would resolve itself.

Rommel was emphatically not anti-Semitic. His son tells a story from the time, at the beginning of the Third Reich, when his father was a battalion commander in Goslar and still far removed from

Hitler's influence; in his youthful naivety he enquired about the 'Jewish' nose of a battalion medical officer. Rommel's circle of friends included Jews, and we do not find him making anti-Semitic remarks of the kind that were reported from other senior officers. Of course, he was not spared the re-education process with which the powers in Berlin tried to imbue all levels of society with the National Socialists' hatred of the Jews. And of course Rommel saw the excesses of the night of pogroms, when the brownshirt mob went on the rampage, as far away as Wiener Neustadt in Austria.

It is highly improbable that an independent thinker like Rommel could have seriously associated himself with the theories propagated by the Nazis about an international Jewish conspiracy. An episode that took place in 1943 is symptomatic of the innocence with which Rommel challenged the attitudes of the Nazi leadership. During a dinner-table conversation, Hitler impressed upon Rommel the loss of international respect that Germany had incurred abroad through its policy towards the Jews. When Rommel suggested that 'Germany's reputation would stand higher in the world if a Jew could become one of our Gauleiters', this caused Hitler great irritation: 'Rommel, you have understood nothing about my intentions.' When Rommel had left the table, Hitler looked at the others with incredulous amazement. 'Hasn't he grasped the fact that the Jews are the cause of this war?' Indeed Rommel had not.

Was he such an innocent as to close his eyes to what was happening to the Jews in Germany? How far the Nazis would take this was as inconceivable to Rommel as it was to many others. When he heard about atrocities in the east, it was not Hitler whom he held responsible, but those around him. A military genius he may have been, but he was still politically naive. His son Manfred, who went on to become Chief Burgomaster of Stuttgart, admits: 'It is true to say that from 1938 on, my father succumbed to the fascination of Hitler. He was relatively slow to recognise the truth.' By then it was too late – for him as well as for others.

'Whether to foe, friend or brother, whether to the sons of Germany, of Italy or of Britain – your manner was chivalrous, humane was the law that prevailed here.' The inscription on the memorial to the German dead of the Battle of Alamein brings a lump to the throat even today. 'Chivalry' is a word that occurs in many descriptions of the desert war. The former adversaries are still agreed today in their characterisation of the war. 'It was a very fair war, a war without blemish', recalls Heinz Blumacher, who fought on the German side. And Charles Squire, who was a member of the British Eighth Army, supports his view: 'We fought according to the rules of war. Civilians, women and children were not affected by the battles.' Many descriptions remind the reader of a medieval tournament. For example, one Englishman tells of a skirmish in which three German and three British armoured cars unexpectedly came up against each other while on reconnaissance. With gun barrels lowered like knights' lances, they charged towards each other. 'Firing furiously, the British vehicles drove through the Germans, then both sides returned to their original positions. There had been no hits and no losses.' The two sides sportingly called it a draw and returned to their own camps.

War without Hate was the title of the book published after the war by Rommel's widow Lucie, and Fritz Bayerlein, his chief-of-staff. And it is certainly true that the German soldiers in Libya were not followed by any SS commandos or SD death-squads, carrying out 'ethnic-cleansing' operations to the rear of the fighting troops. In contrast to 'Operation Barbarossa' in the Soviet Union, civilising restraints were not removed in obedience to orders, the individual threshold of shame did not descend into an abyss. In North Africa there were no mass shootings, no massacres.

'In the desert no one wanted to conquer and loot – they just wanted to fight', wrote the British historian Alan Moorehead. 'This was a clean, clear-cut war. A battle in an empty desert, where there was no civilian population and no political considerations. It was a soldiers' war.' A 'soldiers' war' is governed by rules. One of these is that enemy prisoners shall be treated like human beings. Yet it was undoubtedly the case that the German Wehrmacht high command issued a standing order, which, if obeyed, meant that all senior officers in the armed forces would ultimately violate the rules of war and place themselves beyond the pale of the international community. Soldiers from enemy assault-troops were not to be treated as prisoners-of-war, if they were taken prisoner behind German lines. They were to be shot immediately as 'criminals', so ran the standing order, which naturally applied to the desert war as well. Rommel was among those who received the order from Berlin. What he did with it is reported by his chief-of-staff, General Westphal: 'We burned that order there and then.' In North Africa the old writ still ran.

Moorehead gathered opinions from British soldiers who had been released from German imprisonment. They paint an almost Elysian picture of the desert war: they give unanimous reports of impeccable treatment by the Germans; the British wounded were cared for just as well as the Germans; the prisoners were adequately fed, and even given cigarettes and beer. So extraordinary was the conduct of the opposing sides in Africa that the US commander, General Eisenhower, later expressed incomprehension in his memoirs for the way British and Germans behaved towards each other in North Africa. Eisenhower himself refused to meet the 'Nazi generals' after their defeat. For the British and Germans this was not a problem. After the Battle of El Alamein Montgomery invited the captured acting commander of the Afrika Korps, General Ritter von Thoma, to dinner. And *Generaloberst* Hans-Jürgen von Arnim, Rommel's successor as commander-in-chief, confirmed that 'It had become the custom in the North African campaign to treat enemy prisoners-of-war like gentlemen. Rommel did the same with the British generals after his push through Mechili. The British generals acted in the same way towards captured Germans too.'

Was the war in the desert really no more than an altercation between gentlemen? A noble trial of strength, in which the victor ended by offering his hand to the vanquished? 'Jolly sporting of you, old man!' We should be warned against such nostalgic depictions, too often written in the transfiguring glow of hindsight. Even though (almost) no war crimes were committed in the desert, the clashes were no Sunday afternoon excursions for the heirs to King Arthur's Round Table. When Keitel, during the Nuremberg Military Tribunals, spoke contemptuously of 'Rommel's shooting expedition', this was to

belittle Rommel, not the desert war. Even if General Cramer, the last
commander of the Afrika Korps, bade farewell to the field of battle
with the naive words *Heia safari* (roughly 'happy hunting!'), the
battles for Tobruk and El Alamein were quite emphatically not an
adventure holiday with an 'all-inclusive' programme of activities.

Desert warfare meant blistering heat and huge drops in
temperature; by day, scorching sun and a heat that dried up
everything; by night a pitiless cold. It meant storms that literally
blinded you, sand that seeped into every pore and made breathing a
torture, swarms of flies, which descended on open wounds. Britons
and Germans, Australians and Italians, fought against each other,
but they also fought a common enemy: the desert. And in the desert
war, like others, men died pointlessly. Here, more than anywhere,
war meant dirt, blood and death.

After their talk, the Führer spontaneously decorated him with
the bar to his oak-leaf. Rommel has certainly earned this; he is
not only a great army leader but also a brave man, whose
personal courage has proved him worthy of such a high award.

Joseph Goebbels, diary, 12 March 1943

What strength he radiates! What faith and confidence bind his
people to him!

Rommel on Hitler, 1943

I myself never considered Rommel the military genius that he
was presented as being.

Martin Bormann, secretary to the Führer

The war in North Africa was over. The field-marshal without troops
was now fighting a propaganda war on the home front. There would
have been ample opportunity for him to take up another command,
since, in the summer of 1943, the situation was, to say the least,
precarious on all sectors of the front. The offensive in Russia had
once again come to a halt; and with the breach in the Berlin–Rome

axis following Mussolini's dismissal, a new front had opened up in the south. The Allies were preparing for an assault on what Hitler called 'Fortress Europe'. On 15 July 1943 Rommel was once more given a military assignment of his own: he was appointed commander-in-chief of Army Group B, and German troops under his command began preparations for Case 'Axis' – the withdrawal of Italy from the war. On 3 September, the Italians had signed a secret armistice with the Allies, and when, on 8 September, Italy's surrender was announced simultaneously by Eisenhower and the new Italian prime minister, Badoglio, Rommel's troops immediately occupied northern Italy, while in the south *Generalfeldmarschall* Kesselring was attempting to halt the Allied drive towards Naples.

Rommel's tour of duty in Italy was no more than a brief interlude. He would find his future field of operation further west, in France. On 30 October Alfred Jodl, the chief of Wehrmacht operations, suggested placing Rommel in command of the defensive battle in the west to prevent the invasion they now feared. Rommel had few friends among the General Staff. On 5 November the Wehrmacht chief-of-staff Wilhelm Keitel wrote to the Commander-in-Chief West, *Generalfeldmarschall* Gerd von Rundstedt: 'We have a problem with Rommel because he does not like being subordinate. In North Africa he was very independent. But I believe you are the only man to whom even a Rommel will defer.' That was a misjudgement, as will become apparent. Yet even Hitler was hesitant about entrusting the headstrong field-marshal with an operational command. Thus in the 'Special Assignment West', that Rommel was given on 5 November 1943, his initial tasks were only to examine the state of defensive preparations and develop proposals for offensive operations against the enemy after landing. Once again the chaotic lines of command in the Third Reich were revealed. In his new posting, Rommel remained for the time being under the direct orders of Hitler. His actual superior officer, the Commander-in-Chief West, was not informed of Rommel's assignment nor of his special relationship with the Führer. However, what Rommel did not have was any authority to issue the practical orders that would have been necessary in order the fight the enemy in the event of an Allied landing. All he received was the vague promise that, when the invasion began, he would also be given operational authority.

> Rommel is now being kept close at hand by the Führer. He wants to save him for the next big and difficult job that comes up, and will then post him to where clear-cut but improvisational leadership is most urgently needed.
>
> *Joseph Goebbels, diary, 10 May 1943*
>
> Yesterday I was invited to tea and dinner with Dr Goebbels. Despite the latest heavy losses, Dr Goebbels is full of confidence. That did me good, since my mood has been particularly low lately, because of everything falling apart in Tunisia.
>
> *Rommel, letter to his wife, 11 May 1943*

Rommel went to work with his customary *élan*. Full of eagerness to get on with things he wrote to his wife on 18 December: 'I now want to throw myself into the new job with all my might, and see that it is successfully completed.' In this letter, as in many others, he again expressed his optimism: 'I'm very hopeful that we'll manage it.'

The situation from which he was starting out appeared to justify this optimism. Nominally, 1.3 million soldiers were available to repel an attack in the west. Army Group B comprised some 24 infantry and 5 armoured divisions; approximately 330,000 were under Rommel's command. Yet for the most part these were not fresh troops, but units which were exhausted from fighting in the east and had now been posted to the Atlantic coast for 'rest and recuperation'. Compared to what was happening on the eastern front, the west must have seemed like paradise to these soldiers. Rommel showed a confident face to his men: 'In view of our strong positions, in view of the excellent spirit of our troops, and the new weaponry and combat equipment that have been put in our hands, we can face the coming events with great equanimity.'

Among close colleagues he was far more sceptical. A sober stock-taking of the situation had quickly made clear to Rommel the realist that grounds for optimism scarcely existed. As soon as he had taken up his post, he stated in a discussion with his staff: 'Our own resources are minimal; and there is no prospect of improvement.' Berlin had offered the prospect of 1,000 additional fighter planes in the event of an invasion. But the experience that Rommel, like other army commanders, had had with Göring's extravagant promises, was hardly encouraging. In those critical days, a total of just 500 serviceable aircraft were available; and *Luftflotte* 3, stationed in northern France, consisted of a mere 70 fighters and 90 bombers. Once the invaders had advanced beyond the coastal strip, it would prove very difficult to drive them back into the sea. Rommel had grasped that fact, and concluded: 'Our defence can only be accomplished on the coast itself.' His weapons were mines. 'I want anti-personnel, anti-tank, and anti-paratrooper mines; I want mines to deal with ships and landing craft.' Unlike the 'miracle weapons' so stridently proclaimed by Nazi propaganda, mines were the real weapons with which Rommel wanted to achieve the miracle of a successfully repulsed Allied landing. Rommel remembered North Africa, where his British adversaries had used mines to hold off his assaults on Tobruk for a long time. It was calculated that the opposition had buried a million mines in the desert sand. And this time? In France, 1.7 million mines had already been laid – but in an area infinitely larger than the battle-terrain around Tobruk.

Rommel wanted as swiftly as possible to make good what up to now had been inadequate: the fortification of the coastline. Here he once more exhibited the imagination, the organisational skill and determination to implement a series of brilliant schemes in the form of underwater obstacles, barbed-wire entanglements, coastal artillery equipped with heavy guns, and above all the use of 'Rommel's asparagus'. This was a highly original idea of 'the most important pioneer of the war', as General Meise described his chief. In North Africa Rommel had had wooden tanks built on VW wheel-bases to frighten off the enemy from a distance. Now, in France, he ordered long poles to be rammed into the ground, to make landing difficult on the beaches. In addition, labour squads dotted hundreds of the poles at irregular intervals in the fields inland. Their purpose was to make it impossible for Allied gliders to land and thus to hinder the supply of their troops from the air.

The mines were to be an invisible yet almost insuperable barrier. At the start, 600,000 mines stood ready for laying. The question was: where should they go? Finding the answer to this revealed the fundamental problem that made Rommel's work so difficult: the confused lines of command and the differences of opinion between Rommel and the top military commanders, which reached right up to the commander-in-chief of the Wehrmacht, Adolf Hitler.

Though he has only been working for a short time on the Atlantic Wall, Rommel has achieved an enormous amount. He proceeds systematically and with great exactitude. He does not allow himself to be put off by the general staff people.

Joseph Goebbels, diary, 17 May 1944

We are in the midst of a dire struggle, the decisive battle of this war. In the past weeks and months, extraordinary things have been achieved, and yet we are not as ready as I would have liked. I want even more mines, even deeper obstacles in the water and against airborne troops, even more artillery, anti-aircraft guns, mortars and rocket-launchers.

Rommel in a letter to his son Manfred, 21 May 1944

The Germans knew neither the place nor the time of the Allies' planned landings – and the men in charge could not agree on a single, coherent defensive strategy. Rundstedt expected the landing to be near Calais. He wanted to allow large troop contingents to advance from the coast, and then to crush them – the old formula for success: encircle and destroy. Rommel, on the other hand, was in no doubt that the enemy had to be attacked as soon as they came ashore, and driven back into the sea. This divergence of analysis led to very different strategies. As long as Hitler made no final decision, the German generals continued to fight among themselves. The compromises that were agreed on, after lengthy disputes, served neither side.

One man with whom Rommel indulged in frequent verbal battles was Hans von Salmuth, the commander-in-chief of the 16th Army, because his men were unable to lay mines fast enough for the field-marshal, and at the same time prepare themselves for combat. The already high target that Salmuth had set his men was to lay 15 kilometres (9 miles) of mines per day. 'Make that thirty!' was Rommel's curt and demanding response. The commander-in-chief of Army Group B, who regarded Salmuth as 'lethargic', was thereupon informed by his subordinate that his defensive construction programme was driving his officers insane.

No less heated were the discussions Rommel had with General Baron Geyr von Schweppenburg. The commander-in-chief of Panzer Group West had access to the Wehrmacht's only panzer reserves. Rommel wanted to build these solidly into his coastal defence system. Geyr von Schweppenburg's plan was to hold the units back, so as to be able to destroy the enemy after landing, in operations over a wide area. On this important question, Rundstedt decided not to accept Rommel's view. Once again, things ended in compromise: the panzer divisions were not posted as near the coast as Rommel had demanded, but were held some way inland. It was a fudge that further fragmented the available defensive forces.

> With all his energy and daring, his warmly humane face and clear blue eyes inspired confidence.
>
> *General Hans Speidel, retired*

The amount that the tireless Rommel, with the support of the 'Todt' labour organisation, achieved in barely six months, earned the respect of all his critics. Even Salmuth admitted: 'A new phase began when *Feldmarschall* Rommel appeared.' In May 1944 Hitler congratulated Rommel on his achievements, but did not grant him the reinforcements he requested. Rommel could only put a fraction of his plans into effect, because the necessary equipment failed to materialise, as did the additional panzer divisions he so urgently needed.

'Due to the bad weather conditions, we do not anticipate any Allied action in the next two weeks', declared the German meteorologists on 4 June. But miscalculating the weather was not the only mistake the Germans made. The Allies had carried out adroit deception manoeuvres, while preparing the actual invasion to the last detail. On the defenders' side – faulty judgements, to say nothing of sloppiness, dithering and utterly confused lines of command.

On the evening of 5 June 1944 the chief intelligence officer of the Fifteenth Army, *Oberstleutnant* Meyer, heard in a BBC broadcast the second line of a poem called *Chanson d'Automne*: '. . . wound my heart with dull monotony.' It was the signal to the French resistance: the invasion will start in the next two days. This and other coded messages from London to the French underground fighters were not taken seriously enough. In southern England, more than 2.8 million soldiers stood in readiness for the assault on 'Fortress Europe'; more than 3,400 bombers and over 5,400 fighters would give the Allies unchallenged mastery of the skies; over 6,000 ships of various sizes had been fitted out to transport the troops across the Channel. D-Day, the day of decision, was on 6 June. 'Operation Overlord' had begun. As General Eisenhower declared in his orders to the Allied invasion forces that day: 'The eyes of the world are upon you, the hopes of freedom-loving people throughout the world go with you.'

Emotional as this may sound, his characterisation of the historic significance of that day was certainly more accurate than much of the comment that can still be read today in German history books. To the Nazi leadership then – and to many Germans even now – the events of 6 June were an 'invasion'. Yet an invasion is an assault by hostile troops on a foreign country. The German attack on Poland in 1939 was an invasion, as were the assault on the Soviet Union and the forcible occupation of Holland, Belgium, Denmark, Norway, Yugoslavia, Greece. . . . Almost the whole of Europe had been invaded by the German Wehrmacht. However, on 6 June 1944 no enemy fleet came ashore on a native German coast, to occupy the homeland. The 'invasion' was the liberation of Normandy from its German conquerors; it was the landing of troops from Allied nations.

It was the prerequisite and the prelude to the liberation of Europe from its Nazi occupiers, and not least was it the beginning of the liberation of the Germans themselves from a tyranny which they were unable to put an end to themselves.

At the crucial moment, the top German army commanders were conspicuous by their absence: Salmuth was away hunting for two days, Dollmann, the commander-in-chief of the Seventh Army, was in the process of preparing some paper exercises in Rennes, while the C-in-C of the 21st Panzer Division, Geuchtinger, was spending time in Paris. Hitler was asleep and did not want to be woken before 3 p.m. And when the Führer gave an order, his courtiers obeyed. When news of the invasion reached Hitler's alpine retreat at the Obersalzberg, Jodl, the operations chief, was in any case convinced that the whole thing was a feint. True, Rundstedt urged that he be allowed to deploy the panzer divisions held in reserve, but to do so he needed the agreement of Hitler, who was still asleep. When, in the late afternoon, the Führer had once more taken up the reins of the Reich, he brusquely ordered that the beach-heads be 'cleared'. He too considered the Normandy landings to be a diversionary tactic, aimed at distracting attention from the 'real' invasion elsewhere. Consistent with this, he forbade the deployment of relief forces; these had to watch passively as the German troops, though putting up a tough fight, were forced to yield to the massive superiority of ever more Allied forces coming ashore. And where was Rommel?

> Whenever my father came home for a few days' leave he immediately took me hunting. He wrote a note of apology to my school and took me off. That impressed me incredibly.
>
> *Manfred Rommel*

For the second time in his career Rommel, when most needed, was not at the front: in 1942, when Montgomery's troops broke through the German lines at El Alamein, he was on two weeks' recuperation leave at home; two years later he was again at home in Herrlingen, this time celebrating his wife's birthday. When his chief-of-staff,

General Speidel, informed him about the action on the coast, the field-marshal immediately returned to the headquarters of Army Group B, at La Roche-Guyon, in order to recover the initiative that had been lost in the first hours of the invasion. The coming days and weeks would not only settle the fate of Germany – they would also decide the personal destiny of Rommel, who embodied the dilemma of the top German military in a very acute way.

Here is the story of the highly decorated general, a courageous soldier. He has served his Führer loyally, has not concerned himself with politics, but simply obeyed orders. At the eleventh hour he recognises the criminal nature of the regime and turns his back on the man to whom he had sworn personal allegiance. As a figure of integrity, admired by his own troops and the opposition alike, he declares himself ready to save the Fatherland. He not only knows of the plans to kill the tyrant, but actively supports the plotters, who want to make him President of Germany, if their *coup d'état* is successful. When the plans to overthrow the regime go awry, he takes the responsibility upon himself, protects the plotters, and commits suicide in order to save his family from the vengeance of the Nazis. This is the story that many people have long been happy to believe. Yet it has one critical flaw: at key points it does not correspond to the facts. The story that shows *Feldmarschall* Rommel pulling the strings behind the morally inspired resistance of the Prussian officer-class, the 'secret father-figure of the resistance' who arrived late, but not too late – all this is mere legend. The man who most of all helped to weave this legend was General Hans Speidel, Rommel's chief-of-staff in France. Many theories about overthrowing the Nazi regime have haunted the writing of history, in which, for example, Rommel is said to have planned to arrest Hitler and put him on trial. Then, there was supposedly a joint plan by Rommel and Manstein in July 1943, to occupy the Führer's headquarters. Among German historians today, there is condemnation of the 'irresponsibility' of those who accept Speidel's representation of Rommel's contacts with the resisters. But at the same time, Rommel is said to have achieved an 'inner liberation from Nazism'. It is precisely this that makes Rommel so important to the young generation.

> As a young lad I was keen on the *Waffen*-SS and wanted to join as a volunteer; that particularly annoyed my father.
>
> *Manfred Rommel*

Rommel was not an 'opposition' figure, and certainly not an active member of the resistance; he was not a martyr like Stauffenberg, who was ready to strike down Hitler 'because it is not a question of telling Hitler the truth, but of killing him'. Nor was Rommel like Tresckow, who wanted, above all, to 'show the world and history that the German resistance movement had risked the decisive throw of the dice'.

Nevertheless, Rommel had undergone a critical transformation, which may have historical importance for many Germans, especially German soldiers. The chief-of-staff of the Afrika Korps, *Oberst* Nolte, later described the significance of this change: 'Uncompromising in his condemnation of an immoral, deceitful system that betrayed itself and others, he was the heroic figure the German people needed as a moral beacon after losing the war, who was the symbol of a better Germany, a kindly and humane man, the last representative of fairness in war, a popular leader of his troops, as much respected by his British and American adversaries as by his own men.'

The transformation took place in several stages and put an end to a development which had seen Rommel, the non-political soldier, become the admirer of Hitler. Rommel had always rejected the National Socialist milieu; Hitler alone appeared to him as a figure of radiance in the midst of the Nazi-brown swamp.

Statements by Rommel were recorded, in which, even as early as November 1942, he talked openly among a small group about the necessity for a change of regime. As a soldier, Rommel was annoyed by Hitler's obstinacy, which was leading to senseless loss of life. In December 1943, in a conversation with his former interpreter, Ernst Franz, Rommel made no bones about his pessimistic assessment of the situation and came close to naming some of those responsible: 'The war is as good as lost, and we are facing terrible times. . . .

Unfortunately we are dealing with people at the top, whose fanaticism amounts to lunacy!'

Yet whenever he was in Hitler's immediate presence, Rommel once more fell under his spell. After Hitler had made a speech on 20 March 1944, at Klessheim, near his Berghof retreat, Rommel noted in his diary that the words spoken by the idol he still worshipped, were 'of a wonderful clarity and supreme calm'. It is statements like these that provoked the reproach from Bernd Gisevius, a member of the anti-Nazi resistance, for the 'lack of character in this man, the most convinced Nazi among Hitler's field-marshals'. Yet this verdict is unjust.

> Rommel and Rundstedt, whom the Führer had visited [at their headquarters], made a good impression on him; they are fully in command of the situation and, most important of all, they get on well with each other. But the Führer too, as I have heard from France, left an impression of exceptional freshness and vitality.
> *Joseph Goebbels, diary, 20 June 1944*
>
> Rommel is a wolf-cub; he's no fox.
> *Gerd von Rundstedt, Commander-in-Chief West*

Great significance can be placed on the conversation between Rommel and Hitler at Soissons on 17 June. By now the Allies had been in France for eleven days and were advancing relentlessly. Rommel described the overwhelming superiority of the attackers, both in men and equipment. The 'Desert Fox' was in the same situation as in November 1942 at El Alamein: his own supply-lines had been immobilised, while the opposition was able to throw more and more new forces into the battle. Then as now, there was no prospect of any improvement. Rundstedt, as commander-in-chief, supported his subordinate, Rommel, and called for 'tactical alterations' in the position of his own front line. This was nothing more than a euphemism for retreat. In such instances Hitler only knew one answer: stand firm. Rommel once again had to accept that Hitler was refusing to acknowledge the reality of the situation.

By the time of Rommel's next meeting with the Führer in Berchtesgaden on 29 June, the military situation had further deteriorated. The Wehrmacht had been forced to surrender Cherbourg on 27 June. Driving together to the Berghof, whither Hitler had summoned them, Rommel urged Rundstedt, as the most important man on the 'Invasion front', to put the position to Hitler in realistic terms and to draw the necessary conclusions. These could only be that the war in the west must be brought to an end. Rundstedt agreed: 'I'll present that to the Führer in clear and harsh terms.' In conversation with his deputy intelligence chief, Major Wolfram, Rommel chose an interesting form of words: 'I feel responsible towards the German people.' Now it was no longer to the Führer, but only to the Fatherland that he wished to be answerable.

However, the discussion at the Berghof did not proceed as he had hoped. When called upon by Hitler to report on the military situation in the west, Rommel attempted to explain the overall position: 'The entire world is arrayed against Germany, and the relative strengths . . .'. But Hitler interrupted his field-marshal with the instruction that he was meant to be commenting on the military and not the political situation. Rommel tried a second time – and Hitler once again rebuked him. Only at the end of the meeting did he try a final time. He could not leave, he said, without having talked to Hitler about 'Germany'. Hitler showed Rommel to the door. 'I think you had better leave the room, *Herr Feldmarschall.*' It was the last time that the Führer and his 'favourite general' would meet in person.

There was one benefit to be derived from these three unsuccessful approaches: Rommel had no more illusions. He now knew for certain that Hitler had no intention of suing for peace, either in the east or the west. Yet that was precisely what Rommel wanted to do. In conversations with his staff officers he repeatedly said: 'I will endeavour to exploit my good reputation with the Allies to conclude an armistice, against Hitler's will, if necessary.'

The military situation in the west was becoming ever more desperate. The focus of Allied assaults was Caen, the last obstacle on the road to

Paris. Geyr von Schweppenburg who, in a bleak report to the OKW (Combined Services Supreme Command) had proposed the surrender of Caen, was dismissed as commander of Panzer Group West. The Commander-in-Chief West, *Feldmarschall* von Rundstedt, was awarded oak-leaves to his Knight's Cross – together with a pointed comment on his poor state of health. He was forced to retire, because his reply to Keitel's question about how to solve the problem was: 'Make peace.' The appointment of his successor showed how badly Hitler had reacted to Rommel's behaviour at the Berghof. For it was not Rommel, previously Rundstedt's Number Two, but *Feldmarschall* Günther von Kluge, who became the new Commander-in-Chief West. From the outset, the relationship between the two most important men in the west was bad. Rommel, who was notorious among the general staff for his independent and unconventional decisions, was cautioned by Kluge: 'From now on, even you will have to get used to carrying out orders like everyone else.'

Nonetheless, Rommel managed to persuade his new boss to take a sensible course of action. On 15 July, by which time the Germans had lost Caen, Rommel circulated an internal document to his superior, described as an 'ultimatum' to Hitler, in which he outlined the military situation in his customary realistic and unadorned style: 'Everywhere our troops are fighting heroically; however, the unequal struggle is nearing its end.' His conclusion was: 'In my view, it is necessary to accept the political consequences of this situation.' In this sentence, which Rommel had added in his own handwriting, Speidel and Tempelhoff crossed out the word 'political'.

What was concealed behind this vague pronouncement, Rommel intimated more starkly to his immediate circle. He told *Oberstleutnant* Elmar Warning what he would do if Hitler did not act in the way he wanted: 'Then I'll open up the western front to the Allies, because there is only one important thing to be decided: we must make sure that the British and Americans get to Berlin before the Russians do.' In seeking to muster support for this plan, Rommel now turned to Sepp Dietrich, the commander of the 1st SS Panzer Corps, and took the risk of asking him, one of Hitler's most fanatical followers, 'Would you continue to carry out my orders, even if they were in

contradiction to those of the Führer?' Rommel was gambling for
high stakes and seems to have won, for Dietrich replied: 'You're my
commander-in-chief. I obey only you, whatever orders you give.'
Others whom Rommel spoke to later told of his desperate plans for
an armistice: 'I will try, on the basis of my good standing with the
western Allies, to make a pact against Hitler's will and on condition
that they allow us to march side by side with them against the
Russians.' Rommel's illusions about the Allied war aims were
disastrous. For it was unthinkable that the Western Powers would
join one of Hitler's field-marshals in going to war against Stalin's
armies, alongside 'the damned Germans' – even after Hitler's death.

Even though the experienced soldier von Kluge had been
despatched by Hitler to root out 'defeatism' among the top military
echelons in the west, he recognised that Rommel's assessment of the
situation was correct. He was prepared to sign Rommel's report and
send it to Hitler. But he was overtaken by events.

On 20 July 1944 Count Claus von Stauffenberg detonated a bomb
in the main barrack hut of Hitler's advance headquarters, the 'Wolf's
Lair' at Rastenburg in East Prussia. This 'rebellion of conscience' was
the best-prepared attempt yet to bring Nazi rule to an end, and the
one with most chance of success. Killing the tyrant Hitler was to be
the trigger for all the other plans of the resisters, who had made
advance arrangements both in Berlin and Paris.

The beating heart of the resistance movement was in the War
Ministry, in Berlin's Bendlerstrasse. But in Paris, too, there was an
influential group of officers, who had put in train the necessary
measures for the period after Hitler's death. There is no dispute that
Carl-Heinrich Stülpnagel, Military Governor of France, was among
the conspirators. Nor is there any doubt that *Oberstleutnant* Cäsar von
Hofacker, a cousin of Stauffenberg who was on Stülpnagel's staff, had
tried to win Rommel over to their cause as an active opponent of
Hitler. Less clear is the role played by the senior military officer in
France, *Generalfeldmarschall* von Kluge. He was aware of the broad
intentions of the plotters and had indicated he would lend his support
should they be successful. But when he learned that Hitler had
survived the explosion, he distanced himself from the conspiracy.

However, he was unable to escape Hitler's vengeance. Before the executioner could lay hands on him, he committed suicide. Even if he was not an active participant, it was inevitable that his knowledge of the plot was enough for Hitler to hold him responsible. And what of Rommel? What part did he play in the 20 July plot? What did he know? What did he give his assent to?

> He did not want to accept another command in the west; he said that every shot fired against the Allies hit us, not them.
>
> *Manfred Rommel*

Three days before the attempt to kill Hitler, Rommel was severely injured. On the afternoon of 17 July, as he was being driven from his headquarters at La Roche-Guyon, he was attacked by a low-flying British fighter. By a strange irony, this happened close to a village that bore the same name as the man who had beaten him in North Africa: Montgomery – a hamlet on the Route Nationale 1879, between Livarot and Vimoutiers. The circumstances were typical of Rommel's leadership style. The weather situation on that hot summer day carried great danger; the cloudless sky provided perfect conditions for enemy aircraft. Nevertheless, the field-marshal had set off on a tour of inspection at the front when two British fighter-bombers spotted the little convoy. It was by no means the first air attack that Rommel had been through. *Obergefreiter* Holke, who was sitting in the back as an aircraft observer, suddenly reported enemy planes. Rommel ordered everyone to take cover – but he was too late. The British fighter-bombers dived towards their target, firing from all barrels. Rommel's driver had his shoulder torn out and lost control of the car. A shell shattered his adjutant's pelvis, and the field-marshal himself, hit by a piece of shrapnel, flung himself out of the vehicle. He was found to have a fracture to the base of his skull and other severe head injuries. It was nearly an hour before they could get the badly wounded Rommel to a hospital. The German general's life was saved by a French pharmacist. The beacon of hope that Rommel represented had been extinguished by the British airmen. Yet had he been unscathed, would Rommel have stood with the men of 20 July?

There had been several attempts to win Rommel over to the cause of active resistance. The secretary to the military governor in France recalls a conversation that took place between Stülpnagel and Rommel. In it Rommel had expressed fundamental misgivings about any attempt on Hitler's life. Stülpnagel tried again to draw Rommel into the resistance, through Hans Speidel, Rommel's chief-of-staff, whose brother-in-law was on Stülpnagel's staff. By this time, Speidel, who was confident in his opposition to Hitler, made no secret of his low opinion of the Führer when talking to senior officers in the west. A major on Rommel's staff described the 'mood of total defeatism' at these gatherings – when Rommel was not present. 'In his absence Speidel took over as chairman and the whole conversation revolved around the *arschloch* [arsehole] in the Berghof, meaning Hitler.' Speidel was convinced that Hitler would never make a separate peace with the Western Allies. Rommel thought otherwise, even though he had repeatedly heard from Hitler's own lips that any such peace was out of the question. 'No-one makes peace with me', Hitler had declared – and he was not willing to make peace with anyone either. Nevertheless, up to the day of his injury, Rommel had not given up hope of persuading Hitler to negotiate a separate peace in the west. However much Rommel might have agreed with Speidel's political and military aims, the conclusions that the two men drew from them were very different. Speidel and the officers of 20 July knew that Hitler had to be removed from the equation. For Rommel there was no such *sine qua non*.

The link-man between the conspirators and Rommel was *Oberstleutnant* Cäsar von Hofacker. On 9 July he spoke in person to the field-marshal at La Roche-Guyon. No written record was kept of this or of other similar conversations; the risk of discovery would have been too great. Today we have to rely on the memories of those involved, and on statements made to the Gestapo and to the Wehrmacht's so-called 'Court of Honour'. In these we find many contradictions.

When interrogated by the Gestapo, Cäsar von Hofacker is supposed to have claimed that on 9 July he had informed Rommel's chief-of-staff, Hans Speidel, about the planned assassination of Hitler, and had been assured by Speidel that he would pass the information on to his chief. This conflicts with another version, according to which von Hofacker personally put Rommel in the picture about the whole thing. In a conversation with officers in Paris prior to the attempted coup, Hofacker described how he had revealed to Rommel specific details of the plan. The surviving Paris officers recall Hofacker's assertions that Rommel had given an indication of his support.

It is no longer possible to clear up these contradictions. On 30 August 1944 Hofacker was convicted of high treason. He died an agonising death by hanging at Berlin's Plötzensee prison on 20 December that year.

In the reports from the Central Office of Reich Security to Martin Bormann, Hitler's *éminence grise*, it is true that we find no concrete evidence that Rommel knew about the planned coup. Rommel's pessimistic assessment of the situation in the west is certainly presented in detail, but Hitler did not need a secret service to tell him that. Rommel had never made a secret of his views; they were well known to the Führer from personal conversations he had had with the *Generalfeldmarschall*.

On 4 October the Wehrmacht's 'Court of Honour' met once again in Berlin. It was necessary for this tribunal to find an officer guilty and dismiss him from the Wehrmacht, before he could be put on trial before the People's Court. On this occasion it was Ernst Kaltenbrunner, head of the security services, who led the prosecution against Rommel's chief-of-staff, Hans Speidel. The charge was: having knowledge of and abetting the attempted assassination of the Führer. Speidel denied knowledge of the conspiracy. Two generals, Guderian and Kirchheim, submitted a plea that he was 'not under suspicion'. Through his acquittal by the military court of honour, Speidel escaped the fate of many other members of the resistance movement. After the war he wrote a book, *Invasion 1944. A Contribution to the Fate of Rommel and the Reich*, in which he gave a different version of events. According to this, he was aware in principle about the 20 July plot, but had known none of the details, and thus was unable to pass on any to Rommel.

Today we must assume that Rommel really did know nothing of Stauffenberg's plans, and that when he heard of them after 20 July, he condemned them. He told Kluge that the attempted coup was 'madness'. On 24 July, just after it happened, he wrote to his wife: 'We can thank God, that the outcome was so good' (i.e. that Hitler had survived). But in the shadow of Nazi censorship Rommel could hardly have done other than condemn the plot. Such written evidence is of little value as a demonstration of his actual disapproval. Yet the reverse is equally true: publicly Rommel, like many other high-ranking officers, had distanced himself from the 'traitors'. His declaration of devotion to Hitler, made after the attempt on his life, ('Only one thought rules my mind at all times, to fight and to be victorious for our new Germany'), can hardly be regarded as a genuine oath of loyalty to the dictator. What else *could* a senior officer say after the coup had failed, without putting himself and his family in danger? The '*Heil, Mein Führer*', with which Rommel ends his letter to Hitler, is not sufficient to prove the field-marshal's unshakeable bondage to Hitler.

So if authentic documents from Rommel's hand are not available, or are of limited evidential value to historians, then in answering the question of Rommel's attitude to the attempt on Hitler's life we are at least helped by the statements of those who knew him best and with whom he discussed events without fear of exposure. Rommel's wife Lucie has stated in writing: 'I would like to make it clear that my husband played no part either in preparing or carrying out the coup of 20 July 1944, since, as a soldier, he refused to take that path. Throughout his career he was always a soldier, never a politician.' The time when she made this statement is worth noting: Lucie Rommel did not utter these words in defending her husband against Hitler's thugs, but in September 1945, that is to say at a time when admitting to involvement with the resistance would have carried no risk at all. After the war, quite a few people suddenly discovered a sympathy with Stauffenberg and the number of 'secret' resistance fighters grew hugely. But Rommel's wife stood her ground: her husband knew nothing of the conspiracy, she insisted, and had he known about it, he would have refused on principle to have anything to do with it. The oath of loyalty to Hitler, which, from 2 August 1934 onwards, every German soldier had to swear in person, once again proved to be an obstacle. Every serving officer and man had sworn unquestioning obedience. Since March 1944 the field-marshals of the Reich had been obliged to make a further vow of loyalty to the person of the Führer. Like Rundstedt, Manstein and the other most senior officers in the Wehrmacht, Rommel had once more confirmed his oath of allegiance to Hitler by putting his signature to it. For Rommel, breaking this oath was out of the question. But his unconditional loyalty to his supreme commander did not prevent Rommel from speaking his mind on military matters – and if political conclusions had to be drawn from military questions, because only in that way could the military problems be solved, then the non-political soldier would address the political consequences as well. Rommel was therefore one of the few men in Hitler's immediate entourage who was not afraid to express a dissenting view to the Führer's face. So it was not a lack of courage that held Rommel back from joining the conspirators. It had more to do with his concept of honour and 'loyalty'.

> The field-marshal set his face against the assassination plans, because he did not want to see Hitler made a martyr. His own thinking was to seize Hitler with the help of trustworthy panzer units, in order to bring him before a German court of law and convict him of crimes against his own nation and against humanity. The people who elected him should also sit in judgement on him.
>
> *General Hans Speidel, retired*

I believe that, at the time when my father joined Rommel, relations between Rommel and Hitler were no longer very good. There was a great deal of scepticism. There was a discussion – in February 1944, I think – that Rommel had with Dr Strölin, the Oberbürgermeister of Stuttgart, who was a member of the Goerdeler group. That group was already talking about how Hitler might be removed – preferably by legal means.

Ina Saame, Hans Speidel's daughter

Manfred Rommel tells us that his father certainly had 'considerable sympathy' with the plotters but had constantly argued against the much-discussed tyrannicide. 'He always used to say: "Hitler dead is more dangerous than Hitler alive."' Rommel had expressed his basic attitude to the notion of removing the Führer as the central figure of the Third Reich, in several conversations with Karl Strölin, *Oberbürgermeister* of Stuttgart. Rommel had known Strölin since the First World War, when the two fought in the same unit. There was a relationship of trust between them. It was late in 1943 that Strölin told him for the first time about the persecution of the Jews, and described the consequences that his criticism of those events had had for him, Strölin. During a spell of home leave at Herrlingen in February 1944, Rommel told his wife of another conversation in which Strölin spoke to him of the crimes of the Nazis in the east, of the butchering of the Jews, of the mass shootings and murders. Strölin expressed the hope that the field-marshal might lend his name to a movement for the 'salvation of the Reich'. As Strölin put it: 'Unless that man Hitler dies, nothing makes any sense.' Yet Rommel emphatically rejected this verdict: 'If you hold such a view, then I would be most obliged if you did not air it in front of my under-age son.'

From Rommel's conduct during and after this conversation, historians draw two conclusions:

1. Rommel knew of the things that were being done behind the German front line in the east – even if he may not have been

aware of the true extent of the human annihilation. However,
he did not hold Hitler responsible for these crimes, only the
men around him.

2. Rommel rejected any action against Hitler that had the aim of
killing Germany's dictator. Hitler ought to be arrested and
called to account before a court of law – such was his idealistic,
not to say naive, attitude towards the man to whom he had
sworn his loyalty.

Nevertheless, Rommel did draw one conclusion from these
conversations: he forbade his son to become a member of the *Waffen-
SS* – something that in a fit of youthful enthusiasm Manfred was
considering. But in obedience to his father he decided against it.
Keeping himself and his family out of the toils of the Nazi leadership
and their henchmen was a step that distanced Rommel from the
regime to which he was not a little indebted. The field-marshal took
the next step, too: he developed concrete plans to conclude a
separate peace with the Western Allies and thereby to act in direct
defiance of the orders of the supreme commanders. However, he did
not make the final leap into active resistance.

The reasons why Hitler nonetheless withdrew his favour from his
'favourite general' do not lie in any actual participation in the 20
July attempt on his life. By now the 'greatest military commander of
all time' had come to despise his successful desert general as much
as he did almost all the generals in the Wehrmacht. When the
Führer appointed Hans Krebs as Speidel's successor, on 25 August
1944, he told Speidel that Rommel 'has done the worst thing that
any soldier could ever do in such a situation: seek a way out that is
not a military one. Within limitations, I consider Rommel an
extraordinarily bold and also a clever commander. But I don't think
he's a stayer, and that is the view of all the senior officers.' These
words express disappointment, but no feeling of revenge or hatred, of
the kind that Hitler revealed in his radio broadcast after the
attempted assassination, when he ranted about 'a small clique of
ambitious, ruthless as well as criminal and stupid officers'. Before
this, there was no hint that Hitler intended to hold Rommel

responsible. His attitude towards the field-marshal was admittedly much frostier than before, but it was far from hostile. Nevertheless, Rommel's fate was already sealed.

Generals Guderian and Kirchheim, neither great admirers of the field-marshal, had pleaded in the defence of Rommel's chief-of-staff, Hans Speidel, that he was 'not under suspicion'. When the court of honour concurred with this view, it meant Speidel's acquittal, true enough, but at the same time the witch-hunt against Field-Marshal Rommel began.

There has been much speculation about whether Rommel was the victim of an intrigue among the general staff. He was certainly not short of enemies in the top ranks of the military. Anyone whose career path had risen so steeply, who had enjoyed such public popularity and above all, who owed his promotion to the one man who wielded unlimited power, was bound to attract envy and ill-will. Apart from anything else, the largely close-knit and aristocratic caste of senior officers harboured a latent distrust of the 'upstart' Rommel. He had never been through general staff training – and yet he had risen to the rank of field-marshal. Hitler had backed Rommel and promoted him while other officers were passed over. Rommel had quickly acquired a reputation as a 'typical National Socialist protégé' and nothing clings longer than a bad reputation. Furthermore, Rommel had given the other German generals ample cause for irritation: in front of Hitler he criticised the OKW for 'lacking judgement based on front-line experience', privately he accused Kesselring of sabotaging his supply-lines and indirectly blamed him for Germany's defeat in North Africa. Lastly, Rommel had been consistently successful for a long time, and success breeds jealousy.

The senior men in the Army High Command, Halder and Brauchitsch, continued to have a low regard for Rommel, right up to their dismissal (Brauchitsch in 1941, Halder in 1942), and spoke of his 'pathological ambition' and 'character defects'. Göring had been forced to listen to harsh criticism from Rommel about the capabilities of his Luftwaffe. But after the events of 20 July 1944, certain central figures in Hitler's entourage were of greater importance: intriguers like Keitel and Burgdorf could now try to remove the unpopular competitor from the scene and at the same time find someone to blame for the wretched situation on the western front. But what could the top military brass produce, in order to exploit the post-20 July situation and settle accounts with their rival?

High treason did not simply mean active participation in a coup against the Führer. It was the crime of anyone who no longer believed in the 'final victory'; who was suspected of treating with the enemy; who had information about a planned assassination and did not pass it on. And it was this that the officers seized upon. The key question was posed in the proceedings against General Speidel before the army's 'Court of Honour', on 4 October 1944. Two of the six army generals on the tribunal, Kirchheim and Guderian, wrote in a sworn statement after the war that *Oberst* Hofacker had stated that he had informed Speidel about the 20 July plan to assassinate Hitler. Speidel, so they claimed, had in turn stated that, as a matter of duty, he passed this on to his superior, Rommel. It is a fact that Rommel did not pass on any information about the planned coup. What remains in doubt is whether Speidel really had informed Rommel, or whether he merely claimed to have done so in order to protect himself. By defending Speidel's version as credible, Guderian acquitted him and at the same pointed the finger at Rommel.

After the war, Speidel denied having incriminated Rommel. The man who most strongly supported Speidel's version in the Nuremberg war crimes tribunal, was none other than the head of the OKW, Wilhelm Keitel, who had been despised by Rommel and referred to by most senior officers as *Lackeitel*. As ostensible proof of Rommel's guilt, Keitel pointed to the statement by *Oberstleutnant* Cäsar von Hofacker. However, it can be shown that the record of this statement was not handed over to the OKW until *after* the proceedings against Speidel – in other words at an astonishingly late stage. The trial of Hofacker had taken place as early as 30 August.

We are left with a jungle of conflicting claims, which cannot be disentangled with complete certainty. The sequence of events and the laws of logic would indicate that Speidel's statement, made in his own defence, was reinforced with falsified evidence in order that Rommel could be accused of 'complicity' in the attempt on Hitler's life. 'It's all the work of Keitel and Jodl', wrote Alfred-Ingemar Berndt to Rommel's widow. And Berndt was on just as good terms with Goebbels as he had been with Rommel. Even a Nazi propagandist can occasionally tell the truth.

On 7 October Hitler told the OKW chief, Keitel, to summon Rommel to Berlin for a discussion about where his talents might be applied next. In a telephone call to Berlin Rommel used his physical exhaustion as a pretext to refuse the invitation. As he told his immediate family: 'If I were fool enough to go to Berlin, that would certainly be the last you'd see of me.' Rommel's refusal to present himself to Hitler in person was taken by his adversaries to be an admission of guilt. Six days later the OKW announced that two officers would shortly be paying him a visit. But this time the conversation would not be about new military assignments for the now recuperated field-marshal.

'Please accept my sincere condolences for the heavy loss that you have suffered through the death of your husband. The name of *Generalfeldmarschall* Rommel will for ever be linked with the heroic struggle in North Africa. Adolf Hitler.' Sheer hypocrisy poured from this telegram, dated 16 October and addressed to the field-marshal's widow. For one last time Nazi propaganda abused the myth of Erwin Rommel. News of the idol's death had reached the ears of the world on 15 October. A daily order issued by Hitler read: '*Generalfeldmarschall* Rommel has died as the result of the severe injuries which he suffered in a road accident on his way to the front, while serving as commander-in-chief of an Army Group in the west. His death robs us of one of our best army commanders.' It was the mendacious opening to a campaign that reached its climax with a state funeral on 18 October. The aim of Hitler's stage-managers was not to mount a dignified farewell tribute to Erwin Rommel; instead they put on a macabre spectacle designed to blind people to the disgraceful truth. The genuine grief of the family members was derided in the most repulsive manner. 'As the late field-marshal would have wished it, their courage reminds us all once more of the watchword: fight on to victory.' That was, of course, the last thing that Rommel, driven to his death, would have wanted.

The Nazis had devoted a lot of care to the state funeral on 18 October 1944. Hitler had called for a day of national mourning, but balked at travelling to Rommel's Swabian homeland himself. In the ballroom of the City Hall in Ulm, and in the square outside, thousands of mourners had assembled. Germans all over the Reich saw the newsreel images on their cinema screens. They heard the salute being fired, shattering the silence as the coffin was borne from the City Hall. They saw the crowds lining the streets on the route to the crematorium, they felt a tremor of emotion when the military band struck up *'Ich hatt' einen Kameraden'* ('I had a comrade . . .'), while a wreath sent by Hitler was laid on the bier. High-ranking officers and leading civilians sat in the front row beside the grieving relatives and paid their last respects to the dead man. It was a highly effective production, perfectly executed and utterly phoney. On the swastika-draped coffin lay Rommel's steel helmet and field-marshal's baton. His many decorations were placed on a modest velvet cushion. Four generals stood as a guard of honour with drawn swords. When Lucie and Manfred Rommel entered the hall, the orchestra played a selection from Wagner's *Twilight of the Gods.*

The eulogy was spoken by *Generalfeldmarschall* Gerd von Rundstedt, the highest-ranking officer in the German army: 'Not only the German Wehrmacht, but the entire German people stand with us in deep anguish beside the bier of this dead hero. A harsh fate has snatched him from us at the very moment when the battle is reaching its climax.' The 'harsh fate' had a name: Hitler. The man who was now being heaped with praise had shortly beforehand been forced to commit suicide.

Rommel had written to a staff officer: 'I'm feeling better; I'll be returning to the front in the next few days or weeks.' And then suddenly we heard on the radio that Rommel had died from his injuries. We all said to each other: that can't be right; he has just written to say he would be returning to his job. It made us suspicious. Rommel was the one officer who had always received high praise. The fact that Hitler did not attend his burial – only Guderian – surprised us very much. We thought, there's something wrong here . . .

Wilfried Armbruster, Rommel's interpreter

Rommel had to die, because after the Allied landings in Normandy his advice had been to end the war, that it was lost. Hitler regarded that advice as treason.

Robert M. Kempner, former US prosecutor at Nuremberg

It was a brilliant autumn day on 14 October 1944. But the men whom Hitler had chosen as his envoys had no eyes for the beauties of Herrlingen, as they drove up to the field-marshal's house around midday. Their arrival boded no good. General Burgdorf was the Führer's chief adjutant, having succeeded Rommel's friend General Schmundt, who had been killed by the bomb that was meant for Hitler. His colleague, General Maisel, was in charge of 'matters of honour' in the army's personnel department and anything but an admirer of Rommel. That morning, when Rommel went for a walk with his son, he had hinted at his dark forebodings and said he did not trust either of the two generals. And he had good reason. The field-marshal was already expecting to be held accountable for the failure of German defence against the Allied landings; but now the two men confronted him with 'evidence' of his alleged implication in the attempt to kill Hitler. Keitel had despatched his messengers of death to confront Rommel with a stark choice: if he was innocent of the charges, he should go to Berlin to prove it. If not, then as an officer and a man of honour he should avoid a trial and accept the 'appropriate consequences'. They were to give him a further piece of advice: should Rommel take the second option, he was to choose poison rather than the pistol. Even as a professional soldier, Rommel was not to die by the bullet but by swallowing a cyanide capsule from the stock held by the army personnel department. This would give Hitler's executioners a better chance of disguising the cause of death. For the outcome of the conversation with Rommel was a foregone conclusion even before the two generals set off from Berlin. At that moment the Nazi authorities were already making preparations for the state funeral. As early as 13 October (the day before Rommel's death) the Wehrmacht headquarters in Ulm received the news that a wreath would be arriving from Berlin.

'It is quite impossible for me to express what I could read in his face', Lucie Rommel later said of the moment, around 1 p.m., when her husband came out of his study to tell her the result of the hour-long discussion with Burgdorf and Maisel. With military succinctness, a pale but self-controlled Rommel imparted the dread news: 'I've come to say goodbye. They suspect me of being involved in the plot against Hitler. The Führer has faced me with the choice either of poisoning myself or standing trial before the People's Court. They've brought the poison with them. In a quarter of an hour I'll be dead.' Lucie Rommel begged her husband to defend himself in Berlin. But Rommel refused: 'I know I'll never reach Berlin. They'll get rid of me first.' He assured his wife, who had anyway never believed otherwise, that there was no truth in the accusations, that he had nothing to fear from the People's Court, and that the charges must have been the result of the usual blackmail methods.

Manfred Rommel also describes his father as 'extremely distressed but under control, pale but in command of himself', as he bade his family farewell. Erwin Rommel explained to his 15-year-old son what was about to happen, and why. His final comforting thought was that after his death, the family would be unmolested. 'Hitler asked them to tell me that, in the event of my suicide, nothing will happen to you; on the contrary, you will be well looked after.' By taking his own life, Rommel preserved his family from *Sippenhaft*, the Nazi custom of exacting retribution from the whole family of a 'traitor';

he would be given a state funeral so that 'the secret of his treason could be kept from the German people'. It was important to the Nazis to practise this deception on the public. A memorial was even promised to the man who, in the opinion of the Nazi leadership, really was a traitor.

After his wife and son, Rommel's adjutant, Aldinger, was the third person he told about what had happened and was yet to happen: 'I know very well that Hitler wants me out of the way and that, even if I got as far as Berlin alive, I would be condemned to death by the People's Court.' Aldinger advised him to run for it, but Rommel refused. 'After consulting my wife, I have decided to take the path that I clearly have to take. I feel no guilt. I was not party to any crime. I have done nothing but serve my Fatherland all my life.'

After a brief farewell to his wife, Rommel walked to the waiting car, accompanied by his son and his adjutant. The field-marshal took his place on the back seat, between Burgdorf and Maisel. The small black Opel drove off down the road towards the nearby town of Blaubeuren. Several cars, which had been parked unobtrusively around Rommel's country house, moved off.

A few yards beyond the outskirts of Herrlingen village, Burgdorf asked the driver to stop the car. The driver and General Maisel got out of the vehicle. Hitler's chief adjutant, Burgdorf, handed Rommel the deadly poison capsule, but the poison did not work as swiftly as the field-marshal had assured his wife it would. When the driver was called back to the car ten minutes later, Rommel was still alive. 'I saw Rommel sitting slumped in the car, groaning. I sat him up straight and put on his cap, which had fallen on to the floor.' Then silence fell. Rommel was dead.

After the terrible news of Rommel's death my mother drove to Herrlingen, and by the open coffin Frau Rommel told her of his violent end. She asked my mother to help her remove the medals from the field-marshal's body, they were the *Pour le Mérite* and the Knight's Cross. No filthy hands should ever touch them, she said.

Ina Saame, General Speidel's daughter

> My mother was completely numb. We just didn't know how long our freedom would last, or whether, when the 'play-acting' was over, we would be rapidly deprived of it.
>
> *Manfred Rommel*

At 1.24 p.m. Burgdorf and Maisel delivered the field-marshal's body to the emergency military hospital in Ulm's Wagner High School. During the journey, so the generals claimed, Rommel had suddenly become 'indisposed', probably due to an 'embolism'. They lied with complete assurance. The doctor in charge later told the family that immediate attempts to revive the field-marshal had been unsuccessful. 'Heart failure' was the official verdict in the hastily issued death certificate. The senior medical officer, who did not see the corpse until twenty-four hours after the established time of death, stated after the war that, in view of the symptoms, he had reported his doubts about the cause of death and applied for permission to carry out an autopsy. This was apparently refused. 'I was told to have nothing more to do with the Rommel case. I was relieved of my duties. A short time later I was informed that Berlin had refused an autopsy.' The Nazi regime had no interest in the truth and made sure all traces of it were erased. Rommel's body was to be cremated. No one was to find out the real cause of his death.

> I immediately noticed that the marshal's face looked a picture of health, as though he were asleep. By contrast, his hands had a waxy pallor, and their total rigidity indicated death. That seemed very odd to me.
>
> *Dr Kandler, doctor in charge of the Wagner School military hospital, Ulm, speaking in July 1946*

Lucie Rommel recalled later that, during Rundstedt's eulogy, she considered 'accusing the murderers in the full gaze of the public at the funeral. But what would have been the point? My husband was dead, and now I had to think of my son. They would have killed Manfred too. They knew I was forced to say nothing.'

Thus her protest remained a silent one. She ignored the outstretched hand proffered by General Maisel to express his condolence. As late as March 1945 plans were submitted to Lucie Rommel for a memorial that the Führer was planning to erect over Rommel's grave, in order to keep alive the legend of the 'Desert Fox' and to go on spinning a web of lies around his death. Rommel's widow played for time and delayed making up her mind. In the end it was Germany's defeat and the death of Hitler that finally put paid to this last hypocritical gesture by the Nazis.

> The murder had to be concealed from the nation. By means of the official ceremony for the field-marshal on 18 October in the Ulm City Hall, a political desecration without precedent in history, Hitler attempted to disguise the deed and erase all traces of it.
>
> *General Hans Speidel, retired*
>
> His heart belonged to the Führer.
> *General Gerd von Rundstedt at the ceremony in the Ulm City Hall*

In the person of Erwin Rommel we see clearly the dilemma that faced a responsible general in a totalitarian regime. The root of the word 'general' means 'a man who carries overall responsibility'. Does that mean responsibility for ensuring that military objectives are achieved? Indeed it does. Responsibility for the means employed in the achievement of these objectives? That too. Ultimately responsible, as well, for what his own efforts made possible? By giving stability to a regime whose goal was the destruction of human life, the murder of millions, the extermination of entire peoples – even the annihilation of his own nation? A general who felt bound by his personal oath of loyalty and who thus at the same time made an inhuman policy possible – does such a man meet the demands placed on a 'general' officer? Erwin Rommel, the 'Desert Fox', was a gifted leader of his troops. But did that military genius have a fatal moral flaw?

The tragedy of Rommel was that, never having learned the full extent of the genocide, he represented the soldierly virtues in their most marked form – and in doing so was the servant of a criminal.

It was Rommel's good fortune that there were no special SD squads massacring the civil population behind his advancing troops. Rommel is free of the guilt which other generals in Hitler's Wehrmacht assumed. Yet a form of guilt hangs over him too. It is not guilt in a criminal sense. Rommel shared in the tragedy of Germany because he remained loyal to Hitler, and because, in the belief that he was doing his military duty, he ignored the non-military consequences of his actions. After the war, his wife Lucie declared: 'So ended the life of a man who throughout his life had placed his entire being in the service of the Fatherland.' It is in this self-delusion that the whole tragedy of Rommel lies. As he saw it, he was serving the Fatherland. As history sees it, he served a despot – a despot to whom he had sworn allegiance as his Führer. Like many others, Rommel was taken in by a lie of Nazi propaganda, which presented Hitler's goals as identical with the interests of Germany.

It was still possible for Rommel to have ultimately recognised this identity as illusory. He succeeded in distancing himself from the Hitler he once revered. If it is true that great men, when faced with the consequences of their former actions, are capable of recognising their error and revising their ideas, then Rommel was great. He would have been even greater had he taken the next step and risked active resistance. But Prussian field-marshals do not mutiny, even if they come from Swabia.

Manfred Rommel has accepted the truth about his father's life: 'Secondary virtues like obedience, courage and discipline are wonderful, as long as they serve a primary virtue: the love of truth or the love of mankind. But if they do no more than serve the Führer, Adolf Hitler, and his strange notion of Fatherland, then those virtues become vices.'

> It is clear today that it was far better to lose the war than to win it with Hitler. That was not very easy for a professional soldier to accept. But at the time my father probably suspected it was true.
>
> *Manfred Rommel*

CHAPTER TWO

The Accomplice – Wilhelm Keitel

The war is won, and cannot now be lost . . .

How can you contradict the Führer like that? Don't you see how worked up he gets? What would happen if something like that caused him to have a stroke?

As atonement for the life of one German soldier the death penalty should as a rule be imposed on 50 to 100 communists

You're alive, *Mein Führer*, you're alive!

When an order had been given, then I did what I considered to be my duty, without letting myself be distracted by the possible, though not always *ascertainable*, consequences

I do not dispute that I had knowledge of all those orders, regardless of whether they bore my signature or not

Generaloberst Jodl and I were not always in agreement with the decisions taken by the Supreme Commander, but we invariably carried them out

I believed. I was mistaken. That is my guilt.

Wilhelm Keitel

———————————— * ————————————

We knew he had no real clout. So I didn't regard him as Chief-of-Staff of the Wehrmacht. I never thought of him as such, and in fact he never gave that impression.

Hubertus von Humboldt, officer on the General Staff

As a secretary you get a sort of feeling for what your boss is really interested in. Let's say in music or religion or philosophy or architecture. But no, you felt he was just a soldier.

Hilde Haenichen, Keitel's secretary

In other circumstances, I could well imagine him as head of a large, well-run organisation, though without the very highest responsibility.

Count Johann von Kielmansegg, officer on the General Staff

In many respects he handed the Wehrmacht to Hitler on a plate. And that anxiety to please was summed up in his nickname, *Lackeitel.*

Ewald von Kleist, a brother-officer of Stauffenberg

Keitel was malleable, he was putty in Hitler's hands, as well as being cast in the role of lightning-conductor. He took a lot of flak and had to put up with it all.

Georg Lindemann, member of the anti-Nazi resistance

Keitel always appeared very calm. In the company of others he made a tall, impressive figure, and towered over them in a way. His whole nature was calm and conciliatory. . . . Keitel was a fine man.

Kurt Salterberg, guard in the Führer's headquarters

Constantly in Hitler's immediate proximity, he was completely under his influence. Over the years an honourable, solidly respectable general turned into a fawning, dishonest, mindless servant. Keitel was basically a victim of his own weakness.

Albert Speer

He was a burly, rustic type, who did after all come from a farming family. His father owned land, of course, and he would have liked to have taken it over. He would have been happier as a farmer than as a general.

Karl Böhm-Tettelbach, officer under Keitel

I believe that a man like Keitel could perfectly well recognise cause and effect, and perfectly well see the many contradictions; he could have raised objections if he hadn't feared for his own skin.

Fritz Buchner, aide-de-camp in the Führer's headquarters

As regards charisma, I would rank Keitel with a head waiter or possibly the director of a museum.

Wolfgang Brocke, Keitel's transport officer

Hitler knew he could totally rely on this man; that is why he kept him on, even though he had no illusions about Keitel's qualities as a strategist.

Heinz Guderian, panzer general

The general opinion is that Hitler kept Keitel firmly at his side, because he was convinced of his unquestioning obedience as a soldier and his unswerving loyalty.

Werner von Blomberg, Reich Minister of War 1933–8

He was ambitious yet talentless, loyal yet characterless; he possessed a certain natural astuteness and charm, but no intelligence, nor did he have a strong personality.

Nikolaus von Below, one of Hitler's adjutants

For all his physical robustness, Keitel was a vulnerable, sensitive person, without a trace of brutality or cruelty in his make-up. His pain at the death of his son and daughter, and anxiety about his wife in the air-raids on Berlin, affected him deeply. . . . He was the only one who, after the bomb exploded on 20 July

1944, calmly took Hitler in his arms and, holding him as carefully as he would a child, carried him into the open air. . . .
A conscientious, obedient soldier, too soft and too decent for Hitler, but honest, genuine and co-operative.

Alfred Jodl, Hitler's chief of Wehrmacht operations

One might describe him as a 'sentence-finisher'. He simply watches the Führer's lips and as soon as he sees where a sentence is leading, he is keen to finish it for him. His personnel policy is downright appalling. His servility is so abject that he goes as far as keeping his own brother away from Hitler.

Joseph Goebbels

---------------- * ----------------

In the little German village of Helmscherode, time seems to stand still. Young people head for the towns because farming offers less and less work. Rarely does a car drive down the narrow street. Many houses in this little farming community, in the western foothills of the Harz mountains, look just as they did sixty years ago – in Helmscherode's 'good old days'. That was when the hamlet was still the envy of neighbouring villages; when the squire, who lived on the big estate at the edge of the village, laid out new footpaths, built modern homes for farm-workers and paid for the renovation of the little church; when Helmscherode seemed to benefit from the fresh wind of the 'Thousand Year Reich'. The old folk of the village still clearly remember their erstwhile benefactor. 'He was always very good to us. He made no distinction between rich and poor', says a woman who once worked on the estate. 'He looked after his people', says another appreciatively. No-one seems concerned by the fact that the kindly landowner more than doubled the size of his property during the war – and at the expense of Church lands. They probably feel he earned it.

The little chapel in the middle of the village, romantically overgrown with ivy, is locked most of the time. But anyone who tracks down the key-holder is greeted by a surprise within. Portrayed in oil on canvas, the old benefactor of the village directs his stern and dignified gaze down on to the pews. The picture on the wall of the church shows the Chief of the High Command of Hitler's Wehrmacht, Wilhelm Keitel, in his field-marshal's uniform. The observer cannot help thinking of the inscription on the belt-buckle of every German soldier: *Gott mit uns* (God with us). What is more, outside the church, and charitably hidden by shrubbery, stands a memorial, which the village squire erected to his 'Führer and Reich Chancellor Adolf Hitler' on the occasion of the *Anschluss*, or annexation, of Austria, in the 'Year of Our Lord 1938'.

In Helmscherode time seems to stand still. Only an insignificant shadow is cast over the memory of its most famous son by the fact that the Allies sentenced him to death in Nuremberg in 1946. People do not really wish to hear about the orders he gave, orders which dragged German soldiers into the criminal morass of Hitler's Reich – nor about his instruction to kill 50 to 100 hostages for every dead German, nor yet about his cynical justification for the mass murder of millions of Soviet prisoners-of-war by saying that it was simply 'the destruction of an ideology'. 'He was just a soldier who was obliged to carry out orders', we are told – and to cap it all: 'Of course, he would have preferred to be a farmer.'

At the end of his life, Keitel himself came close to cutting the ground from under the feet of all those, including many in the Wehrmacht, who were still endeavouring to minimise his role in the war. In February 1946 Robert Kempner, the US prosecutor at the Nuremberg war crimes tribunal, heard a knock on his office door. It was Keitel's defence lawyer, Otto Nelte. The American was surprised to hear that Nelte wanted to speak to him alone, without an interpreter or stenographer. Gradually, however, he realised that this conversation did indeed merit confidentiality, since the entire Nuremberg proceedings appeared to have reached a turning point. Nelte revealed to him that his client 'was heavily burdened by having signed Hitler's orders as his all too willing tool', and that he now wished to make a confession. Keitel's aim, said Nelte, was to 'relieve those who had executed his orders of some of their criminal responsibility'. Furthermore, he hoped in this way to escape a 'dishonourable' execution by hanging, and instead to face a firing squad 'like a soldier'. Kempner was, apparently, 'profoundly impressed'. As he later recalled, he interpreted Keitel's proposal as a 'sign of soldierly decency' and as an 'act of patriotism'.

Like all the other defendants, Keitel had earlier rapped out the words 'not guilty' to the court; but the thing which most of all now turned him into a repentant sinner was the screening of a film. This was a compilation of footage of the concentration camps, some parts filmed privately by members of the SS, others by Allied cameramen. It was a document of unrelenting horror. An interpreter at the trial, Lion Le Tanson, remembers today the reactions it provoked: 'Göring said it was a fake, a Russian film. Most thought it had been set up. But others were deeply shocked. Keitel wept as he watched bulldozers piling up the mountains of corpses.' The court psychologist, Gustave Gilbert, heard Keitel's reaction at first hand. 'When I see things like that, I am ashamed to be German', the marshal told him, visibly affected, then hastily added: 'But I didn't know about it.'

After Nelte's visit, Robert Kempner sat there, thunderstruck. He knew, of course, that a confession by one of the principal defendants would help to give the entire trial a firmer moral foundation. Keitel's remorse may have come too late for the victims, but for posterity it might pave the way to the truth. Kempner eagerly speculated whether 'other defendants would follow his example'. But on 23 February 1946 Nelte came to see him again and told him that Keitel had suddenly changed his mind and was not going to make a confession. The reason that the defence counsel gave was that Göring, who Keitel 'still regarded as his superior officer' had 'ordered him' to do this. Nelte said that his client was still of the opinion that a confession was the correct and 'honourable' step, but he nevertheless bowed to Göring's authority. In this way, Wilhelm Keitel threw away his last chance to correct the image that history would form of him. To the last, he clung to that overriding principle to which he was prepared to subordinate all else: absolute obedience.

In contrast to most of the other defendants at Nuremberg, no historian or journalist has dealt in detail with the figure of Keitel. Until the publication of his memoirs, written while in custody, there existed only brief biographical sketches of this man. He seemed to possess too little individuality, and he personified too completely the culmination of an aberrant trend, embodying as he did all the vices of an entire military caste. But this is precisely why Keitel's story is a good example of how a man with no pronounced criminal leanings, with no trace of the demonic in him, can still assume monstrous guilt.

His former subordinates describe his outward appearance as stolid and unsophisticated. In our interviews with them, comparisons ranged from 'ticket collector' to 'head waiter'. Nor was this impression deceptive. Keitel was indeed fundamentally ill-equipped for his position. Anyone reading the memoirs written in his Nuremberg cell, or the letters he left behind, will be astonished by his jejune prose, by the narrowness of his intellectual horizons. It was precisely Keitel's weakness which made him appear predestined for the post of chief-of-staff of the Wehrmacht. He was certainly not as unscrupulous or as criminally inclined as many senior military figures claimed after the Nuremberg Trials, in the search for people to blame for their own failures. Like many, he was simply too weak to accept where his actions were leading. Instead, he took refuge in obedience without limit – not realising, in so doing, how very culpable he had become. It was only in Nuremberg that he came to accept this guilt, albeit assisted by the tireless persuasion of his defence counsel.

His career does provide some clues as to why he ended up where he did. From childhood he seems to have been under great pressure to succeed, and to have known the feeling of being unable to meet people's expectations. At his high school in Göttingen, he had particular difficulty with classical languages. On one occasion, his divinity teacher sardonically alluded to his rustic ancestry, when the class was tackling the Greek text of St Paul's Second Epistle to the Romans: 'Keitel, I'm sure you'd be a hundred times better at taking

St Paul out riding on a pair of fiery steeds than at understanding his theology!' Young Keitel's scholastic difficulties must have been so serious that even in his Nuremberg cell he recalled being proud of his 'smooth transition' to the senior class. His professional career was decided for him by his father. Since Carl Keitel still felt too young for retirement, and had just married a second wife, he was in no hurry to hand the estate over to his eldest son from his first marriage. That is why Wilhelm had to go into the army and, for the first but by no means last time in his life, was obliged to bow to someone else's decision on a matter of vital importance to him. He tells us he wept; and even as a field-marshal he often regretted the opportunity he had missed of becoming a farmer and landowner.

Keitel's first contact with the army produced another disappointment. In the summer of 1899 a regimental doctor judged the 17-year-old's chest measurement too small and was about to send him back home. It was only the intervention of his uncle Paul Keitel, a senior army medical officer, that prevented a humiliating rejection – the first of numerous instances of nepotism in his career. He would later continue this tradition, when he wangled the post of head of army personnel for his younger brother Bodewin. At Easter 1900 Carl Keitel signed his son up with the 46th Field Artillery Regiment in Wolfenbüttel, Lower Saxony. Keitel Junior would much rather have been a cavalry officer, but since in those days an officer's family was responsible for the upkeep of his horses, the financially strapped Keitels opted for something cheaper. So the field artillery was the second choice, but even so, as the recruit was happy to note, 'you could ride there as well'. For the rest of his life Keitel would suffer from a feeling of inferiority among those with more prestigious army careers. He felt at a particular disadvantage in comparison with men who had graduated from one of the officer-cadet colleges. His memoirs are dotted with references to 'typical' or 'supercilious' cadets.

In 1902 Keitel was promoted to *Leutnant*. He was now stationed in Braunschweig (Brunswick), not far from his home, yet far enough for him to be independent. These were probably the happiest years of his life. Undisturbed, he could indulge his passions for horses, hunting and good food and drink. At court balls given by the Prince

Regent of Brunswick, the now tall and well-built officer was a good and popular dancer. However, it seems he was innocent of the vices that typified his comrades and their class: 'No gambling and no fooling around with women', was his motto, or so he told a friend of his youth. As a somewhat rough-hewn but conscientious and industrious character, he seemed assured of a decent career in the Kaiser's army. He had no outside interests to distract him. Neither in those early days as a soldier, nor in later years can we find any evidence that he read anything other than military books. Wilhelm Keitel's world was defined by barrack duty, gunnery practice, manoeuvres, riding to hounds and evenings in the officers' mess. Even his secretary, who first met him two decades later, came to the conclusion that 'he was really just a soldier'. It must be said that in this he was no different from most of his colleagues.

In 1909 Keitel married Lisa Fontaine, whose father owned a brewery and a large country estate near Hanover. For her, Keitel was not exactly a 'good match', since the Keitels' property was nowhere near as large as her own family's. Perhaps this was the reason for the great pride which, from then on, she took in her husband's military career. The well-read, intelligent and musical Lisa made it clear from the outset that she had no fantasies about being the wife of a gentleman farmer in remote Helmscherode. On visits to her husband's home she left the company in no doubt that she preferred the city atmosphere. 'She kept her nose rather in the air', remembers a woman who was employed on the Keitel estate. Lisa Keitel's world was that of high-society receptions and dinner parties. A diplomat who was invited a number of times to the Keitels' home in Berlin in the 1930s describes her as a 'warm-hearted lady', and a 'perfect hostess'.

The First World War gave a boost to Keitel's career. For six months at the front he was forced to face mass warfare and death on an industrial scale. Now with the rank of *Hauptmann* (captain), he was wounded by a shell-splinter and awarded the Iron Cross (First Class). These events – his only front-line experience until the spring of 1945 – left a deep mark on him. In January 1915, his wife Lisa wrote anxiously to her father-in-law to say that her husband's letters 'always sound so sad, and there's really nothing one can do to help'. But two months later she could breathe more easily. Keitel was posted to the General Staff. This was an unexpected promotion and meant that he was no longer in immediate danger of his life. In March 1915, shortly before he took up his new post, Lisa shared her hopes with her father-in-law: 'He's in seventh heaven. Admittedly, he hasn't got his red trousers yet' (meaning the red stripe on a staff officer's uniform trousers) 'but provided he doesn't actually disgrace himself, we can expect them very soon.'

His posting to the level of war planners and strategists who, from the comparative security of their headquarters, determined the fate of front-line units for good or ill, once again triggered Keitel's inferiority complex. Compared with the other staff officers, he lacked five years' advanced training. He complained to his father that he was deficient in his 'ABC and two times table' and was obliged to rely on 'healthy common sense'. In fact he was so successful in compensating for his lack of formal training by working long hours into the night that in 1917 he was promoted to be the youngest senior staff officer in the entire German army.

Wilhelm is still outside Verdun. He's writing a bit more sensibly now, but sadly it doesn't seem to be more than the usual prophecies of doom. . . . His nerves seem to be in tatters. Can't sleep and always these dreadful palpitations.

Lisa Keitel, letter to her mother, 2 August 1916

There is no doubt that Wilhelm Keitel had great talent as an organiser. It was not his job to take strategic decisions; instead he juggled with supply shipments and troop movements. He was one of the first examples of a new type of officer – the military manager. With the increasing modernisation of warfare, specialists like him would soon be in great demand.

At the same time, his acquaintance with Major Werner von Blomberg was to have crucial importance for his future career.

Blomberg, who in 1933 was appointed Minister of War, was four years older than Keitel, and very different from him: educated, with refined literary tastes, and interested in philosophy. Later, when Keitel was Wehrmacht Chief-of-Staff, and after his dramatic breach with Blomberg, he said that he had never really been close to him personally. Yet the two military men shared much more than merely the same colour of uniform. In the slipstream of his older colleague, Keitel's career forged ahead, and when Blomberg's daughter Dorothee married Keitel's son Karl-Heinz in 1938, the two families were regarded by Berlin society as closely allied.

The end of the war, in the chilly autumn of 1918, hit Germany like an earthquake. Most people failed to understand why, after a constant stream of reported victories, they suddenly had to accept defeat. Surely German troops were still deep in Flanders, and far into the Ukraine, while the enemy were nowhere on German soil? Had not the press run endless stories about new offensives, and the imminent 'decisive battle'? Very few knew the truth about the state of the German army and the Kaiser's war economy. So it was that Erich Ludendorff who, from 1916 onwards was *de facto* vested with the powers of a military dictator, was able to sue for an armistice and at the same time spread the legend that the front-line troops had succumbed to a treacherous 'stab in the back'. The generalissimo hastily declared the Communist-inspired mutinies and uprisings to be the cause of Germany's defeat instead of a consequence of it, as in fact they were.

In the final days of the war, *Hauptmann* Keitel was serving in Flanders, with the general command of the Naval Corps; and he had a pretty exact picture of the opposition's crushing superiority, of the first serious breaches in the German front and especially of the enormous supply problems. Nevertheless he was among the first to start weaving tales about the 'stab in the back'. On 10 December he told his father-in-law that 'the flaming red torch [of socialism] flung out from the homeland' was to blame for the fact that 'those immense, victorious battles' had been fought in vain. 'You will be able to judge what conditions were like for us,' Keitel went on, 'when I tell you that in order to carry out my duties I needed a protective pass from the Soldiers' Council and had to agree to fly the red flag from my car; otherwise I would have been disarmed, stripped of my cockades and epaulettes and thrown out of my vehicle.'

It was his political naivety that made him susceptible to counter-revolutionary slogans. Since he was incapable, in the looming collapse of the army supply system, to convert his military expertise into political skills, the sense of being surrounded by rebellious subordinates became more and more deeply ingrained in him. He had actually been forced to tie a red flag to his staff car! The revolution was a trauma that left him, and many others, with a permanent scar. For all conservative opponents of the new republic, there was only one thing to do: wait until the time came to counter-attack. 'But thank God we're still young and healthy enough', the disappointed Keitel comforted himself, 'to rebuild through conscientious and honest labour everything that has been destroyed in a few days of senseless madness.'

His wife Lisa was more realistic. She often spoke openly about the Kaiser's 'monstrous errors' and confessed that she felt very much in sympathy with the 'democratic government'. At the same time she was well aware of the contrast with her husband's opinions: 'The whole thing is particularly depressing for the military', she wrote rather smugly on 5 November 1918, 'not least for someone who has such very old-fashioned Prussian views.' True, her husband's 'old-fashioned Prussian views' reflected the predominant attitude of the entire officer corps. In order to 'come to terms' with their failure on the field of battle, the senior military projected their guilt on to the newly established republic. They fell victim to their own narrow political horizons – and were easy prey for Ludendorff who, with a sure instinct for symbolism, had made sure the armistice document was signed not by generals but by civilian politicians. The peace terms imposed by the victors soon completely hardened the battle-lines in domestic politics. The fury over the 'disgrace of Versailles' and over the revolution of the 'November criminals' was already recognisable as the explosive charge that would destroy Germany's first republic. But until that day came, the officer corps mentally retreated into a 'circle of covered wagons' and kept their heads down. Outwardly, they professed neutrality under the slogan of 'the non-political soldier', but in the barracks and gaming houses hate-filled tirades against the republic were common. Keitel himself talked of the 'mentally sick German people'.

Under the terms of the Treaty of Versailles the republic was only allowed to maintain 100,000 men under arms. Only 4,000 officers were permitted. Even Belgium and Poland had more soldiers than Germany. Beside the feeling of deep humiliation, this resulted, for tens of thousands of former career officers, in the threat of unemployment. 'What will become of men like us', Keitel wrote anxiously, 'is still far from clear.' As a way out, he first joined one of the *Freikorps*, the illegal paramilitary units dedicated to continuing the war in skirmishes on the Polish border. The fateful spirit of those politicised freebooters, which Keitel, like so many future officers in Hitler's Wehrmacht, absorbed there, found expression in his letters. Here he writes about the 'insolent Polish riff-raff' and the 'huge degree of self-denial' required when serving with the often undisciplined *Freikorps*. His long-held desire 'in the near future to say farewell to soldiering for ever' once more became acute. But then he received an invitation to stay on in the new army of the republic, the Reichswehr. He did not hesitate long before saying yes. Whether the decisive factor was his delight in belonging once more to the 'elite', or his wife's refusal to move into the farm in Helmscherode, remains an open question.

Regarding my immediate military future the die has been cast, as I learned yesterday in a personal letter from the Ministry of Defence. On 1 February I will once more have to don my general staff uniform and make myself useful in the *Truppenamt*.

Keitel, in a letter to his father, 20 January 1925

As early as February 1919, the precise reason why Keitel was required to 'stay on' began to emerge. He was invited by the former commander of his unit to go to the Reich Ministry of Defence for a discussion 'about the future army'. His abilities as a planner and administrator had apparently left a favourable impression. But it was not until 1925, after the election of the venerable Field-Marshal Hindenburg as president heralded the beginning of a gradual slide to the right, that Keitel was allowed to get his hands on the levers of secret rearmament. In the *Truppenamt*, or Army Office, which was nothing less than the banned Army General Staff operating under a false name, Keitel co-ordinated the training and equipping of the *Grenzschutz Ost* (Eastern Border Protection Force), a heavily armed militia, which in practice represented an illegal enlargement of the Reichswehr. A report to the government revealed that, since 1927, the secret armouries of this and other shadow-armies had seen a build-up to five times as many rifles and six times as many artillery-pieces as were permitted by the victors at Versailles. It is probable that even these figures were considerably underestimated. The size and strength of the 'black Reichswehr' were 'kept secret even from our own government', as Keitel's secretary recalls. At that time her boss, now promoted to major, was acting on the fringes of legality by renewing contacts from his *Freikorps* days. The *Grenzschutz* was a happy hunting ground for many restless ex-officers who had by now found a new home in the nationalist *Stahlhelm* (Steel Helmet) organisation, in Hitler's SA storm-troopers, or in obscure societies such as the *Jungdeutscher Orden* or the *Werwolf*. It is true that Keitel maintained a cautious distance from these politically motivated adventurers, but he recognised them as 'splendid material' for a new army.

Even so, his position of responsibility revived old fears of failure. Keitel's wife talked about his sleeplessness and 'obsessions'. Her husband had 'no time for anything', worked into the small hours nearly every night and gave his colleagues the impression of being constantly on edge. 'He carries on frightfully', Lisa complained in January 1926, 'and is in a very bad mood.' The 44-year-old Keitel was suffering from serious health problems. In his office in the Reich Ministry of Defence he had started chain-smoking and had put on too much weight. He attributed his phlebitis and cardiac pains to lack of exercise, and realised he was 'completely overstretched'. An exaggerated sense of duty began to dominate his whole personality.

> Wilhelm always talks about being 'carted off to prison'. By that
> he means the Ministry of Defence.
>
> *Lisa Keitel, in a letter to her mother*

As a protégé of his old friend Blomberg who, as head of the
Truppenamt, scarcely made a secret of his animosity towards the
succession of republican governments, Keitel rose in 1929 to be in
charge of the Army Organisation Department. By now he had the
rank of *Oberstleutnant* (Lieutenant-Colonel). In his new post he came
into contact with another illegal method of evading the restrictions
of the Treaty of Versailles: rearmament on foreign soil. In Spain,
Sweden and the Netherlands, German experts were developing the
most up-to-date war equipment: aircraft, tanks and other banned
categories of weaponry. In Japanese shipyards, new types of
submarine were being built to German naval designs. The
Reichswehr even collaborated with Stalin's Red Army. In Russian
training areas, Soviet and German tank crews secretly practised
modern mobile warfare. The object of these activities abroad was not
to establish significant fighting forces beyond Germany's borders, but
first and foremost to gain technological leadership in the armaments
industry. According to secret ministerial papers, this even extended
to preparations for a 'modern gas war'. As it later proved, the
ultimate beneficiary of all this war-gaming would be Hitler. It is no
coincidence that the Wehrmacht's battle-order for the invasion of
Poland corresponded exactly to the plans that Keitel had helped to
draw up under the Weimar Republic.

In 1931 Wilhelm Keitel himself travelled to Russia, in order to
get a picture of the joint operations with the Red Army. One of the
party accompanying him was Walther von Brauchitsch who, ten
years later, would be Hitler's army commander-in-chief during the
invasion of the Soviet Union. Although the trip took place at the
height of summer, the atmosphere that greeted them was frosty.
The Soviet army chiefs permitted no convivial or comradely
contacts with the class enemy. A German officer recalled that

'private contacts with the other side were absolutely forbidden'. Instead, the guests were taken on tours to see demonstrations of the 'capabilities' of communism. The delegation from the Reich Ministry of Defence also visited a number of collective farms and People's Factories. Twelve years previously, Keitel had considered the red flag on his staff car as heralding the destruction of his homeland. Now he felt admiration for the achievements of the 'Bolshevists'. As a farmer's son, the industrialisation of Soviet agriculture made a particularly deep impression on him. Enthusiastically he described to his father what he had seen: 'Only a man who works has a right to live,' Keitel rhapsodised. 'The Red Army is the core of the state and a springboard to the highest offices in government.' Was the red-hater from the *Freikorps* now an admirer of the Soviet empire? No, Keitel had certainly not been converted to socialism overnight. What fascinated him was not the life of Lenin, but the 'possibilities' he perceived in a totalitarian dictatorship. Faced with the annual squabble in the Reichstag over Germany's military budget, the military planners could only gaze with green-eyed envy at the seemingly inexhaustible resources of the Red Army. This army and this state seemed to be capable of waging the 'total war' that Ludendorff had prophesied for the future – a war for which a nation's entire civil society would have to be mobilised. It appeared that dictatorship created the ideal conditions for this. Even Blomberg, Keitel's friend and patron, came back from a Russian trip impressed. 'It wouldn't have needed much', he later confessed, 'for me to have come home a fully-fledged Bolshevist.'

When in Germany, too, a dictator made a successful bid for power, Wilhelm Keitel happened to be on a rest cure in the Tatra mountains of southern Poland. A thrombosis in his right leg and repeated heart attacks had forced him to take time off. At first the convalescent, who was now a full colonel, was sceptical about the National Socialists. He could still remember well the 'arrogance of the SA', who were beginning to compete with the Reichswehr as a second armed force within the state. Like most of the conservative–

nationalist members of his class, he rated Hitler as no more than a 'drummer', who could certainly whip up support among the masses, but lacked the stature of a national leader. In 1933 his miscalculation was no isolated instance. Indeed, the appointment of the leader of the Nazi Party as Reich Chancellor was recognised by only a few of his contemporaries as the fatal break with Germany's past which it was later to prove. He was, after all, the twenty-first Reich Chancellor to have held office since 1919.

Soon, however, Keitel came to like Hitler. The fact that the Führer, on his first day in office, 30 January 1933, appointed Keitel's old colleague Blomberg to be the new Reich Minister of Defence no doubt contributed to this. Blomberg, who had known and admired Hitler since first meeting him in August 1930, wasted no time in setting a course for the future. Within weeks of taking up his post he issued instructions to the soldiers of the Reichswehr to salute the uniform and banners of the Nazi Party; he introduced the heraldic eagle of the party as an element of army uniform and ordered his officers to run weekend training courses for members of the SA and the Nazi Party. The reticence of 'non-political' soldiers was a thing of the past. Keitel also played a part in the measures for training brownshirts. On 17 May he gave a 'big speech to all the Nazi and *Stahlhelm* top brass', as his wife put it, and early in July, at a 'conference of senior SA officers' in Bad Reichenhall, he met Hitler for the first time. Like Blomberg, three years previously, he came back fascinated from his first encounter with the former corporal. Lisa described his transformation in a letter to her mother: 'He was thoroughly rejuvenated, and so full of energy. He talked to Hitler for quite a long time, up in his little house (on the Obersalzberg) and was absolutely enthralled by him. He said his eyes were amazing, and how the man could talk.' It was the seminal experience in the life of Wilhelm Keitel. From the first moment Hitler's powers of suggestion, described by many who saw him, had an overwhelming effect on the politically rather innocent officer. Keitel, not normally a man given to extravagant phrases, in retrospect used terms like 'demon' and 'powerless tool' to characterise his relationship with Hitler.

In April 1934 he was promoted to *Generalmajor* and posted to Potsdam as acting divisional commander. It was a promotion that was in line with his seniority, and for a while it freed him from the wearying desk work of the ministry. Like most army officers he welcomed the end of parliamentary democracy and Hitler's first steps towards bursting the 'fetters of Versailles'. From behind the walls of an army barracks it was easy to ignore the dark side of the totalitarian state. The arrest of political opponents, the abolition of free trade unions, and the first acts of anti-Semitism were virtually unseen amid the joy at the army's 'resurrection'. Even the progressive conditioning of the military to the persecution of the Jews provoked scarcely any resistance. On 8 December 1933 Defence Minister Blomberg ordered the rigorous observance of a boycott of Jewish shops and businesses. Soon all Jews were expelled from the Reichswehr and soldiers were forbidden to marry 'non-Aryan' women. No indeed, the Reichswehr was far from being an island of purity in a brown-tainted swamp, as many military men claimed in retrospect. They accepted, almost without comment, the fact that, from one day to the next, Jewish officers and men, often with decorations for bravery in the First World War, were no longer their comrades-in-arms. It was already the beginning of the Wehrmacht's long history of involvement in the crimes of the regime.

Hitler rewarded the silence of the army leadership with particular generosity. In the eyes of the military, his proclamations about the 'twin pillars of the state', Army and Party, put a welcome end to the 'Cinderella' status they had endured under the Weimar republic. As early as 3 February 1933, the new Reich Chancellor offered the senior generals the pact which ultimately led to the Second World War: the Reichswehr was to remain the nation's sole bearer of arms, provided it helped him to realise his far-reaching foreign ambitions. Someone present at the meeting noted with considerable disbelief that Hitler's goal was '*Lebensraum* in the east and its ruthless Germanisation'. On 30 June 1934 this pact was sealed with blood. When Hitler's close friend, Ernst Röhm, and his senior SA colleagues, wanted to establish a militia-like 'people's army' to supplant the old Reichswehr, Hitler put a bloody end to their unwelcome claims to power. Equipped with weapons from the Reichswehr, and under the pretext of an alleged plot by Röhm to stage a *coup d'état*, SS squads swarmed out of their barracks and murdered over 100 SA officers. Röhm was personally arrested by Hitler in the lakeside resort of Bad Wies-See, and shot a few days later. During this 'night of the long knives' the Reichswehr stood at the ready, and said nothing when the murders were later announced as having been perfectly legal. Despite vehement protests from the officer corps, Minister Blomberg did not even demur when the SS settled old accounts by liquidating two army generals, Schleicher (who had been the last Reich Chancellor before Hitler) and Bredow. Even in 1946, Keitel believed that Schleicher, 'a cat who couldn't leave political mice alone', was personally responsible for his own violent end.

When Keitel's father died on 10 May 1934, the son was once more faced with a decision that would affect his whole future. On 1 October he handed in his request to leave the army, in order to take up his inheritance in Helmscherode. But his wife Lisa and the Commander-in-Chief of the Army, Werner von Fritsch, both raised strong objections. 'My wife and I discussed it back and forth', Keitel recalled in his Nuremberg cell. 'I was drawn to Helmscherode with every fibre in my being, but my wife refused to share the house with my stepmother and my sister, and I couldn't resolve the problem.' What finally decided things – whether it was his wife's intransigence, the family dispute, or the urging of his commander-in-chief – we shall never know. But in the end Keitel withdrew his request and, much to Lisa's relief, moved to Bremen as commander of a division. 'In such ways are human destinies decided', he later commented on this not entirely willing choice.

With the 22nd Infantry Division in Bremen, he established one of the new units which, following the acclaimed termination of the Treaty of Versailles, Hitler described as future guarantors of 'Germany's freedom'. Seven years later the division was among those which captured Sevastopol in the Crimea and suffered heavy losses. As commanding officer in Bremen, Keitel singled himself out for more senior posts, chiefly through his rather ostentatious loyalty to the regime. For example, in March 1935, though with only mediocre gifts as a speaker, he gave a speech to local party chiefs, which ended in 'repeated shouts of *Heil Hitler*'. Apart from this, he was mainly noted for his painstaking observance of army regulations. According to a story circulating at the time, whenever he set off in his staff car for an official reception in the Hanseatic city, his wife had to follow behind by public transport. He would have considered that to take her with him by car would be 'highly incorrect'.

In September he received an invitation from the office of his old friend Blomberg: would he care to accompany the minister to the national rally of the Nazi Party? After the war, Keitel could still describe his feelings in this way: 'I have to say that I was absolutely overwhelmed by the event; the various parades on the Mars Field, the massed ranks of the Party and its many sections.' He was particularly affected by the nocturnal 'light effects' and the 'searchlight dome'. There is no doubt that the elaborately staged mass marches, banner parades and torchlight processions all had the desired effect on Wilhelm Keitel. A revealing light is thrown on the editor of his memoirs by the fact that for publication he heavily abridged Keitel's rapturous description of the party rally – something he otherwise did only with passages of a purely private nature. Needless to say, there is no word to be found, in either the published or unpublished parts, about the promulgation of the Nuremberg Race Laws, which took place at the same time.

His conformist attitude led, in October of that year, to his further advancement, to be the new head of the Wehrmacht Office in the Berlin ministry, which by now was no longer the ministry of 'Defence' but far more appropriately the 'Reich Ministry of War'. Once again, his wife Lisa seems to have been the driving force behind the scenes since, when Blomberg first took soundings, Keitel had given a negative response, on the grounds that he 'wanted nothing to with politics'. However, Lisa argued that 'her health had never been better than in the Berlin climate', and was thus able to persuade her husband to accept the new post. The important thing, for her, was that she expected it would give him better career opportunities – rightly, as it would soon turn out. By January 1936 Keitel was a *Generalleutnant*. That evident lack of decisiveness, which put him at the mercy of other interests, was to dog him for the rest of his career.

When Seeckt was in charge [of the Reichswehr], it's doubtful whether Keitel would have got any further than major.
Nikolaus von Below, one of Hitler's adjutants

He didn't have a martial manner. He was more like an ordinary citizen, a civil servant, perhaps a senior civil servant.
Wolfgang Brocke, transport officer under Keitel

As head of the Wehrmacht Office, Keitel held a key position in the armed forces, on paper at least. His department was in charge of all military intelligence, telecommunications and the administrative duties of the Minister. In practice, however, the three armed services, the army, the air force (Luftwaffe) and the navy led their own lives largely undisturbed by the ministry. The Wehrmacht (combined services) was in the midst of an upheaval which was affecting all the world's armed forces. Whereas in the First World War the army's operations on land formed the core of the operational command, now, with the advance of arms technology, the necessity for a combined command of all the armed services was becoming increasingly apparent. The air force, which until 1918 had been a somewhat exotic appendage of the land forces, had now become a decisive factor.

Yet in the wrangling over spheres of influence in the Third Reich, the establishment of a joint high command over land, sea and air forces encountered stubborn resistance. The Army General Staff, under its chief-of-staff, Ludwig Beck, who was later implicated in the 20 July plot to kill Hitler, bitterly defended every jot of independence against the modernisers from the Wehrmacht Office. In internal discussions he quite openly referred to the reformers as the 'enemy'. Nor did the Luftwaffe have any intention of surrendering its autonomy. Its chief, Hermann Göring, the 'Number Two' to Hitler, commented acidly that he couldn't care less whether he reported to 'Corporal Meier' or 'General Wilhelm Keitel'; he would only take orders from Hitler in person. For this reason, Keitel and Blomberg, together with the gifted strategist Alfred Jodl, fought a lonely battle for a unified command structure, which would meet not only military imperatives but also ideological criteria. 'The concept of the Führer-state', Keitel declared, 'means that the head of state is called upon to take command. This principle extends to all areas and quite naturally it has very particular relevance in the military sphere.'

The fact is that not until the last months of the war was there a united Wehrmacht command – and then it was born of necessity. Up to that point, the duplication of responsibilities led in countless cases to belated and all too often erroneous orders. A genuinely united military body for decision making at the highest level, like the American joint chiefs-of-staff, never existed in Hitler's Wehrmacht. However, the causes of this did not lie, as Keitel believed to the end, in the deep-rooted recalcitrance of the individual services. Hitler himself was to blame. Just as in all areas of government and administration, so too in the armed forces the dictator deliberately avoided erecting clear power-structures. To him, a single 'strong will' seemed more effective than established hierarchies. At the same time, of course, rivalry between his satraps served to reinforce his own position of power. Göring's remark about 'Corporal Meier' illustrated something that would soon be true everywhere in the rank jungle of Nazi power: the final decision always lay with the Führer himself – as referee and sole binding court of appeal for all the paladins and fiefdoms of his dictatorship. On a military level, this would lead to the ignoring of 'expert opinion' and to appalling losses in battle.

As head of the Wehrmacht Office Keitel soon earned a reputation for being a 'yes-man' and party loyalist. In 1936 he and Blomberg drafted an order that all 'politically unreliable' soldiers should be dismissed from the Wehrmacht and immediately reported to the Gestapo. The two old colleagues were agreed that saturating the troops with ideology was a prerequisite for a 'regulated preparation' for war. In 1937 the Minister of War gave an indication to his senior officers of where the journey would take them, with a vague allusion to an 'impending war in the east'. Part of Keitel's job was to cultivate contacts with the Nazi Party and he maintained a vigorous exchange of views with Rudolf Hess, the cranky 'Deputy to the Führer'. In December 1937 the two men launched what amounted to a PR campaign in favour of better relations between the Nazi Party and the army – something which appeared necessary, in view of some outbreaks of violence between SA brownshirts and regular soldiers. As a reward for this schmooze-offensive Keitel was one of the first senior military officers to receive the Gold Party Medal, which was normally reserved for the movement's 'old campaigners'. Now at last he 'belonged'.

Shortly afterwards, this loyalty to the party line catapulted him right into the dictator's immediate circle. What triggered this was an erotic scandal that opened the gates for Hitler's final rise to absolute power. One September morning in 1937 the Minister of War had to forgo his usual ride in the park because his horse had gone lame. Thereupon Blomberg, a widower of 60, decided to go for a walk instead, and found his destiny sitting on a park bench – in the form of 23-year-old Erna Gruhn. 'The damned nag was to blame for it all', was how his adjutant, Böhm-Tettelbach, sarcastically summed up the trivial incident. A passionate relationship was ignited between the field-marshal and the young woman. At Christmas 1937 Keitel was told by his future daughter-in-law, 'Dorle' Blomberg, that her father wanted to marry again. The circumstances were certainly dubious. The minister disappeared with his bride for several days to a remote mountain hotel, and their wedding, which took place on 12 January, was treated as a 'matter of national secrecy'. Hitler and Göring acted as witnesses, but apart from them only the adjutants attended the simple ceremony in the Reich Chancellery. A few months earlier, Göring's second marriage, to the actress Emmy Sonnemann, had been celebrated with a parade of troops, eight brass bands and a 21-gun salute outside Berlin's cathedral. Yet the Blomberg ceremony was kept hidden from the public – except for a brief announcement in a Berlin newspaper.

Then, on 23 January, the Chief of Police in Berlin, Count Helldorf, turned up in Keitel's office. As Keitel remembered it, the official had come into the ministry by a side entrance. He seemed 'very agitated' and 'asked questions about what the Minister's young wife looked like'. To his astonishment, Helldorf discovered that Keitel, who since the engagement of his son to Blomberg's daughter, was after all 'almost one of the family', had never even seen the new Frau Blomberg. Helldorf then produced from his briefcase a document from the Berlin vice squad, laid it on Keitel's desk and revealed to him that Fräulein Erna Gruhn, 'who had officially reported moving from her own home district as Blomberg's wife, had a previous conviction for immorality'. One of Helldorf's clerks had been amazed to see the name Gruhn in the wedding announcement.

The police file has been preserved to this day and is kept under lock and key in the offices of Berlin's Public Prosecutor. It contains not only details of Gruhn being questioned on suspicion of 'procuring' in 1932, but also several pornographic photographs of the young woman. Keitel's appalled reaction on seeing these obscene poses is understandable. Had the field-marshal wedded a woman of easy virtue? Keitel immediately tried to reach Blomberg, but the minister was not in the building. He then demanded that Helldorf should publish the file, which the police chief refused to do. Finally he phoned Göring, who had of course seen the girl when a witness at her wedding, and asked him to examine the embarrassing photos. Helldorf immediately went off to see the Luftwaffe chief, who recognised Blomberg's new wife as the woman in the photos, and from then on events swiftly took their course.

Four days later Blomberg was forced to resign. Yet the affront over his violation of the strict moral code of the Prussian officer corps was only a pretext. In truth Hitler wanted to get rid of the minister anyway, because – with some justification – he saw him as an obstacle in his path towards war. It is the case that Field-Marshal Blomberg, as well as the commander-in-chief of the army, Werner von Fritsch, were still able to maintain a certain independence and had vehemently voiced their opposition when Hitler gave an address about future war aims. The scandal caused by Blomberg's inappropriate nuptials came at just the right moment. Hitler put on an act of being deeply disappointed, reproached Blomberg bitterly and demanded that the marriage be annulled immediately. But the War Minister, who was obviously enjoying a late-flowering passion, refused to comply. Thereupon the Führer, whose one-time affaire with his own niece, Geli Raubal, had long been talked about by those in the know, had a fit of morality and made it clear that in the circumstances the minister had to go.

Blomberg himself later blamed Keitel for his downfall and spread the word that his subordinate had 'betrayed' him in order to further his own career. He claimed that, instead of getting rid of the incriminating file, or at least keeping it under cover until his retirement, Keitel had passed it on to the ambitious Göring, who was known to have his eye on the post of War Minister for himself. Many historians have accepted this version. The truth, however, looks different. Keitel's decision to bring Göring into the loop was entirely appropriate, given the high standing that the Luftwaffe chief then enjoyed in the Wehrmacht. The prestige-hungry paladin did not express any interest in the ministerial post until *after* Blomberg's resignation. What is more, both Helldorf and Keitel assumed that Blomberg personally had no idea about his young wife's past – quite apart from the fact that Keitel was, by nature, anything but a manipulative careerist. No, it was not Keitel's action that triggered the crisis. The fault lay more with Blomberg's naivety; he was in fact aware of his bride's former life, but probably imagined that the whole matter would be handled with the same discretion as was applied to the wedding ceremony. 'These old men with their adolescent urges', Lisa Keitel commented, pointedly recalling the fact that 'the King of England' had recently been deprived of his throne and his dignity through saying 'I do' to the wrong woman.

For Keitel this was the turning point of his life. Immediately after the minister's enforced resignation, he received an order to report to Hitler at 1 p.m. on 27 January 1938 – in civilian clothes. How this appointment came to be made was described by Blomberg at the Nuremberg tribunal. When he went to take his leave, Hitler had told

Blomberg he wanted to set up an independent military staff as the 'Wehrmacht Supreme Command'. At first this sounded as though the Führer had finally decided to put into effect the many proposals for a body capable of issuing orders to the whole Wehrmacht. However, on closer examination it turned out to be no more than a staff of grandly titled aides to Hitler himself. When asked who should be put in charge of such a body, Blomberg said he was unable to give an answer. However, Hitler insisted: whom, he asked, had he had 'beside him' up till then? 'Oh, Keitel', Blomberg replied. 'He has only been looking after my office'; whereupon the dictator shouted gleefully: 'But that's exactly the man I'm looking for!' Apparently the name of this 'ideal' man meant nothing to Hitler at that point, because he immediately went to his outer office and asked for 'General von Keitel' to be summoned.

> A man with the brain of a cinema doorman is no use to me.
> *Hitler to Goebbels, about Keitel, in 1942*

For all the dictator's notorious impetuosity, it may be assumed that the staffing of the Wehrmacht Supreme Command (OKW) was preceded by a rather more detailed examination than a name plucked at random – particularly since, at the Nuremberg Trials, Blomberg came up with a different version, in which it was he himself who had proposed Keitel. Yet the first story told by Keitel's former boss, who never forgave what he took to be treachery by his subordinate, does have a kernel of truth. It was indeed Keitel's weakness that made him interesting to Hitler. What Hitler was seeking was not a man of stature from the general staff tradition, with whom he would have to wrangle endlessly. The prime virtues of the new OKW chief had to be reliability and obedience. Keitel was also well aware that he lacked 'talent' and 'previous general staff training', and suggested that the title of his new post should be 'Chief of Staff of the Wehrmacht Supreme Command', which would have defined his subsequent activity more closely. But for Hitler that would have been 'too little'. So it was that the history of the OKW began with a fraudulent label, one which was probably responsible for putting the bearer of the title 'Chief of the Wehrmacht Supreme Command' in the dock at Nuremberg, along with the other leading war criminals.

> Keitel himself had no predisposition whatever for strategy.
> *Günter Reichelm, colonel in the General Staff*

When Keitel paid his first official visit to the Reich Chancellery, Hitler, as so often, acted the courteous and friendly host. 'You are my confidant and my sole adviser on Wehrmacht matters', he flattered the business-suited general, who we must assume still believed in this apparent show of favour, even though Hitler, among his intimate circle, had for some time described Keitel as having 'the brain of a cinema doorman'. The first question the master and his aide now tackled was who should succeed Blomberg. Keitel suggested Göring – which shows how little he then understood about Hitler's method of wielding power. The Führer rejected the idea on the grounds that the Luftwaffe chief already had enough to do with his Four-Year Plan. Then Keitel threw in the name of Fritsch, the army commander-in-chief. But Hitler went to his desk and pulled out a file sent to him by the Minister of Justice, in which Fritsch was accused of violating Clause 175, which made homosexuality a crime. 'I was appalled by this denunciation', Keitel recalled later. Though it is worth noting that he had told colleagues he had 'known about these things for two years', as Jodl noted in his diary.

The fact is that the accusation against the army C-in-C had been launched by the Gestapo. An alleged 'witness' from among Berlin's rent-boy milieu had reported the general as being a customer of his. The truth was that the youth had conducted his business with an insignificant cavalry captain who happened to have a similar name (von Frisch). Yet the highly embarrassing charge, with which the Gestapo 'confronted' Fritsch, raised the curtain on a kind of low farce in the Reich Chancellery, which was enough to remove Fritsch from the stage as well. Whether Hitler himself had been pulling the strings or had simply exploited a Gestapo foul-up is unclear.

Outwardly he displayed the same shock and outrage as he had in the Blomberg case: 'If this kind of thing is possible among Prussian generals', fumed the petty-bourgeois Austrian, 'then anything in this world is possible.' The spurious outburst was followed by calculated action. The paralysed Army High Command offered no resistance when the dictator now installed himself as Supreme Commander of the Wehrmacht and appointed the pallid and pliable Walther von Brauchitsch in place of Fritsch. This was the true completion of the 'seizure of power'; only now did the Führer possess full totalitarian power – and the necessary accomplices to exercise it.

Henceforth there was to be no Minister of War. With immediate effect, Keitel's OKW was responsible for the administrative duties of the ministry. These included, in addition to the Wehrmacht Office, which was taken over by Jodl, the military intelligence bureau (Abwehr) under Admiral Canaris, the personnel department, prisoners-of-war, military jurisdiction, and the particularly important Office for War Economy and Armaments. It was a vast administrative empire, which would grow even larger once the war started. Yet in practice, aside from pure administration, the OKW chief scarcely had any discretion for a policy of his own, because Hitler reserved all important questions to himself. All that remained for Keitel to do was to implement – to execute, through orders and instructions – the guidelines issued by the 'supreme authority', as he soon came to call Hitler.

> He stayed in the background, behind Hitler, who of course was supposed to be the greatest military leader of all time, and Hitler liked that.
>
> *Hubertus von Humboldt, officer on the General Staff*
>
> He had to be on call, because he would suddenly hear: 'Issue an order', or 'See to it that they get sent a lot more weapons'. He had to be ready. So he had to listen. But he never initiated anything.
>
> *Karl Böhm-Tettelbach, officer under Keitel*

Quite soon after taking up his post, he ought to have been able to see how completely he had become the tool of a gambler. On 12 February he was summoned to the Berghof, 'with no reason given', together with generals Reichenau and Sperrle. This time he wore uniform. When the officers arrived it was revealed to them that the Chancellor of Austria, Kurt von Schuschnigg, was about to arrive on an official visit, and their presence was required 'to provide an atmosphere of menace'. Hitler's Luftwaffe adjutant, von Below, had been given the job of rustling up some generals who looked 'particularly martial'. That afternoon, when the Austrian delegation withdrew for a private discussion, Hitler suddenly bellowed at the top of his voice: 'General Keitel! Send Keitel in immediately!' The OKW chief dashed into the room, out of breath, and asked Hitler what orders he wished to issue. But all he heard was: 'None at all! Sit down.' The object of this display had been achieved. Schuschnigg departed, intimidated by Hitler's threats.

> A proper mess-officer from the Kaiser's time, a fossil, the way German officers are usually portrayed abroad – that was Keitel. You couldn't have had a more suitable figure.
>
> *Fritz Buchner, aide in the Führer's headquarters*
>
> He was a thoroughly imposing sight. Tall, ramrod-straight, serious, fine looking. In purely external terms, he was a real Prussian general.
>
> *Bernd Freytag von Loringhoven, officer on the General Staff*

On 12 March 1938 the dictator reaped the harvest that this drama had sown and drove into Austria at the head of his Wehrmacht troops. Keitel, who was in his retinue, remembered seeing 'tears of joy' running down the face of the former Austrian (Hitler had not acquired German citizenship until 1932). But it was the events of the previous night that particularly stayed in his memory. The army commander-in-chief, Brauchitsch, and some of his senior officers, had telephoned him repeatedly and implored to him to try and dissuade Hitler from ordering the march into Austria. 'I did not for a moment consider even once raising the question with the Führer', Keitel later commented. 'The Führer heard nothing of this. If he had, his verdict on the army commanders would have been devastating, and I wanted to spare them that, and Hitler too.' It was the first time that the OKW chief functioned as hinge between Hitler and the army. By the end of the war he was no longer able to shake off this role. On the eve of the *Anschluss*, two basic patterns of behaviour became apparent: on one hand, the army generals avoided, from bitter experience, dealing face-to-face with Hitler and relied on Keitel's skills as an intermediary – usually to no effect; on the other hand, the OKW chief shielded Hitler from any news which, in his usually correct judgement, would trigger a fit of rage. The march into Austria seemed to confirm the rightness of this tactic. No incidents of bloodshed occurred, nor were there any recognisable signs of an international crisis, as the army commanders had feared.

Only two months later, on 20 May, Keitel, on Hitler's orders, submitted a draft plan for the next raid, the so-called 'Case Green' – and was careful to point out that he had not yet discussed it with the commanders-in-chief of the three arms of the Wehrmacht. Keitel's paper talked of a 'particularly favourable situation' and of 'acting with lightning speed' against Czechoslovakia. Keitel was now one of the first people in Hitler's entourage to hear about new targets for the policy of aggression. He learned that the dictator regarded Germany's strategic readiness for the 'great clash in the east' as 'unstoppable' and that decisive action must be taken in Hitler's lifetime. Keitel raised no objections whatever. True, he later recalled receiving the directives 'not without anxiety'. However, he and Jodl then got straight to work on plans for the invasion.

> In relation to Hitler, he could only be an orderly officer and take orders from him.
>
> *Karl Böhm-Tettelbach, officer under Keitel*

> Keitel's misfortune was that he could not find the strength to resist Hitler's legally and morally indefensible orders.
>
> *Heinz Guderian, panzer general*

Once again loud objections were heard from the headquarters of the army. Ludwig Beck, Chief of the General Staff, submitted a memorandum, in which he prophesied the outbreak and subsequent course of the war with astonishing accuracy. Violent eastward expansion, he said, would automatically precipitate another world war, which Germany, because of her inferior economic base, could only lose. Keitel recommended that Hitler should only be shown the second part of the memorandum, which contained information about the military potential of the European nations. The first section, with its strategic reservations, would, he thought, be immediately rejected by the Führer. Once more, the OKW chief thus acted as a filter, and made sure there would be no final breach with the recalcitrant generals. In the event, Hitler even rejected the second part of Beck's memorandum and delivered himself of another frenzied tirade against the senior military. Alarmed by this outburst of rage, Keitel himself now turned on the departmental heads of the OKW and complained that a development had 'already begun in which the Führer's charges of fault-finding extend to the OKW itself'. He said he would 'not tolerate any officer in the OKW, who indulges in criticism, doubts and carping'. It is significant that, even at the Nuremberg Trials, he knew virtually nothing about the plans for a *coup d'état*, which Beck, Goerdeler, and his own departmental head, Canaris, were hatching in that summer between peace and war.

In the period before the outbreak of the Second World War, Keitel had become a permanent element in Hitler's entourage. There are hundreds of photographs and film-clips showing him in Hitler's immediate presence: usually saying nothing, but constantly poised to come to his master's aid. The deferential body language in these images is alone enough to betray a great deal about the OKW chief. The officer corps soon gave him the contemptuous but accurate nickname of *Lackeitel* (Keitel the lackey). Yet gradually the scope of his job grew beyond that of 'office manager', as Blomberg had put it. Hitler must have recognised that the 'farmer in a general's uniform' was, from his point of view, the ideal occupant for that post. As a result, Keitel is one of the handful of senior officers who, from the beginning of the war to the end, retained their rank and position. With his obsequiousness and limitless obedience he was not only a product of the system, he also initially fulfilled an essential prerequisite for its smooth functioning – the suppression of scruples and reservations in favour of the unquestioning execution of the Führer's will.

It was impossible not to notice the pride with which the OKW chief occupied his position beside Hitler. An acquaintance recalled seeing him with his two sons 'strolling elegantly along the Kurfürstendamm in uniform'. To him, the general and the two young men looked like 'genuine Prussian officers'. Lisa Keitel enjoyed the endless round of social engagements in Berlin. Her husband, writing his memoirs in Nuremberg, stressed how often Hitler summoned him: 'Many were the times when I had unexpectedly to cut short a weekend in Helmscherode, or a few days hunting in Pomerania, to be at his disposal, more often for the sake of a whim than for any justifiable reason.' His satisfaction with what had been achieved made it all the easier for him to ignore the dark side of the regime. Thus he did not want his promotion to full general on 10 November 1938 to be overshadowed by the burning of synagogues the previous night, and rejected with annoyance a report from Admiral Canaris which gave full details of the murder and arson perpetrated by the Nazi mob. As it was, he read only with great reluctance the regular reports by the Abwehr's foreign desk on the terror-tactics of the Gestapo. Instead, Keitel preferred to occupy himself with the 'spirit' of the troops, a spirit which he, a former lieutenant in the Kaiser's army, tried to help develop, by banning participation in any celebration of the 80th birthday of Wilhelm II.*

---

* After his abdication in 1918, the Kaiser lived on in Dutch exile until his death in June 1941. He remained a focus of royalist sympathies in Germany and, as such, a potential threat to Hitler.

Once the Sudetenland and, in the spring of 1939, the remainder of Czechoslovakia, had fallen into Hitler's hands without a shot being fired, the OKW began preparing for the invasion of Poland. Despite unambiguous warnings from Paris and London, both Hitler and Keitel firmly believed that the Western Powers would once again sacrifice their ally. 'England is decadent and France pacifist', the OKW chief told General Georg Thomas, clearly expressing his master's views. 'They'll make threatening noises', Keitel went on, 'and then once again they'll accept a *fait accompli*.' He blocked proposals by the Army High Command to examine the likely course of hostilities in the west in a hypothetical 'war-game', as a means of dissuading the dictator from launching an attack on his objective. After one conversation with Keitel, the diplomat Ulrich von Hassell was appalled by his 'back-of-an-envelope calculations', which were clearly no more than an echo of Hitler's words. Though privy to the political plans of his warlord, the shallowness of Keitel's understanding of them is shown by his reaction to the statement that now the Red Army would mobilise as well. 'Oh, really? Against whom?' was his irritated riposte.

With the invasion of Poland, the Wehrmacht became further enmeshed in the crimes of the regime. From the very first days of the campaign the army commanders received an ever-increasing volume of outraged reports about the bloodthirsty activities of the SS *Einsatzgruppen* behind the front line, who were systematically hunting down and killing Jews, aristocrats and even Catholic priests. Yet the refusal by the majority of the army to countenance these atrocities did not have any consequences – on the contrary: by their very inaction the commanders-in-chief made themselves silent accomplices to mass murder. On 12 September, while on the Führer's train behind the front line, Canaris remonstrated to Keitel about the crimes committed by the SS, but the OKW chief dismissed this brusquely with the comment that 'if the Wehrmacht want nothing to do with this, they must accept that the SS and Gestapo will step into their shoes'. It appears that Keitel had already fully accepted and adopted the equivalence of military objectives with the criminal extermination plans, just as he had taken to using Hitler's weasel words. He told the quartermaster-general of the army how the occupied areas of Poland would have to be 'cleansed of Jews, Polaks and other riff-raff'. But in a later conversation with Canaris he revealed that, in saying this, he certainly had to overcome his own moral concerns. During the preparations for the phoney attack on the Gleiwitz radio station by SD agents (dressed in Polish uniforms), which was to be the pretext for invading Poland, Keitel had declared: 'I personally don't hold with such things, of course. But it is the Führer's will and that's that.' His only initiative in the early days of the Polish invasion was to ensure that war was formally declared on the enemy, if only retrospectively.

Up till now, the orders to the troops largely avoided any violation of international law, but the conduct of the soldiers began to display the fateful consequences of six years of Nazi propaganda. As can be seen in the records of the army courts martial, numerous atrocities against the civilian population went unpunished. Particular attention was attracted by the case of Major Salah. The officer had murdered five Polish women and had been sentenced to death by a court martial. The army commander-in-chief, von Brauchitsch, had insisted that the sentence be carried out. However, after some to-ing and fro-ing, Hitler personally decreed that the man should only receive a prison sentence. The message sent out by this and similar decisions did not fail to have an effect. Members of the 'master-race', in their triumphant advance, should not feel bound by either law or morality.

Within the Wehrmacht Keitel increasingly identified himself as an exponent of amorality. At the start of the Polish campaign, his colleague Franz Halder had remarked with some sympathy that the OKW chief was 'no longer up to the job', but as time went on, Keitel's unconcealed support for Hitler's violent methods and his ostentatious servility attracted increasing hatred. When the army chief, Brauchitsch, refused to write the foreword to an illustrated book entitled *With Hitler in Poland*, Keitel immediately sprang into the breach, thus avoiding a snub to the dictator. Von Hassell noted that Keitel was 'enslaved', and that General Reinicke, who was known to be particularly loyal to the regime, had got himself nicknamed 'the little Keitel'. In July 1940, when the military commander in Poland, General von Gienanth, once more enumerated the atrocities of the police and SS against Polish Jews, he received a 'rude letter' back, telling him 'once and for all to stop meddling in matters' that were no concern of his.

It was immediately after the victory parade in Warsaw that Hitler and his assistant had their first row. Admittedly, this had nothing to do with questions of morality, but was simply about whether the troops had recuperated sufficiently to be ready for the next bout of plundering. Keitel took the view of the army C-in-C, Brauchitsch, that the units were in urgent need of rest in order to regain their strength. Hitler, on the other hand, wanted to launch a strike against France that very winter – and only later backed down from that. People can still remember the hell-fire and damnation that the dictator brought down on Keitel. Apparently Hitler hurled 'violent accusations' at him, became 'abusive' and levelled the 'seriously damaging charge' against him of 'supporting an opposition movement among the General Staff'. Keitel thereupon wrote Hitler a pained letter requesting a front-line command, but a few kind words from the dictator, and the warning that this was no time for 'over-sensitivity', seem to have been enough to persuade the OKW chief to stay. Once again Keitel bowed to a stronger will. After the war he admitted that he was 'no match for Hitler's personality'.

The brief Scandinavian campaign in the spring of 1940 would be something of a baptism of fire for the OKW. In Poland operations had still largely been directed by the Army High Command under Brauchitsch; but in Denmark and Norway the necessity to fight with army, navy and air force in close co-operation meant that this time the OKW had to take control. The fact that this finally proved successful was chiefly the work of operations chief Alfred Jodl, the man behind Keitel. When the mountain troops under General Dietl got into serious difficulties at Narvik, where the British had landed a task force, both Hitler and Keitel lost their nerve. Hitler wanted to abandon Narvik and order Dietl to march his troops across the border into neutral Sweden, where they would be interned. On 19 April 1940 Jodl wrote in his diary: 'Crisis worsening. OKW chief leaves the conference room; a further leadership shambles threatens, since Hitler insists on getting into every detail.' It was only Jodl's urging that Dietl should be ordered to hold on that finally enabled the Germans to drive the British out of northern Norway. And the lesson that Hitler drew from the success of his 'stand firm' order would later have dire consequences, especially on the eastern front. Alfred Jodl, whose official title was 'Chief of Staff, Wehrmacht Operations', moved more and more into the role of Hitler's strategic adviser, which Keitel was only too happy to hand over to him. At situation conferences the OKW chief increasingly restricted himself to listening to and agreeing with Hitler's expositions.

With the launch of the invasion of France, the preparation for which Keitel participated in as dutifully as he did in all the dictator's wars of aggression, Hitler's entourage for the first time occupied a specially built 'Führer headquarters'. Thousands of cubic yards of concrete went into the construction of a gloomy complex of bunkers on a mountain ridge west of the Rhine, near Bad Münstereifel. On the morning of the first day of the campaign, Hitler and his staff moved in. In terms that were reminiscent of the blood-and-thunder novelist, Karl May, he named the complex '*Felsennest*', or 'rocky eyrie'. The weeks spent in this headquarters proved to be a foretaste of the permanent life in the bunker, which would begin in less than a year – a life in surroundings that were as spartan as they were martial. Jodl later described it as 'a mixture of monastery and concentration camp'. The interminable situation conferences, at which Hitler often involved himself in operations right down to company level, began at midday and generally lasted deep into the night. Alone among the Führer's immediate entourage, Keitel never managed to adapt, even later on, to the dictator's eccentric daily rhythm. Instead, he rose early and was always at his desk by 9 a.m. Although, at over 60, he was the oldest officer in the Führer's headquarters, he probably had the least sleep. It was the same old pattern. He tried by hard work and excessive conscientiousness to rid himself of the feeling that he was not up to the job. As Jodl analysed it in his evidence at Nuremberg, it was particularly after disputes with Hitler that Keitel genuinely 'sought refuge in work'.

Admittedly, the western campaign scarcely gave rise to any disputes. The French bogeyman who was brought to his knees in only six weeks was the same enemy against whom in the First World War the German army had vainly thrown itself for four long years. All the warnings of the Army General Staff about the numerical superiority of the French had proved groundless. Like many other officers, Keitel could only explain this victory by the extraordinary gifts of their supreme commander. The term 'the greatest military leader of all time', which Keitel coined in this period, probably represented his own deep conviction. It is also significant that it was Keitel who, in the first Wehrmacht report, expressly named Hitler as supreme commander.

As a reward for his Byzantine panegyrics, Keitel was allowed to conduct the armistice ceremony in the Forest of Compiègne in exactly the same railway carriage in which imperial Germany had sued for peace in 1918. He described it as 'the climax of my life as a soldier'. To the strains of the German national anthem Hitler and the leaders of the Third Reich stepped aboard the saloon carriage of French Railways. Immediately behind the dictator, next to Göring and Brauchitsch, walked Wilhelm Keitel. At that moment he had probably ceased to dream of farming his broad acres in Helmscherode. His address to the French negotiator, General Huntziger, was recorded at the time and is one of the rare speeches of Keitel to have survived. On the old shellac disc can be heard the clipped, staccato voice of a man who is having difficulty in restraining his emotion.

Reading from a script which Hitler had had a hand in drafting, he informed his audience: 'It was in this train that the German people's years of suffering began. All the dishonour and humiliation, all the human and material misery that can be inflicted on a nation, had its origin here. Bad faith and perjury had joined forces against a people who, after four years of heroic resistance, had succumbed to the sole weakness of putting their trust in the promises of democratic statesmen.' This was of course the purest rhetoric of the 'stab-in-the-back' myth, which the Führer had propagated in countless speeches – the false but, for many Germans, seductive thesis that 'treachery in the homeland' was all that had led to defeat in the First World War. Yet even against the background of the war that was now raging, Keitel, acting as a spokesman for the dictator, produced an extraordinary statement: 'On 3 September 1939, twenty-five years after the outbreak of the Great War, Britain and France, once again without any reason, declared war on Germany. Now the verdict of arms has been passed. France is vanquished.' To the ears of the defeated French, these words may have sounded like a victor's derision. But presumably Keitel must himself have believed in the phrase 'without any reason'. As someone who had listened endlessly to Hitler's sententious torrents of words, the OKW chief had long ago become largely detached from reality. He sometimes reproduced his Führer's thought processes word for word. Even in his memoirs Hitler's phraseology and choice of words can be recognised, for instance, when German preparations for the invasion of Poland are dressed up as being 'for purely defensive purposes', or when the author asserts in all seriousness that, before being invaded by Germany, the Dutch and Belgians had 'forfeited' their neutrality by permitting British aircraft to overfly their territory.

On the evening after the signing of the French surrender, a party was held in the officers' mess at the Führer's headquarters. At the end the conquerors gave emotional voice to the Bach chorale *Nun danket alle Gott* (Now thank we all our God). When it was over Hitler shook hands with his aide and left the room without a word. A short time later, on 19 July, Keitel, along with nineteen other generals, was presented with the baton and insignia of a field-marshal. The OKW chief had not, of course, proved himself 'in the field', as some army commanders rather acidly observed on his promotion; yet in the general euphoria of victory, the overwhelming reaction to this surfeit of gold braid was one of celebration. At the moment when Keitel saluted with his baton for the first time, he was indeed one of the few people privy to his master's next objective in the war. A few days earlier Hitler had remarked in passing: 'Now we've shown what we're capable of. Believe me, Keitel, compared to this, a campaign against Russia would just be a sandbox exercise.' Late in July 1940 Keitel was one of the chosen few at the Berghof, to whom Hitler announced his 'firm decision' very soon to 'destroy Russia's capacity to exist'. In these discussions there was no talk of having to beat Stalin to the draw. Furthermore the theory of a pre-emptive war, which Keitel himself put forward, is contradicted by the fact that, in the exuberance of victory over France, the Wehrmacht's top brass did not consider the Red Army any match for them. The obvious shortage of good officers and the heavy Soviet losses in the winter war against Finland were still a regular topic of conversation. Furthermore, it was known that only a few years earlier Stalin had had thousands of his best staff officers liquidated in a bloodthirsty purge. And in any case, had not a crushing defeat been inflicted on the Russian army in the First World War, at a time when France was still undefeated?

The majority of senior officers shared Hitler's view that the Soviet Union was 'a giant with feet of clay'. Only a few far-sighted individuals, among them men like Beck, Halder and Canaris, could clearly foresee the catastrophe. Surprisingly, Keitel was an early opponent of the eastern campaign, though his anxiety was chiefly about the fragmentation of German forces, which were already committed from Norway's North Cape to the Mediterranean. In principle, he had no objection to taking on the hated communists; but he felt that as long as Britain remained unconquered, it would be wiser to wait. He drafted a cautionary memorandum, which he sent to Hitler, and even found an ally in Ribbentrop, who assured him he was also against opening up a new theatre of war in the east. However, an alliance between the craven Keitel and the basically powerless Foreign Minister was hardly going to pack much punch. Even their alternative suggestion, that Hitler might like to meet Stalin in person to discuss their differences, never really had a hope of being accepted. In fact the Führer impatiently swept aside the anxieties of his two yes-men. Keitel was forced to endure another withering lecture; he pleaded in vain for a transfer but then returned dutifully to his post. He was at least allowed a few weeks leave. They would be the last he ever took.

Once back at his desk, he began all the more zealously to prepare for the new campaign. His return to work was perhaps made easier for him by Hitler's generous 'endowment', a transfer of more than a million Reichsmarks to his account 'for military services'. Keitel now issued a stream of written instructions, which added up to nothing less than a campaign of annihilation. In doing so he crossed the threshold to becoming a full accomplice. It was the moment when orders bearing Keitel's signature finally dragged the Wehrmacht into the maelstrom of crime. 'Our harshness in the east will be considered mild in the future', was how the warlord exhorted his OKW planners. On 13 May 1941 this guideline was implemented through the 'Decree on the Exercise of Military Jurisdiction'. 'For acts committed by members of the Wehrmacht against enemy civilians, there is no obligation to prosecute, even when the act constitutes a military crime or offence.' In plain language this meant that no matter whether German soldiers looted, raped or murdered, no military court was obliged to punish such crimes. On 6 June this removal of all rules of civilised conduct was followed by the 'Guidelines for the Treatment of Political Commissars' – a positive order to commit murder. 'The originators of barbaric Asiatic methods of fighting are the political commissars. Action of the severest kind must therefore be taken immediately and without further ado against these people. Consequently, if they are captured while fighting or offering resistance, they must on principle be disposed of immediately with firearms.' It is significant in this and all further orders for the liquidation of Soviet political officers, that nowhere are any precise instructions to be found as to how a 'commissar' was to be recognised among the prisoners-of-war who were expected to be taken. Mere suspicion was enough. Finally, on 23 June, the 'Guidelines for Conduct of Troops in Russia', the army marched with the unambiguous assignment to act 'ruthlessly' against 'Bolshevist agitators, irregulars, saboteurs and Jews'. It was the first time that measures against Jews were decreed in military orders.

This is the only way to explain how orders like the 'commissar order', the decree on the treatment of prisoners-of-war and inhabitants of enemy territory, and other such instructions, could have been issued to the troops. For this weakness, Keitel had to pay with his life at Nuremberg.

Heinz Guderian, panzer general

> At the time we regretted that Keitel was so totally under Hitler's influence, that he was nothing but a compliant instrument without a will of his own.
>
> *Albert Speer during the Nuremberg Trials*

At the time, even people outside the army were aware that a Rubicon had been crossed with those orders. The diplomat Ulrich von Hassell noted on 16 June that the Wehrmacht command had 'already fallen for the Hitlerian ploy of transferring to them the odium of this murderous rampage, which up to now was borne by the SS alone. That appalling little corporal!' The fact that not one senior officer did the decent thing by resigning, or at least protesting strenuously, illustrates how deeply both the OKW and the Army High Command were already mired in crime. Those who tolerated the killings in Poland were only a step away from active participation. Certainly, the criminality was apparent to the chief of the General Staff, Franz Halder, who dreamed of reforming the system from within and of eliminating, if not Hitler himself, then the SS and Gestapo, who were the real perpetrators of the terror. Later, there were countless courageous men even among the middle-ranking and junior commanders who simply ignored criminal orders from their superiors, or at least mitigated their harshness. Yet all too often such orders were carried out. Even if only a proportion of the Wehrmacht became murderers themselves, every soldier now had to confront the fact that they were fighting side-by-side with murderers.

The man principally responsible for the barbaric orders issued to German soldiers was of course the supreme warlord, Hitler. In Russia he was at last fighting the war he had always wanted – the battle for 'existence or oblivion', for 'victory or annihilation', as he quite openly described it. However, all the senior military were tarred with the same brush; they became accomplices. When, like Keitel, they subsequently invoked their oath of loyalty and the imperatives of military discipline, they conveniently forgot that in the same Prussian army that Hitler was so fond of presenting as the model for the Wehrmacht, obedience to immoral orders was considered a serious offence. The drafting and issuing of criminal instructions really had nothing to do with any traditions of soldiering, let alone Prussian ones. On the contrary, officers like Keitel had long since abandoned the firm ground of military principle. The OKW chief had so completely absorbed Hitler's injunction to wage a 'war of annihilation' that he acted accordingly, even when not carrying out a direct order from the Führer. When Admiral Canaris submitted a document to Keitel, objecting to the fact that more than three million Soviet prisoners-of-war had died in captivity, the OKW added a handwritten note in the margin on 23 September without any prior agreement from Hitler: 'These concerns are based on the soldier's notion of chivalrous warfare. What we are doing here is destroying an ideology. That is why I approve the measures and take responsibility for them.' He even described as 'very appropriate' the operations of the *Einsatzgruppen* behind the front line, for which Wehrmacht soldiers provided transport and security cover. Changes in the murderous treatment of prisoners-of-war, of whom over two million died in German camps in the first year of the Russian war, were only ordered when it became clear that a swift victory in the east was no longer possible and that the prisoners would be needed for forced labour. Similarly, the 'commissar order' was only revoked in 1942, when it was shown not to be undermining the morale of the Red Army but rather strengthening it.

There is no surviving evidence to indicate that Keitel ever had any scruples or a bad conscience about the orders he signed. In his memoirs he pushed all responsibility on to Hitler and pointedly quoted a dictum of the Führer: 'I do not require my generals to understand me, but I demand that they obey my orders.' Even in hearings after the war, when he did at least admit a degree of shared responsibility, we do not find a word of regret over the fate of the victims. If Jodl is correct in describing Keitel as a 'thin-skinned and sensitive human being', then he must also have been a master at suppressing his feelings.

The only occasions when the OKW chief appeared genuinely shocked was when he was the object of one of the Führer's outbursts of rage. This happened again at the end of 1941. In the late summer of that year the warlord had already throttled back German arms production in anticipation of imminent victory over the Soviet Union; but by the winter the Wehrmacht had, for the first time, been fought to a standstill. Close to the gates of Moscow, caught in deep snow and freezing temperatures, the infantry of Army Group Centre suffered a heavy defeat. Faced with this first débâcle, which at a stroke put the entire success of the Russian war into question, Hitler attempted to put the blame for it on his generals. The army commander-in-chief, von Brauchitsch, was dismissed with a few bleak words, and the dictator himself took over the post. After this, Keitel felt it incumbent on himself to offer a kind of vow of loyalty 'on behalf of all members of the OKW'. Yet even the devoted OKW chief, who had nothing to do with the strategic failures, had to act as a lightning-conductor and became the target of another of the dictator's hysterical fits of rage. The precise point at issue is not recorded. But it seems that the dressing-down was so violent that even Ulrich von Hassell in Berlin got wind of it. 'Hitler and Keitel had a tremendous row', he noted in his diary, 'during which Hitler made such absurd accusations against Keitel that he went into a deep depression and started muttering about suicide. . . . The matter has no significance, of course, but it *is* at least symptomatic.' At the Nuremberg Trials Jodl also recalled the consequences of that scene. He had found the field-marshal at his desk, writing a letter of resignation. His service revolver lay beside him, which Jodl claims to have 'taken away from him'.

In his memoirs Keitel tells us that he faced the question of suicide 'more than once', and finally decided against it because he was afraid of being accused of 'cowardice and deserting the flag'. When Hitler later committed suicide in his Berlin bunker, Keitel called it 'utterly incomprehensible and the final disappointment'. Yet the moment when he himself sat in his office, depressed and with a loaded pistol on his desk, impressed itself deeply on Wilhelm Keitel's psyche. As to his own thoughts that evening, he never said anything. The only hint we get is a conversation with General Warlimont (then Deputy Chief of the Wehrmacht Staff), who was asked by Keitel whether he thought remaining in his job could be 'reconciled with his self-respect'. Was all this simply the result of being insulted by Hitler's tirade, or was it a cry for help, when his conscience could no longer rest easy in face of the mass crimes?

There is no doubt that, in Hitler's Reich, Keitel was one of those 'in the know'. His excuse at Nuremberg, that he had been misused 'for purposes which were not ascertainable', does not tally with the facts. The logistical assistance given by the army to the *Einsatzgruppen* was provided with his guarantee. The entire complex of orders, which co-ordinated the war of annihilation in the east, bore his signature. What is more, Admiral Canaris was still keeping him regularly informed about the state of the Abwehr's knowledge; he sent in reports on mass shootings and, from 1942 onwards, about the gas chambers as well. Sometimes the Abwehr boss ingeniously disguised his reports as documents stolen from foreign agents, because he knew how reluctant the field-marshal was to read complaints from the German ranks. If it is true that most of the 'squaddies' at the front were still bound by 'Führer Order No. 1', which stated that no one should know more than he needed for his immediate assignment, then the OKW chief, by reason of his position alone, was one of the best-informed soldiers in the Wehrmacht.

His reaction to the grave crisis during the winter battle for Moscow was simply to place even more faith in Hitler. At situation conferences it was quite common for the field-marshal to intervene in a debate with the words 'the Führer is absolutely right'; without even having followed the gist of the discussion, as Count Johann von Kielmansegg, an officer on the General Staff, remembers. Keitel's shibboleth, 'The Führer cannot be wrong', also originated in this period, when the shortage of winter clothing for the front-line troops gave rise violent arguments at headquarters. The order to the troops to hold their ground in a blizzard outside the Soviet capital, which cost the lives of 10,000 German soldiers, was praised by Keitel as proof of 'the Führer's iron energy'. In his memoirs he was still completely imbued with this spirit when he claimed that, without Hitler's personal intervention, 'in 1941 the German army would inescapably and inevitably have suffered the fate of 1812', referring to Napoleon's disastrous retreat from Moscow. He even hailed as a stroke of genius Hitler's quite unnecessary declaration of war on the USA following the Japanese attack on Pearl Harbor. He recalled feeling as though freed from a nightmare.

With the end of the Wehrmacht's aura of 'invincibility', resistance by partisans and saboteurs began in many parts of the occupied territories. The need to combat this enemy 'behind the lines' triggered another avalanche of orders from the OKW, which were no less brutal than the instructions issued in the run-up to 'Operation Barbarossa'. This second wave of terror orders signed by Keitel began with the 'Night-and-Fog' decree of 7 December 1941. This specified that anyone suspected of 'a punishable act against the German Reich', if not immediately sentenced by a military court, was to be taken to a German camp – by night or in fog, and without their relatives being informed. In France alone over 7,000 men and women disappeared, initially without trace, as a result of the order. After the war Keitel justified this wholesale abduction by saying that the French resistance had been started by 'shady riff-raff' and was only in retrospect glorified as 'the heroic achievement of patriots'. Then in 1942 came ever more ruthlessly worded instructions for 'combating gangs' in which, for example, troops were 'obliged to employ all means without restriction in this battle, even against women and children'. Keitel impressed upon the front-line commanders that in the occupied countries 'a human life' was of little value and that 'unaccustomed harshness' was therefore appropriate. 'As atonement for the life of one German soldier', ran the OKW orders, 'in these cases the death penalty for 50 to 100 communists must generally be considered applicable.' How 'communists' were to be distinguished from other inhabitants of occupied areas, the order did not explain.

> I do not dispute that I had knowledge of all these orders, regardless of whether they bore my signature or not, nor that Hitler had discussed them with General Jodl and me, nor that I passed them on to the relevant arm of the Wehrmacht and supervised their execution.
>
> *Keitel in his memoirs, 1946*

It was behind the eastern front, most of all, that the second wave of terror orders left behind a ghastly trail of blood. Since the Wehrmacht units almost always failed to track down genuine partisans, they set fire to whole villages in 'reprisal' and on many occasions murdered innocent hostages. This brutalisation of the war, ordered by Hitler through Keitel, led to huge loss of life, especially among the rural population. Around one-fifth of the population of White Russia (now Belarus) died during 'Operation Barbarossa', either directly in the fighting, through starvation, or in terror campaigns by the occupiers. Between 1941 and 1945 a total of *twenty million* Soviet citizens lost their lives. In the end the hatred sown in those years rebounded on the nation that had caused it. The acts of vengeance by Soviet troops when they invaded Germany remained among the unhealed traumas of the postwar generation.

In his memoirs and also in the Nuremberg Trials Keitel defended himself by arguing that many of the terror orders had been preceded by a long tug-of-war with Hitler, and that he tried to indicate this by introducing the orders with the words. 'After long consideration, it is the will of the Führer . . .'. However, the surviving minutes of situation conferences tell a very different story. On 1 December 1942, for example, we find no mention of any resistance by Keitel to Hitler's demand that even women and children were to be 'ruthlessly shot down'. There is merely Jodl's sarcastic remark that these orders now gave German soldiers a free hand to fight any way they liked: 'They can hang people, hang them upside down or quarter them.' Keitel, on the other hand, was full of praise for how 'everyone is working so well together now' behind the front line. There is no record in the minutes of any objections, even in the mildest form. Albert Speer was surely correct when he observed that Keitel had 'abandoned any opinion of his own', and was now nothing more than a 'fawning, dishonest, mindless servant'.

> Keitel was very accommodating and was clearly more strongly influenced by Hitler than my husband was.
>
> *Luise Jodl, wife of Alfred Jodl*

While the Stalingrad disaster was unfolding, Keitel showed a further example of his inner degradation. In a conversation with the new army chief-of-staff, General Kurt Zeitzler, who, like Manstein, was trying to convince Hitler that the trapped Sixth Army could only be saved by an attempt to break out, Keitel promised to 'make a formal case for this plan to the Führer'. However, in the crucial situation conference the OKW chief 'did a complete U-turn'. As an eyewitness recalled, he went excitedly to the map-table, pointed to the position of the Sixth Army, surrounded by circles of red and said: 'We'll hold out, *Mein Führer!*' Keitel thus shared responsibility for the tragedy that was played out in the days that followed, for a quarter of a million German soldiers. Henceforth, every one of Hitler's orders to 'hold out' was defended by the OKW chief. When Rommel's army in North Africa asked for permission to retreat, when in June 1944 an entire army group was facing annihilation in Normandy, or when Model's divisions were about to be encircled in the Ruhr in 1945 – each time Hitler gave the order to 'stand firm', Keitel backed him up and the armies were decimated. In each case the decisive situation conferences followed the same pattern. Hitler used ideological arguments to counter all suggestions of a more flexible form of warfare, and then at the critical moment asked the OKW chief for his opinion. Keitel's views, 'uncritical waffle' as Halder called them, never differed from those of the Führer. Instead, the field-marshal supported his supreme commander in the pointless search for scapegoats. The usual routine after a battle had been lost was, before anything else, to dismiss the commander of the army in question.

This ensured a serious shortage of senior officers in the long retreat of German forces. After the surprise landing by the Allies on the Anzio beaches in Italy, Keitel actually summoned fifteen young officers from the defeated divisions to the Berghof, where they had to spend three days explaining to him and Hitler the reasons for the débâcle, in what amounted to a full-scale interrogation.

In the face of steadily worsening news from the battle-fronts, Keitel, like Hitler, succumbed to ever more lunatic hopes, to which he lent emphasis by an outward show of toughness. Within the OKW, where of course a large number of officers were still working and seeing the real evidence with their own eyes, Keitel introduced a note of fanaticism that was unusual even for him. In a sudden outburst at a meeting, he said there was 'no room' in the Wehrmacht Supreme Command, for 'pessimists and defeatists', and that was simply because his colleagues wanted to debate strategic alternatives to Hitler's 'fight to the end' tactics. In the spring of 1944, when a German collapse in the east was looming as clearly as the inevitability of an invasion in the west, he told Sonthofen officer-cadets in all seriousness that it was still just a question of 'hanging on' until the enemy's front line 'crumbled'. If this did not succeed, he went on, there would be 'nothing left for the German people but the annihilation which threatens it'. The idea that liberation, even 'from inside' by a *coup d'état*, might be possible, never occurred to the field-marshal – he would instantly have classed that as high treason.

Hence, it is a particularly nice irony of history that Keitel, of all people, was the one who ultimately made possible the attempt on Hitler's life on 20 July 1944 – albeit unwittingly. The man who would plant the bomb, *Oberst* Count Claus von Stauffenberg, had managed to get through the outer security ring of Hitler's 'Wolf's Lair' headquarters, carrying a briefcase packed with explosives. But he still had to pass the checkpoint of the inner security ring. He knew that any luggage carried by officers who were not members of Hitler's closest circle would be checked for fear of assassination attempts. But Stauffenberg had a solution to hand: he just had to find someone to escort him to his target. Kurt Salterberg, who was then a guard on the inner security ring, still has a vivid memory of the young colonel with the eye-patch heading for the wooden hut where, unusually, the conference was to take place – and he was 'accompanied by Keitel'. So the OKW chief was practically carrying the bomb that was intended to release Germany from tyranny! 'We had standing instructions', Salterberg goes on, 'not to check any persons arriving with Keitel, who wanted to enter the inner security zone.'

Tragically, Stauffenberg's briefcase bomb missed its target. It was the last-minute transfer of the meeting to the lightly constructed barrack hut that saved the lives of most of those present. Had the bomb gone off inside the concrete bunker, it is unlikely that anyone would have survived. '*Mein Führer*, you're alive!' were Keitel's first words after the detonation. Jodl recalled that it was the field-marshal who then 'took Hitler in his arms and very calmly, and as gently as if he had been a child, carried him out into the open air'. The OKW chief then dashed to the telephone and implored all the commanders of Germany's military regions not to obey any orders from the conspirators in Berlin. Alfred Jodl, who received a head wound, later expressed the belief that Keitel did this with such energetic zeal that, had the OKW chief himself been seriously injured in the blast, events in Berlin might well have taken a different course. It is significant that, even after the war, Keitel was unable to evince any comprehension of the motives of the men of 20 July. He called Stauffenberg 'an uncontrollable religious fanatic'. In Keitel's eyes, Field-Marshal von Kluge, who had not even been among the inner circle of the conspiracy, 'retained to his death the arrogance of a college cadet'. For many others, who wanted to prove to the world that another Germany still existed, the field-marshal's verdict was as curt as it was ignorant: they were, he said, nothing more than 'moaning pessimists'.

On the very day of the explosion, he began setting the scene for Hitler's counter-strike. General Fellgiebel, in charge of military intelligence, had been closely involved in the plot and had made sure that communications with Hitler's headquarters were cut off before the coup. Keitel arrested him personally on the spot. The same evening Keitel arranged the details of the revenge campaign with Himmler, the SS supremo. The Wehrmacht then set up a 'Court of Honour', which was to discharge from the army everyone suspected of complicity in the plot, so that they could be brought before the so-called People's Court. This far from 'honourable' tribunal, of which Keitel himself was a member, handed over a total of fifty-five officers, including eleven generals, to the court presided over by the hanging judge, Roland Freisler. The OKW chief later defended his role as a judge in the army's Court of Honour by saying that 'there were demonstrably no miscarriages of justice'. Photographs of the conspirators being executed on the gallows were handed round at situation conferences. On 24 July Keitel and Göring issued a joint order making the stiff-armed 'German salute' compulsory for all Wehrmacht soldiers – as a sign of 'steadfast loyalty' to the Führer. It rather looks as though Keitel's great activity following the attempted coup can be traced back to his old aversion to the 'snooty-nosed' officers from the cadet colleges with whom he worked. Now he wanted to prove that he, the self-made Wilhelm Keitel, was a better 'soldier of the Führer' than they.

The field-marshal did indeed rise noticeably in Hitler's favour. Only now was he wholly convinced of Keitel's 'loyalty', the dictator remarked a few days after the attempt on his life. On 1 September he added further praise, that Germany had 'an institution that is the envy of every nation in the world – the Supreme Command of the Wehrmacht'. Such eulogies probably now made it easier for the OKW chief to issue orders that actually targeted his own troops. A document bearing Keitel's signature was headed 'Rules for the Conduct of Officers and Men in Times of Crisis'. With a date in late January 1945 it was directed against 'deserters' and 'defeatists' in the Wehrmacht. From now on, courts martial were permitted to pass death sentences, even on officers. Senior officers were urged, in cases of 'cowardice in the face of the enemy' to 'make use of firearms' without hesitation. According to these frenzied instructions, any officers who without authorisation gave orders to retreat, were 'to be arrested immediately and, if necessary, disposed of on the spot'. Keitel did not even shrink from offering a bounty of 'up to 500 marks' to anyone denouncing a deserter. He also held the threat of *Sippenhaft* (punishment of family members) over all those who were no longer prepared to sacrifice their lives to Hitler's deluded madness: 'Anyone who is taken prisoner', the field-marshal warned, 'without being wounded or having demonstrably fought to the last bullet, has forfeited his honour. . . . His relatives will be held liable. All payment of entitlements or social assistance to the relatives will cease. This is to be announced immediately.' Rock bottom was reached with the order that refugee columns were to be forced to turn back, 'if necessary, by armed force'. The inhuman death throes of the 'Thousand Year Reich' produced further monstrous losses. The tens of thousands who died fighting against herds of tanks and swarms of dive-bombers, armed with no more than grenade-launchers and carbines, were now joined by the victims of the military police and kangaroo courts. Military historians calculate that 25,000 Wehrmacht soldiers were executed for 'desertion' or 'subverting military discipline' – more than in all the Allied armies put together.

This bloodlust came close to being followed by mass destruction though the latest 'miracle weapon' in the Wehrmacht's arsenal. The code-name '*Tabun*' was given to the most deadly nerve gas to be produced during the Second World War. No gas masks then in use were effective against this colourless and odourless killer. The Germans knew it to be far more murderous than any poison gas their opponents possessed, because they had tested it on Soviet prisoners-of-war in a Wehrmacht laboratory inside the fortress of Spandau. By the end of the war 12,000 tons of the gas canisters were in storage. As the front-line fighting approached the first of these stores, Keitel decided, after consulting Hitler, that no *Tabun* was to fall into enemy hands. Did the warlords, as they faced the abyss, want to keep this last trump up their sleeve? Be that as it may, Albert Speer tells us about a discussion in the Führer-bunker beneath the Reich Chancellery in Berlin, in which Goebbels and Ley argued strongly in favour of deploying *Tabun*. But instead of handing the arsenal over to the advancing Allies, the grenades filled with nerve gas were now to be shipped in trucks to a remote location deep in Germany – despite the risk that any attack by dive-bombers would create an appalling catastrophe. The fact that no such disaster occurred is probably due solely to the swift advance of the enemy, which prevented the OKW chief's orders from being carried out.

On the Führer's final birthday all his courtiers assembled one last time in the catacombs of the Berlin bunker. Their congratulations were offered in the tone of condolences to one bereaved. Keitel claimed that on that day he finally urged Hitler to take some 'decisions that cannot be postponed'. In his memoirs he records the words of the Führer's refusal: 'Keitel, I know what I want. I will fight outside, inside or behind Berlin.' Yet even the belated fit of common sense that prompted Keitel to ask the dictator for 'decisions' seems to have been a retrospective invention of the field-marshal. How else can one explain why, even in those very last days of Hitler's Reich, he once more displayed the energy of an out-and-out fanatic? Or why he and Jodl together planned to evacuate the visibly faltering Hitler from Berlin to Berchtesgaden, by force if necessary? Or why, like the last herald of the god of war, he sought out the scattered remnants of German divisions, in order to persuade the long since defeated troops to 'liberate' the encircled capital of the Reich? Hubertus von Humboldt, then a staff officer with the 'Wenck Army', in which Hitler and Keitel placed completely false hopes, recalls the field-marshal's brisk manner when he turned up at the forestry camp, which served as the army's last field headquarters. 'General Wenck listened to him and said: let the man blather on. None of it makes any sense.'

> It was quite clear that Keitel was no Supreme Commander of the Wehrmacht, as far as leadership goes. Nor did he feel that he was. He always leaned on his boss. It was Hitler who was in the driving seat; Keitel would have a quick talk with the chaps, then draft the order in writing, or get someone to do it, and then put his name to it.
>
> *Hubertus von Humboldt, staff officer*

There is no doubt that, in the final days of the war, Keitel's tenuous grasp of reality finally took on the characteristics of paranoia. When the remains of the 'Army Group Vistula' failed to 'liberate' Hitler from Berlin, he explained this in all seriousness as 'a lack of will'. On 28 April he vainly requested permission to land in an aircraft on Berlin's Heerstrasse, which was already being fiercely fought over, in order to submit one final report in person to Hitler. So on 30 April – as Soviet troops were already forcing their way into the government district – his obsession with duty made him radio a situation report to the man who had determined his destiny. Shortly after 1 a.m. he reported from outside the pocket of German resistance, 'the attacks on Berlin have made no further progress at any point'. It was the field-marshal's last report, and the closest to the truth for a long while. Admittedly Keitel did not know that Hitler, in one of his last fits of rage, had accused even him, the most compliant of his followers, of treason. When bidding farewell to his personal pilot, Baur, Hitler told him bitterly: 'They ought to put on my gravestone: "He was the victim of his generals!"' On 1 May 1945 the Reich Broadcasting Service announced that Hitler had 'fallen' in the battle for Berlin. Even this epitaph was a lie. The truth was that the dictator, and his bride of a few hours, Eva Braun, had taken their own lives in the bunker.

Most Germans, preoccupied with their own problems, listened to the broadcast with no obvious signs of regret. But Wilhelm Keitel, as conscientious as ever, reported to the man whom Hitler had nominated as his successor, the new Reich President, Grand-Admiral Dönitz, based in the northern city of Flensburg. But as soon as he arrived at the grand-admiral's headquarters, the aide realised how little weight he carried without his master. It was Jodl, not Keitel, who was given the task of contacting the units that were still fighting, and who was summoned to conferences. Dönitz even tried to dismiss the field-marshal and almost succeeded. The Reich President also chose to place the signing of the German surrender in the hands of Jodl. On 7 May, in Reims, the old city of the French kings, the operational chief of the German armed forces drew a line under Hitler's unsuccessful grab for world domination. The following day, 8 May, the guns would fall silent in Europe. Yet Stalin was unwilling to settle for that. He felt that the Red Army had borne the main burden of the war, and insisted that the surrender ceremony be repeated in territory under Soviet military control. The location chosen for the rerun was the officers' mess of a Wehrmacht pioneer barracks in the Berlin suburb of Karlshorst.

> He really didn't look as if he had lost the war. . . . He was too much of a soldier to show his feelings . . .
>
> In a way he symbolised the Wehrmacht Supreme Command. For the signing, we wanted the man who had been Number One in the Wehrmacht. I would say that made a big impression.
>
> *Howard Smith, US observer at Karlshorst*

Since this ceremony had only symbolic value, Dönitz sent the OKW chief as his representative. In the end Keitel was once again only given a walk-on part on the stage of international politics – just as, at Hitler's Berghof in 1938, he had been wheeled in to scare Schuschnigg. On the morning of 8 May Keitel landed at Berlin's Tempelhof airfield in a British military aircraft. Yet 'Hour Zero', as the Germans were already calling it, began with a delay. The victors' tug-of-war over the niceties of protocol held up the start of the historic act until after midnight. After endless waiting, in the early hours of 9 May Keitel and his entourage were summoned into the hall. 'We heard an odd noise', the Soviet correspondent Anatoly Mednikov recalled, 'and couldn't figure out where it was coming from. It sounded like someone hammering nails.' It was the boots of Keitel and his adjutants. The field-marshal had told them to 'keep a straight back'. As had been previously agreed, the Allied officials sitting at the green conference table made not the slightest response when the OKW saluted them with his marshal's baton. The smartly executed salute froze into an awkward gesture. Thus the impression made by Keitel in his last official act before the newsreel cameras was exactly that expected by the victors: a blinkered Prussian squarehead. After the signing, the field-marshal resignedly awaited instructions from the victors. 'What will happen next?' he asked his Luftwaffe liaison officer, Karl Böhm-Tettelbach. 'They'll now take us prisoner and shoot us', was his glum reply.

> There is no doubt that Field-Marshal Keitel embodied an attitude, which can be described as one of great dignity, yet very rigid, very disciplined. Wearing his best uniform with the red stripe on the trousers further reinforced this impression. As he entered the hall for the surrender ceremony he gave a salute with his field-marshal's baton. That certainly made him appear very arrogant and self-important.
>
> René Bondoux, member of the French delegation at Karlshorst
>
> The worst thing for him was losing his field-marshal's baton; he kept on asking to have his baton back.
>
> Lion Le Tanson, interpreter at Bad Mondorf internment camp
>
> He was a 'yes-man'. He readily agreed to everything, in order to protect his own position.
>
> John E. Dolibois, Keitel's interrogation officer at Bad Mondorf

Just five days later, Keitel was indeed arrested in Flensburg, at the insistence of the Americans. He had not taken the chance to put an end to his life, as so many of the guilty senior Nazis had chosen to do. In a letter to his son he wrote that, as one of the defendants in Nuremberg, he wanted to 'perform this final duty before the nation and posterity'. For all that Keitel, on the witness stand, played down and glossed over his own role, his open admission that he stood four-square behind every order he signed made a lasting impression on many observers. Unlike the majority of his co-defendants, he did not struggle to 'save his neck', as his defence counsel pointed out, but only 'to save face'.

> You will know my fate, the trial will last for weeks yet. It is a severe test of my nerve and is my final duty to the nation and to history.
>
> *Keitel in a letter to his son Karl-Heinz, 12 January 1946*
>
> It is a tragedy to be forced to realise that the best I had to give as a soldier, my obedience and loyalty, was exploited for purposes I did not recognise; and that I did not see there is a limit even to the performance of soldierly duty. That is my fate.
>
> *Keitel in his closing plea to the Nuremberg tribunal*

Even though he allowed Göring's veto to dissuade him from making a full confession, his closing words in the trial must still be one of the most remarkable statements by a German officer at the end of the war: 'I believed. But I was mistaken, and was unable to prevent what should have been prevented. That is my guilt . . . I pray that from a clear recognition of the causes, of the disastrous methods and of the terrible consequences of this war, the German people will find the hope of a new future in the community of nations.'

> The death sentence was no surprise, but the method of execution was a terrible blow. I must ask you . . . to help in petitioning for clemency, with the aim of changing the execution into a soldier's death by shooting.
>
> *Keitel in a letter to his defence counsel, 1 October 1946*

The judges did not accede to his request that he be executed by firing squad. On 16 October 1946 Keitel was the second prisoner, after Ribbentrop, to mount the wooden scaffold in Nuremberg. His last words were: 'It was all for Germany, *Deutschland über alles!*'

> No, he had no sense of guilt; he kept on insisting that the Wehrmacht knew nothing about it. . . . It was the *Waffen-SS*, it wasn't us.
>
> *Lion Le Tanson, interpreter at Bad Mondorf*

CHAPTER THREE

The Strategist – Erich von Manstein

Steadfast in loyalty

The environment in which I grew up was the world of Prussian soldiering

A war is only lost when one gives it up as lost

If every commander who thought his situation hopeless were to surrender, then no one would ever win a war

As a messenger in the First World War you, *Mein Führer*, should in fact know how long it takes for an order to reach the most forward troops!

I am firmly resolved to defend the honour of the German army

Field-Marshal von Manstein will always stand loyally at the disposal of the legitimate power

Prussian field-marshals do not mutiny

Erich von Manstein

———————— * ————————

Loyalty – the word was always on everyone's lips, even the Mansteins and the Kluges used it to stifle all their doubts.

Albert Speer

Whatever objection Manstein raised, it was not the answer of a field-marshal.

Claus Schenk, Count von Stauffenberg

My father mistook Hitler's true nature. He believed he could exert a lasting influence through rational argument.

Rüdiger von Manstein

Manstein was a soldier pure and simple, and had absolutely no feel for politics.

Georg Lindemann, member of the German resistance

Manstein's failure and his guilt lay in the fact that in the years 1933–1945 he never developed beyond what was demanded by Prussian–conservative German tradition.

Andreas Hillgruber, historian

He was an impressive authority with great military experience, and that is how he was regarded by the members of the [postwar] Defence Committee.

Ulrich de Maizière, Inspector-General of the Bundeswehr

He was a military figure of exceptional stature. What distinguished him were high intelligence, enormous strategic ability, bold decisiveness, great vision and an immediate grasp of essentials.

Hans-Adolf von Blumröder, staff officer under Manstein

We considered the hated von Manstein our most dangerous opponent. His technical mastery of every, and I mean every, situation was unequalled. Things would perhaps have gone much worse for us if every general in the German Wehrmacht had possessed his stature.

Marshal Rodion Malinovsky, Soviet army

Manstein was always the typical militarist Junker, whose conduct was instinctively modelled on Ludendorff in its brutality and indiscriminate methods.

Franz Halder, 1946

Deep down in Manstein there was really a very sensitive core of decency and humanity, which at times he tried to disguise by a rather abrupt manner.

Rudolf Graf, staff officer under Manstein

Manstein is anything but a supporter of the National Socialist regime. But for the moment we can't do anything about him, because we need him; at least the Führer says we do.

Joseph Goebbels

Of course, Manstein frequently went back on his ideas. You see, if I wanted to save men's lives and do so successfully, I had to manoeuvre back and forth. Then Hitler would often say: we're not even going to discuss it.

Hans-Georg Krebs, staff officer under Manstein

There was no commander-in-chief who argued with Hitler as much as Manstein did.

Count Johann Adolf von Kielmansegg, officer in the operations division of the Army High Command (OKH)

Von Manstein was a troublesome operational thinker whom Hitler deliberately prevented from evolving.

General Adolf Heusinger

———————————   *   ———————————

There was no doubt that the man in civilian clothes was a professional soldier. The elderly gentleman at the rostrum made his points with military succinctness and objectivity. With his finely chiselled features, striking nose and silver-grey hair, it was his bearing and choice of words that most revealed the tradition from which this expert witness came. Self-assured, and with the precision of a Prussian officer, he explained to the Federal German Defence Committee where he stood on one of the most controversial questions of the postwar period: conscription or a professional army?

Eleven years after the end of the war the dispute over legislation on military service had created a deep divide – right across party lines and throughout the population of the young republic. What was the point of military service in the age of the atom bomb, some people asked. Others feared that a professional army would threaten to become a state within the state. The only thing clear was that, within the framework of NATO, the Federal Republic had to make a contribution to collective defence, one way or another. The politicians in Bonn hoped for an answer to this vexed question from military experts who themselves had previously been professional soldiers – in Hitler's Wehrmacht.

On that day, 20 June 1956, the Deputies of the Federal Parliament were anxious to hear what direction would be proposed by the adviser whom Hitler had considered the 'best brain' among his generals. The speaker began with a lengthy analysis of the security situation, talked about strategic power-groupings in the Western Alliance, described Western Germany as the most threatened country in NATO and came to the conclusion that compulsory military service was unavoidable. But it had to be of an adequate length: at least eighteen months, preferably two years.

In saying this, Field-Marshal Erich von Manstein aligned himself with the plans of the 'Blank Office', the forerunner of Federal Germany's new Ministry of Defence, and named after Theodor Blank, a labour leader who would become its first minister. He was grateful for Manstein's military counsel. At the age of 69, Manstein certainly did not want to play an active role in running the Bundeswehr, but he considered it his duty to place his knowledge and experience at the service of the new army – a force which was there to defend a democratic state and never again to wage a war of aggression on behalf of a criminal dictatorship.

> Parliament believed that it should listen to the military experience and judgement of such a great strategist, in order to come to a sensible answer on the Bundeswehr.
> *Ulrich de Maizière, Inspector-General (retired) of the Bundeswehr*

Just twelve years had passed since Hitler, at a crucial point in the war, had dismissed Field-Marshal von Manstein and condemned him to inactivity. Even so, the dictator owed some significant successes to this Prussian army commander: first and foremost the defeat of France in 1940, the greatest triumph in German military history; then the conquest of the Crimea; and the stabilisation of the eastern front after the disaster of Stalingrad. These were martial achievements that even earned the respect of his opponents. Marshal Rodion Malinovsky, commander-in-chief of the Soviet southern front, passed this judgement on his opposite number: 'We considered the hated von Manstein our most dangerous opponent. His technical mastery of every, and I mean every, situation was unequalled. Things would perhaps have gone much worse for us if every general in the German Wehrmacht had possessed his stature.' The British military historian, Sir Basil Liddell Hart, saw him as 'the most able of all German generals'. And in the USA, *Time* magazine made the German field-marshal the subject of a cover story on 10 January 1944, while the war was still raging. Such high praise fed the myth of Manstein the 'military genius' – an army officer whose career typified a whole stratum of conservative Prussian generals, most of whom either rejected Nazism or kept their distance from it, but who nevertheless became efficient tools in Hitler's hands.

> Manstein was imaginative and always ready to put up a fight. It was thanks to his clever and tireless performance that the officers of the General Staff were acquitted.
> *General Siegfried Westphal on Manstein's evidence at the Nuremberg Trials*

> Purely on questions of military command Hitler did listen to me to some extent. But even in those matters I had endless arguments with him.
>
> *Manstein giving evidence at the Nuremberg Trials*

It was still very early in the morning of 31 March 1944 when Manstein was hastily woken from a snatched sleep in his headquarters on the eastern front. The Führer's staff had cabled to say that one of Hitler's personal Condor aircraft would shortly be landing near Lvov to take the commander to the Führer. Manstein knew what this meant. He had suspected for some time that it would happen sooner or later. Everyone was expecting it – the officers on his staff, and the generals in the Army High Command (OKH). It was in the air. And now the moment had come.

Only the evening before, the OKH had sent a telex to Army Group South to say that its commander-in-chief, Field-Marshal Erich von Manstein, was being suspended from duty 'to allow his health to recover'. Was sickness a ground for dismissal now? Manstein was suffering from a cataract but had repeatedly postponed the long-overdue eye operation. Yet his health was certainly not so bad as to render him incapable of command. There were other reasons behind his dismissal. It was the nadir and the endpoint of a long series of gruelling confrontations with Hitler.

In fact, a year previously the Führer, as supreme commander, had already intended to remove this awkward general, who never made any secret of his views – and that was at a time when an entire army was bleeding to death in Stalingrad, and the southern front in Russia was threatening to collapse. Yet Hitler hesitated. He still felt he could not do without the man who had fought and won so many battles, whose battlecraft was capable of turning round apparently hopeless situations. With Manstein, Hitler had planned great offensives, to conquer Palestine and push on into India, to create a world empire by force of arms. But these were delusions which, by March 1944, even Hitler had long ceased to discuss. On the battlefields of Russia the German army was being worn down in tough rearguard actions. The time of big offensives was finally over – and with it, so Hitler reasoned, the time of a field-marshal who, while remaining outwardly loyal to him, was not a convinced devotee. Field-Marshal Erich von Manstein had outlived his usefulness.

The end came with another argument around the map-table. Once more a large army formation had been encircled; this time it was the First Panzer Army near Kamenets-Podolsk. Once again Hitler insisted that not a foot of ground should be yielded. Once again Manstein asked for permission to break out. Only in the rarest cases was Hitler willing to give in to such pressure. But this time Manstein was not prepared to be fobbed off yet again with flimsy arguments. He threatened to resign – and it worked. Hitler conceded. It was the last of Manstein's 'lost victories', as he would later call all his successes. For Hitler had finally had enough of trying to work with this gifted but obstinate military man.

On 31 March the Führer received Manstein in the main hall of his mountain retreat, the Berghof, where, on a clear day, an outsize picture window gave a view as far as Salzburg. The warlord appeared to be in a jovial mood. Despite all their differences, he had always behaved correctly towards Manstein, had never become abusive or insulting. He valued the abilities of this Prussian officer as much as he mistrusted the man. But in this encounter there was no hint of mistrust – on the contrary: Hitler had pleasant things to say, praised Manstein's achievements and awarded him one of the highest military honours, the swords added to the oak-leaves of his Knight's Cross. Then the dictator came to the point.

As Manstein noted in his diary, Hitler told him 'he had decided to put someone else in command of the Army Group (it was Field-Marshal Model). He said that in the east the time for large-scale operations, for which I was particularly suited, had come to an end. What was now necessary there was to hold on grimly.' There was, Hitler said, no question of a crisis of confidence between himself and Manstein. No, he had always had 'the fullest confidence' in him and would never forget that it had been Manstein who had drafted the operational plans for the victorious French campaign and had conquered the Crimea. Manstein must have felt he was listening to his own obituary. Then Hitler wished his guest good luck with his eye operation and assured him he would be employing him again soon, as 'Commander-in-Chief West'. Manstein was dismissed – a field-marshal without a job.

At the same time, even in the hopeless military situation of spring 1944, Manstein still saw chances of an honourable draw, if only the eastern front could be held long enough. Several times Manstein had toyed with the idea of pre-empting Hitler's decision to remove him. The two military leaders differed too greatly over how the war ought to be conducted: with mobile operations, as Manstein wanted, or by clinging stubbornly to fixed positions, as Hitler insisted. The gulf between them could no longer be bridged, but to the very end, a sense of duty and obedience prevented this soldier, deeply rooted as he was in the tradition and virtues of Prussia, from doing what he should have done – resign, or even give his active support to a coup against the tyrant. To Manstein, Hitler embodied the 'legitimate' authority of the state, to which he saw himself, as a 'non-political soldier', bound by obedience and loyalty. That is what he had been taught as a cadet in the Kaiser's day. And that is how he acted as commander-in-chief of an army group on the eastern front: as a soldier, so he believed, he had to perform his duty, nothing more – to misquote Brecht: 'First comes obedience, then morality.'

> I am first and foremost a soldier.
>
> *Erich von Manstein*
>
> He wasn't a political general.
> *Hans-Adolf von Blumröder, staff officer under Manstein*

Soldiering was part of Manstein's life from the cradle; his education did the rest. Born on 24 November 1887 in Berlin, he was the tenth child of the Lewinskis, an old Prussian family of the officer class, but he was adopted at birth by the Mansteins. Frau Manstein and Frau

Lewinski were sisters, and since Hedwig von Manstein's marriage had produced no children, it had already been decided that if the tenth Lewinski child was a boy, he should bear the name of Manstein. Then, on 24 November 1887, the Mansteins, at their home in Rudolfstadt, read a telegram from Berlin: 'A healthy son was born to you today. Mother and baby well. Hearty congratulations. Helene and Lewinski.' From then on the child's formal appellation was 'von Lewinski named von Manstein'.

The Mansteins were of the old Prussian nobility. Since the days of the great Electors they had provided officers for the army, and they offered their adoptive son an upbringing in the tradition of the Prussian officer corps. From his earliest years Erich von Manstein wanted to serve the Prussian monarchy as a soldier, just as his forefathers had done. He had come into what he described as 'a certain soldierly inheritance'. He attended a school in the then German city of Strasbourg – 'with more application', one schoolmaster wrote, 'he could achieve far better things'.

> Just as I was christened with water from the River Spree, so was Berlin later to become my home, and there is no doubt that from time to time people see something of the Berliner in me.
>
> I am by nature happy, because I am an indefatigable optimist and have no complexes.
>
> *Erich von Manstein*

Then in 1900 Manstein's army career began with the rigorous training of the imperial cadet corps in Plön and the chief cadet academy at Lichterfelde, a suburb of Berlin. Obedience, a sense of honour, comradeship – these were the watchwords drilled into Manstein when, in 1906, he joined the 3rd Prussian Regiment of Foot Guards, as a subaltern. This forcing house of elitism had already produced Field-Marshal Paul von Hindenburg, who later became president of the interwar republic, and was related to Manstein by marriage, and General Kurt von Schleicher, the ill-starred last Chancellor of the republic before Hitler. Pictures from this period show a slight and rather undersized boy who, as he later told his children coyly, was always given the 'lady's' part at dancing class and in plays.

Lichterfelde cadets commanded great respect and one of the high points of Manstein's youth came when he was chosen as a page for the wedding of Crown Prince Wilhelm and the Russian Princess Vladimir. The following year he attended the silver wedding celebration of the Kaiser and his consort. When war broke out in August 1914, the young Manstein had to interrupt his staff college course in Berlin, which is why the man who, in the Second World War, was 'the Allies' most dangerous adversary', did not have the benefit of a properly completed staff training. But as an adjutant in a battalion of fusiliers he demonstrated the scope of his military gifts. In the words of his commanding officer he was 'the best adjutant I ever had'.

Manstein went off to war with enthusiasm and took part in the capture of the Namur fortress, in the battles of the Masurian Lakes on the eastern front, as well as the Somme and engagements at Soissons and Reims, and between the rivers Marne and Vesle. He was only wounded once, in the autumn campaign in Poland; on 17 November 1914, in close combat near Kotowice he was hit by two bullets – one in the shoulder and one in the sciatic nerve. From then on Manstein had no feeling in his right leg. After six months in a military hospital in Wiesbaden, he spent the rest of the war in various staff posts, but fought in the final German offensive in July 1918, until the collapse and surrender in November put him into a severe state of shock. For Manstein, the eclipse of imperial Germany meant the traumatic loss of a value system that was inseparably bound up with the monarchy. 'When the Kaiser gave up his crown on 9 November 1918, for the troops this was the end of the world.' Like his forebears he had sworn an oath to the King of Prussia. In his eyes the army was 'royal', and without the monarch it was 'no longer conceivable'. The loss of the old world weighed all the more heavily on him because it brought chaos and anarchy. 'With the armistice and revolution', Manstein wrote, 'my military youth came to an end. The King and Kaiser, to whom we owed allegiance, was replaced by the concept of *Reich*, an abstract and, one might say, a mythical concept.'

Even more abstract, in his view, was the new, democratic form of government. Manstein had been transferred as a captain to the new army of the republic, the Reichswehr, but like most officers from his background he regarded the Weimar constitution with scepticism and disapproval. Yet he held to the maxim of General Hans von Seeckt who, as commander-in-chief of the Reichswehr, wanted to be seen as non-political and, as he put it, acting 'in the spirit of silent, selfless performance of one's duty'. For Manstein, obedience, loyalty and performance of duty remained primary virtues throughout his life. At the same time, from the beginning of his career, he left no one in doubt that he felt called to higher positions – both for reasons of prestige and from a need to take on responsibilities. In the meantime Manstein had organised his personal life to suit his ambitions. In January 1920, while staying with relatives in Silesia, his eye was caught by a young woman named Jutta Sybille von Loesch. Three days later he asked for her hand. The marriage, from which he had three children, lasted throughout his life.

> He wanted to make something of himself, he had things to say, he wanted to represent something.
> *Count Johann von Kielmansegg, officer in the operations division of*
> *the OKH*

Manstein had never lacked self-confidence and assertiveness. It is true that in the eyes of older colleagues he may have seemed rather brash and presumptuous, but it was precisely those qualities that helped him advance swiftly in the officer corps. In the autumn of 1929, as a newly promoted major in the operations division of the General Staff, the nerve-centre of the Reichswehr, Manstein immediately embarked on the first-ever mobilisation plan for the army. With meticulous precision he calculated all the dispositions –

and uncovered shocking weaknesses. His counter-proposal immediately convinced his superiors. The work had to be reviewed by *Oberstleutnant* Wilhelm Keitel, later Chief of the Wehrmacht Supreme Command, from whose department the draft plan was issued. Keitel had to work hard to catch up, a fact which earned the ambitious young Major von Manstein both the respect of his more able peers and the lifelong envy of the mediocrities. Up to the day of his dismissal and beyond, Manstein and Keitel were bound by a relationship of mutual dislike.

Among quite a number of his contemporaries and many higher ranking officers, the professionally superior Manstein was never particularly popular. He had a reputation as an arrogant know-all, who did in fact know more about a lot of things, was quicker on the uptake, more precise in his formulations. Time and again he proved that he was someone to be reckoned with, the man of the future. 'From then on', Manstein wrote after the war, 'my opinion as a member of the operations division carried a certain weight.' The younger officers admired the 'wonder-boy of operations': 'He didn't even have to think, he just rattled the stuff out.'

There is no doubt that his well-founded analysis of the mobilisation plan singled him out for higher things in the General Staff. But the tradition of the Reichswehr required that officers had to serve at regular intervals with the troops. From October 1932 to January 1934 Manstein commanded a battalion in Kolberg. In this attractive little town on the Baltic he enjoyed the 'most beautiful and carefree years' of his career. He was scarcely even concerned about what took place in distant Berlin on 30 January 1933. The conservative Prussian battalion commander saw Hitler's seizure of power less as a threat than as an opportunity to help Germany return to 'its former greatness' – with a strong army. Most of all, what drew him to the new man in power was his promised intention to revise the Treaty of Versailles. In those years there was scarcely anything that worried Manstein more than the nightmare vision of an attack by neighbouring countries on an almost defenceless Reich. For this reason he found it no great hardship to bid farewell to the republic. Having attended a number of sessions of the Reichstag he had been 'disgusted' by the 'undignified squabbling' between the parties. His devastating summing-up of the republic after fourteen years was: 'External impotence and internal turmoil.' 'The only way out was a temporary dictatorship by the leader of the strongest party. Furthermore, if old Hindenburg accepted this solution, then for us soldiers the matter was settled.' It seemed as simple as that. 'Democracy' was a dirty word.

It is true that the uncouth behaviour of Hitler's party was anathema to Manstein, a man who described himself as 'a real "gentleman" in the good sense of the word', but for the moment he only wanted to admit to the changes that were presumably for the better: the reduction in unemployment, for example, or Hitler's foreign policy successes. And what about the concentration camps, the persecution of the Jews and of everyone who did not share the ideas of the man now wielding power? In 1949 Manstein claimed: 'In almost all cases it is true to say that I never became aware of these things.' For a long time Manstein's mind remained closed to the depth of the gulf between his Prussian conservatism and Hitler's National Socialism, although at an early stage he did come into conflict with the racial policies of the Nazi regime and protested openly against a decision by the Reich Ministry of Defence. On 28 February 1934 the minister, Werner von Blomberg, had decreed that the 'Aryan clause' should also be applicable in the army. Manstein, who that month had become chief-of-staff of Military District III in Berlin, was outraged. On 21 April he protested in a memorandum to his superior officer, *Generalleutnant* Ludwig Beck, head of the *Truppenamt*, in other words Chief of the General Staff. No other German officer had dared to say a word against the 'Aryan clause'. So was this an act of resistance?

It required moral courage to oppose the clause and as a strategist Manstein knew that in this case a frontal assault offered practically no prospect of success. He therefore dressed up his protest in terms that were intended to leave no doubt as to his ideological soundness: 'That we all affirm National Socialism and racial ideas without exception is beyond any doubt. However, in my view, we should not forget the soldiers' honour which until now has bound us indissolubly together.' Manstein only objected expressly to the *retrospective* application of the clause. That it should apply in the future seemed to be less of a problem for him. There was certainly no mention of future arrangements in his memorandum, yet it was still sufficiently explosive to drive Blomberg apoplectic with rage. A Prussian officer turning against his minister? Blomberg was so furious that he wanted to discipline the rebellious Manstein. 'It was only Fritsch [the commander-in-chief of the army] who prevented that', Manstein explained in 1949.

The driving force behind this measure of 'racial policy' saw and heard Manstein for the first time in the spring of 1934, when tension was threatening to escalate between the Reichswehr and the SA under Ernst Röhm, whose ambition was to turn it into a 'People's Army'. For a long time Hitler had watched the conflict boiling up but had done nothing. Now, in late March, he saw that the time was coming when he must make a pronouncement. In the Defence Ministry in Berlin he assembled the top brass of the Reichswehr, the SA and the SS, to make it clear that only one body was the 'arms-bearer of the nation' – and that was and would remain the Reichswehr. What followed was the usual monologue about the injustice of Versailles, the need for rearmament and for living space for the German people.

Hitler's speech did not fail to leave its mark on Manstein. 'I cannot deny that it made a strong impression.' Despite Hitler's judgement of Solomon, the tensions between SA and Reichswehr remained. The army continued to feel threatened, and even Manstein feared 'the worst': a *coup d'état* by the brownshirt storm-troopers. As a precaution he sent his three children, Gisela, Gero and Rüdiger off on holiday to their grandmother's house in Silesia. As Gisela remembers: 'He expected to be arrested any day.' The SA had set up machine-gun positions in the building opposite Manstein's office.

On 30 June 1934 Hitler put a bloody end to the crisis with the first big wave of killings under his rule. Although satisfaction was felt by many officers in the Reichswehr at finally being rid of their SA competitors, they were simultaneously outraged by the murder of two army generals, von Bredow and von Schleicher. Manstein gave his backing to an attempt to persuade his GOC to lodge a protest with the Minister of Defence, von Blomberg. But the initiative ran into the sand. In any case, the uproar had quickly died down. No matter how seriously Manstein regarded these crimes, a coup by the Reichswehr was, to his mind, quite out of the question. 'A retrospective and violent reaction by the Reichswehr against Hitler's breach of the law would have meant civil war.' Intervention by the army would have 'granted to armed force the right to control the administration of government'. Army and politics, he believed, should keep out of each other's business. Thus, the officers of the Reichswehr did not even venture to protest against the slaying of two of their comrades. They remained silent – and accepted the fact that, after the death of Reich President Paul von Hindenburg on 2 August 1934, they were required to swear an oath of personal allegiance to Hitler.

> The man isn't my cup of tea, but he certainly knows his stuff.
> *Adolf Hitler*
>
> A cooling of the Hitler–Manstein relationship wasn't possible. It had always been cool.
> *Count von Kielmansegg, officer in the Operations Division of the OKH*

Manstein did distance himself from National Socialist ideology. Nevertheless his career prospered. Hitler was rearming and experts were in demand. On 1 July 1935 Manstein reached the top job in the Operations Division and on 1 October 1936 he was promoted to *Generalmajor*. As Chief Quartermaster he was now working in the innermost circle of army commanders – with the aim of one day inheriting the post of Chief of the General Staff from the man he greatly admired, General Ludwig Beck.

After his numerous postings, Manstein had counted on a settled job in Berlin. He bought a house for himself and his family in the Thielpark district. The Mansteins were firmly established – their neighbours were upper class with a sprinkling of film stars and wealthy financiers. However, this Berlin idyll lasted only a few years. 'One morning', Manstein's daughter tells us, 'my father received a phone call. He was being posted from Berlin to Liegnitz [now Legnica in Poland] with immediate effect.'

That was in February 1938, and it came as a profound shock to Manstein. Still more disturbing was the background to his sudden transfer. With a double blow Hitler had rid himself of the top army brass. Even though Manstein was able to see some justification for the dismissal of the defence minister, Werner von Blomberg, who had married a young woman with a dubious past, the fall of the army's commander-in-chief, Baron Werner von Fritsch, came like a punch in the face. Manstein regarded Fritsch as 'a man of great military ability, straightforward character, soldierly bearing and comradely attitude'; yet he had been falsely exposed as a 'homosexual' through a cunningly engineered intrigue, discredited and dismissed from his post. This meant that Manstein's job was also vacant. As a close colleague of the sacked commander-in-chief he was part of the circle of senior officers who advocated an army that was independent of government, and whom Hitler suspected to the last, since they were not National Socialists but Prussian conservatives.

Wilhelm Keitel, the newly appointed chief of the Wehrmacht Supreme Command, was prominent among those strongly in favour of having his rival Manstein despatched to provincial Silesia. In Liegnitz Manstein was to take command of the newly established 18th Infantry Division. Nominally this was a step up, but in practice he was being sidelined. He had always wanted a division of his own – but not at that moment, when he might have been on the point of getting his ideas on the Wehrmacht command structure accepted, in preference to Keitel's. And not now when he was considered a certainty to succeed Beck as Chief of the General Staff. 'This put an end to all that. The most honourable assignment for any staff officer, to be permitted to take over the seat at which men like Moltke, Schlieffen and Beck had worked, was dead and buried for me.' When handing over, Manstein pressed the key of his safe into the hand of his successor, Franz Halder, and said curtly: 'Here! You can read yourself into the job. *Auf Wiedersehen.*' With that he turned on his heel and left Halder standing there.

'It's impossible to describe how shattered and downcast my father was', Manstein's daughter Gisela remembers. 'We simply couldn't talk to him. My mother tried to cheer him up. She said that Liegnitz was in Silesia, after all, and certainly an attractive city. Up till then we only knew its railway station, where you could buy the famous Liegnitz gingerbread and cucumbers. So Mother fetched the Baedeker guidebook and all it said was: "Liegnitz, dormitory town at the foot of the Riesengebirge mountains. Not worth a stop"! My father just said. "You see, I told you so . . .".' Deeply disappointed, Manstein sold the house in Berlin he had only recently bought, to a director of the AEG company. 'My father swore never to go back to the ministry', says Gisela, 'and in fact never return to Berlin at all.'

> He never talked about his feelings. He wasn't the kind of man to complain about anything.
>
> To him his job was a duty, the rest of the time he just enjoyed life at home.
>
> *Gisela Lingenthal, Manstein's daughter*
>
> My father's military assignments left him neither the time nor the energy to worry much about other things.
>
> *Rüdiger von Manstein*

Yet before Manstein took up his new job in Liegnitz, his talents were once again needed in Berlin. On 7 March 1938 Hitler summoned Beck and Manstein to the Reich Chancellery. The Führer had a surprise in store for them: he intended to move troops into Austria. Manstein only took five hours to work out the marching orders. On 12 March the Wehrmacht marched into Austria, and the following day Manstein flew to Vienna to prepare for the integration of the Austrian army into the Wehrmacht. It was his last act as a member of the Army High Command.

From Liegnitz Manstein watched Hitler taking an increasingly aggressive road to war, and saw how his friend and mentor, General Beck, was clearly finding himself in conflict with these plans. In a series of memoranda, Beck warned that any action against Czechoslovakia could mean a European war. He considered Hitler to be a man without scruples and proposed to *Generaloberst* Walther von Brauchitsch, the commander-in-chief of the army, that all the top Wehrmacht officers should resign *en bloc* if the Führer persisted with his warlike intentions. In an appeal to Brauchitsch's conscience, Beck told him: 'It amounts to a lack of stature and of awareness of one's responsibility, if in times like these a soldier in the highest position only sees his duties and tasks in the limited context of his military assignments, without being aware of the higher responsibility to the nation as a whole. Extraordinary times demand extraordinary action.' In this situation Beck did not even shrink from the idea of a *coup d'état*. But Manstein implored him to stay in his post – despite differences of opinion with the 'political leadership'. It was precisely in times like these, Manstein urged, that men of Beck's calibre were needed. Both the officers remained true to themselves: Beck resigned when no general was willing to follow him in his opposition to the war. Manstein stuck obediently to his post, even though he had grave doubts about Hitler's determination on war. His fundamental position was that a soldier must subordinate himself, and should not attempt to challenge the primacy of politicians.

> The danger of an unprovoked attack came chiefly from Germany's eastern neighbours, principally Poland.
>
> *Erich von Manstein*

Manstein did his duty assiduously, and in the unopposed march into the Sudetenland he led his troops south of Budovice. His career took priority. But once home he sought relaxation from soldiering in his hobbies – classical music (especially Mozart), history, learning languages and gardening. 'When my father came off duty', his daughter Gisela remembers, 'he immediately changed out of his uniform, even before saying hello to us. He never talked about his job. That was taboo. He certainly didn't like men who were always talking shop, or told stories about the glory days of the Franco-Prussian War.'

Yesterday's campaigns were of no interest and, after all the bloodless 'battles of flowers' that Hitler had won, Manstein did not believe in fighting another proper war: 'We knew that since 1938 Hitler had been negotiating to get rid of the Polish–German border problem. But the generals were not told how the talks were going. On the other hand we knew of Britain's guarantee to Poland. None of us were so blind as not to recognise this as a deadly warning. For that reason we were convinced that there would not be a war. We recalled a statement by Hitler that he would never unleash a war on two fronts.'

Manstein would be proved wrong. On 31 August 1939 at 7 p.m. Army Group South, commanded by Gerd von Rundstedt, received the order to attack Poland. As Rundstedt's chief-of-staff Manstein worked out plans for the attack on Warsaw, and when the fighting came to a successful end in October, the Rundstedt Army Group was transferred to the west, where Hitler was pressing for the launch of an offensive against France and the Low Countries. On 23 November 1939, at a 'command reception' on the Obersalzberg, Hitler informed his senior generals and admirals, Manstein among them, that the hour had come: 'My decision is unalterable', he barked at his military elite. 'I will attack France and Britain at the earliest and most favourable moment. Violating Belgian neutrality is of no significance. Nobody will raise the matter when we've won.' Then he warned his generals, whom he enjoyed disparaging as 'scaredy-cats' who used 'Salvation Army' methods: 'I will stop at nothing and will destroy anyone who opposes me.' He was directing this threat at the OKH leadership, at Franz Halder and Walther von Brauchitsch who, like most generals, considered an offensive in the west unwise, not to say reckless. The military wanted to gain time; they hoped for a political solution, for a peace that did not have to be fought for. But

Generalleutnant von Manstein was in more of a hurry. As he saw it, a German attack was unavoidable if the Allies were not to launch an offensive themselves. But the blow must be struck by the spring of 1940 at the latest, since: 'With the question-mark of the Soviet Union constantly at our rear . . . we could not wait until the Western Powers had gained superiority over us.'

After the successful assault on Poland, the way to defeat France was surely quite obvious. As early as 27 September 1939, Hitler told the commanders-in-chief of the three arms of the Wehrmacht the direction in which to launch their strike: through Belgium and towards the Channel coast, more or less as Count von Schlieffen had proposed in 1905 – but that was a plan which, when put into practice in 1914, had stalled at the Marne. Barely three weeks later Halder, the chief of the general staff, presented his battle-orders to the Führer. Hitler's ideas had been taken fully into account, but this did nothing to improve his mood: 'But that's just the old Schlieffen Plan!' The OKH drafted new plans, and Hitler had them changed again until, on 10 January 1940, something happened which meant that all the tactical planning had to be scrapped. A German courier aircraft had to make an emergency landing near the Belgian town of Malines. On board was the chief-of-staff of the 7th Air Division who was carrying in his briefcase top-secret operational plans for the attack in the west. This incident created an immediate crisis in the senior ranks of the Wehrmacht. We know today that the material picked up by the Belgians was not of great importance. But at the time the worst was feared. A new invasion strategy was drafted and once again Hitler was dissatisfied: the OKH's planning, he ranted, was like 'the ideas of a war-college student'; the generals might have read their Clausewitz, but not enough Karl May.* Where was the effect of surprise?

At the same time, when a spell of bad weather offered the opportunity to think through the plans once more, *Generalleutnant* von Manstein who, as chief-of-staff of Army Group A, was certainly not charged with planning the western offensive, nonetheless came

---

* This best-selling author of implausible Wild West novels was one of Hitler's favourites. (*Tr.*)

up with a completely contrary idea. As soon as he had first studied the OKH's battle-orders, their weak points hit him in the eye. So, in the Elector's palace in Koblenz, on the banks of the Rhine, he began to work out an alternative strategy which was intended to make possible the apparently impossible: a swift and conclusive victory over France. Strong armoured forces of Army Group A were to break through at the very point where they were least expected – through the supposedly tank-proof Ardennes forests – in a rapid curving movement through Sedan and towards the Atlantic coast. At the same time, Army Group B would attack the Belgian strongholds, thus luring the French and British formations into an advance into Belgium. This 'sickle-cut', as Churchill called Manstein's plan, was intended to separate the French and British armies and cut off their retreat. It was the idea of *Blitzkrieg* – lightning war.

In a series of seven memoranda, Manstein pointed out the advantages of his plan. But the OKH would have none of it. Generals Halder and von Brauchitsch had serious reservations. The concept was too risky, they claimed, and basically no more than a self-centred attempt by Army Group A to enhance their own importance. Manstein's idea was not even submitted to the Wehrmacht Supreme Command for consideration. There was a strong possibility, Halder feared, that Hitler would be impressed by this audacious scheme. In fact, Hitler himself was already thinking about attacking through Sedan. But he was not sure whether such a thrust could succeed.

Not a word was spoken about Manstein's plan until 29 January 1940, when Manstein's colleagues had an opportunity to introduce the plan to an officer in Hitler's most intimate circle. On a fact-finding visit by Hitler's chief adjutant, Rudolf Schmundt, he was informed by to two staff officers, *Oberst* Günther Blumentritt and Major Henning von Tresckow, about Manstein's improved assault plan. On 4 February an army adjutant, Major Gerhard Engel, noted in his diary: 'Schmundt went to Koblenz and came back very impressed by a longish discussion with v. Manstein. The latter expressed strong doubts about the operational plan put forward by OKH. Schmundt was very excited and told me he found that Manstein had the same ideas about the concentration of force as the Führer is always talking about, only Manstein's are in a much more precise form.'

> Behind my back Manstein sought to establish contact with Hitler and succeeded.
>
> *Franz Halder, as retired Chief of the General Staff*

What needed to be done now was to arrange a meeting with Hitler, without arousing Halder's suspicions. This was provided on 17 February 1940 with a specially organised 'working breakfast' in the Reich Chancellery, with the newly appointed army commanders. Afterwards Hitler called Manstein into his study. With the help of a large situation-map Manstein explained his plan in detail. That evening he commented in his diary on Hitler's 'staggering knowledge about military and technological innovations in every country. . . . I presented the gist of the memorandum we had sent to the OKH. Found him in complete agreement. He was altogether astonishingly well versed in these matters and had the same point of view as we had put forward from the outset.' Four days earlier, when Schmundt had first told him about Manstein's proposal, Hitler had made up his mind to shift the weight of the attack southwards, on to Army Group A. 'But genius though he was', as Manstein claimed in his diary, 'he lacked the necessary detail that could be provided by a general with real operational training and imbued with the same will to victory.' Manstein gave Hitler the arguments he needed to challenge the generals, whom he derided for their over-cautiousness, and to take the wind out of their sails. The 'sickle-cut' idea won the day. Hitler later remarked with Olympian condescension: 'Of all the generals I discussed the new western invasion plans with, Manstein was the only one who understood me.' Yet for all Manstein's recognised ability, this gifted general still appeared suspect to Hitler: 'There's no doubt he's exceptionally bright, with great operational talent; but I don't trust him.'

Franz Halder, the Chief of the General Staff, had a similar opinion of Manstein, who was already being treated by officers as the 'Chief-of-Staff in waiting'. Halder now made his move – and posted his unwelcome rival to distant Stettin, on the Baltic. There Manstein was to take over as General Officer Commanding the 38th Army Corps, which was then only a skeleton unit, and still had to be built up. For the second time in his career Manstein had been promoted into a siding.

> The western offensive has started! And I'm sitting at home, after having fought so hard for it to be carried out in just this way.
> *Manstein, personal war diary, 10 May 1940*

On 10 May 1940, at 5.35 a.m. the German assault on France and the Low Countries began. Manstein spent that day at home with his family in Liegnitz, Lower Silesia. The offensive he had planned led to a successful breakthrough: the German panzer divisions swept through Luxembourg, Belgium and the Ardennes into France, smashed through the French lines and showed the advantage of highly mobile warfare. By 20 May German tanks were already in Abbeville, at the mouth of the Somme and on the coast of the English Channel. The armoured columns stormed ahead at such lightning speed that even the generals were mystified by the success of their own troops. *Generaloberst* Gerd von Rundstedt, commanding Army Group A, toyed with the idea of halting the panzers, while the OKH advocated continuing the advance. Hitler intervened in the dispute, in order to demonstrate his authority as Supreme Commander of the Wehrmacht, and issued the order to halt. The defeated British forces succeeded in getting back to Dunkirk, from where they escaped across the Channel to England. It was the first of Manstein's 'lost victories'.

Manstein himself commanded the 38th Army Corps during the western campaign and at the beginning had the task of funnelling as many as 21 divisions simultaneously through the narrow passes of the Ardennes mountains. Not until 5 June did the real war start for his corps, with a 'battle assignment'. His formations crossed the Somme and went on pursuing the enemy until, as Manstein put it, 'the final collapse ensued'. During the fighting he frequently put in an appearance among the infantrymen on the front line. 'Our GOC liked an honest answer more than subservience', recalled Rudolf Graf, then Manstein's principal aide-de-camp. 'Equally he hated people waffling on. Anyone who didn't get straight to the point could be sure of getting pretty rough treatment.'

In France Manstein and his staff preferred to occupy châteaux – and time and again had the same unpleasant surprise. The owners had always fled. And yet he would so much have liked to converse with them, mused about history, and enjoyed French hospitality. He did not like being so obviously regarded as the enemy – he of all people, who knew exactly how a 'gentleman' should behave, and who made every effort not to seem like an arrogant victor.

At 35 minutes past midnight on 25 June 1940 the guns fell silent. In the First World War the German warlord, who now claimed to be the undisputed 'greatest military leader of all time', had himself lived for month after month through the inferno of trench warfare. Now the 'ancestral enemy' had been laid low in only six weeks. The signing of the surrender document on 22 June in the Forest of Compiègne was for Hitler the 'happiest day' of his life. He now fancied himself superior at last to his procrastinating generals.

The 'sickle-cut' plan, without which this lightning victory would have been unimaginable, laid the foundations of Manstein's reputation as an 'operations genius' and made him a legend in military circles for the rest of his life. Yet for all his satisfaction in the part he had played in the greatest triumph in German military history, the post that matched his strategic brilliance continued to be denied him. Manstein was assigned the 56th Panzer Corps – a highly mobile formation with which, during the invasion of the Soviet Union, he completed a daring 240-kilometre dash in five days and, on 27 June 1941, captured the key town of Daugavpils in Latvia. How greatly the war in the east differed from that in the west, Manstein was able to see from an order issued by Hitler, which affected his corps, along with all the others. Even before the first shot was fired, Manstein informed the commander-in-chief of the

Army Group, *Feldmarschall* Wilhelm von Leeb, that he could not carry out the 'Commissar Order'. It was, he said, 'unsoldierly' to 'dispose of commissars by the bullet immediately and as a matter of principle', as the order specified. This order, Manstein stated at the Nuremberg war crimes tribunal, 'was the first instance when a conflict arose between my duty to obey and my conduct as a soldier. I ought in fact to have obeyed.' What he failed to see was that the Commissar Order exposed the criminal nature of the war being waged in the east. Only a week later, he had already forgotten the order. 'When I took over the Eleventh Army, it was already a matter of history to me.' As the new army commander, Manstein did not think it either necessary or possible to forbid once more the carrying out of the order. The risk of losing his job was too high. He satisfied himself with reports from his generals to the effect that the order was not being put into effect within the Eleventh Army. In fact, though, fourteen commissars were shot under Manstein's jurisdiction, and five others handed over to the SD. Manstein claimed that this had been without his knowledge, but in 1949 he was convicted of war crimes by a British military court in Hamburg.

Manstein took command of the Eleventh Army on 17 September 1941, succeeding the fatally wounded *Generaloberst* Ritter von Schobert. Word had already got round about his aloofness. In the war diary of the Eleventh Army we read: 'We are getting a new commander-in-chief. He's a "gentleman" and rather difficult. But one can talk frankly to him.' To officers and men who did not know him better he sometimes gave the impression of being chilly and detached. 'He didn't seem particularly sociable', recalls Hans-Adolf von Blumröder, who served on Manstein's staff in 1943 and 1944. 'He lacked the warmth of a paternal commander. He had difficulty in displaying his inner feelings.' To quite a few people he seemed not only reserved but also very pleased with himself and his abilities. 'Manstein liked to make it clear to others that he was cleverer than them', said Count Johann Adolf von Kielmansegg, senior staff officer in the army's Operations Division. But this apparent arrogance may actually have been due to the fact that his sight was not very good. 'His eyes were bad, and when soldiers saluted him he often didn't notice and so he didn't salute back', observed *Hauptmann* Günter Reichhelm, then aide-de-camp to Field-Marshal Model. Manstein's daughter Gisela has another explanation for the effect her father had on other people: 'He was, by nature, a man of few words, very reticent and even shy. He was not someone who enjoyed parties. But with people he knew well, he was easy and relaxed.' Those people included the officers on his staff, with many of whom he built up friendships that lasted beyond the end of the war. He would play bridge with them in the evenings and they got used to the fact that, just as in their work, he demanded speed and precision from them.

> When Manstein spoke to his men, they always felt they were able to do anything he demanded of them.
>
> *Theodor Busse, Manstein's Chief-of-Staff*

As the new army commander on the southernmost flank of the eastern front, Manstein had the task of capturing the Crimea and its stronghold, Sevastopol. The conditions were not favourable. To Manstein, accustomed to fighting on the move, the Crimea offered no space to deploy his strengths and exploit the mobility of his troops. Furthermore, the Soviet forces arrayed against him on the Crimean front were superior to his in numbers and weaponry. It had been difficult enough for him to breach the 'Tartar ramparts' across the narrow isthmus linking the Crimean peninsula to the mainland; but storming the fortress of Sevastopol on its southern coast claimed even more casualties. The first assault had to be called off, and to make matters worse Stalin launched an offensive aimed at recapturing the Crimea. Strong Soviet formations landed near Feodosiya and forced Count Sponeck, commander of the 42nd Army Corps, to abandon the Kerch peninsula on the eastern tip of the Crimea. He did so on his own initiative, even though in December 1941 Hitler had forbidden any soldier to retreat by so much as a step. Manstein, furious at having been informed of the retreat only after it had taken place, immediately relieved Sponeck of his command. Sponeck demanded an opportunity to justify his action before a military tribunal. But instead of reinstating Sponeck, the court's president, Hermann Göring, sentenced him to death. Manstein's attempts to speak up for his subordinate met with refusal from Keitel. Hitler did in fact reduce the sentence to imprisonment, but Sponeck was shot in July 1944 on the orders of Himmler. The Sponeck case showed Manstein clearly how tragically the conflict between conscience and obedience could end. By deciding to dismiss Sponeck, Manstein had opted for obedience.

Manstein had estimated that the second assault on Sevastopol would take eleven days. It lasted a whole month. And that was after deploying a massive arsenal of weapons, including the biggest that Germany possessed: the rail-mounted 'Iron Gustav' gun with a calibre of 80 centimetres (about 2ft 8in), which could hurl 7-ton shells at the beleaguered city. On 1 July 1942, after a devastating bombardment and a high casualty toll on both sides, a victorious Manstein marched into Sevastopol. His Eleventh Army took nearly 100,000 prisoners.

When Greater German Radio announced the fall of Sevastopol, Hitler had just sat down to a lavish dinner with his closest associates, in his 'Führer headquarters'. 'When the special announcement came through on our little radio set in the dining-room,' noted Henry Picker, who transcribed all Hitler's 'table talk', 'Hitler got up and so did all his dinner guests, who then stood and gave the German salute as the national anthem was played.' That evening Manstein wrote in his personal war diary: '1 July 1942. Sevastopol taken! Special radio announcement about it and about my promotion to Field-Marshal. Very thankful to God and to all those who gave their blood for this victory.' Hitler had sent a congratulatory telegram and created a new decoration, the Crimea Shield, to honour the Eleventh Army. 'It is indeed a unique experience', we read in Manstein's memoirs, 'to savour the taste of victory on the field of battle.'

A short time later, in the Führer headquarters, Hitler handed Manstein his field-marshal's baton. Words of praise were spoken but the talk was not just of victories and new objectives. At breakfast Manstein asked his Führer what was happening to the Jews. At the very moment when thousands were being murdered every day in Auschwitz-Birkenau, Hitler (as recorded by Picker) replied that 'their own state ought to be created for them. He had thought about Palestine, and then the island of Madagascar. But a Jewish state must be controlled by Germany. He had therefore settled on the Lublin district of Poland, where the Jewish state can be under our control.' Not a word about 'extermination'. Manstein appeared satisfied with this answer, and did not press the matter further.

It was precisely at this time that he came dangerously close to Hitler's programme of extermination. On 20 November 1941, Manstein signed a military order stating that 'the Jewish-Bolshevist system' must be 'stamped out once and for all. Never again must it be allowed to invade our European living space.' The order went on to say that 'every soldier must fully realise the necessity for harsh retribution against Jewry, as the intellectual vehicle of the Bolshevik terror.' So, was Manstein a perpetrator?

This order, which chiefly applied to the battle against the partisans, was based on a model of similar severity. On 10 October 1941, the commander-in-chief of the Sixth Army, *Generaloberst* Walter von Reichenau, emphasised the racial politics underlying the order. At the end of October a call had gone out from the OKH to all armies and army groups, to issue orders along similar lines. Manstein made the Reichenau order even harsher, by indulging in anti-Semitic phraseology. True, he did not talk about the physical destruction of Jews, nor, as Reichenau had done, of 'Jewish sub-humanity', but he did want to 'eradicate the Jewish-Bolshevist system'. On the other hand, Manstein toned down the order by instructing his officers to 'take the severest measures against arbitrary and exploitative behaviour, against lapses into undisciplined savagery, and against any violation of military honour'. Before the court in Nuremberg, Manstein claimed not be able to recall the order. Whether he issued it because it would further his career, and because he wanted to enhance his chances of becoming commander-in-chief of the army, remains a matter for speculation. What is clear is that he did not *have* to sign the order.

In the Crimea Manstein, as an army commander, had total authority for the first time over occupied territory which became the scene of organised mass shootings. Between June 1941 and March 1942, *Einsatzgruppe* D of the SD, operating under Otto Ohlendorf along the Black Sea coast and in the Crimean peninsula, murdered at least 90,000 Jews, gypsies, communists and members of other persecuted groups. Ohlendorf described his relationship with Manstein's Eleventh Army as 'excellent'. The army supplied the *Einsatzgruppen* with vehicles, and it can be shown that Manstein had at least one meeting with Ohlendorf in the Crimea. Nevertheless, Manstein insisted that he had no knowledge of the killing operations. 'As for the *Einsatzgruppen* and their assignments', he stated at his trial in Nuremberg, 'all I knew was that they were intended to prepare for a political administration, in other words for a political scrutiny of the population in the occupied areas.' Nothing more than that?

Several of the officers on Manstein's staff knew enough to be able to put their superior fully in the picture. For example, the Quartermaster of Manstein's army group, *Oberst* Eberhard Finckh, who later took part in the 20 July attempt to assassinate Hitler, knew about the murders, yet he remained silent. He is reported as telling another officer: 'The field-marshal must keep his mind clear for the problems of his operational command. As it is, he is constantly in dispute with Hitler over professional matters. If he is to be burdened with these things as well . . . then this is likely to lead to difficulties that could very soon end in his dismissal. And we all know the field-marshal is indispensable, even more so after a successful coup.' Clearly Finckh was working on the assumption that Manstein would protest against the mass killings. Was this just a precautionary statement to further the building of the Manstein myth?

Manstein certainly heard about atrocities behind the front line. But did he actually believe the reports? In autumn 1943 his aide-de-camp, Alexander Stahlberg, told his superior about rumours that in the area to the rear of Army Group South, which Manstein was commanding at that time, the SS were engaged in the mass shooting of Jews. Apparently 100,000 had been massacred in a forest area. Stahlberg described Manstein's reaction as one of 'outrage'. 'He reacted angrily. He said "What you've just told me is so unbelievable that I refuse to accept it. What would you do with 100,000 corpses?"' Manstein reminded his ADC of the opening of the Berlin Olympics in 1936, when there were 100,000 spectators in the stadium. 'Now just think of that mass of people', Manstein had said. 'How do you propose to bury all those? It's a vile propaganda trick. I refuse to listen to such stuff!'

There is no documentary evidence of a killing operation with 100,000 victims on one day in 'a forest area' to the rear of the Army Group. In 1987 the East Europe Institute in Munich stated in an expert opinion, given at the request of Manstein's son Rüdiger: 'The slaughter of such a large number of Jewish inhabitants of the USSR "in a forest area" can be ruled out with a probability bordering on certainty.' However, that does not mean that Manstein knew nothing. It was rather that he did not want to believe things that seemed to him inconceivable.

As far as the field-marshal was concerned, that was the end of the matter. He suppressed the things he did not want to see, and concentrated on his job as an army commander. 'I can only say', Manstein insisted after the war, 'that preoccupied as I was for years with the heaviest of assignments at the front, I had no opportunity to see how much the regime was going off track, nor to appreciate Hitler's true nature, to the extent that seems obvious to us today. . . . The anxieties and the tasks that battle brought us allowed us little time to reflect on more general questions. . . .' According to one of the prosecution charges at his trial in 1949, Manstein had, in full knowledge of the murder operations, ordered, approved and permitted the handing over of Jews to the SD. But no proof of this was available. On this count at least, Manstein was acquitted for lack of evidence. Addressing the court, he said: 'We soldiers shared with the German people as a whole the inability to see through the true character of the regime.'

Yet in Manstein's case it was an 'inability' that defied his actual knowledge. This is proved by the account given by Ulrich Gunzert, then a captain in army education who, at the time of the Crimean campaign, was seconded to the headquarters of the Eleventh Army. He witnessed how, on the Tartar defensive wall across the Crimean isthmus, SD men shot down Jewish men, women and children with sub-machine guns. 'Lying in a deep pit were several layers of bodies', Gunzert remembers. 'After each salvo the SD men climbed down into the pit and finished off those who were still alive, with pistol shots to the head. It was mass murder. The terror in the faces of those people waiting in the pit to be murdered is something I will never forget.' When he tried to intervene, an SD man stopped him with the words: 'Clear off, this is none of your business!'

Back at HQ, Gunzert reported what he had seen to his commanding officer. 'I begged Manstein to do something about it. But he demurred. He said he had no authority in the rearward area; and anyway he now had other things to worry about. Manstein took refuge in the limits of his military powers and ordered me not to speak to anyone else about it. It was an abdication of his responsibility, a moral failure.'

With the capture of Sevastopol, if not before, Hitler saw Manstein as a kind of 'secret weapon' for tricky assignments such as the capture of Leningrad, the second largest Soviet city, which was very well defended. In October 1942 Manstein wrote in his diary: 'I propose an assault to capture the estuary of the Volkhov, so as to cut off Leningrad's supply-line across Lake Ladoga, starve the city and thus avoid having to make a difficult frontal attack on the fortifications.' By now, however, the Red Army had once more gone over to the offensive. 'Operation Northern Lights' was postponed indefinitely.

At the time when he was besieging the starving city of Leningrad, Manstein was hit by the 'severest blow' of the war. On 29 October 1942 his son Gero was killed at the age of only 19. He was a lieutenant, and had been in action near Lake Ilmen, not far from his father's headquarters. When placing the announcement of his death, Manstein asked to have his son's baptismal motto printed. Taken from the Acts of the Apostles, it was: 'And he went on his way rejoicing.' When the editors of the *Völkischer Beobachter* (the official Nazi newspaper) refused to print this pious quotation, Manstein, who had a strong Christian faith, protested. On 22 November 1942, the announcement appeared in the party organ – but without the line from the Bible.

The father did not remain in mourning for very long. A brief stay with his family in Liegnitz, then it was back to the front line where, on 20 November 1942, an order reached him from OKH, which was to have far-reaching consequences. The formation under Manstein's command, now renamed 'Army Group Don', was immediately to move off towards Stalingrad. There he was to go to the assistance of the Sixth Army, also under his command, and 'restore the cohesion' of the German front. The next day, Manstein set off in a private railway carriage on a five-day journey that was repeatedly interrupted by partisan attacks. On arriving in Novocherkassk, about 100 miles from Stalingrad, he started on the toughest assignment of his career.

When Manstein stepped out of the train, the ring of steel had long since closed and the entire Sixth Army, as well as part of the Fourth Panzer Army, were trapped. As chief of an Army Group, he now found himself for the first time in his career facing the task of deploying his talents at a higher level than ever before. But his first telephone conversation with Hitler revealed the basic dilemma: Manstein tried in vain to obtain overall command of all troops in the southern sector of the eastern front and to have a free hand in his own operations. However, Hitler categorically refused to countenance a retreat: the front along the lower Volga must, he said, be held at all costs; what was at stake were the oilfields of the Caucasus. For the Sixth Army to break out and escape was out of the question – Stalingrad must be held, no matter what the cost.

To begin with, Manstein appeared to share this view. Although he was aware that 'airborne supply of the 6th Army, even when flying is possible, can currently provide only one-tenth of the daily requirement of fuel and ammunition' (as he wrote in his diary on 24 November 1942), Manstein reported to the OKH in Berlin: 'I do not propose a break-out by the 6th Army, which is anyway impossible today and for the next few days. We can only risk leaving 6th Army there for as long as adequate supplies by air can be guaranteed. This is the critical factor.' However, Manstein let it be known that he would request a break-out by the Sixth Army, should insufficient troops be available to relieve the besieged forces by an offensive. Manstein then radioed to the commander of the trapped Sixth Army, *Generaloberst* Friedrich Paulus, to tell him 'we will do everything we can to get you out of there'.

Why did Manstein initially back Hitler's decision to leave the Sixth Army in Stalingrad to await rescue? He knew that the pocket could not, as Göring had promised, be supplied from the air. Yet he reckoned he could guess what Hitler's reaction would be if he had ordered an immediate break-out. 'The Führer still wouldn't have given an inch', he wrote in his diary on 25 November 1942. 'But if I too say I will try to hold out, then, if nothing is left except to try and break through, he will be more likely to listen to me than if I had given up right away. And in any case the break-out cannot take place immediately (28.11 at the earliest).'

> There are only two ways to go: one is that ordered by the Führer – to hold on to the last cartridge. The other would be to pick a moment to break out, when we still have the strength and resources to do so.
>
> *Manstein's personal war diary, 26 November 1942*

But Manstein would soon realise how unrealistic his hope had been. Hitler refused to be dissuaded from his decision; he insisted that it was impossible to abandon the territory that had been so hard won in the summer offensive; in the coming year it would simply have to be reconquered with even larger forces. Manstein now wrote in his diary: 'I cannot accept this reasoning.' What mattered, surely, was simply to save the situation, and above all rescue the Sixth Army. On 26 November Manstein noted: 'Detailed discussions with Paulus, whom I am preparing for the break-out. Führer still refuses.'

Report to the Führer that I regard a break-out by the Sixth Army as the last chance of rescuing at least the bulk of the troops.

Manstein, personal war diary, 26 November 1942

I would like to hear some other suggestions from you, *Herr Feldmarschall.*

Hitler, on Manstein's proposal to order a break-out by the Sixth Army, November 1942

By this time the most favourable moment to attempt a break-out had passed with no action taken. What remained was a slim prospect of a successful offensive to relieve the garrison. In those fateful days of late November, Manstein's ADC, Stahlberg, describes in his memoirs how Hitler telephoned his field-marshal to announce: 'In the spring we're going to march across the Caucasus. And I'm thinking of putting you in command of the spring offensive. You will then link up in Palestine with Field-Marshal Rommel's army, which will join you from Egypt. Then with our combined forces we'll march on to India and there finally decide the war with a victory over Britain.'

All hopes rested on a relief attack on Stalingrad. On 1 December Manstein had given the order for 'Operation Winter Storm' – code-name for the relief offensive under *Generaloberst* Hoth. As soon as Hoth's tanks came within 30km (18 miles) of the pocket, combat units of the Sixth Army were to go into action and fight their way through to the liberators. Through the breach thus created, convoys of trucks were to be funnelled, carrying 3,000 tons of supplies, as well as 30 buses to transport the wounded out of the pocket. Hitler and Manstein were agreed on this point. According to Manstein 'Winter Storm' would be followed by 'Thunderclap', the break-out by the Sixth Army. Hitler had been told about 'Winter Storm'. But Manstein did not want to inform him of 'Thunderclap' until Hoth's thrust had been successful.

On 12 December, four days later than planned, Hoth launched his relief attack, initially with two panzer divisions. He was hampered by ice and snow, and came up against far superior enemy forces. Despite stubborn Soviet resistance and high losses, his tanks managed to get within reach of Stalingrad. On 19 December Manstein telexed Paulus an urgent order: '57 Panzer Corps shortly to commence "Winter Storm" attack.' Units of Paulus' Sixth Army were to fight their way out, link up with Hoth's tanks and thus establish a supply corridor. Exactly when 'Operation Thunderclap', the actual break-out, was meant to begin, Manstein left open. As he explained in his memoirs: 'The Army Group . . . opted for this form of order, in order to avoid an anticipated veto by Hitler.' Manstein still hoped that while the relief attack was actually in progress, Hitler would give his permission for the break-out. But he never did.

Hoth's panzers battled forward for 60km (36 miles) then, exactly 48km (29 miles) short of Stalingrad, the assault stalled under heavy Russian fire. Now the only thing that could help Paulus was if Manstein ordered a break-out on his own authority. But Manstein did not give the order. Even though he had just been put in command of an Army Group, Hitler would immediately have reversed the order and dismissed him. However, Manstein did try several times to persuade Hitler to order the break-out, as is clear from the relevant entries in his war diary:

19 December 1942: Report to OKH that break-out by 6th Army must be ordered.
With Zeitzler I issue orders for 'Winter Storm' and make preparations for 'Thunderclap'.
21 December 1942: Discussion [Chief of Army General Staff].
Tell him it is finally time to make decision about break-out by 6th Army . . .

On 22 December Manstein noted resignedly: 'All my urging for a decision on 6th Army has been useless.'

Meanwhile, on the middle reaches of the Don, another crisis had arisen. The Red Army had broken through the front line of the Italian Eighth Army, fighting in alliance with Germany, and was pushing westwards. Now the fate of two German army groups was in the balance: Army Group Don and Army Group A (under Kleist), which was meant to capture the oilfields of the Caucasus. One and a half million men were in grave danger of being cut off. All German forces had to be mobilised. For this reason Manstein ordered Hoth to call off the attack and turn round. Hoth's Sixth Panzer Division was to plug the gap in the front. But with only two divisions left, a successful attack on Stalingrad was no longer conceivable. The attempt to liberate the Sixth Army had finally failed. The break-out was never ordered. Manstein later insisted that he would have supported Paulus, had the latter risked a break-out. But after the war Paulus saw it differently: 'Someone who then believed he was unable to give me the order or even permission to break out, has no right today to write that he had wanted me to break out, and would have backed such a move.'

The fate of the Sixth Army was sealed. Nevertheless, Manstein refused to consider a surrender. Paulus' troops were to go on tying down the Soviet forces until he had the situation on the southern flank of the front under control once more. Essentially Manstein's view was: 'If every commander who considered his position hopeless chose to surrender, then no one would ever win a war.'

> In that case I'll fight a decisive battle in southern Russsia, at the end of which you'll be able to get oil from wherever you want!
> *Manstein to Hitler on being given unrestricted operational freedom,*
> *December 1942*

The dramatic worsening of the situation in Stalingrad was conveyed to Manstein on 12 January 1943 by *Hauptmann* Winrich Behr who, on Paulus' personal orders, arrived to describe the wretched conditions of the besieged soldiers and to request permission to surrender. All that mattered now, Behr told him, was to save men's lives. The Sixth Army had long ago lost any military value. Manstein sent Behr on to the Führer's headquarters, where he was to describe the conditions to Hitler at a situation conference. When Behr returned, Manstein listened to his report in silence: Hitler had forbidden any surrender; the men of the Sixth Army were to go on fighting to the bitter end.

Once Manstein had stabilised the front line, on 22 January, he attempted once more to persuade Hitler to allow the surrender. On the same day he noted in his diary: 'Paulus asks me to query possibility of negotiations. Discussion with Führer. We have to fight on, since the Russians would not keep to an agreement anyway.' Hitler's obstinacy almost caused Manstein to resign. Since he had become a commander-in-chief and was receiving operational orders direct from the Supreme Command, he realised that 'Hitler was failing as a military leader'. Even so, he did not draw the obvious conclusion. A field-marshal, he said, cannot just pack up and go home. He is committed to obedience and loyalty. On the tragedy of the troops bottled up in Stalingrad, Manstein remarked after the war: 'Perhaps this loyalty was given to a man who did not deserve it, yet even so that loyalty and devotion to duty remains a paean of German soldiery!'

In this crisis-ridden period, when Manstein was fighting along a 700-km (420-mile) front with 32 worn-out divisions, he received a visit by a young major from the army's Organisation Division. The officer wanted to talk to Manstein about the reserve situation and the status of newly established units. His name was Count Claus Schenk von Stauffenberg. Manstein did not know him personally but he knew his reputation as one of the most gifted younger officers on the General Staff. What Manstein did not know was Stauffenberg's real aim in meeting him – a *coup d'état* staged by the army.

Like others in that group of patriots who saw that the Reich was on a fatal path to the abyss, Stauffenberg had placed his hope on the Commander-in-Chief of Army Group South. In Manstein's headquarters at Taganrog a dangerously explosive conversation took place, which was overheard through a half-open door by Manstein's ADC, Alexander Stahlberg.

Stalingrad was not the first failure of leadership, Stauffenberg declared; the Russian campaign was a string of blunders, and the blame lay with Hitler. Manstein nodded in agreement. It was when discussing the 'command structure' that he got the best reception from Manstein. After all, the field-marshal himself held the view that, as in the First World War, the whole eastern front should be placed under one military commander-in-chief. Only four days earlier, on 22 January, Manstein had confided to General Zeitzler, the army chief-of-staff: 'If the supreme commander [Hitler] also takes on the duties of his subordinates, and if at the same time he is burdened with all the worries of politics and government, and if his will alone can create the means to power, then in the end even the greatest genius finds himself faced with an impossible task. I consider it essential that the Führer puts the trust in his generals that they merit, gives them the freedom of action that they need in order to command, and thus gains the respite without which operational decisions cannot mature. I consider it equally essential that for the whole conduct of war in all theatres, he only listens to one adviser, and puts his faith in that man's judgement. It's the only way it can work.'

Manstein assured Stauffenberg he would put a strong case to Hitler for a unified Wehrmacht command. But Stauffenberg was not satisfied with that. If need be, he warned, the step of appointing a Commander-in-Chief East must be forced on Hitler, before the war ended in disaster. Yet Manstein refused to countenance this idea. For him, illegal activities were out of the question. He had once written to his mentor, General Beck: 'A war is only lost when one gives it up as lost.' When Stauffenberg persisted, Manstein apparently admonished him: 'If you do not stop this business immediately, I'll have you arrested.' In 1962 Manstein denied having made this reproach and described it as 'totally inaccurate'. On the contrary, he said, he had made every effort 'to help Stauffenberg, as a valued younger colleague, by letting him voice his justified anxieties. At worst I may have advised him in his own interest to be more cautious in what he said, since not every commanding officer would listen as I did to his criticism of Hitler.'

Manstein did listen – and it would not have been difficult for him to grasp that Stauffenberg wanted to win his support for a *coup d'état*. When *would* Manstein have been prepared to act if not when confronted by a catastrophe on the scale of Stalingrad? Stauffenberg was bitterly disappointed. The coup would be too late, Manstein argued, since the Allies were going all out for an 'unconditional surrender'. But it would also be too early in the sense that the German people were not yet ready for it; Hitler was still too popular. There was no possibility of a spontaneous revolt by front-line troops. After a conversation lasting more than hour, Stauffenberg left Manstein's room depressed and downcast. 'The generals all know the truth', he concluded. 'Yet only a very few of them are willing to take action!' And in more unequivocal terms: 'Those fellows are either shit-scared or brainless. They just don't want to know!' Manstein mentioned Stauffenberg's visit in a letter to his wife: 'Being confided in is always very touching, but how am I expected to change things that lie outside my authority and capacity?'

As they said goodbye, Manstein advised Stauffenberg to arrange to be transferred to the front line, in order to get away from the 'unpleasant atmosphere' of the Führer's headquarters. 'Much as I like him', he wrote to his wife, 'and pleasant and intelligent though he is, he is simply too clever for these difficult times; he sees the risks and the negative side to clearly. I see it all myself too, of course, but I can come to terms with it.'

On 6 February 1943 Manstein himself plunged into the 'unpleasant atmosphere'. He made his way to the Führer's head-quarters – with the intention of pressing Hitler to appoint a sole commander-in-chief for the eastern front. But putting himself forward for the post, as both Stauffenberg and now General Erich Fellgiebel had urged him to do, was very far from Manstein's mind. 'My appointment only makes sense if I receive the summons, that is to say, if the necessary trust is placed in me; for that to happen, my advice in the operational sphere has to be accepted. To push oneself forward in any way at all, even if it be only by putting one's name down for a lecture on this subject, in my view amounts to destroying that trust from the start. And without it one can serve neither the Führer nor the cause.' At best the basis of trust between Hitler and his field commander was fairly fragile. Once already, during the winter crisis of 1941–2, the warlord had refused to appoint Manstein as 'Chief-of-Staff of the Wehrmacht', on the grounds that 'he may have a brilliant brain, but he's too independent a character.'

At the very beginning of their conversation, Hitler had a surprise up his sleeve. It was anticipated that he would seek a scapegoat for the defeat at Stalingrad. But Hitler opened by saying: 'Gentlemen, I'd like first of all to say a few words about Stalingrad. I alone bear the responsibility for Stalingrad.' Manstein was impressed by these 'soldierly' words and felt the moment was opportune to raise the question of a unified command. 'There was a very frank discussion of the command question, but no result', he wrote in his diary that evening. 'Having a Wehrmacht chief-of-staff is, of course, scuppered by G[öring]'. Manstein chose not to pursue the matter. 'A dictator cannot not be compelled to do anything', he later told the Nuremberg tribunal. 'The moment he gives way, even once, to such pressure, his dictatorship is finished.'

Around the map-table, the differences continued. Manstein urged that the troops should be temporarily withdrawn from the central and northern Donets region, and regrouped in readiness for a new offensive. But in Hitler's mind the mere idea of abandoning conquered territory without a fight was anathema. He ordered Manstein to offer head-on resistance, not to give any ground and to hold out stubbornly to the last cartridge. Manstein warned that the man who wants to keep everything runs the risk of losing everything! The discussion lasted four hours at the end of which Manstein had achieved at least partial success: Hitler allowed him to pull back the First and Fourth Panzer Armies from the Donets region, in order to rest and prepare for a counter-strike. Manstein's plan to withdraw the Fourth Panzer Army in a large-scale chess-style 'castling' move was successful. In mid-February he launched his counter-offensive. It brought Hitler his last victory in the east – and once again reassured Manstein that in open combat in the field, with mobile operations, even critical situations could be brought under control.

Just before the start of the offensive Hitler arrived unexpectedly at Manstein's headquarters in Zaporozhye. 'Oh yes, "Effendi" shows once again what a nose he has for anything that will be useful to him for propaganda', Manstein joked. He had taken to calling Hitler 'Effendi' (a Turkish word meaning 'lord' or 'master'), after hearing a prayer muttered by a Crimean Tatar: 'Thanks be to Allah and Adolf Effendi.' Five situation conferences were held in three days, in the course of which it became clear how deep was Hitler's distrust of his army commanders in general and of Manstein in particular. In their strategic thinking they were worlds apart. Hitler demanded that he hold out at any cost. But in view of the superiority of the Red Army, Manstein opted for mobility, tactical withdrawal and surprise strikes, which meant pulling back his troops in order to gain some freedom of action, so that he could attack again. When Soviet tanks came to within 80km (50 miles) of Zaporozhye, the discussions came to an abrupt end. Hitler flew back to his Rastenburg headquarters in East Prussia. And now, for the first and only time, Manstein had a free hand. Success quickly followed. On 19 February 1943 the two Panzer armies in Manstein's Army Group thrust forward into the Donets region and recaptured Charkov and Belgorod. It was only the mud caused by the thaw in March that eventually brought the assault to a standstill. The front line was now close to where it had been a year earlier. Hitler told his press chief, Otto Dietrich: 'I was the one who recaptured Charkov, not Herr von Manstein!'

> Manstein may be the best brain the General Staff has produced. But he can only operate with good, fresh divisions, not the debris we are left with now.
>
> *Adolf Hitler, 1943*

Manstein did not yet believe the war was lost. Even though he no longer actually expected a victory in the east, in the spring of 1943 he still cherished the hope of a military stalemate – as a basis for negotiating with Stalin, who was waiting with increasing impatience for the Western Allies to open a second front, and might at that time have been prepared to make a separate peace with Germany. As long as this way seemed to be open, Manstein was unwilling to risk a big new offensive, but wanted to continue with the tactics he had applied up to now. That Hitler would never agree to a 'draw' with the Soviet Union, that he could contemplate nothing but victory or defeat, was something Manstein could not grasp. Hope of an undecided outcome remained what it always had been – the illusion of a strategist used to thinking rationally, who could make nothing of the irrational workings of Hitler's mind.

There were no circumstances under which Hitler was prepared to give up conquered territory without a fight, least of all the Donets basin with its steelworks and coal reserves. Without this region, Hitler claimed with great exaggeration, German war production would collapse. The Russians, he stated dramatically, would 'simply bleed to death as long as we defend every foot of ground'. With his threadbare arguments Hitler prevented Manstein from deploying his forces with mobility, the only chance of succeeding against enemy superiority. The often wearisome debates between Manstein and Hitler always revolved around the same contentious points: to hold out, not to hold out, how long to hold out . . . Hans-Georg Krebs, a captain on Manstein's staff, was once present when his superior was arguing with Hitler over the situation. 'Needless to say, Manstein's ideas tended towards retreat. If you want to conserve your forces and fight successfully you have to be mobile. But Hitler frequently interrupted him and said: "We'll have no talk of that!" This often had the effect of reducing Manstein to silence. When he could see he wasn't getting anywhere, he simply stopped talking. That was the trouble with Manstein; if he considered someone to be of unsound mind, he said nothing. To him, Hitler was the ignorant First World War corporal, who imagined he knew a thing or two and that he could do anything.'

As a military professional, Manstein granted that Hitler 'no doubt had a certain eye for operational opportunities' and 'an astonishing knowledge and memory', but no more than that. 'Taken over all, he lacked precisely that military skill that is based on experience, for which his intuition was simply no substitute.' In Manstein's view

Hitler overestimated the power of his own will, his impact on the troops – and culpably underestimated the strength of the opposition. After one situation conference, at which Hitler once again imposed his own will, *Hauptmann* Krebs heard Manstein complain: 'My God, the man's an idiot!' Manstein saw what damage the 'idiot' was doing on the front lines, how he was gambling with what the Prussian field-marshal considered their greatest asset – Germany itself. Nevertheless, he refused either to resign or to raise a hand against Hitler.

Manstein remained in his post because he really did consider himself indispensable. He never gave Hitler any cause to doubt his loyalty. It was only on military questions that he contradicted the supreme commander; politics remained off limits, true to Manstein's motto: war is war, and politics are politics. And as he was well aware, he could wage war with greater skill than almost anyone. Manstein did not place himself centre stage, but he was always conscious of his ability and, as General Günther Blumentritt observed, would even go so far as to 'describe the ideas that Hitler came up with as nonsense'. Hitler, for his part, never placed real trust in Manstein, though he rated his military abilities very highly. And Hitler always maintained decorum. He never belittled Manstein in front of others, even though the latter could deliver a scathing put-down: 'As a messenger in the First World War, you, *Mein Führer*, should certainly know how long it takes for an order to reach the most forward troops!' In military matters Manstein gave Hitler as good as he got. *Generaloberst* Heinz Guderian characterised him as prickly. 'He had his own opinions and expressed them.' In this, too, Manstein differed from the other army commanders. 'No-one picked arguments with Hitler like Manstein', Count von Kielmansegg remembered. But even Manstein only very rarely succeeded in convincing Hitler. Sometimes he had the impression he was looking at 'an Indian snake-charmer'. 'I cannot recall ever seeing a look in a man's eye that so expressed the power of his will.' Hitler and he, Manstein confided to his diary, were on two different planes. 'Consequently, one never gets to a result.'

To Manstein, Hitler was like a second front, which taxed his strength just as much as the operational command of his troops.

For his decisions had not only to make sense militarily, but more importantly had to find favour with Hitler, to comply with his will. In the spring of 1943 both Hitler and the Army High Command were pressing for an offensive before the Red Army had recovered from their defeat at Charkov. The adversary had to be forced into action. An opportunity for attack was presented by the Kursk salient on the Soviet front – scene of the greatest tank-battle in history. Code-named 'Citadel', it was to be the last German offensive in the east.

The Army Group Centre under Kluge would advance from the north, and Manstein's Army Group South from the south, trapping the Soviet troops in a pincer movement. The first orders for 'Citadel' had already been issued on 13 March. Yet Hitler hesitated; he wanted to wait until new tanks had been delivered to the troops. Manstein was impatient, and advised attacking as quickly as possible. The sooner it happened, the less time the Soviets would have to build up a strong defence, and the less would be the danger of a major Soviet assault on the Donets region. But Hitler would not be moved, and the month of April slipped ineffectually away. 'Manstein was furious', recalls Baron Hubertus von Humboldt, then a captain on Manstein's staff. 'In telephone calls to Kurt Zeitzler, the army chief-of-staff, he pointed out that every day we lost reduced our chances of success, and that the attack was bound to fail if there was any further delay.' The date for the attack was postponed from mid-May to mid-June.

In this phase of inactivity, when the fronts scarcely moved, Manstein found a little more time to devote to riding his horses, which he had had sent from Silesia to his headquarters in Russia. He was a very keen horseman and tried to arrange things so that he could ride at least once a day – usually accompanied by his ADC, Alexander Stahlberg. The latter was a cousin of Henning von Tresckow, a colonel on the General Staff, who had excellent links to the Führer's headquarters. Manstein had already heard through another contact, *Generalfeldmarschal* Wolfram von Richthofen, that a 'smear campaign had been mounted against him, probably by Göring and Keitel'. Those two men were using every means to prevent him being appointed Commander-in-Chief East, which would have made him a figure of considerable power. Joseph Goebbels, the propaganda minister, was another who had a strong aversion to the commander of Army Group South. 'Manstein', he averred, 'is anything but a supporter of the National Socialist regime.'

He wrote in his diary for 2 March 1943: 'When the Führer made his trip to the southern front, he had actually intended to dismiss Manstein, but for the moment he has not put this intention into effect. As it is, we have to be careful with the top Wehrmacht and Reichswehr brass. We have precious few good friends among that lot.'

However, what came to the ears of Stahlberg, through his cousin von Tresckow, was the most sinister rumour yet: 'Among his closest associates, Hitler has recently been given to loud outbursts of rage whenever the name Manstein is mentioned.' Tresckow quoted his source in the Führer's HQ as saying that Hitler knew Manstein often went riding in the afternoons with his ADC. Hitler had said it would be 'an easy job to get rid of both of them with a "partisan ambush"'. Was he really about to assassinate the field-marshal on the eve of a crucial operation like 'Citadel'? The truth behind this remains unclear. But by now a state of icy formality existed between Hitler and Manstein.

On 1 July 1943 the long wait for 'Citadel' ended. Hitler had finally made up his mind to attack – but too late, as it turned out. The Red Army had made use of the time to erect a massive defensive structure. There was no longer any prospect of surprise. 'Manstein must have seen what was happening', recalls Count Johann von Kielmansegg. 'But to us in the Operations Division he didn't make it clear how the danger of the whole operation was growing greater by the day, so that we got the impression that it would all be OK.' On 4 July the battle that had been awaited since April finally began. The Germans attacked with 1,081 tanks and 376 assault field-guns. Manstein's units thrust deep into the Soviet defences but failed to make the decisive breakthrough. On 12 July, at the critical climax of a costly battle, Manstein received an order from the

Führer's headquarters to report next day to Hitler, along with Field-Marshal von Kluge. Manstein still believed he had scored a partial success, because he had not yet called up his reserves. However, once the Allies had landed in Sicily on 9 July, Hitler decided to break off the offensive and move some of his forces over to Italy. 'Citadel' had failed.

Following the announcement of the Führer's decision, three field-marshals, Kluge, Rommel and Manstein, ruthlessly analysed, over a bottle 'of the best French red wine', how dramatically the situation had deteriorated over the past few months. As Alexander Stahlberg remembers it, Kluge said quite frankly to Manstein: 'It will come to a nasty end. And I repeat what I have said before, that I am prepared to place myself under your orders.' Rommel joined him in this: 'The end of the war will be one big disaster. If the Allies land in the Balkans as well and finally on the Atlantic coast, then the whole house of cards collapses.' Manstein retorted. 'It's not nearly that bad yet. Hitler will give up supreme command, rather than fail.'

'He'll never give up supreme command', Rommel countered. 'I clearly know him better than you do, Herr von Manstein.' There was a short pause, then Rommel assured him: 'I too am willing to put myself under your command.' As the meeting broke up, Rommel turned to Stahlberg, who had been listening to the whole conversation, and said: 'Your field-marshal is a brilliant strategist. I admire him. But he's fooling himself.'

Rommel was right. At no time did Hitler consider giving up overall command of the eastern front, voluntarily or otherwise. The dictator would have seen this as an abdication of power. Manstein was certainly confident enough to see himself as the ideal replacement as supreme commander on the eastern front. But he still shrank from bringing his own name into any discussion with Hitler, even though all the other senior officers saw him as first choice and were suffering from Hitler's blunders as a commander. 'The situation whereby the commanders-in-chief of the army groups are only informed about the overall situation through reports from the Wehrmacht [combined services]', Manstein wrote to General Zeitzler, 'is just as intolerable as the lack of any intellectual exchange between the most senior officers.' It was only in the creation of a sole commander-in-chief for the eastern front that Manstein saw a chance of saving the German Reich by reaching a military stalemate. But was this enough of a reason for him to accept the idea of a *coup d'état*?

This is precisely what was proposed to Manstein on 8 August 1943 by *Oberst* Baron Rudolf-Christoph von Gersdorff, sent as an emissary by *Feldmarschall* von Kluge. Before Gersdorff set off for Manstein's headquarters in Zaporozhye, Kluge had instructed him: 'Tell Field-Marshal von Manstein that after a *coup d'état* I would offer him the post of Chief of the Wehrmacht General Staff – in other words the combined general staffs of the army, navy and Luftwaffe.'

On his arrival in Zaporozhye, Gersdorff began his mission as planned, with a confidential conversation which, even forty years later, Gersdorff could remember verbatim. Gersdorff, with psychological astuteness, opened with the topic which Manstein was itching to talk about: the senior command structure of the Wehrmacht. He conveyed Kluge's anxiety that the conflict between the OKW and the OKH, together with Hitler's amateurish leadership meant that the collapse of the eastern front was only a matter of time. Someone had to make it clear to Hitler that disaster was inevitable unless some change was made in the military command. 'I'm of the same opinion entirely,' were Manstein's words, quoted by Gersdorff in his memoirs. 'But I'm not the right man to tell Hitler. The enemy propaganda is saying that I am the one who wants to challenge Hitler's authority, and I can do nothing to stop that. He now regards me with nothing but distrust. Only Rundstedt and Kluge can take on such a mission.'

It is quite true that at that time Manstein's name featured frequently in the English-language press and broadcasting. Reuters news agency reported that Manstein was going to be put in overall command, and in the USA *Time* magazine even put him on their front cover on 10 January 1944 – which only served to stoke up ill-feeling among his adversaries in Hitler's circle, Goebbels, Göring and Himmler. Goebbels wrote in his diary for 11 March 1944, without being specific: 'The Führer appears to have no idea how shoddily Manstein has behaved towards him.'

Gersdorff now took the plunge: 'Perhaps you and all the field-marshals should go to Hitler and hold a pistol to his chest.' At this, Manstein apparently retorted flatly: 'Prussian field-marshals do not mutiny!' But never before in history, insisted Gersdorff, had Prussian field-marshals found themselves in a comparable situation; any means was justifiable to preserve Germany from catastrophe.

> *Manstein:* Your lot want to bump him off, I suppose?
> *Gersdorff:* Yes, like shooting a mad dog.
> *Manstein:* Then count me out. It would be the end of the army. . . . I'm first and foremost a soldier. . . . If something like that happened inside the army, it would be certain to lead to civil war.

Manstein was convinced that if Hitler were forcibly eliminated, the war could no longer be fought, let alone won. When Gersdorff saw that he could not change Manstein's mind, he put the question to Manstein that Kluge had bidden him to ask: after a *coup d'état*, was Manstein willing to take over the post of Chief of the Wehrmacht General Staff? In replying, Manstein chose his words with Sybilline opacity: 'Please convey my thanks to Field-Marshal von Kluge for the trust he places in me. Tell him that Field-Marshal von Manstein will always stand loyally at the disposal of the legitimate state authority.'

How much truth is there in Gersdorff's account? Would a field-marshal discuss such explosive subjects with a liaison officer he scarcely knew? Could it be that Gersdorff's approach had been much less direct? When Manstein was giving evidence to the Nuremberg war crimes tribunal, his defence counsel, Hans Laternser, asked him: 'Did members of the 20th July Plot try to sound you out?' Manstein replied: 'I was not aware of it. . . . Now, in retrospect, I realise that various attempts were made to sound me out, apparently to probe my position. On one occasion, *Oberst* von Gersdorff came to see me and, as he subsequently told me, had with him letters from

1 Erwin Rommel with one of his tanks en route for the Scarpe sector in France, 1940.

2 Rommel on his most important promotion: 'Being made a field-marshal is like a dream to me', he wrote to his wife on 23 June 1942.

3 General Ramcke of the *Fallschirmjäger* (paratroops) reporting to Rommel in North Africa, October 1942.

4 Rommel with his wife Lucie and son Manfred, September 1944.

5 A Nazi spokesman offers hypocritical condolences to Rommel's widow, October 1944.

6 Wilhelm Keitel (standing, left) at the signing of the French surrender at Compiègne, June 1940. He called this 'the climax of my life as a soldier'.

7 Hitler with Keitel ('the very man I'm looking for'), at his 'Wolf's Lair' HQ in 1941. Hitler told Goebbels a few months later that Keitel had the 'brain of a cinema doorman'.

8 Keitel (right) with Jodl (centre), Chief of Wehrmacht Operations, and Göring, at the 'Wolf's Lair' in 1943.

9 Keitel signing Germany's surrender to the Russians in Berlin, 9 May 1945. He still maintained his Prussian bearing, 'as though he'd swallowed a broom-handle', one observer remarked.

10 Erich von Manstein after his promotion to field-marshal in July 1942. A contemporary described him as 'very much a "gentleman" and rather difficult'.

11 Inspecting Sevastopol after its capture, Manstein 'savoured the feeling of victory on the battlefield'.

12 Manstein (left, leaning forward) at a situation conference with Hitler at his HQ in Zaporozhye early in 1943. Afterwards Manstein described the Führer as an 'idiot'.

13 The last time Manstein saw his son Gero, whose death in action soon afterwards in October 1942 was 'the heaviest blow in this war'.

14 Friedrich Paulus in 1941. He was then a lieutenant-general on the Army General Staff.

15 Paulus with Hitler at the map-table in May 1942, when he was commanding the Sixth Army.

16 German troops at Stalingrad, following the failed attempt to break out of the city in November 1942.

17 Paulus as a prisoner of the Russians on 1 February 1943. Hitler raged: 'The man ought to have shot himself.'

18 Ernst Udet (front row, centre) in 1918, with other recipients of the *Pour le Mérite* (the 'Blue Max'), then Germany's highest award for gallantry.

19 Udet (left) in 1933, with the actress Ehmi Bessel and his friend Carl Zuckmayer, whose postwar play, *The Devil's General*, was based on Udet's life.

20 Udet performing a stunt near ground level, for the film *Wonders of Flight* in 1935.

21 Udet (right) in 1937, with Gen. Erhard Milch, Permanent Secretary at the Reich Ministry of Aviation, where Udet then headed the Technical Office. Though once a personal friend, Milch was instrumental in Udet's downfall.

22 Udet with Field-Marshal Göring, head of the Luftwaffe, at a military air display in 1938. Göring told Udet that the Nazi regime needed his name.

23 'Udet, my dear friend . . .' Hitler and Göring at Udet's state funeral on 21 November 1941. The fact that he had committed suicide was hushed up.

24 Patriot or traitor? Admiral Wilhelm Canaris as head of the Abwehr, the military intelligence service of the Third Reich.

25 Canaris with his deadly rival, Reinhard Heydrich, head of the Security Service. Canaris played along with Heydrich, fearing that Heydrich would take his place if he were removed.

26 Canaris (left) on a visit to the Eastern Front in 1941. Canaris' staff not only leaked information to the Allies and helped Jews to escape, but made several attempts on Hitler's life, almost certainly with Canaris' knowledge.

Goerdeler,* I believe, and Popitz,** which he was to show me if he thought I would be open to the idea of a *coup d'état*. But since I had always held the view that to push Hitler aside or remove him altogether while the war was on would have inevitably led to chaos, he did not even show me those letters. Of course, I now realise that they were trying to sound me out. At the time, though, I never gave any commitment to anyone to be a part of such an enterprise.'

In Manstein's diary we find no indication that Gersdorff had talked about an attempt on Hitler's life. And it would certainly have been too dangerous to put anything in writing. There was too great a risk that his diary might fall into the hands of the security services. Nonetheless, his notes show with what dangerous frankness Manstein spoke to Gersdorff about 'failures of leadership'. Hitler, Manstein wrote, 'should not be running everything himself'. He ought to work with a Chief of the Wehrmacht General Staff, or else take over supreme command of the Luftwaffe and navy and take joint control with the chiefs of staff of the three services. Hitler's task as 'civilian and military Führer' was chiefly one of 'political leadership of the nation, which is lacking, of running the foreign policy aspects of the war, which includes the occupied territories, and of managing the war economy and arms production. But in military policy he should only take the fundamental decisions.' All this, said Manstein, would have to be put to Hitler by Kluge. He, Manstein, could not do it himself, 'since foreign propaganda is making me out to be the man who wants to take power'.

At that point in time, Manstein told Gersdorff, there could be no thought of peace, since the opposition believed they had victory within their grasp. However, every opportunity to negotiate must be seized, and Hitler must do this – no one else. 'The army must on

---

* Carl Goerdeler (1884–1945) was Mayor of Leipzig and a junior minister in late Weimar governments. From 1935 onwards he came into conflict with the Nazis and played a leading part in plans to oust Hitler. He wrote numerous policy papers and was the first choice for the post of Chancellor after Hitler's removal. When the Stauffenberg coup failed, Goerdeler was arrested and tried. He was executed in February 1945.

** Johannes Popitz (1884–1945) was a senior civil servant in the Weimar finance ministry and continued to serve under the Nazis. However, he joined the conservative opposition to Hitler and from 1938 worked closely with Admiral Canaris and Hans Oster of the Abwehr. After the July 1944 plot he suffered the same fate as Goerdeler.

principle have nothing to with such things', Manstein insisted. 'It owes its allegiance to the flag and has a duty to obey; it will always be the one element that remains loyal. Any idea that senior military officers should involve themselves in questions of political leadership would mean abandoning the basis of military subordination, and this will always rebound against the army itself.'

It was the trap that Manstein had set for himself: he wanted to be 'just' a soldier and absolutely nothing else, and 'as such I did not use my tunic to conceal a dagger'. Brought up in the tradition of the Prussian officer corps, Manstein saw himself bound to give his loyalty and obedience to the 'legitimate authority of the state', which also meant to Hitler, 'the only man who commands the trust of the nation and its soldiers, the man they believe in. No-one else would have that' (diary entry for 8 August 1943). At no time would Manstein have entertained the idea of a *coup d'état*, let alone the assassination of the 'legitimate' head of state. Caught up in the conflict between conscience and obedience, Manstein remained true to his family motto, 'Steadfast in loyalty'. He pointed to his responsibility to his troops and the duty he had to perform as an army commander. He believed that a *putsch* would lead to civil war within the army. The thought that Hitler's demise might save millions of people from death never occurred to him. General Dietrich von Choltitz, whose courageous action later saved Paris from destruction, explained his dilemma, torn between service as a soldier and resistance, in this way: 'The enemy's superiority, which I have had to fight against for years, has now risen from 3 to 1, to 20 to 1. Faced with this, it is a ludicrous idea simply to drive into Hitler's headquarters and kill him, while millions of Russians are lined up against me, ready to swarm into Germany. As commander of an Army Group I am answerable to the German people and cannot for one moment considering imposing a change of leadership by force. . . . I do not have the right to put my men at risk through my own disobedience. . . . If such a change, which in many respects is necessary, and which, indeed, I would heartily welcome myself, is being planned, then it must be carried out by men at home in Germany, who have the opportunity to get close to Hitler, and who in any case are in a much better position to envisage the political consequences. I myself must stand by my men, whom I have to lead and whose fate I share.'

Manstein's conversations with representatives of the military resistance all followed the same pattern. He understood the situation very well and did not reject a coup on principle. But he did not want to be personally involved. On 25 November 1943, when *Oberst* Henning von Tresckow of Army Group Centre, who was on good terms with Manstein, tried once more to persuade the field-marshal to act, he was confronting a man who, as he put it, saw only one possibility: to go on fighting under Hitler, in the hope of at least reaching an honourable draw. Tresckow tried to convince Manstein that Hitler was leading Germany to perdition. 'We, on the other hand, have it in our power to stop him in his tracks. If *we* don't do it, no one will.' At one of these discussions with Tresckow, a staff officer, Hans-Adolf von Blumröder, heard Manstein say: 'For God's sake, Tresckow, give me a rest from your stupid politicking!'

Tresckow's visit on 25 November 1943 was the last attempt by a member of the anti-Nazi opposition to win over the commander-in-chief of Army Group South as a figurehead of the resistance. As far as the coup was concerned, Manstein was a lost cause. According to his mentor, *Generaloberst* Beck, the disappointing behaviour of his one-time protégé, the 'wonder-boy of operations', could be explained by his character. In March 1944, when Manstein was dismissed, Beck observed soberly: 'Although I thought highly of Manstein for a long time, I do not in any way regret his removal.'

Given his tolerant attitude towards the resistance, without himself doing anything to help it, Manstein was far from being alone among German generals. Quite a number of the senior military, first and foremost Field-Marshals Rommel and von Kluge, would have welcomed the overthrow of Hitler. But they refused to act. Manstein's resistance to Hitler did not extend beyond hard-fought battles over the map-table.

> Retreat may be masterly, but winning is in the opposite direction.
>
> *Time magazine, January 1944*

After the great tank-battle of Kursk, the initiative passed irrevocably to the Red Army. With battle-fronts of up to 900km (540 miles) wide, Manstein's Army Group was constantly exposed to attack. Almost daily, new crisis points developed, gaps in the front line had to be plugged. Yet as each hole was patched up, another was torn open. The Red Army seemed untameable – like a hydra-headed monster. Manstein urged a shortening of his overstretched fronts. But Hitler would not budge: not a foot must be yielded, just hold on, hold on. . . . Time and again he involved himself in the operational command of Army Group South. Whenever Manstein tried to convince him with military arguments, Hitler cited economic and political imperatives. Sometimes Manstein would admit resignedly: 'I get nowhere against this dialectic.' In August 1943, he protested to the OKH: 'If the Führer thinks he knows a commander-in-chief who has stronger nerves, shows more initiative, is more resourceful, and sees ahead more clearly, then I am only too willing to hand over my post. However, as long as I am in this position, I must be given the chance to use my brain.' Once again he tried to win Hitler over to the idea of a unified high command on the eastern front, and in view of the dramatically worsening situation, he no longer shrank from proposing himself as candidate for the post of Commander-in-Chief East. 'If, *Mein Führer*, you were to consider my good self in this connection, I personally guarantee you that . . . I would bring the front to a halt.'

Hitler replied that *he* was the only one able to control his unruly generals. A disillusioned Manstein wrote in his diary: 'There can now no longer be any doubt about the seriousness of the situation, and that the army is finished. . . . For the umpteenth time I put it to the OKH that we can't go on like this. . . . Everyone is getting tired of fighting not only the Russians but also the wilful blindness of those at the top.'

Hitler still hung on to Manstein. But the voices demanding his dismissal were growing ever louder. Ever since Stalingrad, when Manstein considered it impossible to supply the besieged city from the air, he had sensed that Göring was an enemy. In league with Goebbels and Himmler, the Luftwaffe chief saw Manstein as a new military power-centre, a potential rival in the battle for Hitler's favour. As early as April 1943 the Minister of Propaganda, Joseph Goebbels, had noticed that in the territories across which the German army was retreating, Manstein had introduced 'more humane treatment of the inhabitants'. On 19 October of that year, Goebbels expressed his doubts even more clearly in his diary: 'Manstein is anything but a supporter of the National Socialist regime. But at the moment we can't do anything about him, because we need him; at least so the Führer claims.' Scarcely a week later Goebbels thought he could see a gratifying change of mood in Hitler: 'The Führer is planning a major change of personnel to relieve the emergency on the southern front. He wants to put in *Generaloberst* Model to replace *Generalfeldmarschall* Manstein and give him command of the Army Group.' But two months later Manstein was still in post. Goebbels grew increasingly impatient to see that 'the Führer has not yet removed him from his job. Everyone now refers to him as "Marshal Backwards".'

The tensions between Hitler and his field-marshal became ever more acute the more massively the Red Army advanced against the German fronts. On 27 January 1944, after a conference of the Nazi leadership in Poznan Castle, Poland, Hitler lectured the senior officers of the three armed services on the need for loyalty and obedience. To Manstein this was an 'unbelievable' affront. As Manstein told his ADC, Stahlberg, he could 'bear it no longer', when Hitler ended by rambling on about a final hand-to-hand battle in which his loyal field-marshals would stand at his side. Hitler got more and more carried away with this vision until Manstein voiced the ambiguous remark: 'That's just how it's going to be, *Mein Führer!*' Hitler reacted with outrage: '*Herr Feldmarschall*, I must ask you not to interrupt when I am giving an address. You would not tolerate such behaviour from your own subordinates.'

The outburst made waves. In his activity report, Hitler's chief adjutant, Rudolf Schmundt, stated: 'In connection with this intervention, and with the various recent causes of tension, the question is once more being considered, as to the replacement of *Feldmarschall* Manstein in his command.' As it happened, Manstein's comment could hardly be heard, and not all those in the hall took it as a criticism of Hitler. Percy Ernst Schramm, who kept the OKW's war diary, said that Manstein's heckling was only picked up in the first few rows, amid the general muttering. However, there is no doubt that those controversial words were grist to the mill for Manstein's opponents.

While Goebbels, Göring and Himmler continued to plot against the field-marshal they saw as their rival, the crisis at the front turned into a disaster. West of Cherkassky, a new Stalingrad was looming. The Red Army had encircled six German divisions – 56,000 men. Attempts to liberate them had got bogged down. Then, without obtaining Hitler's consent, Manstein ordered a break-out. During the night of 16–17 February 1944, tens of thousands of German troops, with a courage born of desperation, overran the Soviet positions. Manstein's independent action had saved thousands of lives, for the moment. And Hitler gave his – retrospective – approval to Manstein's order.

The 'greatest military leader of all time' distrusted his generals. More than any of them, it was Manstein, clearly his superior in military skill, and a former confidant of Beck and Fritsch, of whom Hitler was suspicious to the very end. In the spring of 1944 the relationship between the supreme commander and his generals became several degrees colder. General Seydlitz, one of the German commanders who had been taken prisoner at Stalingrad, was appointed by the Soviets to be vice-president of a propaganda organisation, the 'National Committee for Free Germany'. He wrote to field-marshals and senior generals, calling on them to abandon the fight against the Soviet Union and join the 'Free Germany' movement. For this reason, Hitler's chief adjutant Schmundt felt it necessary for the field-marshals to assure the Führer of their absolute loyalty by swearing an oath of allegiance. At first Manstein resisted the idea of signing such a document. The oath sworn by the army to Hitler in 1934, following the death of Hindenburg, was surely as valid as ever. But Manstein's signature was of particular importance to Hitler, and so in the end he put his name to the text which came, dripping with emotion, from Goebbels' pen, and which was read out to Hitler by Field-Marshal von Rundstedt at the Obersalzberg on 19 March 1944: 'We, the field-marshals of the army have, with grave concern and distress, now come to the certain view that *General der Artillerie* Walther von Seydlitz-Kurzbach has committed a despicable treason against our Sacred Cause. . . . More than ever will it now be our task to implant the high ideals of your philosophy in the army, so that every soldier in the army will fight the more fanatically for the National Socialist future of our nation. We know that only an army imbued with National Socialism will survive the test of endurance, which today stands between us and final victory. Please accept, *Mein Führer*, this declaration by the field-marshals of your army as testimony of our unwavering loyalty.' Hitler appeared deeply moved. He told his propaganda minister that the oath was 'very forthright, very unambiguous and totally National Socialist'.

However, the Berchtesgaden oath did nothing to alter Hitler's fundamental distrust of the senior military in general and of Field-Marshal von Manstein in particular. The intrigues of Goebbels, Göring and Himmler had already seen to that. For example Himmler, the *Reichsführer*-SS, had reported to Hitler on 29 March 1944 that he was making two new *Waffen*-SS formations available for the southern front, but that he had the gravest reservations about putting them in the hands of Manstein. Goebbels noted with satisfaction: 'The Führer was profoundly impressed by Himmler's arguments.'

Not long afterwards, Manstein's adversaries achieved their objective. Once again, an entire army had been bottled up; this time it was the First Panzer Army, near Kamenets-Podolsk. On 25 March 1944 Manstein saw Hitler at the Obersalzberg, and told him he was going to order a break-out. 'Hitler very opposed to it', Manstein wrote in his diary. 'Much to-ing and fro-ing with irrelevant assertions about why things had taken this turn, which he [Hitler] blamed on the retreats in recent months, while I say that it was bound to happen, because we had always been forced to put our forces in the wrong place, in order to hold our positions.' The discussion became heated. The views of Hitler and Manstein collided more violently than ever. Afterwards, Manstein requested Hitler's chief adjutant, Schmundt, 'to tell the Führer that I would ask him to entrust the command of the Army Group to someone else, if he finds himself unable to concur with any of my opinions'. At the 'evening situation conference' Hitler agreed to Manstein's earlier demands. The successful break-out by the First Panzer Army was Manstein's last 'lost victory'. Six days later he was dismissed.

> Manstein was the most important operational figure in the Wehrmacht. He would have been the obvious choice to command the whole eastern front.
>
> *General Hans Speidel, retired*

From his home in Liegnitz, a civilian Manstein watched the situation deteriorate dramatically on all fronts, but was powerless to intervene. All he was left with was the vague hope that, as Hitler had promised, he would soon be able to take up another command. Hitler would call for him soon enough, when the water was up to his neck. Manstein still believed that, as the best army commander, he was indispensable to Hitler.

After an operation on his right eye, he did everything he could to hasten his recovery. Manstein wanted to be ready when his Führer summoned him. Even now, freed from the burdensome responsibilities of an Army Group command, the idea of a coup against Hitler was unthinkable to him – it would be an illegal act against the 'legitimate' authority of government. He was taking a sea-bathing cure on the Baltic island of Usedom, when he heard about the attempt to kill Hitler on 20 July 1944. Two days earlier, driving between Liegnitz and Breslau, his aide-de-camp Alexander Stahlberg had told him about a planned assassination: *'Herr Feldmarschall*, I feel obliged to report that today or in the next few days, the Führer is going to be killed.' Manstein took this on board, but merely replied: 'Well, now we both know something, don't we, Stahlberg!' The SD security service found nothing to suggest that Manstein was implicated in the conspiracy. 'The cleverer generals have been biding their time', Goebbels remarked, 'and Manstein is one of them.'

By August 1944 the field-marshal had not been given a new posting, and he realised that for him the war was probably over. He had still not been appointed Commander-in-Chief West. Disappointed, he told General Heinz Guderian: 'By now the post of C-in-C West has been filled twice, and nearly all the army groups have new commanding officers, without my being made use of. I must conclude from this that the Führer does not intend to deploy me. You know how much I hate this inactivity.' Hitler had absolutely no thought of re-appointing Manstein, 'the best brain that the general staff has produced'. 'If I had forty superbly equipped assault divisions with which to deal the enemy a decisive blow', Hitler said in March 1945, 'only then would I consider Manstein as commander of those troops. But in the present situation I can't use him. He lacks faith in National Socialism. That means that he is incapable of withstanding the pressures an army commander is subject to in today's military situation.'

> Manstein was anything but a Nazi, and there were unbridgeable differences between him and Hitler.
> *Ulrich de Maizière, former Inspector-General of the Bundeswehr*

Manstein abandoned hope. As the Soviet front moved ever closer, he instructed his aide-de-camp, in the autumn of 1944, to purchase an estate in Pomerania. The fact that in this war millions of Germans would soon be driven from their East Prussian homeland, and that large parts of Pomerania would no longer belong to Germany, was beyond Manstein's powers of imagination. In October 1944 the man who was 'fooling himself', as Rommel had said, wrote in a congratulatory birthday telegram to the aged First World War field-marshal, August von Mackensen: 'I trust that you will live to see our ultimate victory!'

The relentlessly advancing Soviet army soon taught him a different lesson. Only now, in the last months before Germany's collapse, did he come to accept that the war was finally lost. Manstein fled from Liegnitz to Berlin, applied at the Army High Command in Zossen for a posting, even if only the command of a battalion. 'He insisted on being given something to do', remembers

Rüdiger von Manstein, who saw out the last days of the war at his father's side. 'He didn't want to sit around idly, when the situation at the front was so serious.' But the Army High Command had no idea what to do with the field-marshal. There was no longer a job for the 'most dangerous adversary of the Allies'.

Manstein's escape route took him to Achterberg, the estate on Lüneberg Heath belonging to *Generaloberst* Baron von Fritsch, and on to Schloss Weissenhaus in Holstein. This was not far from Plön where, after Hitler's suicide, his successor Grand-Admiral Karl Dönitz was in command of the remnants of the Wehrmacht in the north. In company with another dismissed officer, *Feldmarschall* Fedor von Bock, Manstein presented himself to Dönitz and urged him to withdraw the 'Armies of the Eastern Front' gradually back to the vicinity of the American and British fronts. He made no mention of finally bringing the war to an end. It seems, instead, that Manstein was pinning his hopes on a break-up of the wartime alliance between Russia and the West. Perhaps that might open up new opportunities for Germany to negotiate . . .

For the new 'Head of State' Karl Dönitz, the arrival of the retired army commander was opportune. 'On 1 May I gave orders for contact to be established with Manstein', Dönitz wrote after the war. 'I now intended to ask him to replace Keitel as head of the Wehrmacht Supreme Command.' Clearly Dönitz hoped that with Manstein's help he could negotiate a 'better surrender' and save as many soldiers as possible from becoming prisoners-of-war of the Soviets. Manstein refused. Even in those dying days of the war he was still the last hope for a number of officers. *Feldmarschall* von Bock, who had been severely wounded in a dive-bombing attack, made a plea from his deathbed: 'Manstein, save Germany!'

There was nothing left to save. Manstein saw the surrender of the Wehrmacht as the one disaster that he, as an army commander, had always tried to prevent. On 8 May 1945 he informed Field-Marshal Montgomery's headquarters of his whereabouts. He did not want to hide away like a criminal. Perhaps a use would after all be found for him, if the victors' forced alliance did fall apart, as he thought it might. In Holstein

Manstein survived another eye infection, which almost proved fatal. He had not yet recovered when, on 26 August 1945, British officers drove up in jeeps to the Schloss Weissenhaus to arrest him. The field-marshal's foster-son, Dinnies von der Osten, a stepson of the late Field-Marshal von Bock, recalls an 'undignified scene': 'The officers hustled Manstein down the stairs and amused themselves by twirling his field-marshal's baton around. Manstein showed no reaction. He refused to demean himself.'

I never had the impression that he was a broken man. I actually think his Christian faith was too strong for that. When you have firm faith you don't topple over that easily.

I was surprised at how unmilitary he was. Although he had a strong personality, he was a perfectly normal man, a very ordinary father, just as a boy would expect a father to be.

Dinnies von der Osten, Manstein's foster-son

In 1949, after four years as a prisoner of the British, Manstein was charged before a military tribunal with war crimes committed in Poland and the Soviet Union. The trial in Hamburg's Senate House was the last case to be heard against a senior Wehrmacht officer. Perhaps surprisingly it provoked sharp protest in Britain. Churchill spoke of the 'belated proceedings against elderly German generals'. There were objections in both Houses of Parliament – and they led to action: Lord Bridgeman and Lord De Lisle and Dudley set up a defence fund for Manstein, to which Churchill, no longer prime minister, was the first to make a donation. The fund would enable Manstein to be defended by a British barrister, in front of a British military tribunal. In fact Manstein's defence was undertaken, without a fee, by a respected MP from the governing Labour Party, Reginald Paget. There were seventeen charges to be answered. On seventeen occasions, the prosecution claimed, Manstein had, in the course of the war in the east, violated the principles of the Hague Convention on Land Warfare. Manstein was sentenced to eighteen years' imprisonment. On the eight most serious charges, referred to by Paget as the 'Jewish charges', the court acquitted him. In 1953, following protests by Churchill and Montgomery, Manstein was released early from Werl prison in Westphalia, on grounds of ill-health.

> Had I not known he was a field-marshal, I would have assumed him to be the rector of a university.
>
> *Reginald Paget, Manstein's defence counsel*

His conduct during the postwar years was typical of the way many senior generals behaved. Like them, Manstein was anxious to absolve the Wehrmacht – and thereby himself as well – of any political responsibility under Hitler's evil regime. His statements to the Nuremberg War Crimes Tribunal and in his trial in Hamburg were his personal contribution to creating the myth of a Wehrmacht with 'clean hands', and they gave rise to a new legend of the 'stab in the back'.

This time it was not the people at home who had attacked an undefeated army from behind, this time it was the 'Führer' who had brought about the catastrophe. Manstein claimed that the dictator, by involving himself in the conduct of the war, had prevented the Wehrmacht from carrying all before it. If Hitler had just allowed his generals to get on with it, the war would not necessarily have resulted in Germany's defeat. With good reason, as he saw it, Manstein entitled his memoirs *Lost Victories*.

Instead of victory or defeat, he had longed dreamed of an honourable draw. He failed to recognise that Hitler could only contemplate triumph or destruction, all or nothing. He equally failed to see that it was impossible for him, as Hitler's general engaged in total war, to avoid being dragged into politics. Manstein saw himself as a 'non-political soldier' and applied all his powers to 'the art of military command'. Conscientious to the point of self-sacrifice, he did what he was best at: waging war – without grasping the criminality of Hitler's aims in the east. Therein lay the dilemma of this military man, as the *Frankfurter Allgemeine Zeitung* wrote in its obituary of him in June 1973: 'Perfecting the art of military leadership, which is meant to prevent senseless horror and atrocity, but is powerless to do so, becomes a farce when the political leaders are so dominated by a criminal mind that by his high degree of skill the officer prolongs the slaughter of war.'

In the end the catastrophe came and with it his own realisation that 'his background and upbringing' had not prepared him for the challenges of Hitler's dictatorship. Right to the end Manstein had closed his mind to crucial insights: he could not accept that military victory was no longer possible, and that he had served political ambitions which no sensible person could share. This incapacity demonstrated what Manstein had always been: a genius at the map-table, but a strategist who did not think politically. True, he argued with the dictator on military questions, but he failed to support organised resistance. While other officers were planning tyrannicide, he clung to the notions of obedience and duty, and served a warlord who deliberately led Germany to its doom, true to his motto: 'Germany will either be a world power, or it will be nothing at all.' Having had it drummed into him at the Lichterfelde cadet school, he gave unquestioning obedience to the ruling power – even when the head of state was Adolf Hitler. Despite his own inner reservations towards the Nazi regime, he let himself be misused for ends that were not his own. By not recognising Hitler's true nature and goals, and by placing his abilities in the service of a criminal, in the mistaken belief that he was serving the 'Fatherland', Manstein contributed to the destruction of the Germany which he, as a military commander, believed he could preserve.

> This brilliant soldier and great army commander was a man of nobility in the truest sense of the word – an example to us in every respect.
>
> *Theodor Busse, Manstein's chief-of-staff*

> We soldiers shared with the German people the inability to perceive the true character of the regime.
>
> *Erich von Manstein*

Field-Marshal Erich von Manstein died on the night of 9/10 June 1973, as the result of a stroke. Soldiers of the postwar German army, the Bundeswehr, on whose formation and development he had been consulted, bore his coffin to its burial place on the Lüneberg Heath. He was a soldier – no less, but no more than that.

CHAPTER FOUR

The Captive – Friedrich Paulus

As a soldier, I stand here as I have always done: awaiting orders

I must accept my fate as God ordains

I know that the history of war has already delivered its verdict on me

Germany is still strong; it will fight on to success

I was a soldier and believed at the time that I was serving my nation precisely by obeying orders

Where Stalingrad is concerned, some people act as if no one existed except Hitler and myself – no Army High Command and no Army Group either

I am neither an easterner nor a westerner. I am German

Friedrich Paulus

———————————— * ————————————

We ask ourselves whether *Generalfeldmarschall* Paulus is still alive at all. As things are, there is of course nothing left for him but an honourable soldier's death. Fate has placed him in a situation where, precisely because so many men have already died, he must sacrifice fifteen or twenty years of his life, in order to keep his name alive for thousands of years to come.

Joseph Goebbels

How can a man watch his soldiers die and defend themselves courageously to the last man – how can he then surrender to the Bolsheviks? What hurts me so much is that the heroism of so many soldiers is wiped out by a single spineless weakling. In this war no one else is ever going to be made a field-marshal.

Adolf Hitler

Thus the only possibility would have been to face Hitler with the complete withdrawal of the army from Stalingrad, particularly when the Supreme Command remained silent for thirty-six hours. It was more probably a kind of loyalty to Hitler, which caused Paulus to ask for permission for his army to break out, since he was in radio contact with the Army High Command.

Erich von Manstein

Every sentence that he spoke or wrote was carefully weighed. He expressed every idea with clarity, so that no doubt could arise. If Reichenau was a decisive commander-in-chief who relished responsibility, and was distinguished by his toughness, iron will and daring, then Paulus was the exact opposite. Even as a young officer he was known in his circle of colleagues as 'Cunctator', the waverer.

Wilhelm Adam, principal adjutant of the Sixth Army under Paulus

History has never yet granted a military leader the right to sacrifice the lives of his soldiers when they are no longer able to fight.

General Hans Doerr

Paulus was respected as one of the leading strategic minds in the German army and the German General Staff. On the other hand, there was always a worry about whether he would have the same abilities as a commander-in-chief as he had as Chief of the General Staff.

Philip Humbert, principal aide-de-camp of the Fourth Army Corps

Whether *Feldmarschall* Paulus really did himself a favour when he got taken prisoner and lived through all those times in Russia, in Dresden and at the Nuremberg War Crimes Tribunal, is a question that is certainly worth asking.

Winrich Behr, principal aide-de-camp in Sixth Army HQ

Paulus argued that there had to be a neutral, independent Germany.

Heinz Beutel, Paulus' adjutant in the GDR

The conduct of *Generalfeldmarschall* Paulus was impeccable – correct relations with the authorities, public declaration of sympathy with the Soviet Union, rejection of all Nazi propaganda. But at the same time he strictly refused, while a prisoner-of-war, to take any political decisions.

Leonid Reshin, Russian journalist

To my mind, any soldier in a situation like that is not a criminal but a tragic figure, for whom one may often have compassion but never hatred.

Erich Mende, former minister in the German federal government

He once said he couldn't help the fact that he would go on living.

Erna Eilers, Paulus' housekeeper

The wrong man in the wrong place.

Paul Jordan, former staff officer in the Sixth Army HQ

---------------------- * ----------------------

East Berlin, 26 October 1953. In the 'action plan' of Department I of the Ministry of State Security we read: 'The subject will be greeted by a delegation in Frankfurt-an-der-Oder. Responsible: *Generalmajor* von Lenski. The task of the delegation is to collect the subject by car and drive him to Berlin. In Berlin a reception will be held at the Ministry in Schnellerstrasse. A small dinner will be given, attended by Comrades Matern, Stoph, Hoffmann, Maron, Müller, Homan, Dölling, Korfes, Bechler, Kessler and others. After the meal there will be a confidential discussion between the subject, the Minister and the *Generalleutnanten* Heinz Hoffmann and Vincenz Müller.'

The 'subject', as he was described in the action plan of the GDR state security, was no less a personage than the former field-marshal of the German Wehrmacht, Friedrich Paulus. Ten and a half years as a prisoner-of-war in Russia lay behind him when, on 26 October 1953, shortly after 11 a.m., he set foot on German soil once more, at the frontier railway station in Frankfurt-an-der-Oder.

A decade earlier, on 2 February 1943, at 12.35 p.m., a radio message had been received by the Wehrmacht's Army Group Don. The message said: 'Cloud-base 5,000 metres. Visibility 12 kilometres, sky clear, small scattered clouds, temperature 31 degrees below zero, mist and red haze over Stalingrad. Weather-station signing off. Give our regards to the old country.'

Two days previously the battle for Stalingrad had come to an end. It was the beginning of the end of the Wehrmacht's campaign in the east. Today, history scarcely remembers the names of the victors in this mighty battle. But it knows the name of the vanquished: Paulus. It is a name that is inseparably linked with Stalingrad.

Stalingrad: in the German language this word has come to be more than just a geographical entity. The city has become both a symbol and a legend. It conjures up images that are as diverse as the viewpoints of the men who see them in their mind's eye. There are places where the number of victims was incomparably greater – Auschwitz or Hiroshima. There are defeats suffered by the Wehrmacht, which were of greater strategic importance: Moscow, El Alamein, Kursk, Normandy. But that city, more than 1,200 miles south-east of Berlin, has become synonymous with the failure of the Wehrmacht's triumphant model of *Blitzkrieg* warfare.

It was there, in November 1942, that at least 260,000 German, Italian, Hungarian and Romanian soldiers of the German Sixth Army were encircled by eight Soviet armies. Two and a half months later the Soviet troops were still able to round up some 91,000 enemy, completely exhausted both mentally and physically, and despatch them in long convoys to PoW camps situated far behind the front line. Years later, when their repatriation was finally negotiated, only 6,000 were still alive. However, of the twenty-three generals taken prisoner in Stalingrad, only one failed to return to Germany: he was *Generaloberst* Walter Karl Heitz, who died of stomach cancer in a Moscow hospital on 6 February 1944. The commander-in-chief of those troops, Friedrich Paulus, who was promoted by Hitler to field-marshal, even as his army was in its death throes, survived his capture by fourteen years, one day and eight hours. Because of Stalingrad, he would become the most controversial commander in German military history. Even after more than half a century, opinions on Paulus are deeply divided: hero or traitor? A loyal general who held out, as Hitler demanded, or a mere opportunist? A pawn in the game of Cold War chess or a truly tragic figure? Today a former aide-de-camp in the Sixth Army sums it up like this: 'Paulus would have saved himself a lot of trouble if he'd followed the example of General von Hartmann.'

Hartmann, who commanded the 71st Infantry Division, moved up to the main fighting line after his formation had been virtually wiped out, and went on firing at the Soviet attackers, without any cover himself, until he was killed by a shot in the head.

On 8 November 1942, Adolf Hitler was addressing a group of the Nazi Party's 'old campaigners' at the Bürgerbräu beer cellar in Munich. 'I wanted to reach the Volga, and in fact one city in particular. It happens to bear the name of Stalin himself', the Führer mused. 'But you mustn't think I marched there just for that reason: . . . No. It's at a very important point on the map. That's what I wanted to capture.'

And then he told a lie: 'Y'know, I don't want to boast, but we've got it.' They had not got it, and they never did get it – that 'point on the map'. To the very end, the Red Army went on bitterly defending a bridgehead only a few hundred yards wide on the northern bank of the Volga at Stalingrad. The Soviet 62nd Army, with 75,000 men of the workers' militia, 7,000 young *Komsomol* (Soviet Youth) members and quite a number of women, held off the Wehrmacht's most battle-hardened formation. The Sixth Army had already earned a reputation by conquering the capital cities of Warsaw, Brussels and Kiev. But Stalin's order no. 227 was clear enough: 'Not one step backward . . .' Troops of the NKVD, Russia's equivalent of the SS, made sure it was enforced. For five long months the battle raged from street to street, from house to house, around the docks, on the banks of the Volga, at the main railway station and in the factories. In the words of Arthur Schmidt, Chief-of-Staff of the Sixth Army, it was a battle the like of which 'none of the troops involved have ever experienced in this war'. It was a slaughter that went on until everything lay shattered. Stalingrad turned into a dubious myth of martial heroism and 'eager' self-sacrifice. As Hitler's army adjutant, Major Gerhard Engel, put it: 'Stalingrad was declared a "shrine" and was compared with great battles of antiquity, like Cannae or Thermopylae.'

But the hell of Stalingrad was no Thermopylae and Paulus, promoted to field-marshal at the eleventh hour, was no modern Leonidas. His soldiers were not defending the threshold of their homeland, but stood as conquerors in the heart of another country. They were not there because the law or the moral precepts of the state required it, but because their Führer had ordered it. And the field-marshal did not die fighting shoulder to shoulder with his troops, but walked with his officers into captivity. The end was rather prosaic. The final report of the Soviet 64th Army to its headquarters reads as follows:

On the evening of 30 January elements of the army, who had been engaged in relentless fighting with the southern enemy formations, forced their way into the centre of Stalingrad. The

38th Motorised Rifle Brigade, in co-operation with the advancing 329th Pioneer Battalion, came up against particularly stubborn enemy resistance in the Square of the 'Fallen Fighters', which came from two buildings in Lomonossov Street. From interrogating a prisoner who had been captured when a building was overrun, it was learned that these buildings formed a stronghold guarding access to the city's main department store, the basement of which provided accommodation for the staff of the Sixth Army along with its commander-in-chief.

In the night of 30–31 January 1943 the department store building was sealed off by elements of the 38th Motorised Rifle Brigade and the 329th Pioneer Battalion. Their telephone links were cut off. On 31.01.43, during an exchange of fire with the guard of the army staff, Paulus' personal adjutant came out of the basement at 6 a.m. and stated that the senior German officers wished to negotiate with ours.

Up to that point the commander-in-chief and his chief-of-staff, *Generalmajor* Arthur Schmidt, had consistently refused to negotiate. The Soviet offer of surrender terms on 8 January was countered with the statement that any Soviet peace envoys would be driven back by German fire.

But now the principal adjutant of the Sixth Army HQ, Oberst Wilhelm Adam, walked with a Russian negotiator, Lt-Col Vinokur, second-in-command of the 38th Motorised Rifle Brigade, through the subterranean catacombs of a shell-blasted department store in the centre of Stalingrad, in order to work out the terms of surrender by a German field-marshal.

Born on 23 September 1890 in the small town of Breitenau-Gershagen in Hessen, Friedrich Wilhelm Ernst Paulus grew up in the household of a typical minor functionary of the Kaiser's era. This respectable middle-class background shaped the rest of his life. His father was the accountant in a reformatory and his mother was the daughter of its director. Equipped with such virtues as correct behaviour, exactitude and a deep-rooted consciousness of the

German nation and its hierarchy, as well as an almost archaic notion of loyalty, coupled with above-average intelligence, the young Paulus seemed absolutely predestined for a military career. He attended the Wilhelm High School in Kassel and passed his leaving examination in 1909. In his final report his career choice is noted as 'officer in the Imperial Navy'. However, His Majesty's Navy had exclusive ideas about their young officer cadets. Noble blood, or at least a father who was a leading industrialist, were more important qualifications than ability, aptitude or achievements. The son of a minor Hessian functionary saw his application turned down. Later in life, Paulus never spoke about this crushing rejection. But it is very clear that he took it as a social slight. Initially he decided to take up a legal career. In the winter term of 1909 his name is to be found on the matriculation list of the Faculty of Law at the Philipps University in Marburg. Nevertheless, his leanings were still in a military direction. The army needed officers and their selection procedure was less hampered by class prejudice than that of the navy. On 18 February 1910 Friedrich Paulus, then aged 19, was made an ensign in the 111th Baden Infantry Regiment in Rastatt. In 1911, after passing through military academy at Engers, he was given the coveted lieutenant's commission. Considerable influence on his career can be attributed to his marriage in 1912 to an aristocratic young Romanian woman, Elena Constance Rosetti-Solescu. Coca, as his wife was usually known within the family, came from a wealthy and respected Boyar family who attended the court of the Romanian monarchy. It was an unusual alliance, for both parties. But for the young lieutenant it provided access to the highest social strata of old Europe – a world that would soon disappear.

In August 1914, when the first global war of the twentieth century began, Lt Paulus was serving as battalion adjutant in his Baden infantry regiment. It is a characteristic of his career that Paulus was usually posted to adjutancies, and later to staff positions. Even as a young officer he was already becoming known for an almost pernickety conscientiousness in handling planning assignments. In the recollection of his class colleagues from that period the verdict on Paulus is unanimous: a typical staff officer of the old school, tall, elaborately well-groomed, occasionally over-modest, likeable, with exquisite manners, exceptionally gifted and interested in things military, a slow, deliberate worker at his desk, and passionately keen on war-games and planning exercises at the map-table or in the sandbox, in which he showed considerable operational talent, though he certainly revealed a tendency to think over every decision thoroughly and carefully before he drafted the appropriate orders. Paulus never gave any thought to his health; he worked all through the night, keeping himself awake with coffee and endless cigarettes.

The loss of the First World War, which he ended as a captain and staff officer, but even more the fall of the German monarchy, had a profound impact on Friedrich Paulus as a soldier and a monarchist. The disgrace of defeat caused him personal anguish, yet his attitude to war as a means to political ends remained unaffected. A document from 1937 provides retrospective evidence that in the years 1919–20 he served in an illegal militia or *Freikorps*, known as 'Frontier Protection East'. To what extent he was involved in this fighting, which bordered on civil war, can only be guessed at today. Sadly, there is a fundamental lack of available sources for this period. Friedrich Paulus was never a great letter-writer, nor did he even keep a diary. The man who carefully weighed up every decision three times over, never really revealed himself. The few retrospective studies from the last years of his life concern themselves exclusively with explaining the decisions he made as the commander in the battle for Stalingrad. For this reason his biography remains fragmentary to this day.

In October 1922 he was posted to Berlin for what was known as an 'R-course' for staff officers. In spite of all his talent, one of the commanding officers at that time, General Heim as he later became, accused Paulus of 'a certain lack of decisiveness in tricky situations'. Among his class colleagues he was given the Latin nickname 'Fabius Cunctator' – the 'waverer'. In the papers left by Paulus there is what was known as a *Bierzeitung* (drinkers' journal) – a scurrilous document of the kind written by students at the end of a stage of their course. Even here, the 41-year-old major is described as an extremely painstaking, almost pedantic officer; and as the 'noble lord', the 'fine, slim gentleman', the 'major with sex-appeal'. All in all, Paulus appears in those years as the archetypal, highly educated and yet totally non-political staff officer, of the kind preferred by the Reichswehr high command – 'staff officers have no names', as they used to say.

After various postings as a teacher of tactics and as 'deputy assistant commanding officer' in the 100,000-strong Reichswehr, Paulus was promoted to the rank of *Oberstleutnant* (lieutenant-colonel) in 1933 and given command of the 3rd Motorised Division in Zossen, the military base near Berlin. Later this division formed the core of the German panzer forces. It was during this posting that Paulus saw Hitler seize absolute power. Although he was instinctively opposed to 'that proletarian' and his 'People's Party', he felt rather drawn by what Hitler promised, particularly since the 'lack of discipline and order' in the Weimar Republic had been abhorrent to him. The part played by Friedrich Paulus in the emergence of what was then new to the army: the *Panzertruppe*, or armoured forces, is often overlooked. The organisation, command structure and types of deployment of this 'instrument of *Blitzkrieg*' were permanently shaped as much by him as by generals Guderian and Nehring. In this the 'non-political' staff officer could rely on the undiluted goodwill of that infantry veteran, Adolf Hitler. The dictator was thinking in a modern way and displayed an understanding of technology when he assigned top priority to this innovative arm, and to the newly developed Stuka (*Sturzkampfbomber*), the dreaded dive-bomber of the Luftwaffe. The plane's perfection marked the birth of the highly successful *Blitzkrieg* – lightning warfare – and Paulus played a decisive role in it.

In passing judgement on the military elite of the Nazi Reich, the focus today is generally placed on their relationship with the anti-Hitler resistance. Objectively speaking, this criterion is historically and morally correct; subjectively, however, it is questionable, to say the least. During the years of the Weimar Republic Paulus remained no more than a captain for twelve long years, before rising to major. After Hitler had taken power, Paulus was promoted to *Generalmajor* (major-general) within eight years. It is obvious that as a professional officer Friedrich Paulus must have regarded the new head of state as the man who furthered his career.

On the outbreak of the Second World War *Generalmajor* Paulus was Chief-of-Staff of the Tenth Army, under *Generaloberst* von Reichenau. In this man Paulus came up against one of the most unusual, brilliant and controversial commanders in the German Wehrmacht. The 'pairing' of Paulus with Reichenau proved to be the almost ideal combination for the leadership of an army. Walter von Reichenau had benefited from a wide-ranging education and was well up in the latest technology. In the First World War, as an artillery officer and then on the general staff, he had carefully observed the increasing industrialisation of war and drawn the appropriate lessons from that. In the years between the two world wars he had travelled extensively through Europe, the United States and South America. He was the embodiment of a new type: the political soldier. As early as 1932 von Reichenau had made cautious advances to the Nazis. With help from his uncle Friedrich von Reichenau, a retired ambassador and chairman of German Nationals Abroad, he succeeded in gaining direct access to Hitler. When the Nazis seized power in Germany, Reichenau's political gamble came off: with Hitler in charge, Reichenau tried to exploit to the full the opportunities for pushing through his ideas for a modern military policy. He realised that the brownshirt masters would raise the professional army to a new level, and not just in the short term. Historians of this period are right when they present Reichenau and the then army minister, Werner von Blomberg, as the men who not only drew the army closer and closer to the regime but also typified the phenomenon of the new 'political soldier'. At the same time, Reichenau felt obliged to add to his unbounded ambition by shining as a sportsman, whether at tennis, riding, cross-country running, shot-putting, swimming or pistol-shooting. Despite the early toll that this took on his body, he

insisted on savouring life to the full. As a general he engaged in
political argument; as a field commander he was always up with his
troops; in Poland he did not hesitate to lead them in swimming
across a river, and later in Russia personally fought in a battle in
order to gain control of a difficult situation. He was not a likeable
man, but undoubtedly a daring and uncompromising one, whose
ruthlessness towards himself and others amounted to the
abandonment of all traditional codes of behaviour.

Paulus once said jokingly of Reichenau, that this man did
everything that he, Paulus, was actually built for – riding, sport and
the like – while he was left to do the work. That was certainly not
meant to be derogatory. It was part of the job of a chief-of-staff to
take the workload away from the commander-in-chief. And Paulus
had always been a man who liked sitting at his desk and brooding
over maps. Reichenau, the charismatic commander, found in Paulus
the reliable staff support that allowed him to go off on his escapades.

As Chief-of-Staff of the Tenth Army, which was later renamed the
Sixth Army, *Generalmajor* Paulus witnessed breathtaking victories in
Poland, Belgium and France. The victory parade in Warsaw and the
acceptance of the surrender of the Belgian army under King Leopold
III in the Château of Anvaing on 28 May 1940, were certainly
experiences which gave Friedrich Paulus the feeling that Adolf Hitler,
as Führer and Reich Chancellor, had completely liberated the
German people from the 'disgrace of Versailles'.

Under Reichenau the Sixth Army gained the reputation for being
an elite unit. Paulus was considered one of the few high-ranking
staff officers who could draw on years of relevant experience in the
development and tactical deployment of armour. In the late summer
of 1940, with an eye to the impending Russian campaign, the
supreme commander of the army, *Generaloberst* Franz Halder, chose
Paulus, by now promoted to *Generalleutnant*, to be senior
Quartermaster on the Army General Staff. That meant that he
ranked in third place after the then Commander-in-Chief of the
Army, *Generalfeldmarschall* von Brauchitsch, and the Chief of the
General Staff, Franz Halder. Paulus would now be based in the
elaborate underground complex known as 'Maybach I/II', in Zossen.

Paulus carried out his functions with an adaptability born of practice, and a constant awareness of the next career move. It is true that his attitude to a war against the Soviet Union was sceptical, but he did not reject the idea out of hand. Paulus did not enquire about ultimate responsibility, but concentrated on the job in hand, which he realised was a personal opportunity. At about this time, one of his two sons, Ernst Alexander Paulus, a lieutenant in the 6th Panzer Regiment, heard these words spoken by an instructor in the panzer training school in Wünsdorf: 'There are two men in the German army who are recognised as having very great operational talent – von Manstein and Paulus.' When Ernst asked if that was not rather an exaggeration, the reply was that in the army personnel office great long-term careers were predicted for both of them.

Like many military men, Paulus had become, whether consciously or not, a compliant tool of the Nazis' policy of conquest. When the new Senior Quartermaster took up his post in September 1940, he found himself confronted with a task that would test his skills as a planner to the full: the drawing-up of a battle-order against the Soviet Union. Developing such plans is one of the principal assignments of a staff officer, and Paulus took it up as a military challenge. It was he who was chiefly responsible for the planning of 'Operation Barbarossa', which encompassed in operational terms the destruction of the Soviet armed forces. The central risk of the campaign was, as he could see, in securing German supply-lines.

In the Army High Command opinions were divided as to whether the Soviet Union was planning an offensive for 1941, or whether the very extensive deployment of the Red Army, in anticipation of German intentions, should be interpreted as a purely precautionary defensive measure. In the event, the Soviet formations stationed on Russia's western frontier were taken completely by surprise when the Wehrmacht launched its assault on 22 June 1941.

It was inevitable that when working out a battle-plan like that, despite all the regulations on secrecy, it would be discussed in general terms within the Paulus family circle. His sons, both panzer officers, had in any case picked up rumours in their units that they would be having a go at the Soviet Union in the near future. Paulus' wife Elena Constance was, for all her loyalty to her husband, a woman of independent mind. The daughter of a Romanian aristocrat, she had already judged the invasion of Poland to be an unforgivable crime. To make war on the Soviet Union was, in her view, a glaring injustice. Paulus himself had had Soviet Russian officers among his students at the war college. Because of the international connections of his wife's Rosetti-Solescu family, many Russians visited his mother-in-law's home in Baden-Baden. For all his personal sympathy with the Russian mentality, Paulus found communism, let alone Bolshevism, wholly unacceptable as a form of social organisation, and he retained this fundamental attitude even in the last controversial years of his life, spent in Russia and East Germany. In 1940–1 Paulus, as Deputy Chief-of-Staff of the Army, had clearly accepted the argument that an assault on the Soviet Union was the only way for Germany to extract a reasonably favourable outcome from the war. According to statements by members of his family and close friends, on the few occasions when he discussed the assault on Russia, he never attempted to justify it by saying that Germany had to forestall aggressive Soviet intentions.

In any case, Paulus was not the sort of man to put his career at risk by openly opposing Hitler's decisions. He had been trained as a soldier and, true to his understanding of the military profession, he regarded political decisions, such as the one to invade Russia, as an area that soldiers should keep away from. Following the triumphant campaign against France, the Reich that Adolf Hitler had created stood at the zenith of its power, and the staff officers of the Seeckt and Schleicher schools did not feel obliged to dwell for one minute on the diplomatic implications or political problems on the home front.

In the midst of preparations for the eastern offensive, originally scheduled for May 1941, the Yugoslav army staged a coup against the Prince Regent, Paul, and his pro-Axis cabinet. This meant that all the timetables had to be scrapped. Paulus was despatched to Budapest to discuss a joint operation against Yugoslavia, with the Hungarian Minister of War and chiefs of staff. Hitler and the senior members of the German General Staff considered Paulus the right man to carry out such a sensitive diplomatic and military mission, which also involved Romania. For not only did he have superb manners and was known for his self-control, but thanks to his wife he had useful contacts in Romania, which was now allied with Germany. For example, a cousin of his wife was Court Chamberlain to the Queen Mother, Helena, who was by no means friendly towards Germany.

The April campaign against Yugoslavia and Greece, organised at short notice with support from Hungary and Romania, was not the only reason for the momentous decision to postpone 'Operation Barbarossa'. In addition to the need to secure the south-eastern flank of the invasion of the Soviet Union, the Wehrmacht was committed to another theatre of war: after Germany's Italian allies had suffered several defeats in North Africa at the hands of British and Commonwealth forces, Mussolini had been forced to request the despatch of a German expeditionary force to Libya. The commander of these troops was the charismatic *Generalleutnant* Erwin Rommel, who had been a colleague of Paulus when they were both serving in the 13th Infantry Regiment in Stuttgart. Rommel, who had won his *Blitzkrieg* spurs as a panzer general in the invasion of France, had no intention of adopting a defensive stance in the task assigned to him. Even before the majority of his troops had come ashore in Tripoli, his advance assault units had recaptured almost the whole of Cyrenaica, the western part of Libya, thereby dangerously extending his supply-lines. Despite all the positive aspects which the newsreels from Goebbels' propaganda machine were able to present from the distant war-zone, the staff officers in the Army High Command became increasingly concerned: was it possible under sensible planning, which took account of German resources in men and equipment, to run two offensives simultaneously – one against British forces in North Africa, the other against a massive nation in the east? In the opinion of Franz Halder, Chief-of-Staff of the Army High Command, North Africa, and with it the whole Mediterranean region, could only be a secondary theatre of war, if Germany was to pick a serious fight with the Soviet Union. But every theatre of war develops its own dynamic and a figure like Rommel, the 'Desert Fox', created new circumstances almost daily with his daringly aggressive operations.

On 23 April 1941 *Generaloberst* Halder noted in his diary: 'Therefore necessary to sort matters out in North Africa with all speed. After much consideration, I decide against flying down there myself. I can't act merely as a fact-finder there. If I turn up in North Africa I want to have the right to issue orders. The C-in-C of the army, on the other hand, is worried and puts up the pretext of problems with the Italian High Command. Of course his real reasons are different; perhaps it is better to send Paulus off, who's on good terms with Rommel from the time they served together. He may be the only man with sufficient personal influence to rein in this soldier who has gone stark mad.'

On the evening of 25 April 1941 Paulus and several officers of the General Staff flew via Rome to North Africa. He found the *Panzergruppe Afrika*, as Rommel's force was then called, in a pretty difficult situation, due in particular to its over-extended supply-lines. He observed at first hand how Rommel's attack on the port of Tobruk ground to a halt against strong British defences.

Paulus spent two and a half weeks in North Africa. On 11 May he submitted his report to Halder: 'Situation in North Africa very unsatisfactory. By exceeding his orders, Rommel has created a situation in which it is currently impossible to keep him adequately supplied. Rommel is not up to his job.' To his family Paulus was even more frank about his former comrade-in-arms: 'That Swabian numbskull . . . acts as though he doesn't need to listen to anybody.'

Paulus, who had long wanted a field command of his own, considered at the time whether he should suggest to the Army High Command a change of leadership in North Africa, and take over command of the *Panzergruppe Afrika* himself. His wife's comment on this has been recorded: 'Stay out of it! What good will it do you if the British nab you in Africa . . .'

In the early hours of 22 June 1941 the plans for the 'Barbarossa' operation became reality. The *Blitzkrieg* model, so successfully tested by the Wehrmacht in the west, was now expected to prove its worth in the endless expanses of Soviet Russia. However, the initially breathtaking success of the invasion was soon to reveal the flaw in German operational planning: the culpably irresponsible underestimation of the length of supply-lines needed, of the vast area to be covered, and of Soviet resources. By November, when the Russian winter had begun to bite, the illusion of a swift victory over the 'giant with feet of clay' was shattered. The German armed forces, spoiled by success, found their Achilles heel cruelly exposed. Equipped by the industrial output of practically an entire continent, the Wehrmacht's infantry divisions were driving across the vast Russian landscape in as many as 100 different types of truck. Belgian spare parts were useless in French troop-carriers. German infantry ammunition could not be used in looted Czech sub-machine guns. With typical thoroughness, the Germans went on improving every prototype for an up-to-date combat tank, so that even as late as the autumn of 1942, no tank had gone into full-scale production. What is more, the troops were only kitted out for a summer campaign. In a *Blitzkrieg* of that kind, winter uniforms were regarded as superfluous ballast. 'Operation Typhoon' has gone down in history as the greatest battle of encirclement ever fought (45 Russian divisions, totalling 673,000 troops, were taken prisoner), yet the assault on Moscow was a miserable failure. The Wehrmacht had forfeited once and for all its aura of invincibility. What is more, Hitler was becoming more and more directly involved in the strategic dispositions of his generals. The man who had been a mere infantry corporal in the First World War felt called upon to make decisions about the deployment of armoured groups and infantry battalions operating 1,200 miles from Berlin. The General Staff, an institution created by Scharnhorst and Moltke, soon degenerated, without significant resistance, into a group of high-ranking yes-men.

In the second year of the war Hitler tried to seek a conclusive victory on the southern flank of the Russian front. The objective of the German manoeuvres were the Caucasus oilfields of Baku, Grozny and Maikop, without which, Hitler was convinced, the German panzer armies would be deprived of their mobility. It was no longer a question of winning the war, but of being able to go on fighting it at all. This notion was by no means far-fetched in view of the fact that of about 30 million tons of crude oil produced in the USSR in 1938, nearly three-quarters came from the Baku area, and a further 16 per cent from the north Caucasus oilfields around Maikop and Grozny, and in Dagestan; barely 10 per cent came from other parts of the Soviet Union. Hitler was now clearly preparing for a long war – a war also being waged against the Anglo-American forces, equipped from virtually inexhaustible resources. Once the USA had joined the war in December 1941, the raw materials situation had become the critical factor in the dictator's strategic calculations.

As 1941 turned into 1942, the advance of Army Group South ground to a halt near Rostov, and the former commander of the Sixth Army, *Generalfeldmarschall* von Reichenau, took over command of the Army Group. This brought Friedrich Paulus to a turning point in his life. His name was proposed, probably by Reichenau himself, as his successor in command of the Sixth Army. On 1 January 1942 Paulus was promoted to full general, and given the task of commanding the most battle-proven force in the Wehrmacht: the Sixth Army – subduer of cities.

What may have ultimately persuaded Hitler to make this key appointment remains obscure. It is probable that, among other things, he wanted to ensure Reichenau's loyalty. At all events, the sacred law of seniority within the army was thrown into complete disarray. Paulus had never had independent command of a regiment, let alone a division or an army corps. His last posting to the front line, or at least to a staff posting with a fighting unit, had been eighteen months before. Even after the war, Paulus' former instructor, General Ferdinand Heim, considered it an unpardonable error in Hitler's personnel policy to entrust Paulus with an army on the eastern front. Paulus had always been a desk-man, Heim claimed, and lacked practical skills.

A few days after Friedrich Paulus' appointment as commander of the Sixth Army, Field-Marshal Reichenau died unexpectedly from a stroke. From then on the Army Group was under the command of

Field-Marshal Fedor von Bock, the 'Soldier of Misfortune', as a later biographer dubbed Paulus' new superior. A little later Hitler issued his Directive No. 41, which would set the goals for the summer campaign: the central objective of the German offensive was 'finally to destroy the remaining Soviet forces left alive and as far as possible to deprive them of the sources of energy required for the prosecution of the war. . . . In any event, an attempt will be made to reach Stalingrad itself or at least to subject it to the impact of our heavy weaponry to such an extent that it ceases to function as an armaments and transport centre.'

Only after the successful conclusion of this phase of operations would the actual advance into the Causasus region take place. Before any thought could be given to that, the Sixth Army under its new commanding officer immediately found itself caught up in heavy defensive engagements on the southern flank of the eastern front. The army came through these battles around Charkov with comparatively low casualties, thanks to a combination of skill and luck. They earned a Knight's Cross for the 51-year-old Paulus, and those who had hitherto expressed the view that the staff officer was out of his depth in a front-line command were temporarily reduced to silence. A photo of the army chief appeared in the newspapers and the name of Paulus was on everyone's lips. For a short time he seemed to be, like Rommel and a handful of others, a gift to the Nazi propaganda machine. The Sixth Army had become famous under Reichenau, and for a time, thanks to Paulus, its reputation seemed to rise to almost mystical levels. It is this period that provoked Hitler's enthusiastic boast that with the Sixth Army he could 'storm Heaven itself'.

Starting on 28 June 1942 the German offensive rolled steadily on in a south-easterly direction. The Wehrmacht gained some small and middling victories, but it never succeeded in achieving what had been planned: to engage the opposing Soviet divisions in a decisive battle. After the initial successes – on 3 July alone the Sixth Army took 40,000 prisoners – Hitler issued the notorious Directive No. 45. All good military sense was now finally abandoned: in Hitler's mind the adversary was already prostrate. He gave orders that the two successive operational objectives should now be captured simultaneously, and split his forces on the southern flank of the eastern front. The Seventeenth Army, the Third Romanian Army, together with the First and Fourth German Panzer Armies, were now re-formed as Army Group A under *Generalfeldmarschal* List and given the task of invading the Caucasus through Rostov-on-Don. The Sixth Army was ordered to swing north-east and take Stalingrad. This plan made no provision for building up reserves. Hitler's generals knew the risk but said nothing – not even General Paulus.

Later he was reproached for this. He, more than any other army commander, must have recognised the irresponsible madness in Hitler's conduct of the war. In fact, exactly the opposite was the case: he was thoroughly familiar with the basic assumptions in the operational planning of the Russian campaign, and he was aware, from his knowledge of the overall situation, of how the army formations were being led. Paulus stated that, in view of the millions of troops on the move, no army commander-in-chief could get an appreciation of the total situation and therefore he should not be given freedom to take decisions that went beyond the performance of the tasks assigned to him. This judgement proved fatal and led to the death of tens of thousands of German soldiers.

> If General Paulus did not seize that last chance when it was offered, if he hesitated and finally failed to risk the venture, then it was surely because he felt the weight of responsibility upon him.
>
> *Erich von Manstein*

On 21 August 1942, with a fighting strength of more than 300,000, the Sixth Army, under General Paulus' command, launched an assault from a bend in the River Don on the city that bore Stalin's name.

Countless books have now been written about the battle on the Volga, and studying it is compulsory at a number of military academies. The Germans made war in a way that overstepped all bounds in its hubris, but they failed to overcome the resistance of the defenders.

While keeping up a determined resistance, the Soviet troops fell back to the suburbs of the city on the Volga. This shift of the fighting into the city completely nullified any strategy devised by the German General Staff. Having advanced so far eastward, and with inadequate cover on its flanks, the army was caught up in a battle of attrition, fought from house to house. The classic elements of *Blitzkrieg*, designed to gain control of large areas and then crush the opposition, were no longer effective. It was scarcely possible to deploy the Stuka dive-bombers of *Generaloberst* von Richthofen's 4th *Luftflotte*, because in the murderous street fighting no clear front line could be made out from the air. In the jungle of buildings tank formations became easy prey for the opposing infantry. Though by the middle of October 1942, nine-tenths of the city was in German hands, the Soviet 62nd Army was grimly defending a narrow strip of terrain along the bank of the Volga.

> It's going very slowly, yet every day we make a bit of progress. It's all a question of time and manpower. But we will see the Russians off.
> *Paulus in a letter to General Schmundt, 7 October 1942*

The Russian commander General Chuikov directed operations from a command-bunker on the bank of the Volga, which was sometimes as little as 100 yards from the main fighting line. Instead of being able to report the capture of the city, Paulus was forced to accept that, whereas his total force including non-combatants numbered 260,000, he was left with a fighting strength of only 25,000 men. Despite repeated demands, he received no significant reinforcements. Only five battalions of assault pioneers, each numbering 600 men, were assigned to him, to enable him to capture the final group of factory buildings in the industrial district. After two days of fighting, these units had been wiped out – and the factories were still in

Soviet possession. During the last days of October and early
November Paulus and his chief-of-staff, *Generalmajor* Arthur
Schmidt, were getting increasing indications of an imminent Soviet
counter-offensive which could put his army in mortal danger. On
both flanks of the front, the adjoining Italian and Romanian armies
could see unmistakable signs of a heavy concentration of Soviet
forces, which were well placed to break through the extended
eastward bulge of the front and trap the German attackers in
Stalingrad. Aware of this predicament, the Sixth Army HQ requested
permission in late October to call off the fruitless assaults on central
Stalingrad, to withdraw the army to a position between the Don and
Chir rivers, and to bring up the 14th Panzer Corps as reserves. All
three proposals were flatly rejected by Hitler. On 7 November
German monitoring of Russian radio traffic reported another
dramatic change in the enemy dispositions. Everything pointed to a
major Soviet offensive on the right and left flanks of the Sixth Army.

> As a well-schooled staff officer, Paulus made a sober assessment
> of the situation. He was thoroughly aware of the deadly danger.
> But to act in defiance of the orders he had been given went
> against all his military training. Thus, for Paulus – as for many
> older officers – there was from the start a stark conflict between
> responsibility to his men and obedience to military orders. After
> a severe inner struggle, military obedience won.
>
> *Wilhelm Adam, principal adjutant in the Sixth Army under Paulus*

During a lecture he gave to officer-cadets of the People's Police in the
GDR in May 1954, Paulus described the Stalingrad situation as follows:

The Russian preparations for an attack were clearly aimed at
bottling up the Sixth Army. The army's HQ, in agreement with the
various army corps, despatched continuous reports and requests to
our superiors in Army Group B . . .
    Army Group B shared the view of Sixth Army HQ, but was
unable to get this accepted by the OKW [Wehrmacht Supreme

Command]. The Army Group kept on passing back the decisions of the OKW, which were essentially these:

(a) In the light of their overall assessment of the Soviet forces, the OKW did not consider that an enemy attack constituted a danger to the Don front.

(b) For the sectors of the Don front held by allied armies, the existing reserves behind the front line (including the 48th Panzer Corps behind the Third Romanian Army) were sufficient.

(c) In this situation the important thing was first to complete the assault aimed at clearing the enemy from their remaining positions in Stalingrad, in order to neutralise this danger point.

(d) The Luftwaffe would be deployed over the areas of Soviet advance as soon as troops were seen to be occupying these areas.

When the anticipated Soviet offensive was finally launched on 19 November, there was such a dense snowstorm that the German *Luftflotte* 4 could not go into action for several days. The much-vaunted reserve, the 48th Panzer Corps, was in a sorry state: the 22nd Panzer Division consisted of just 42 tanks, the 14th Panzer Division was expected to fight without its supporting infantry regiments, and the 1st Romanian Panzer Division was quite simply unfit for combat.

In the literature about Stalingrad, blame for the Soviet breakthrough on 19 and 20 November is repeatedly placed on the ill-equipped and poorly motivated Romanian, Hungarian and Italian troops. That is unfair, since those units often put up bitter resistance. But the massive assault which swept over the German front line on the morning of 19 November 1942 was something which even rested, well-equipped elite Wehrmacht units in combat strength would have been unable to stand up to. Soviet troop concentrations of a size never before seen were on the move: 900 factory-fresh tanks of the superior T-34 type, 13,500 field-guns and grenade-throwers, 1,250 rocket-launchers of the kind known as 'Stalin's organ', because of their distinctive booming noise, and 1,100 anti-aircraft guns, had turned the Red Army into a potent attacking force for the first time in the Second World War. The Soviet fighter squadrons could put more than 1,000 planes into the air. To provide punctual transport for reinforcements, six railway branch lines had been specially built, with a total length of 660 miles; and a further 1,175 miles of existing track and 293 bridges had been repaired. No less than 142,000 wagons loaded with troops and equipment were despatched to Stalingrad alone.

On 19 November 1942 the multiple prints of edition 637/42 of the German weekly newsreel were distributed to cinemas throughout Germany. Shots of the fighting in Stalingrad were accompanied by this commentary: 'What was once the capital of the Volga region has, with the exception of a few districts, been wrenched from enemy hands. The German Wehrmacht stands on the Volga.'

Before the majority of prints had reached the cinemas, the situation in the area between the Volga and the Don was looking completely different. The next day Paulus was obliged to report: 'Strong Russian forces have attacked the adjacent army to the west and achieved a deep incursion on both sides of Kletskaya and Blinov, though the terrain on either side of Baskovsky is being held. . . . We must expect the Russians to attempt to widen these breaches, especially with armoured forces. It is uncertain whether the Romanian troops are capable of putting up stronger resistance.' The reply came back from the OKW by return: 'Whatever happens, Sixth Army must hold Stalingrad and present position. Counter-measures against enemy penetration already initiated.'

At about 14.45 hours on 20 November an order went out from Sixth Army HQ to all the corps under its command: 'The Army will cease its attacks in Stalingrad and hold its present positions. It is bringing up forces in the rear of its west flank in order initially to form a defensive front there. A later attack across this front to the west is planned.' In plain language this instruction to dig in meant that Paulus and Schmidt already knew the fate that awaited the army, even before the leading tanks of the Red Army closed the ring of steel at Kalatch two days later.

On 22 November an advance division of the Soviet 26th Armoured Corps captured the bridge over the Don at Kalatch and thus not only cut off the supply-line to the Sixth Army, but also severely restricted its tactical freedom of movement. The small German rearguard was inadequate to drive back the Soviet bridgehead. A relief attack by the 14th Panzer Corps was immediately ordered, but because of shortage of fuel it could not be carried out. By this time the supply situation of the encircled army was already so bad that they were not even able to defend themselves against the encroaching Russians. At the moment when the ring was closed, Paulus' command-post was situated outside the pocket that was being formed. On the evening of 22 November, on instructions from the Army Group, he was moved by air to Gumrak. Paulus and his staff flew into the 'cauldron'. A 'Führer Order' was issued by Hitler in person, tying the army firmly down in Stalingrad: 'The Sixth Army must know that I am doing all I can to help it and to send relief.'

From then on the saying went round among the rank and file of the besieged troops: 'The Führer'll get us out!' But the words were written on lavatory walls. During the night of 23–24 November General Paulus appealed directly to Hitler in a radio conversation, and begged for freedom of action: '*Mein Führer*, since the receipt of your radio message on 22 November, developments have completely reversed the situation. . . . Enemy breakthroughs are imminent. Ammunition and fuel are running out. Many of our batteries and anti-tank guns have fired their last shell. The chances of adequate and timely re-supply are nil. In a very short time the army will face destruction unless all our forces are combined to strike a crushing blow against the enemy now attacking from the south and west. To do this it is essential to pull all divisions out of Stalingrad and call in strong forces from the north. . . . This will admittedly mean losing a lot of equipment, but at least it will conserve the majority of our valuable combat troops and some of our equipment. . . . Because of the situation I ask again for freedom of action. All the generals commanding the Sixth Army join me in this view.'

The next morning, in reply, the Sixth Army HQ received a 'Decision of the Führer', the highest and most stringent category of order, ending with the following words: 'Present Volga front and present northern front to be held under all circumstances. Supply by air.' When the text of this order was announced, the general commanding the 51st Army Corps, *General der Artillerie* Walther von Seydlitz-Kurzbach, sent a memorandum to Paulus, his commander-in-chief, pleading to be permitted to mount an immediate and independent break-out. The request culminated in the words: 'If the army is to be kept intact, then it must get a different order issued, or else immediately take another decision itself.'

The desperate situation was reflected in the closing sentence: 'If the Army High Command does not immediately reverse the order to hold out in defensive positions, then your own conscience as commander makes it your duty to the army and the German people to act on your own discretion. The total destruction of 200,000 fighting men and their entire equipment is at stake. You have no other choice.'

Ever since then there has been argument over whether the decision to keep the Sixth Army fighting and dying in the streets in the first few days after the encirclement was a mistake on the part of the army commanders and thus of the commander-in-chief, Friedrich Paulus. 'Resistance' would have been tantamount to 'treason' – something which from today's perspective would be seen as an act of patriotism. But to do that, Paulus would have had to deny everything he was brought up to believe.

> We may assume with certainty that Paulus put his faith in the promises made by Hitler and Göring, that supplies would be maintained. Paulus may also have been influenced by the fact that not only Germany but all the combatant nations were watching the battle of the Sixth Army. This battle suddenly seemed like a test of personal worth, which he, Paulus, had to pass.
>
> *Otto E. Moll, journalist*

Long after the end of the war, in conversations with his son, Paulus spoke out about Stalingrad and especially about General von

Seydlitz's memorandum: 'The General's part seems to have been exaggerated. However, once the catastrophe had taken place, that is not surprising. People made a legend of it! Of course we were all in favour of a break-out, including my corps commanders. I had framed my appeals to the High Command in correspondingly unambiguous terms. But without a knowledge of the overall situation, simply to get an entire army to abandon its assigned position was quite out of the question.' What might have resulted from an over-hasty retreat by weakened troops from the built-up and thus relatively secure positions around Stalingrad had been shown at the very beginning of the siege. On 24 November General von Seydlitz withdrew some of his troops on his own initiative, in order to shorten the front. Most of these units – in particular the 94th Infantry Division – were caught by the rapidly advancing Soviets and virtually wiped out. What is more, Paulus stated, he had called a meeting to decide between break-out or defence, which was attended both by Seydlitz and his chief-of-staff, Clausius (the man who had actually drafted the memorandum). 'I said to Seydlitz: "If I give up command of the Sixth Army now, there is no doubt that the Führer will appoint you, as *persona grata*, to be commander-in-chief in my place. I ask you: would you then break out against Hitler's orders?" After some thought, Seydlitz said: "No, I would defend."'

We can be sure that Hitler had found out about the division among the army commanders, since his subsequent decisions did at least demonstrate a certain subtlety in his personnel policy: he promoted Paulus to *Generaloberst* (full general), thus ensuring his loyalty. At the same time he assigned to Seydlitz direct responsibility for the northern sector of the pocket and thus kept him quiet. The general was now hardly going to act on his own initiative in direct defiance of a 'Führer Order'.

What is more, Hitler ordered *Generalfeldmarschall* Erich von Manstein, who enjoyed the highest reputation in the Wehrmacht as a tactitian, to assume command of the newly formed Army Group Don. His initial task sounded simple and inspiring: to restore the 'old situation' and thus free the Sixth Army from its trap. For this purpose an assault group of the Fourth Panzer Army under *Generaloberst* Hoth was to advance from the Kotelnikov area towards Stalingrad, and restore a land link with the besieged army. The air-bridge, so grandly promised by Göring and Richthofen, never in fact came to anything. At its peak, the quantity of ammunition and food flown into the pocket only reached 40 tons per day, which represented some 15 per cent of what was actually required. Hoth was unable to start his attack until 12 December, due to a lack of available forces. The 6th Panzer Division, with 136 tanks, had to be urgently despatched from France; and the 23rd Panzer Division arrived from the Caucasus in a weakened condition, with 96 tanks and armoured cars. Nonetheless, in the period from 19 to 23 December, these units had fought their way up to within 30 miles of the perimeter of the Stalingrad pocket. Then they ran out of steam. At the same time the Russians launched a major offensive against the Italian 8th Army on the northern flank of the Army Group Don. The whole Army Group began to waver. Both Manstein and Paulus realised that if the Red Army succeed in pushing their advance as far as Rostov-on-Don, they would be threatened with a 'super-Stalingrad'. Furthermore, the units of the 17th Army and 1st Panzer Army stationed in the Caucasus would also be cut off. Manstein decided to call off the attempt to relieve Stalingrad and instead to concentrate on securing the retreat of the Army Group Caucasus. It was a sentence of death for the army of *Generaloberst* Paulus, which at that point was tying down eight Soviet armies and thereby covering the retreat from the Caucasus.

> After the failure of the attempted relief operation and the non-appearance of the promised assistance, it was simply a matter of playing for time, so as to make it possible to rebuild the southern sector of the eastern front and to rescue the large German forces located in the Caucasus. If we did not succeed in this, then the entire war would have been lost.
>
> *Friedrich Paulus*

The remaining course of the siege is quickly told: no more attempts were made to relieve the Sixth Army; the Luftwaffe was never able to deliver the supplies so blithely promised by Göring; several times the Soviets offered surrender terms, and each time they were flatly rejected by the army command. Under ceaseless Russian attack the Stalingrad pocket dwindled in the end to a few city centre blocks. On 13 January 1943 the ADC of the Sixth Army HQ, *Hauptmann* Winrich Behr, left the pocket in one of the last aircraft, with orders from Paulus and Schmidt to see Hitler in his Rastenburg bunker and personally describe the army's hopeless position. Behr had the additional assignment of handing over Paulus' war diary, together with his wedding ring and signet ring, and a farewell letter addressed to his wife, Elena Constance. In it he wrote: 'My beloved Coca, you will get this letter when my fate has finally been clearly decided, or is still uncertain for a while. As a soldier, I stand here as I have always done: in obedience to orders. What my fate will be, I know not. I must accept it as God ordains.'

On 22 January 1943 the Russians began their decisive push to destroy what was left of the Sixth Army. The end now really did seem to have come, and Paulus begged Hitler – incidentally, against Schmidt's vote – for permission to order a cease-fire. When Hitler refused, Manstein telephoned him to make the same request, but he too was given the brush-off: as a matter of honour, there could be absolutely no question of surrender. That evening Hitler cabled the Sixth Army to say that in its battle it had 'made a historic contribution in the most colossal struggle in German history!' With that the army was finally written off, and the last attempt 'to put a limit on the death-toll' had failed. Even in the Sixth Army HQ there were signs that things were closing down.

On 30 January, the anniversary of the Nazi seizure of power in 1933, there was further communication between Paulus and Hitler: '*Generaloberst* Paulus to Führer: on the anniversary of your taking power the Sixth Army salutes its Führer. The swastika flag still flies over Stalingrad. May our struggle be an example to generations living now and to come, never to surrender even in a hopeless situation. Germany will then be victorious. *Heil Mein Führer*! Paulus.'

Hitler replied as follows: '*Mein Generaloberst Paulus!* Today the German people looks with deep emotion upon its heroes in that city. As always in world history this sacrifice will not be in vain. Clausewitz's creed will find its fulfilment. Only now does the German nation comprehend the full burden of this struggle and will make the supreme sacrifice. In my thoughts I am always with you and your men. Yours, Adolf Hitler.'

> True to its oath of loyalty to the flag, and mindful of its great and important mission, the Sixth Army has held its position for Führer and Fatherland to the end, to the last man and the last round of ammunition.
>
> *Paulus in his last situation report to Army Group Don,*
> *31 January 1943*

The following night Hitler made sure his call for a Clausewitzian sacrifice was absolutely foolproof: he promoted the 52-year-old *Generaloberst* Friedrich Paulus to *Generalfeldmarschall*. A German field-marshal does not surrender, he goes down with his men: such was Hitler's cynical calculation. In propaganda terms the sacrifice of the Sixth Army would only make sense if there were no survivors.

> Your orders are being carried out; long live Germany!
> *Paulus' reply to Hitler's order not to surrender*
>
> I suppose this is meant as an invitation to suicide. But I won't do him [Hitler] that favour.
> *Paulus after his appointment as field-marshal*
>
> What personally hurts me the most is that I promoted him to field-marshal.
>
> *Adolf Hitler*

He made it so easy for himself! . . . The man should've shot himself, like the generals who used to fall on their swords when they saw that the game was up.

Hitler on 1 February 1943

On the morning of 31 January, in the ruined department store in the centre of Stalingrad, the procedures for surrender were negotiated between the chief-of-staff of the Soviet 64th Army and, on behalf of the Sixth Army staff, the CO of the German 71st Infantry Division. Paulus did not take part in the talks. Apathetically he awaited the end. Before being taken prisoner he said briefly to a staff officer: 'Yes, I know, the history of war has already passed judgement on me.'

When Paulus entered the room, he said '*Heil Hitler*'.

Lev Bezymensky, military interpreter

In the report on his capture by Soviet troops we read: 'At the request of Major-General Laskin, that the Northern Group should issue the order for resistance to cease, Paulus stated that he was not in communication with that formation and was not its commander. He said that the previous evening, after the broadcast speech by Reich Marshal Göring to mark the anniversary of the Nazi seizure of power, he had announced that he was no longer in command of the troops, that he was a "private individual" and had appointed commanders of the two sectors of the Stalingrad pocket. The only thing he demanded of all those under him, he said, was that, if they were forced to surrender, all officers and men should be armed as long as they stayed in the area. After his departure, matters would be in the hands of the commanders of the North and South Groups.'

This means that when Hitler sent his radio message with the intention of calling on the army commander-in-chief to die a hero's death, the man he promoted to field-marshal was already a private citizen, albeit one who desired continued armed protection for his army, but a man who had no intention of ending his life with a final bullet through the head. Hitler appeared to lose his reason when he heard of this: 'How can a man watch his soldiers die. . . . How can he then surrender to the Bolsheviks? What hurts me so much is that the heroism of so many soldiers is wiped out by a single spineless weakling. In this war no one else is ever going to be made a field-marshal.'

We must anyway bear in mind the fact that the commander in Stalingrad had the choice, either to live 15 or 20 years longer, or to gain a life of several thousand years of undying fame. In my view the choice cannot have been a difficult one.

Joseph Goebbels, diary, 2 February 1943

There is still the question of whether *Generalfeldmarschal* Paulus is still alive, or went voluntarily to his death. The Bolsheviks insist that he is in their hands. For the army this represents a grave moral setback.

Joseph Goebbels, diary, 4 February 1943

In his first session of questioning before General Shumilov and Major-General Laskin, the prisoner emphasised his new status:

Shumilov:	Please present your papers.
Paulus:	I have a military pass.
Shumilov:	I mean confirmation that you, Field-Marshal, have been promoted to field-marshal.
Paulus:	No such confirmation exists.
Shumilov:	Did you receive a telegram about your promotion?
Paulus:	I received Hitler's order by radio.
Shumilov:	May I report this to my Supreme Command?
Paulus:	Yes. Herr Schmidt, my Chief-of-Staff, can verify it.
Shumilov:	Who was taken prisoner with you?
Paulus:	The Chief-of-Staff, *Generalleutnant* Schmidt, and a colonel from the Sixth Army staff.
Shumilov:	Who else?

Paulus: I have given the names of the others in writing to the negotiators . . .

Shumilov: What persuaded you to lay down your arms now?

Paulus: We did not lay down our arms, we were exhausted; we couldn't go on fighting. After your troops had broken through and were advancing on the remnants of our troops, they had nothing left with which to defend themselves – no ammunition – and that is why we stopped fighting.

Shumilov: Did you order the Southern Group to lay down their arms?

Paulus: I gave no such order.

Laskin: That order was issued in our presence by Major-General Roske, commander of the 71st Infantry Division. The order was passed on to the troop formations.

Shumilov: And did you confirm the order to lay down arms?

Paulus: No. He acted on his own initiative. I was not in command of the Southern and Northern Groups; no troop formations were under my orders. It was Herr Roske who took the decision to lay down arms.

Shumilov: Did you order the Northern Group to surrender?

Paulus: No.

Shumilov: I must ask you to do so.

Paulus: I have no right whatever to give any orders.

Shumilov: But you're the commander, aren't you?

Paulus: I cannot give any surrender order to troops who are not under my command. I hope you understand a soldier's position, his obligations.

Shumilov: Every soldier must fight to the end; the superior officer can order the men under him to cease fighting, if he sees that people are dying for nothing.

Paulus: That decision rests with the officer who remains directly with his troops. That is what in fact happened with the Southern Group, in which I happened to be.

Shumilov (to the interpreter):   Tell the Field-Marshal that I am now inviting him to dine with me, and afterwards he will be taken to the front-line staff.

There are two remarkable things about this dialogue: firstly the extreme courtesy of the Soviet general – after all, German troops had spread war and murder all over his homeland; and secondly, the odd indifference displayed by the German prisoner. Was this simply weakness or an abdication of responsibility?

> Does the prospect of one's own death or the probable destruction or imprisonment of one's own troops release a commander from his military duty to obey orders? Today, let each man, on his own account and in his own conscience, find the answer to this question.
>
> *Friedrich Paulus*

Paulus' road to captivity took him in early February 1943 by train to the Krasnogorsk camp near Moscow, in April to the monastery of Suzdal and in July to the Voikovo camp for senior officers. Copies of most of his letters have survived. Initially his main concern was to maintain an appearance in keeping with his status. After all, when he was taken prisoner the field-marshal was still wearing the insignia of a *Generaloberst*. One of the first letters he wrote was addressed to the military attaché at the German embassy in Ankara:

My dear Rhode, I have been taken prisoner with only the clothes I had on. That is why I am asking you to do me a favour and buy some things for me . . . (3) Six pairs of field-marshal's epaulettes, (4) a general's peaked cap size 58, (5) a service uniform (ask my wife about the one I had tailor-made in Paris) . . .

   With thanks in advance for doing me this service, and best wishes.

Yours, Paulus.
My address: Prisoner-of-war camp 27, USSR. Paulus, 25.02.43

It was no doubt also in the interests of Soviet propaganda that Paulus quickly received his insignia. In later photos from his period in captivity he is always seen in field-marshal's uniform. All he lacked was his field-marshal's baton, since these were always presented by the Führer in person.

> Germany is still strong; it will fight on to success.
> *Paulus in 1943, while a prisoner of the Russians*

Up till the summer of 1944 Paulus was careful to keep his distance from anything political. He followed subsequent events on a map in the canteen and soon realised that for Germany the war was lost. Even so, he could not bring himself to yield to pressure from Soviet officers, German communists and activists in the 'National Committee for Free Germany' and, by joining the 'League of German Officers' (*Bund Deutscher Offiziere*, or BDO), to give a signal for a rapid ending of the war. In 1943 Paulus' relationship with the 'anti-fascist movement' was one of great suspicion and reticence, although his values were changing rapidly. In retrospect, he described his attitude in this way: 'Consistent with maintaining my position as an army commander, I did not consider I was justified, as a prisoner-of-war, in intervening in the destiny of my Fatherland – that is to say under the guise of collaboration with an enemy of Germany.' He feared the stigma of delivering the 'stab in the back' to the German nation. While Paulus, in a deep moral struggle with himself, accepted his share in the blame for the wretched end of the Sixth Army, he remained unshaken in the conviction that the responsibility he bore was only military, not political.

On 24 July 1944 the prisoners in the 'generals' camp' of Voikovo heard about the failed attempt on Hitler's life. Many of the conspirators were men Paulus knew and admired, such as Generals Beck, Fellgiebel and Olbricht, and *Oberst* Stauffenberg. However, when his friend Field-Marshal von Witzleben was executed by strangulation at Plötzensee prison on 8 August 1944, Paulus could no longer remain detached. He signed an appeal 'to the German officers and men in captivity and to the German people' and broadcast a message on the 'Free Germany' radio station: 'Germany must renounce Adolf Hitler and give itself a new government, one which will end the war and create conditions that will enable our people to carry on their lives and to establish peaceful, indeed, friendly relations with our present adversaries.' This was an astonishing change of heart for the man chiefly responsible for planning 'Operation Barbarossa'.

In this way the Soviet Union had gained a figurehead among the German PoWs for their own purposes, and Paulus had abandoned his neutrality. Hitler was beside himself with rage. Since Paulus was now making these public statements, the propaganda myth of the field-marshal who stood shoulder to shoulder with his grenadiers, fought in Stalingrad to the last cartridge and died with his army, could no longer be maintained. The 'Hero of Stalingrad' was alive, and he was Stalin's prisoner. Paulus' wife, Elena Constance, resisted pressure from the Nazis to denounce him. Together with her son Ernst and daughter Olga, she was imprisoned under the harsh Nazi law of *Sippenhaft*, by which whole families were held guilty of the alleged crime of one member. Their suffering did not end until Dachau concentration camp was liberated in April 1945.

The 'League of German Officers' won the figure of Paulus to its ranks at a moment when its aims were already proving illusory. The Red Army stood at the eastern frontier of the German Reich, and Stalin would not have dreamt of stopping there. Even the various calls for a German surrender, which Paulus drafted and signed, failed to have any effect on the Germans. The war ended with unconditional surrender.

Early in 1946 the eminent prisoner returned to the glare of world publicity with a bang. On 11 February the Soviet Chief Prosecutor at the Nuremberg war crimes tribunal, Rudenkov, announced that Field-Marshal Paulus would appear in court that very day as a witness for the prosecution. At about 2 p.m. he stood facing his former superiors, Jodl and Keitel. Paulus' appearance had been carefully planned by the Soviets; it was timed to have maximum effect on the proceedings and, what is more, was kept secret until the very last minute. Even when Paulus was in Germany, in a country house near Plauen in Saxony, preparing for his court appearance, no one had any idea of the statement he was about to make.

The one-time General of Infantry Erich Buschenhagen, in a letter written in 1959 to Paulus' son, Ernst Alexander, reconstructed the field-marshal's journey to Nuremberg:

20.01.46: F-M Paulus and General Buschenhagen transferred from Lunovo camp to an MVD [Soviet Secret Service] safe-house in Moscow.

01.02.46: At noon flew from a Moscow military airfield in a special MVD plane with Major-General Pavlov, Lt-Col Georgadze and three lieutenants, via Allenstein and Küstrin [former German towns now in Poland] to Berlin (Staaken airfield). Then drive by car via Potsdam to Babelsberg, stay the night in a house in the Kaiserstrasse (later named Leninstrasse).

03.02.46: Sunday – first attempt to travel to Plauen. Failed because car broke down in the Ravensberg hills beyond Potsdam.

04.02.46: Drive in a new car brought up from Dresden, through Treuenbritzen, Leipzig, Altenburg, Zwickau, and Reichenbach to Plauen. Stay in a house called 'Torterotot' in Mommsenstrasse (now called Antifa-Strasse).

11.02.46: Set off early from Plauen along the Hof autobahn to Nuremberg. Arrive about 10 a.m. at the International Military Court in the Palace of Justice in Fürther Strasse. In the afternoon F-M Paulus is examined as a witness. Spend the night in a building on a housing estate outside Nuremberg, occupied by Russian guards.

12.02.46: Morning, cross-examination of F-M Paulus. Afternoon, General Buschenhagen examined as a witness. Evening, drive back to Plauen.

13.02.46 onwards: Nerve-racking wait in Plauen for the promised 'reunion with family'.

28.03.46: Unexpected night drive to Dresden.

29 and 30.03.46: In Dresden-Neustadt.

31.03.46: Flight from Dresden to Moscow. Accommodated in the MVD house in Gorki Street. About a week later, transferred to a dacha in the suburb of Tomilino, south-east of Moscow.

On the day before Paulus' court appearance, the Russian photo-journalist Yevgeny Khaldei had used photos to explain the seating arrangements in the courtroom. Those most shocked to find Paulus making statements against them, were the accused senior commanders of the Wehrmacht. Hermann Göring told his defence counsel to 'ask the filthy swine if he knows he's a traitor'. When Paulus entered the courtroom, took the oath and began answering General Rudenkov's questions, some of the accused could scarcely be restrained. They were ordered to keep quiet by US military policemen. The statements by the witness did not reveal any sensational new details about Hitler's war planning, but his appearance in person was alone worth more than any number of documents. Paulus made accusations in particular against Göring, Keitel and Jodl. Even though some of the accused showed sympathy for Paulus, most condemned him – as though they had decided that they would not employ a man like that in the next war.

> You cannot speak of Paulus and myself in the same breath. . . . An enormous number of men were shot on his orders. He is responsible for his actions, since he was the general commanding the Sixth Army and deputy to the Chief of the General Staff.
> *General Walther von Seydlitz speaking to German generals in Russian captivity, in connection with the Nuremberg Tribunal*

The only man who could claim a points victory was defence counsel for the Wehrmacht Supreme Command, Dr Hans Laternser: when in cross-examination he questioned Paulus about the fate of his soldiers as prisoners of the Russians, it was the moment the Soviet prosecutors had most feared. They objected to this question being allowed in court. The Austrian journalist Joe Heydecker seized the opportunity to talk to Paulus about this outside the courtroom. At first Paulus dodged the question by referring to the Soviet objection raised in court, but then he gave this reply: 'Tell their mothers and wives that the prisoners are doing fine!' This appeared in all the papers the next day. For being so inquisitive, Joe Heydecker was on the point of losing his accreditation as a trial reporter, though the Americans prevented this from happening.

After his stay in Germany Paulus did not return to the generals' prison camp. Personal quarters were put at his disposal in Tomilino, a small village about 30 miles from Moscow. It was a typical Russian dacha with a garden. But his wish to see his wife during his short stay in Germany did not come true. Elena Constance Paulus died in November 1949 without ever seeing her husband again. For Stalin Paulus was a jewel in the crown of victory. He placed at his prisoner's disposal an adjutant, a personal doctor and a cook. (Naturally these three secret service men all watched each other as well as their charge.)

> He is too soft and indecisive. He has lately appeared very nervy, and has become such a fusspot and a moaner that many of the generals go out of their way to avoid him.
> *Verdict on Paulus by German generals while in Russian captivity*

Friedrich Paulus put down on paper his views about the war and gave lectures to Soviet generals. Although he was the highest ranking German prisoner-of-war in the USSR, he was not, as so many other generals were – among them the chairman of the BDO, General von Seydlitz – tried before a Soviet court and sentenced to 25 years in a labour camp. Stalin himself gave orders that Paulus should be left unmolested. He even made arrangements for the field-marshal to go on a health cure in Yalta. But Paulus wanted to get back to his family and announced that he wished to play a part in the reconstruction of Germany. He drafted petitions to Stalin and to Beria, the head of the secret police. This was not just a prisoner making an application to the head of state; it was Marshal Paulus writing to Marshal Stalin. There is no evidence in the records that Stalin considered this approach impertinent. At worst it might have provided some amusement to the dictator.

It was while he was a prisoner that his great transformation took place. He admitted that the German assault on the Soviet Union had been in breach of international law. He admitted following a man who disregarded all loyalty and therefore deserved none himself.

Otto E. Moll, journalist

In 1948 even the notorious chief prosecutor at the Moscow show-trials, Andrei Vyshinski, put in a word for the eminent prisoner. Stalin replied to every enquiry by saying that he alone would decide when the field-marshal was to be released.

One morning in 1951 the Soviet Union's most distinguished prisoner was found at his country house in a state of collapse. In the days that followed, the 60-year-old field-marshal refused to leave his bed or to eat. He spoke to no one. The patient was suffering from severe depression. For years he had done all he could to secure his return to Germany, had written letter after letter to Stalin. To the Soviet dictator Paulus represented a human trophy of incalculable value, the living reminder of his greatest victory: Stalingrad. But now the generalissimo began to fear that his favourite bird might die in his gilded cage. He decided to release Friedrich Paulus. Yet it was important to choose the most favourable moment in order to make the maximum political capital out of the field-marshal's repatriation. This would take time, and before a decision could be reached, Stalin died. In the Kremlin a power struggle began among his potential successors.

On 27 September 1953 Walter Ulbricht, the President of the communist state of East Germany, the so-called German Democratic Republic, stopped in Moscow en route to a health cure on the Black Sea. At short notice the Soviet authorities arranged a meeting between Paulus and Ulbricht. The private conversation between the two men lasted more than an hour and a half. The next day, before continuing his journey, Ulbricht had a meeting with a representative of the Central Committee of the Soviet Communist

Party. What Ulbricht had to say about his exchange of views with Paulus was this: Paulus had expressed the wish to settle in the GDR and take up a post in a government body or state-owned industry. Paulus was also prepared to make a political statement in public. This statement should, in Comrade Ulbricht's view, be restricted to a summary of the hard lessons learnt in the war which had led Germany to catastrophe.

A short time later, Paulus wrote: 'As commander of the German troops in the battle for Stalingrad, which was so fateful for my Fatherland, I came to know all the horrors of a war of conquest, not only for the people of the country we invaded, but also for my own soldiers. The lessons learnt from my own experience, as well as from the events of the entire Second World War, have brought me to the realisation that the destiny of the German people cannot be built upon notions of power, but only in lasting friendship with the Soviet Union as well as with all other peace-loving nations. . . . . I do not want to leave the Soviet Union without saying to the Soviet people that in blind obedience I once came to their country as an enemy, but now I take my leave of this country as a friend.'

This statement was printed in *Pravda* on 24 October 1953.

On 26 October that year Friedrich Paulus arrived in East Berlin. He had decided to live in the GDR from now on. This decision may have been influenced by the death of his wife in 1949, the justified fear of being the subject of public controversy in the Federal Republic, and his obvious reservations about Adenauer's policy of military integration in a system of western European alliances. Paulus was no communist, nor did he wish to see a communist Germany, but he did want 'the peaceful future of a united and peaceful Germany'. The deciding factor was probably that the GDR offered him better opportunities. As head of the nascent Office of Research into War History, in August 1954 he began teaching a course in warfare at the People's Military Police Academy in Dresden. He took an active part in planning the Office of Research and lectured on the Battle of Stalingrad and the Schlieffen Plan. The GDR showed its gratitude by giving him a house in Dresden's exclusive Weisser Hirsch district and privileges such as a gun licence, hunting rights and a police-financed Opel Kapitän car. The growing National People's Army provided the field-marshal with one of its young officers, *Hauptmann* Beutel, as his adjutant. His luxurious home was protected by the guard battalion of the Dresden mechanised rapid-response force of the People's Military Police (from March 1956, the 7th armoured division of the National People's Army). In his correspondence with the leaders of the 'Workers' and Peasants' State' he always used as his letterhead: 'Friedrich Paulus – *Generalfeldmarschal* of the former German army.'

> Paulus was no communist; he didn't want a communist Germany, though he did want a 'peaceful future for a unified democratic Germany'. He was obliged to pursue this goal in his new homeland – the GDR.
>
> *Thorsten Diedrich, journalist*

The GDR succeeded in winning over the field-marshal for their political ends. Ulbricht and the political administration of the People's Military Police set great store on his 'patriotic attitude' and his rejection of Adenauer's integration with the West, whose objectives Paulus, after ten years of one-sided information and absence from Germany, denounced as 'dangerous'. The GDR leadership wanted to use those who had served in the war to create a kind of pan-German military caucus against the NATO treaties. In July 1954, Paulus, whose articles and lectures had a lasting influence, attacked the Paris treaties publicly for the first time at an international press conference, and in December of that year in an interview with the East German radio station, Deutschlandsender. As the principal speaker he addressed officers of the former Wehrmacht and *Waffen*-SS at meetings in East Berlin on 29–30 January and 25–26 June 1955, as well as smaller gatherings, and expressed the view that those who had fought in the war bore a high responsibility for a democratic Germany, and opposed the military commitment of the Federal Republic to a western alliance.

In the eyes of his former colleagues, Paulus (the German name for Paul the Apostle) had become Saulus (Saul of Tarsus). For his own part, he continued to believe he had remained true to himself. However, when it came to his attitude towards rearmament in the GDR, to the Sovietisation of Eastern Germany and to the dictatorship of the communists in power, or how he envisaged a unified Germany – on this he never uttered a word, even to trusted friends. When making preparations for a gathering of former officers, he was deeply hurt by letters of refusal from former colleagues, among them *Generaloberst* Franz Halder, who accused him of treason against Germany and of making common cause with the enemy. Equally painful were the enquiries from relatives of those who had fought at Stalingrad, wanting to know the whereabouts of their sons, brothers or husbands. He replied to them conscientiously, to the best of his knowledge. All this sapped his health and increased the unhappy burden of responsibility that weighed on him. In an opening address to an officers' conference he tried to outline his political creed thus: 'With the bitter lessons we drew from the so-called policy of strength, and our general feeling of responsibility for the present state of the German nation, we express our conviction that we need no new military treaties, which set the fateful division of Germany in stone; we need instead an understanding between the Germans of east and west, and between Germans and other nations. We want a strong, respected, sovereign and independent Germany without occupying troops, a Germany whose territory is guaranteed by a general security agreement of all European states and the Great Powers and whose frontiers are guarded by national armed forces, subordinate only to the German people.'

A short time later, a 'bugging' report by the Stasi (state security service) quoted him as saying: 'I am neither an easterner nor a westerner. I am German.'

> Paulus was obsessed by the idea that one day there could be a German Reich, a Germany, not two divided strips of territory.
>
> *Baroness Olga von Kutzschenbach, Paulus' daughter*

He was frequently rumoured to have played a personal part in building up the national armed forces of the GDR, though there is no evidence that he did so. On the contrary, to the end of his life the renowned field-marshal remained an alien being in the 'Workers' and Peasants' State'. The Ministry for State Security set up a dense network of informers around him and his social circle. To the communist spooks, surveillance of Paulus was known as 'Operation Terrace'. In a comprehensive report of August 1956, we read among other things: 'it is clear that he is not, nor has he ever been engaged in the build-up, training, or leadership of the People's Military Police. He does not have, and has never had, any links with commanding officers or units; only his living expenses were met from the funds of the Ministry for National Defence by means of a salary for a non-existent job.' Suffering from a serious illness, Paulus vanished from the political limelight at the end of 1955. He was stricken with progressive and incurable brain disease, which, while leaving his mental faculties unimpaired, led to total paralysis of all muscular movement. This medical syndrome could perhaps be said to symbolise the life of Friedrich Paulus.

On 1 February 1957, the 14th anniversary of the defeat at Stalingrad, the field-marshal died in Dresden, in a state of deep depression. On 6 February, after a modest funeral, attended by relatives and members of the National Council of the GDR, as well as a small delegation from the Ministry of National Defence, his mortal remains were cremated in the Dresden suburb of Tolkewitz. At the request of his family, the urn was taken to Baden-Baden, where Friedrich Paulus found his last resting place beside his wife Elena Constance, whom he had seen for the last time in the spring of 1942.

It is impossible to deduce from official statements what Paulus really thought and felt. He was a very private person – and, especially after Stalingrad, was very conscious of his part in history. As a field-marshal of the Wehrmacht he bears the stigma of the army commander often demonised for his loyalty to Hitler. He was then derided for being a 'communist'. Yet neither accusation really defines Paulus. From today's standpoint, this tall, introverted man embodies rather a character sorely tested by fate, and one who recognised himself as a tragic figure in German military history. Caught between the burden of responsibility for the catastrophe of Stalingrad, and the political pressures of a new society he did not fully comprehend, Paulus sought new ideals both in the east and the west, but always remained an outsider. Returning from the Soviet Union was for him like coming home to a land of strangers. His patriotic hopes for a single, peaceful Germany, and his attempt to apply his personal experience to achieving this, were simply exploited. The man who helped to write two tragic episodes of German history died alone.

On 6 February 1957 a member of the Stasi staff closed the Paulus file with the comment: 'The subject "Terrace" was a one-time field-marshal of the former fascist German army. With his death on 1 February, surveillance of the subject was terminated.' Friedrich Paulus was never accepted by postwar Germany.

Before the troops and the officers of the Sixth Army and before the German people I bear the responsibility for having obeyed the order from the Supreme Command to hold out, up to the moment of disintegration.

Friedrich Paulus

I feel only sympathy for him.

General Alfred Jodl at Nuremberg

CHAPTER FIVE

The Aviator – Ernst Udet

Flying becomes a passion. Once you have mastered it, you can never let go again . . .

You cannot dwell on the fact that, for every man you shoot down, a mother weeps

The reports about events in Germany are exaggerated. . . . There have been a few cases of Jews being badly treated, but those have been given undue importance

Hitler will not lead Germany into war

We were soldiers without a flag. We have unfurled our flag again. The Führer gave it back to us. For the old soldiers, life is worth living again

For the sake of flying you sometimes have to make a pact with the Devil. But you must not let yourself be devoured by him

I am nothing more than a ghost in uniform

But I must keep going. Soon the great night will begin, and then all of life is submerged

Ernst Udet

————————————— * —————————————

At about 05.15 hours I observed *Oberleutnant* Udet's red aircraft cause a DH [De Havilland] 9 to break up and shortly afterwards bring a second plane, a DH 2, down in flames.

Signed: Göring, CO of Baron von Richthofen Squadron
Hermann Göring

Udet is a master of the skies and feels as much as home there as a motorcyclist does on the highway. . . . We are pleased that German technology is advancing unceasingly and that we have pathfinders like Udet in the air industry. German aviation is bound and gagged, but it can never be killed off.

Würzburger Volksblatt (newspaper)

Hitler quite rightly regarded Udet as one of Germany's great aviators. Unfortunately he also saw him, quite mistakenly, as one of Germany's leading experts in the field of aircraft technology.

Erhard Milch, Permanent Secretary in the Reich Ministry of Aviation

If only I knew what Udet thought he was doing. He has turned the entire Luftwaffe programme into a shambles. If he were still alive today, I would feel obliged to say to him: 'You are responsible for the destruction of the German Luftwaffe.'

Hermann Göring

A divinely gifted artist in his field, a man whose skills as a pilot place him in a uniquely exalted position. 'Speak to me no ill of the masters' is today the wake-up call to our German youth; they certainly do not despise the airman Ernst Udet, they look skywards to him with admiration and enthusiasm as one of their great exemplars.

Die Luftwelt ('Air World' magazine)

Udet lives in a medium-sized apartment that he has filled with flying and hunting trophies, and with those souvenirs that one collects or is given in the course of an active and much-travelled

life. On one wall hung several photos of beautiful women. I took
five shots, then Udet took five. Udet won . . .

Charles Lindbergh

He radiated so much charm, such good nature and enthusiasm
for flying. He could drink enormous quantities and the next
moment be completely sober.

Adolf Galland, fighter pilot

We liked each other after exchanging only a few words, and
together finished off our first bottle of cognac.

Carl Zuckmayer, playwright

Absolutely no need to worry about your job. Your excellent staff
will do whatever is necessary. In any case, have asked Milch to
look after things as well.

Hermann Göring

Whenever he and Göring got together, they talked about old times.
Any discussion of service matters was scrupulously avoided.

Advocate-General Christian von Hammerstein

He had to battle against Milch's intrigues, he had to cope with
Göring's excessive demands, he had to try and reconcile the
differing views of a vast staff. It was too much for him.

General der Flieger (Air Force General) *von Seidel*

He was not a straightforward person, very vain and easily
offended.

Erhard Milch, Permanent Secretary in the Reich Ministry of Aviation

———————————— * ————————————

Only a few of those present knew what had really happened. In the
grand reception room of the Ministry of Aviation a nervous hush
reigned, broken only by the monotonous hum of the newsreel

cameras, capturing every detail of the scene that had been so meticulously staged.

Beside a coffin placed on a catafalque several officers stood motionless, with drawn swords. Their faces picked up the reflection of four flaming torches flanking the coffin on black columns. The assembled mourners bristled with famous names, called in by the skilled stage-managers of this state funeral. Adolf Hitler was there, and the great flying aces of the Luftwaffe. Emmy Göring was there, the 'First Lady' of the Third Reich, and behind her the diplomatic corps and leading figures from the Nazi Party. The last to make his appearance was Hermann Göring, *Reichsmarschall* and commander-in-chief of the Luftwaffe, glittering like a peacock in a pale blue uniform, tan-coloured boots and a gilded ceremonial belt. To the strains of Beethoven's *Eroica* symphony, he ascended the steps to the podium, his spurs jangling. The *Reichsmarschall* cleared his throat and spoke:

We must now take our leave of you. It is impossible to grasp the idea that you, my dear Udet,* are no longer here among us. We cannot understand it, for your character was so forceful, so invigorating and so cheerful. You were so full of vitality that we almost feel you are still with us. And remain among us. The Almighty has called you to Him and now you can join those others who died before you. And now . . . I simply cannot say more . . . my best comrade, farewell!

Göring's closing words could hardly be heard. His voice broke. And as the overweight Reich Marshal came down the steps, the band struck up quietly with *Ich hatt' einen Kameraden*. Göring sang along, with tears in his eyes. Adolf Hitler stepped forward and shook the hand of an elderly, heavily veiled woman. Paula Udet maintained her composure with difficulty. The drama being played out here was the mendacious climax of a production in which even the grieving mother had to play her role.

---

* Although originally a French name, probably Huguenot, the German pronunciation is 'Oodett'. (*Tr.*)

The officers lifted the coffin and carried it through the crowd outside in the street. The procession of mourners was formed: at the head marched the standard-bearer, the band, those carrying wreaths, and the adjutants. Then followed the coffin and finally the solitary figure of *Reichsmarschall* Hermann Göring.

Five days earlier the German News Bureau had reported: 'On 17 November 1941 the Air Armourer-General, *Generaloberst* Ernst Udet, while testing a new warplane, suffered such a severe accident that he died from his injuries on the way to hospital. The Führer has ordered a state funeral for this officer who perished in such a tragic manner in the performance of his duty.'

The death of a pilot: Germany mourned. Until 1945 most people believed the fairytale of his heroic death for *Volk und Vaterland*. Ernst Udet had been a famous man. He had clocked up innumerable flying hours and performed breathtaking stunts in the lofty skies. Children loved the man 'who could waggle his wings' and, if the mood took him, could pick up a handkerchief from the ground with his wingtip. On the cinema screen he had entertained young lovers by playing airborne rescuer to mountaineers in peril. Berliners remembered him spending endless nights in the city's bars, where he was always among the last to leave. And they knew him from newsreel reports in which he was often to be seen – at the side of Hermann Göring and the Führer.

Udet's friend, the émigré German playwright Carl Zuckmayer, was in the United States when he read in the newspapers of the airman's tragic death. It prompted him to start writing his drama, *The Devil's General*. It was to become synonymous with Udet. Zuckmayer made no secret of the fact that the hero of the play, 'Harras' was based on his Luftwaffe friend.

The play became one of the most frequently performed works on the postwar German stage. Udet was transformed into his literary *alter ego*, the pilot Harras. 'General or circus clown. I'm a pilot and nothing else', the latter insisted. A pilot, and if he flies for Hitler, so be it. He becomes more and more enmeshed in the criminal machinations of the regime, until he admits resignedly that he has become 'the Devil's general'. Heroically he takes the consequences and kills himself by deliberately crashing his aircraft. With this play Zuckmayer created a memorial to Udet; but not until more than 20 years after he had written down the first lines in a kind of intoxicated frenzy did it dawn on him to question Udet's motives. In 1966 he rewrote the play and finally withdrew it from the stage altogether. Too often his work had been mistakenly understood as an apology 'for a certain type of fellow-traveller'.

Who was Ernst Udet? One of the Devil's generals? Or someone who resisted domination by the Devil?

> I've fallen in love with flying. I can't ever escape from it. But one day the Devil will get the lot of us.
>
> *Ernst Udet*

His war had been the one from 1914 to 1918. The aura of being the most successful fighter pilot after the 'Red Baron', Manfred von Richthofen, clung to him like a second skin and during the interwar period it gave him privileged access to the rich and the powerful. Charming and *galant* he certainly was – a man whose open and friendly manner almost no one could ignore. Yet at the same time he was thoughtless and irresponsible. He passed the years of the Weimar Republic as a stunt flier and film star. He was not a military man, a life spent marching in step was not for him – until the year 1935, when he joined the newly created Luftwaffe with the rank of *Oberst* (equivalent to Group-Captain in the RAF). On Hitler's instructions and under the command of Hermann Göring, he co-ordinated the arming and equipping of the Luftwaffe for the second world conflagration, the end of which he would not live to see. When he died he was only 45 years old. He left behind him a mountain of unpaid bills in Berlin's exclusive Horcher restaurant, several illegitimate children and a Ministry of Aviation which his appalled successor described as 'the Augean Stables'.

It was in 1896 that the German pioneer of flight, Otto Lilienthal, crashed to his death while attempting to fly a glider. That same year, in Frankfurt-am-Main, Ernst Udet was born. The day of his birth, 26 April, was a Sunday. His parents Paula and Adolf Udet were proud of their first son. His mother affectionately called him 'Erni'. Soon after his birth the family moved to Munich, where Erni grew up into a typical Bavarian scallywag. His scholastic performance was less than brilliant. In the opinion of his teachers at the Theresien High School on Kaiser-Ludwig-Platz, the boy had too many crazy ideas in his head. 'He picks things up quickly, but forgets them again with equal ease, is interested in everything but at a rather superficial level, is able to talk easily and pleasantly on many subjects. . . . But what eludes him is a depth of seriousness and painstaking exactitude in all his work.' So ran the report on his first year in the upper school. Erni's interests lay outside the gloomy walls of that seat of learning. He was a talented draughtsman, very keen on photography and most of all on flying. His boyhood heroes included the Wright Brothers, who had achieved the world's first powered flight in 1903.

Fired with enthusiasm for the first international aviation exhibition in the autumn of 1904, Erni and some friends founded the 'Munich Aero Club'. Udet Senior allowed them to use the attic of his house for 'pilots' meetings', and the boys met every Wednesday after school, built model aircraft and talked shop. The 'Gustav Otto Aircraft Works' in the Munich suburb of Milbertshofen exerted a magical fascination. Here, with their noses pressed against the perimeter fence, the members of the 'Aero Club' watched the first biplanes in amazement and admired their daring pilots. Sometimes they were allowed to help, turning a propeller by hand to start the motor. In 1909 the French pilot Louis Blériot succeeded in making the first aerial crossing of the English Channel. For the youthful Munich aviators the River Isar served as the 'Channel' which had to be 'conquered' with model aircraft. On 9 January 1909 Erni Udet gained his first 'qualification': 'The official pilot's certificate of the Munich Aero Club was obtained by Herr Ernst Udet, aviator, on a Dornier monoplane built by MGW. The same covered the prescribed distance of 3 metres in the presence of the Chairman and Secretary.'

During the summer holidays of 1910, in his holiday home in the village of Aschau, Udet built his first full-scale glider from bamboo and linen. In wild leaps he hopped down a slope with the makeshift kite until it broke into pieces. The 'Aero Club' aviators, who had hurried over to witness the event, had a suitable explanation ready to give the jeering villagers: in that particular area the earth's magnetism was so strong that it made flying impossible.

The youth's fantasising was a thorn in the flesh of his schoolmasters: 'Though intelligent and not ungifted, his performance has been no more than mediocre. This is due largely to his distractedness and inattention. His head is full of other ideas, and he is particularly obsessed with aviation. He is determined to build a monoplane himself and later to become an aviator.' The fact that he was not moved up to the next class was of little concern to Erni. Nor, it seems, to his parents, since the school noted that they had never got in touch about the matter. He was left to his own devices. True, his father, who by now was running a prosperous small factory making boilers and central-heating equipment, tried to prepare the son for a career in the family business. He had little success, since Erni did not envisage a future among water-pipes and bathtubs.

With much sweat and tears he managed to pass his *Mittlere Reife*, the basic school-leaving examination, in 1913. His well-to-do father rewarded him with a motorcycle – presumably as a 'sweetener' to get him into the family firm. For the moment, however, the lad contented himself with wandering wistfully around the Gustav Otto Works, until finally one of the pilots took pity on him and invited him up in an aircraft for the first time. This maiden flight was to be the first of innumerable sorties.

Wer fliegt da so früh mit dem Morgenwind?
Das ist der Udet, das fröhliche Kind
(Who flies in the morning breeze like a lark?
It's only our Udet, the bright young spark).

Ernst Udet

In 1914 the time for playing games was over. With the shots that felled the Austrian Crown Prince Franz Ferdinand in Sarajevo on 28 June, the delicate equilibrium, which had kept Europe teetering on the edge of war for years, was shattered. In Munich, Berlin, Vienna, Paris and elsewhere, the crowds cheered the outbreak of a conflict in which years of pent-up aggression were released. Infected by the general euphoria of war, Udet immediately volunteered for service. 'Too short', was the succinct verdict at the reception centre for volunteers. Short he may have been, but he was also tenacious. Day after day he reported to the Munich branch of the German General Automobile Club, which was organising despatch-riders for the front. Since he was one of the few people who owned a motorcycle, he was finally taken on. At first he was posted as a driver with the 26th Infantry Division in the military administration of Strasbourg, and soon after that to the vehicle pool at Namur, in Belgium. The ordinary soldiers mocked the despatch-riders as 'gasoline hussars' and 'gentlemen drivers'. But their activities were certainly not without danger. During a gun-battle, Udet and his motorcycle plummeted into a shell-crater and he was wounded.

In October the army terminated its contracts with the volunteer despatch-riders. Once again the thwarted serviceman sat twiddling his thumbs in Munich. His father realised that something now had to be done. With a generous injection of cash and a new fitted bathroom for Gustav Otto, he managed to secure Ernst's admission to the Oberwiesenfeld flying school and by April 1915 Ernst Udet had a civil pilot's licence in his hands. On 4 September of that year he entered service as a pilot with the 206th Artillery Division – he still did not fire a shot in anger, since the pilots were mostly unarmed observers. However, Udet's transfer to Field Flying Section 68 at Habsheim would soon provide a very different experience. The Dutch aero-engineer Anthony Fokker had developed a machine gun that enabled pilots to fire between the blades of their propellers, thereby turning the skies into a battlefield. In December Udet found himself in his first air battle with a French Caudron biplane. Although he had the chance, Udet could not bring himself to shoot his opponent down. In his autobiography, *A Pilot's Life*, published in 1935, he described this duel as a seminal experience: 'It was as if the horror had turned the blood in my veins to ice, paralysed my arms and torn all thought from my head with one blow.' And later: 'However, he who wishes to remain a man among men, must in the moment of decision have the strength to stifle in himself the fear that animals have. For the animal fear in us wants to go on living at any price. And any man who gives in to it is lost to the community of men, where honour, duty and faith in the Fatherland prevail.'

The soft-heartedness, which he later enjoyed making such play of, did not survive for long. With ruthless ambition he proceeded to stamp out his weakness. He set up a dummy aircraft at the edge of the airfield and repeatedly dived down to shoot at it until he had markedly improved his hit-rate. Then finally he won his first aerial victory. 'I cannot describe the feeling I had then; I could have whooped out loud for joy and pride.'

From now on he kept a meticulous account of his triumphs. In *A Pilot's Life*, he dutifully notes every 'kill'. The climax came when he shot down three enemy planes in a single day. He avoided taking leave or going sick, so as not to be ousted from his top position in the list of kills. The war seemed like an adventure novel.

The flying corps was the new elite of the Kaiser's army. The pilots presented themselves as 'Knights of the Skies'. They were the men who could raise themselves above the misery of the trenches, where their contemporaries were losing their lives in the hundreds of thousands.

Thanks to the personal identification marks on their aircraft, they often knew with which adversary they were dealing. Without false modesty they painted overblown mottos on their machines. Udet's was '*Du doch nicht*' (roughly: Oh no you don't!'). '*Le voilà, le foudroyant* – Here comes the thunderbolt', warned one of his French antagonists.

For as long as they lived, they cultivated the myth of a chivalrous comradeship of the air. In 1916 Udet found himself in a duel with the French flying ace, Georges Guynemer. They fought it out for eight minutes, until Udet's machine gun jammed. He struggled helplessly with the weapon. Guynemer flew in close, saw his opponent's problem – and turned away. That at least was the version of the story repeated time and again by Udet, even though others claimed, more prosaically, that Guynemer was also having trouble with his ammunition belt.

The dream of 'genuine comradeship' was one that the airmen continued to share with their former opponents, even after the war. In 1928 Udet met the famous French pilot René Fonck, who signed his photo with the words: 'The more we fight one another, the more we are able to understand the true fellowship of the air.'

The fact was, however, that the war in the air had long since become a grim struggle for life and death. Udet was one of those who saw his entire flight wiped out in a very short time. The loss of friends and colleagues would make him shrink from close relationships for the rest of his life. But at the same time he acquired the privileged status of a man who was born lucky. He was counted among the heroes, and heroes were courted.

At carefully staged events in Berlin known as 'comparison flying', the aircraft manufacturers vied for the pilots' favours. Entire floors of the leading Berlin hotels were booked. The Pfalzwerke company took over the whole of the Adlon hotel on Pariser Platz, while Fokker held their receptions at the Bristol. And when a pilot opened his wardrobe, he sometimes found in it – surprise, surprise – a fur coat.

Even at the battle-front the pilots knew how to exploit to the full the aura that surrounded them. The looted champagne seldom ran out, and in requisitioned châteaux there were always opportunities for rowdy parties. It was the kind of life that very much appealed to the young Udet. His colleagues called him *Kneckes*, 'Shorty'. They liked the perky, sunny-natured young man, who was up for every prank. Carl Zuckmayer, the playwright, recalled their first meeting. 'We liked each other after exchanging just a few words, and together finished off our first bottle of cognac.'

We lived better than the other troops in every respect. We were adequately fed, better equipped and had more free time. But most important, we were spoiling for a fight and felt we were the elite. . . . Flying in the measureless firmament, often having to fend for ourselves entirely, gave us a feeling of superiority over the little creatures down there on earth, and the trivial activities they pursued. We had our own special kind of pride.

Hauptmann Hermann Steiner, on the pilots of the First World War

Udet was now bringing down one enemy plane after another. He moved higher and higher up the ranking of successful pilots. On the body of a shot-down enemy airman a photo of Udet was found, with the caption: 'The ace of aces.'

On a rainy November day in 1917, at Le Cateau in northern France, he received his accolade from the 'Red Baron', Manfred von Richthofen, commander of the 1st Fighter Squadron and the most successful fighter pilot of the First World War. 'How many kills do you have now, Udet?' – 'Nineteen acknowledged, and one more reported, Sir.' – 'Then I'd say you're about ready for us. How would you like that?'

With Richthofen's squadron Udet became familiar with a new dimension in aerial combat. Of the 'Red Baron' it was said by colleagues that he hunted the British like boar in the forest. Richthofen once wrote to his mother: 'Dear Mama, One's heart beats faster, when one's opponent, whose face one has only just seen, plummets down enveloped in flames.' He lived for flying, and flying meant shooting down the enemy. Only a few miles behind the front line, the pilots were housed in barracks and went up to fight air battles as often as three times a day. The enormous physical and mental strain was too much for Udet. A painful ear infection forced him to take some home leave. This pilot's affliction would be with him for the rest of his life. Back home in Munich he and his family were able to celebrate his award of the highest decoration, the *Pour le Mérite* (the famous 'Blue Max') for having shot down twenty of the enemy. It was his entrance ticket to the military aristocracy. With his breast swelling with pride, Udet strolled along the streets of Munich with his girlfriend and delighted in the fact that the guards outside the royal palace had to stand to attention and salute him. All of a sudden the pint-sized pilot was walking tall. On 21 April 1918 news reached him of the death of Manfred von Richthofen. After the latter's successor, Reinhard, also met his death, Udet took temporary command of the famous fighter squadron. But who would be the new squadron leader? Guesswork got people nowhere. Could it be Udet, who by now had no less than forty kills to his credit? At the very least, another member of the Richtofen family, Lothar, was in the frame, for the pilots were certain that the new CO would be someone from their own ranks. The suspense was broken by a telegram – with a surprising message: 'In accordance with order no. 178654 of 8 July 1918, from the General Commanding Air Forces, *Oberleutnant* Hermann Göring is appointed commanding officer of the Richthofen fighter squadron.' So it was Hermann Göring, who with twenty-one kills had, like Udet, won the *Pour le Mérite*! But something was not quite right about those statistics; some of his colleagues muttered that Göring had heavily embellished his record of successes. Whatever the truth of the matter, the man thus honoured contented himself for the moment with a brief visit to his new squadron and then went off on leave. The unstable character of this swaggering air ace, whom Udet was later to call 'Ironsides', was something he would come to know all too well.

> The generation I belong to was shaped by the war. It struck us in our formative years. The weak ones were shattered by it. They were left with nothing but a paralysing horror. But in *us* – and I am speaking for nearly all front-line troops – the will to live became tougher and stronger. A new kind of will to live, one which knows that an individual existence means nothing, the life and future of the community means everything . . .
>
> *Ernst Udet*

The news that an armistice had been signed in the French town of Compiègne hit the German fliers like a bolt from the blue. Did this mean all their sacrifice had been for nothing? Together with his squadron, Hermann Göring flew to Aschaffenburg, near Frankfurt, and tried in vain to hide their aircraft in a papermill before the victors seized them. For one last time the comrades-in-arms sat boozing in the town's monastery *Bierkeller*, and Göring shouted with great emotion: 'Our hour will come again!'

The following day Ernst Udet was discharged from the service. With sixty-two kills to his credit he was the most successful German fighter-pilot to have survived the war.

What now? Back in Munich, Udet shared the fate of all those returning from the war. The airmen plunged from the heroic fantasy world of the war years into hard reality, which for most of them meant unemployment. Some were able to secure jobs as civilian pilots, others flew around under orders from the illegal militias, the *Freikorps*. Ernst Udet first managed to find a billet as a motor mechanic at the Gustav Otto factory. The only thing he really knew about was flying. Yet with the signing of the Versailles Treaty there was scarcely any opportunity to realise his aerial ambitions: Germany was not permitted to possess any military aircraft, and civil aviation was heavily restricted. For six months no aero engines or components, let alone aircraft, could either be manufactured or imported. At a stroke Germany's aviation industry had been reduced to the conditions of the ballooning Montgolfier brothers.

Udet, whose optimism was undimmed, set off with his friend Robert Ritter von Greim in search of aircraft, in order to put into practice an idea that he hoped would, in the years to come, be converted into hard cash: air displays on a grand scale. On 10 August 1919 thousands of people crowded on to the Oberwiesenfeld near Munich. The programme was spectacular: nosedives, looping the loop, rolls, flying upside down. . . . Udet was in his element. The climax of the event was a mock air battle between the 'Knights of the Air', in which Udet and von Greim chased each other across the sky in a series of breakneck aerobatic feats.

In 1920, however, the two daredevils were brought rapidly down to earth by hard reality. On 10 January that year the terms of the Versailles Treaty came fully into force. Close on 15,000 aircraft and 28,000 aero engines were called in and destroyed; a million square metres of aircraft hangars were razed to the ground. For the moment the dream of a stunt-flying career was shattered.

Udet now had to make a living in other ways. He tried his hand as a racing driver, then as a commercial pilot. This did not bring in enough for him to exist on, yet his relish for the good life remained as great as ever. Munich was experiencing a bohemian renaissance. In the artists' bars and clubs around Schwabing, Munich's Chelsea, everyone was whooping it up – and in the middle of it all was Ernst Udet. He called his capers 'ground-level aerobatics' and riding his motorbike through the door would chase the hostesses on to the tables. In bars like Maxim or the Odeon he was almost part of the furniture. He made new friends between bar and dance floor and caricatured them wittily in his notebook. One of these was the poet Joachim Ringelnatz, with whom he engaged in marathon drinking sessions. A new job would come along in good time.

It happened sooner than expected. In 1921 Udet was approached by the brothers Heinz and Wilhelm Pohl. They told him that Wilhelm had made a fortune in America and would put up the money for a new company called Udet-Flugzeugbau (Udet Aircraft Construction).

There was still a ban on building aircraft in Germany, but that did not worry the carefree Udet. He and his friends acquired a small workshop in Milbertshofen, blacked out the windows and laid down mantraps, Wild West style, to keep out uninvited visitors.

They were not the only people busily bypassing the terms of the Versailles Treaty. In Bremen, for example, Heinrich Focke and Georg Wulf were knocking together their aircraft in a basement. This was precisely the intention of the armed forces chief, General von Seeckt, who announced in 1920, when the German flying corps was officially disbanded: 'The air arm is not dead, its spirit lives on.'

By 1922, when the first machine developed by Udet-Flugzeugbau, the U-1, was rolled out, the conditions imposed by the Allies had already been relaxed to such an extent that the aircraft could be shown in public. Commercially, Udet's output was not a success. His technicians certainly came up with numerous new models – but not even Udet's celebrated name could sell them. By 1925 no more than twenty-seven aircraft had found buyers. The firm went into liquidation, leaving a massive debt of 800,000 Reichsmarks owed to its bankers, Merck, Finck and Co. The huge sum would be repaid by a guarantor, but the proprietors of the firm refused to say who that was. It is not hard to guess, though, that like many others the company was being financed, through devious channels, by the German government. For the government had long ago found ways and means of producing, behind closed doors and beyond the frontiers of the Reich, arms that were banned under the Treaty of Versailles. Since 1924 it had been running a secret air force camp in the Russian town of Lipetsk, where fighter pilots could be trained, undisturbed by visits from the Allied control authorities.

It was in 1924 that the Udet factory produced its first big seller, the Flamingo. But by that time the restless Udet had already become bored with aircraft production. He wanted to return to his old life, free and unburdened by organisation, account books and planning. He wanted to recapture the good old days of aerobatic flying. With another friend, Walter Angermund, he went back into show business.

In the second half of the 1920s one air show followed another in quick succession. In just three months in 1926 Udet put on displays in Krefeld, Würzburg, Karlsruhe, Mannheim, Chemnitz, Villingen, Fürth, Berlin, Traunstein, Stuttgart and Hof. 'Udet takes to the air' – this headline was enough to get huge crowds on the move. Walter Angermund handled the organisation of the extravagant spectacles, while Udet did what he loved most: flying. And if the endless round of air displays got a bit tedious, he would fly privately: under the Rhine bridge in Düsseldorf, under Munich's Isar bridges or between the spires of the Frauenkirche cathedral.

> Udet was flying. You search for superlatives, to describe in some small way the experience that Udet gave us yesterday with his flights over the Breitenau field, to pay some small tribute to the performance that Udet achieved. But there is nothing to compare it with. All you can say is: Udet was flying.
>
> *Bamberger Tageblatt* (newspaper)

The air shows made him famous, but not rich, even though his stunts were big box-office. Angermund, who knew his irresponsible friend all too well, suggested that the takings be placed in a deposit account. 'I'd rather have the cash. But give it to me in 1,000-mark notes. That way it lasts longer', was Udet's reply. But not even large denominations helped him to hold on to his money. Udet spent it hand over fist. In 1925 alone his flying circus and competitions earned him around 140,000 marks – an enormous sum for those days. But even that was not enough. Udet loved to act the big spender; without batting an eyelid he would buy a drink for everyone in the bar. But his creditors were usually on to him faster than he could escape them. In December 1926 he wrote to the Mayor of Villingen, an old town in Baden-Württemberg: 'I apologise for not yet having said anything about settling the bill for hydrogen supplied by Rheinfelden for the air display held there. I am under such financial strain that I am having difficulty in raising the necessary sum of 75.30 marks. If it is not possible for you to undertake the settlement of this account yourself, then I must ask for your forbearance.'

Income from advertising activities improved the situation in the short term. A toy manufacturer had named one of its model aircraft after Udet and gave him a share in the profits. On behalf of the Rotbart razor-blade company, he bombarded bathers in the Baltic and the North Sea with little beach balls bearing the words: 'A smooth shave – happy all day. Best wishes, Udet.' He founded a company called Udet-Schleppschrift GmbH, and towed advertising slogans printed on fabric behind his aircraft.

'We mustn't let them get us down,' was how Udet shrugged off the unpaid bills, for which his frequently alternating female companions were in large part responsible.

Shortly after the end of the war he had planned to start living a regular life, by marrying his first love, Lo Zink, the daughter of a well-to-do Nuremberg businessman. True to form, the Udet wedding was celebrated in riotous fashion. Yet the marriage had probably been a matter of obligation. During the war, in a moment of melancholy, he had had the letters 'LO' painted on his aircraft, and had visited the girl whenever he went on leave. But Lo's father made the daredevil suitor very unwelcome and obstinately refused even to be introduced to him. Nonetheless he was obliged to finance the young couple's extravagant lifestyle when they moved into a spacious three-bedroom apartment in Munich's Widenmayerstrasse. As early as 1923 the marital bliss was already over. Udet wanted his freedom back. Ever the gentleman, he insisted that Lo had given him the push. The separation was finalised without much fuss, and Udet took rooms in the exclusive Vier Jahreszeiten (Four Seasons) hotel, which he furnished to his taste throughout. The walls were covered with the identification markings and propellers of enemy aircraft, photos of pilots and women, as well as a target at which, as his alcohol intake rose, he would shoot less and less accurately with an air gun.

Very soon he was seen with a new female companion at his side: the Countess Einsiedel, a sophisticated *femme fatale*, who liked to be photographed in Udet's plane wearing a leopard-skin coat. After leaving her husband, she moved in with Udet at the Vier Jahreszeiten – bag and baggage, along with her children and their nursemaid. But as suddenly as she had swept into his life, she swept out again. In February 1927, she packed her belongings and went off with her new beau, a racing driver, leaving astronomical debts behind her. Udet never let himself get upset by the enormous bills that the countess ran up at the Vier Jahreszeiten. She had after all written him IOUs, little handwritten notes which, of course, were entirely worthless. Udet celebrated her abrupt departure with a well-lubricated stag party in Garmisch-Partenkirchen.

In the roaring twenties, she was not the only woman who had found gratification with the charming aviator. But few of his affaires ended so smoothly. One amusing weekend in Garmisch almost proved fatal for the inveterate skirt-chaser. When the lady he was visiting, whose name Udet never revealed, found another woman's photograph in his wallet, she had an attack of hysterics and rammed a large nail into his chest. Bleeding profusely, he just managed to get to the nearest doctor. 'I don't run after women. But they run after me. What d'you expect me to do?' he confided with a wink to his friend and mechanic, Erich Baier. One affaire followed the other; none lasted.

Because of his louche lifestyle he became known as a 'colourful character'. Occasionally he would go round bars performing on the 'musical saw'. Then he was seen with a nail through his lip, like an Indian fakir. In the jet-set resort of St Moritz he fitted his Flamingo with snow-skids and terrified hotel guests from their balconies by scraping past them with inches to spare. Breakfast in Berlin, a lunch of trout on the Eibsee lake, and cocktails in St Moritz – that was the kind of day Udet enjoyed.

> What is bravery? I sit in my plane, shut both eyes tight, and then wiggle the joystick a bit. Somehow or other, it seems to work . . .
>
> *Ernst Udet*

Yet, for all his outward exuberance, the joker was haunted by a desperate restlessness, which he attempted to quell with ever greater quantities of alcohol. He was seldom seen without a bottle, but rarely was he drunk. He could put away unimaginable quantities of liquor. Later on, he even had a small bar installed in his cockpit, so that he could keep himself supplied during flights. He recklessly claimed he flew better when drunk. He ratcheted up ever greater risks in his aerial stunts: nosedives with the propeller idling, loops at very low altitude, taking off in a glider from the Zugspitze, Germany's highest mountain peak – nothing seemed too daring. His aircraft appeared always to be accompanied by an invisible guardian angel. Others who copied him were less fortunate. Quite a few of his colleagues lost their lives performing aerobatics. At an air show in Karlsruhe in 1926, he took off with a parachutist, a 20-year-old student named Otto Fusshöler. The young man jumped out at a height of 1,250 feet, but his parachute failed to open and he fell to his death among the crowd. Udet never said anything publicly about this and many other accidents, although he lost a number of good friends.

He seemed to want constantly to better his own performance, and always gambled with the same stake: his life. And he always won. Just as he had done in the First World War, he came through every sortie unscathed.

His years as a stunt pilot seem to have been the happiest in Ernst Udet's life. In 1928 a collection of his caricatures and cartoons of his friends and acquaintances from this period was published under the title *Break a Leg*. It featured among others the aircraft builder Junkers, and the celebrated American pilot, Charles Lindbergh. Udet had also portrayed himself at the controls of his Flamingo, flying at speed with a bottle of cognac slung around his neck. Under the picture he had written the rhyme: *Wer fliegt da so früh mit dem Morgenwind? Das ist der Udet, das fröhliche Kind*, which might be freely translated as: 'Who flies in the morning breeze like a lark? It's only our Udet, the bright young spark.'

In Berlin he met the actress and film-maker Leni Riefenstahl, who asked him on the spur of the moment whether he would like to be in her film. He certainly would. In *The White Hell of Piz Palü* he played the part of a pilot who flies to the rescue of a couple of lovers, caught by a snowstorm in the mountains – a trite plot, but a heart-stopper nonetheless. The critic of the *Berliner Zeitung* praised the epic directed by Arnold Fanck (Riefenstahl played the lead and assisted with the direction), as a 'hymn to humanity at its noblest and to a selfless readiness to help others'. In just four weeks over 100,000 movie-goers had stormed the Ufa-Palast cinema in Berlin. In Germany alone the film grossed over a million marks.

Udet found film appearances to his liking. *The White Hell of Piz Palü* was followed by *Storm over Mont Blanc* – another drama of love and passion in the high Alps. This time Leni Riefenstahl plays the daughter of an astronomer who meets a weather observer at night. When the lover gets into danger, who comes flying to his rescue? Ernst Udet.

In 1930 Udet and his friend, the cameraman Hans Schneeberger, known as 'Snow-flea', mounted a filming expedition to East Africa, entitled 'Strange birds over Africa'. Using film and still cameras they took some remarkable pictures of wildlife. When Udet swooped down and almost brushed the earth, a lioness jumped up and tore one of the wings with her paw. This African adventure enriched his repertoire of exciting stories, with which he effortlessly enthralled astonished audiences in the bars of Berlin. Visitors to his apartment in Berlin's Pommersche Strasse were amazed to see the walls covered with African souvenirs, animals' heads, shields, spears and masks.

The Germany to which Ernst Udet returned from Africa in 1931 had a very different face. He had flown unconcernedly through the years in which the seeds had been sown, which were now yielding their brownshirted crop. In 1923 he had been in Munich and had seen Adolf Hitler and his supporters playing at being revolutionaries in the Bürgerbräu beer hall. Hermann Göring, his squadron comrade from the First World War days, had been among those marching at the head of the brownshirt guard. Udet's only worry on that day, 9 November 1923, had been about his fleet of aircraft. The Nazi rebels had eyed them longingly. When the revolt was crushed and Göring had fled to Sweden, Udet had been among those who called for his expulsion from the veterans' association of the Richthofen Squadron – a disgrace which the conceited airman was never to get over. Udet's attitude towards the National Socialist movement was one of indifference and incomprehension. As late as 30 March 1936, when the SA donated aircraft to the Luftwaffe for a fighter squadron, which thenceforth was to be named the 'Horst Wessel' squadron, Udet noted in his journal: 'Are we meant to be grateful for the name Horst Wessel?' His tradition was that of the 'Red Baron', the recollection of heroic dogfights in the skies over Flanders. Yet three of the men who had been stationed on the western front, no great distance from Udet, were now marching side by side once more. Following the Reichstag elections on 14 September 1930, the Nazi Party celebrated a landslide victory. And one guest was very welcome among Hitler's aides: Erhard Milch, the architect of Lufthansa, Germany's national airline, who was now actively seeking membership of the party. This was still being denied him, since Hitler believed Milch could serve him better by staying under cover. However, as a fallback, an honourably low membership number had already been reserved for him.

Udet ignored the changes taking place in his homeland and flew away from them. In any case, his display flights abroad were considerably more profitable than in an economically prostrate Germany. As early as 1931, in search of new aircraft, he shipped his Flamingo over to the United States and travelled with it. Among the planes he was shown was the Curtiss Hawk, an ideal aircraft for steep dives. Udet was thrilled. He had found the perfect aircraft for spectacular aerobatics. The object of his desire would cost him US$ 18,500 – an exorbitant price, which Udet could not possibly raise. Unless someone were to give him a financial leg-up.

Back in Germany he prepared for his next adventure: *SOS Iceberg* was the title of a film that was to be directed, once again, by Arnold Fanck. Udet set sail for Greenland with a motley crew: pilots, cameramen, actors and actresses (including his latest girlfriend, Elloys Illing, nicknamed 'Laus'), three polar bears and two seals from the Hagenbeck Circus.

The footage from Greenland was probably the most spectacular shot with Udet. He took off from icebergs that were already breaking up under the skids of his aircraft, and sank with it into the icy water. Making friends with the native Eskimos was something that left a permanent impression on him. He made a last wish come true for an old man who wanted to fly just once like a bird. The happy singing of the old fellow, who died the following night, was indelibly imprinted on Udet's memory. It was with this experience that he concluded his book, *A Pilot's Life*. The final sentence is pregnant with meaning: 'But I must go on. Soon the great night will begin and then all of life is submerged.'

However, the great night was only just descending over Germany. On the eve of the Nazis' seizure of power, Berlin's high society had a date at the Press Ball. At the Ullstein table, the champagne was flowing. Udet's friend Carl Zuckmayer recalled later: 'The atmosphere in the overcrowded rooms . . . was very strange. . . . Everyone could sense something in the air, but no one quite wanted to accept it. That afternoon, the Schleicher government had resigned. . . . People were going about in a mixture of grim apprehension and frantic gaiety; it was eerie and macabre . . . Udet and I, who had been served several glasses of cognac, were soon in a state where we didn't care what we said. "Will you look at those creeps", said Udet, pointing to the guests. "They've all taken their gongs and ribbons out of mothballs. A year ago they were still out of fashion." It was true that in many buttonholes and on many chests there were war decorations that previously no one would ever have worn at a press ball. Udet unfastened his *Pour le Mérite*, which he always wore beneath his white tie when in full evening dress, and stuffed it in his pocket. "I tell you what," he suggested, "let's both drop our trousers and hang our bare backsides over the balustrade." But the truth was, we were in no mood for humour . . .'

He was a real old warhorse, who knew how to drink, but never lost the plot. He was always full of amusing ideas and could tell jokes better than anyone I know.

Ernst Udet was a lovely man.

Actress Ilse Werner

Shortly afterwards word spread through the reception that Hitler had been appointed Reich Chancellor. The two men, together with Zuckmayer's wife and Udet's mother, left the party to go to Udet's favourite Propeller Bar. 'Not another word about Hitler', whispered Udet to Zuckmayer, 'it would spoil the old lady's evening.' At the bar counter they drowned their sorrows in double brandies.

The following Monday, 30 January, Udet's *Pour le Mérite* was back in its customary place. From a window of the Adlon hotel he watched the torchlight procession of the SA storm-troopers, which provided the new men in power with a dramatic backdrop to their victory. From now on, Udet's Prussian decoration would be more than useful to him.

He was not alone in making this calculation. At Berlin's Tempelhof airport a deputation of twelve First World War air heroes lined up smartly to welcome Hermann Göring, whose appointment as Minister of Aviation was anticipated. Göring walked past the group of civilians and only saluted the SA guard of honour that had paraded for him. This made it clear upon whom the new elite was relying. Yet Göring did need the big names, the heroes of the First World War. To this end he even swallowed the disgrace of his expulsion from the Richthofen Association. A party to celebrate the 25th anniversary of the German Aero Club was a further occasion for establishing friendly relations. Indeed, all those awarded the *Pour le Mérite* had got together and were listening eagerly to the tempting offers from the brand-new 'Reich Commissioner for Aviation'. Even Udet found something to interest him. 'He's recruiting people. He promised me the money to buy two Curtiss Hawks.'

Yet he still seems not to have been ready to march in the Nazi ranks. On 21 April 1933 some unique film footage was shot at a memorial ceremony for the 15th anniversary of the death of Manfred von Richthofen. At the Invalides cemetery a delegation of the German Air Sport Association laid a wreath. Three bearers of the *Pour le Mérite* marched at their head. Two of them were parading in their new Luftwaffe uniforms. In their midst Ernst Udet stands out in his dandified outfit of morning coat and top hat, with an elegant silk scarf slung around his neck.

Effective from 1 May 1933 Ernst Udet, pilot, became member no. 2010976 of the National Socialist German Workers Party, otherwise known as the Nazis. A few weeks earlier, when asked whether he would fly for the party, he replied: 'Depends how much they're paying.' He is said to have celebrated joining the party by downing a massive quantity of brandy and practising the *Heil Hitler* salute.

The new *Genosse* ('partner' or 'comrade'), as party members were known, was more than welcome. He was well known and popular, had travelled widely and was a man of the world. When the German Aero Club issued an invitation to twenty-five members of the British Parliament, Udet was the focus of the gathering – a charming *bon vivant*, who drew caricatures for the guests and entertained them with tales of his adventures. He was an excellent mouthpiece whenever it was necessary to convey to suspicious foreign countries the harmless nature of the change of regime in Germany. Another trip to America was scheduled, with flying displays in Los Angeles and at the World Fair in Chicago. And this time he would not return empty-handed. All it needed was a call to Curtiss. The German Ministry of Aviation had already transferred the money to purchase two Hawks. Göring had kept his word.

Now it was time for Udet to meet his obligations. To questions from critical journalists he replied in grandiose terms: 'In other countries Hitler's position in Germany is either misunderstood or misinterpreted. Hitler is not doing what *he* wants, but what is wanted by the 40 million Germans who stand behind him. The reports about what is going on in Germany are exaggerated. One thing is clear: the Kaiser will not return to the throne; that time is past. There have been a few cases of Jews being badly treated, but those have been given undue importance. The German Jew who attends to his own affairs and is a good citizen will not be molested. And all the rest, who were not in the communist party, will go on living as normal and will be left in peace. Things had reached such a point that something had to be done to halt the growth and spread of communism.' On the next occasion he was presumptuous enough to declare: 'Hitler will never lead Germany into war. He is anxious to rid the population of certain undesirable elements and to cleanse the country of revolutionary ideas, but every nation has the right to do that.'

Were these merely phrases he had learned by heart, or were they his actual convictions? It is difficult to know what to make of Udet's speeches in the United States. He had never been seriously involved in politics, let alone with ideologies. Nevertheless, he mouthed the jargon of the new masters whose service he had entered. In private he struck a different note. For instance, he asked Clifford Henderson, director of America's National Air Races: 'Do you think I could find a worthwhile job here? And maybe an American girl I could marry? Those damned Nazis. When I'm at home, I'll be a good Nazi too, but . . .' On his journey back to Germany he confided to his mechanic Baier that Göring had invited him to work for him in the Ministry of Aviation. He said he would probably take up the offer.

On 25 October 1933, he flew his 'welcome aboard' present, a Curtiss Hawk, to the aircraft test centre at Rechlin.

Later, Nazi propaganda would dub him the 'Father of the Stuka'. In his eulogy Hermann Göring wallowed in nostalgic memories: 'In those days you were the first to talk about dive-bombers. I have to say, I suddenly saw the brilliance of the idea, saw its endless possibilities . . .'

However, the fact is that as early as 1930 Ernst Heinkel had built the He-50, which had dive-bombing capabilities. For years this type had been undergoing trials at the secret flight-training camp at Lipetsk in Russia. And just two weeks before Udet turned up at Rechlin, Göring had issued orders for the first Stuka (dive-bomber) units to be established in Schwerin. In view of the limited sources of raw materials and fuel in Germany, the Stuka's high strike-rate seemed to be the recipe for the future. To popularise it, they needed Udet. For with his brilliant talent as a pilot, he was the man who could get an aircraft of that type accepted, even against resistance from within the ranks of the Luftwaffe. He enjoyed promotional work. And the unerring machine was very much to his taste, both as a fighter pilot and stunt flier.

> The German nation must become a nation of airmen.
>
> *Hermann Göring*

On 1 April 1934 he demonstrated the Hawk to 120,000 spectators in Hamburg. The enthusiasm of reporter from the *Hamburger Fremdenblatt* could not be restrained:

Now the engine roars with a force that drowns everything. Udet's miracle-machine howls away with its 750 h.p. The German master-pilot provides a spectacle never before witnessed. Like a prehistoric insect of gigantic size and power, the machine cuts through the air, and shoots at unimaginable speed vertically into the sky, pierces the clouds and vanishes. And then something strange happens. Like a fatally wounded eagle it drops out of the clouds once more, and plunges, again vertically, at a speed of over 360 m.p.h. towards the airfield. We hold our breath; an incredible tension reduces the tens of thousands of spectators to silence. Has something gone wrong? Engine failure? It seems that the metal eagle must at any moment bore into the earth with fantastic force! Udet dives down from a height of about 10,000 feet. Then the engine bursts into life with a fortissimo wail; strained to breaking-point, its last reserves of power used up, the aircraft swoops up again only feet away from the runway. The crowd utters a gasp of relief. But the daredevil Udet is off again heavenwards, to new flights.

He was flying in a new outfit. On 10 September 1935 the 'new German Luftwaffe' presented itself at the 'Reich Party Freedom Rally'. In March Hitler had officially announced the existence of a German air force, the 'secrecy' of which had in any case only been a formality. In Nuremberg the fighting forces of the air put on a show with great relish. A huge mock-up of a power-station had been built on the Zeppelin field and was attacked by squadrons of aircraft. The climax of the demonstration came when an aircraft screamed down out of the heavy, grey clouds and reduced the power-station to rubble and ashes. The pilot was Ernst Udet.

Udet, the aerobatic artist, film star and tearaway had turned into a propaganda pilot for Hitler. In June 1935 the *bon vivant* had exchanged his casual flying clothes for the uniform of the Luftwaffe, which he joined with the rank of *Oberst*. The aircraft designer Ernst Heinkel later recalled how astonished he was to see Udet in full rig for the first time: 'For the sake of flying, you sometimes have to make a pact with the Devil', was the latter's cryptic reply. 'Only you must not let yourself be devoured by him.'

Those who knew him reacted with amazement at this change of heart. The transformation from hedonist to well-disciplined officer seemed much too abrupt. Would the same Udet who could squander thousands of marks in a single night now be satisfied with the meagre pay of a Luftwaffe colonel? Was this man, who since the end of the First World War had walked away from any but the most short-term commitment, now joining the ranks of the armed services?

He had flown for the Fatherland, for cheering audiences, for money. Now he was flying for the party. However, he would soon experience at close quarters what it meant to cross swords with the new masters.

His friend Walter Kleffel, a journalist with the Ullstein press and, at the microphone, a fluent commentator at numerous Udet air shows, became caught up in the ruthless machinery of Nazi 'clean-ups'. In one of his reports he had used the unambiguous term 'dive-bomber' (*Sturzbomber*, as opposed to the more innocuous-sounding *Sturzkampfflieger* or 'low-level combat aircraft'). A little later the Gestapo were at his front door, accusing him of having betrayed a state secret. The background to this absurd allegation was that the Reich Minister of Propaganda, Joseph Goebbels, was conducting a hate campaign against the liberal Ullstein newspaper group, as a prelude to a 'take-over' of the company. Kleffel was helpless to defend himself against the charges. In October he was sent to Dachau, the Nazis' first concentration camp, near Munich. In desperation he tried to get in touch with Udet. His prominent friend would surely be able to help him. But it was no use; Udet did not lift a finger. When Kleffel was released from the concentration camp in 1939, he met Udet once more, and again begged him for help – but again there was no response. A colleague of his from the Aviation Ministry had not wanted to be seen with the convicted visitor, or so Udet weakly justified himself.

It was a case of old friends versus new ones; and the latter knew how to make skilful use of Udet's popularity. In 1935 German cinema-goers had a last chance to admire him on the screen. The film, *Miracle of Flight*, already bore the clear fingerprints of the new men in power.

In accordance with a directive from the Minister of Education, Bernhard Rust, young people's interest in aviation was to be strongly promoted at school and in leisure time. The action of the film chimed with the new ideal of the young pilot. A boy whose greatest desire is to become a pilot like his dead father meets Ernst Udet, who takes him under his wing and trains him. Needless to say, the climax of the film takes place in the Alps, where the flying hero rescues his young friend from danger on the mountainside.

Udet's public appearances in 1934 and 1935 were to be the last of their kind. After that he left the entertainment business. He had been appointed Inspector of Fighter and Dive-Bomber Aircraft. What followed was a comet-like rise on Göring's coat-tails. In the summer of 1936, Göring made him head of the Technical Division of the Reich Ministry of Aviation. It appears that Udet resisted the idea: 'I know nothing about production. I don't even know anything about large aircraft. They're not for me, they're not my style.' Göring dispelled his anxieties: 'What matters is having lots of ideas. For the rest of it, you'll be given as many people as you need. What we need most of all is to have your name in the public eye. At the moment, that's worth more than almost anything.'

Göring made absolutely no secret of the direction in which technical developments were heading. On 20 May 1936 he announced in Berlin: 'I dream of possessing a Luftwaffe which, if ever the hour should strike, will descend on the enemy like a corps of vengeance.'

For Carl Zuckmayer and Ernst Udet, who had been close friends for many years, 1936 was the year of parting. 'Shake the dust of this country from your feet, go off round the world and never come back', Udet ordered his friend. 'And what about you?' asked Zuckmayer. 'I'm in love with flying – I can never escape from it. But one day the Devil will get the lot of us.' They would never see each other again.

Only once more did Udet attempt to avert the destiny in whose hands he had willingly placed himself, and to escape from the clutches of the Nazi regime. A friend of his, an American pilot named Eddie Rickenbacker, who had flown in the First World War, received a letter from Udet asking him, through the US Army Air Force, to let the German authorities know how glad people would be to see the popular Udet as Air Attaché at the German embassy in Washington. But this vague attempt came to nothing. Udet remained in Hitler's Germany.

It is hard to describe this man. Short, stocky, fit, with small hands and feet, fair hair, which admittedly time had not left him much of, a strong, expressive face, and bright blue eyes which radiated determination, but also humour. Yet as soon as you thought you had the measure of him, he changed, and you had to start over again.

Al Williams, US flying ace, on Udet

By April 1937 Udet was a major-general; in November 1938 he was promoted again, to lieutenant-general. When he got the general's white collar-tabs he was as thrilled as a little boy, and at a rowdy party danced the cancan on a table.

As head of the Technical Division the massive burden of aircraft development and production for the entire Luftwaffe was placed on his shoulders. In order to grab the biggest slices of the aircraft industry's cake, the individual companies fought among themselves like tinkers. The trio of Heinkel, Messerschmitt and Junkers kept their greedy eyes on every new contract, every new aircraft type. Messerschmitt and Heinkel in particular, though both brilliant designers in their own way, showed scarcely any interest in longer-range planning and found in Ernst Udet a credulous client, who all too quickly could get carried away by new ideas. Yet his task was to keep the aircraft designers on a common course and steer the jumble of new developments along orderly lines.

He himself saw things very differently: what he wanted was to be the Luftwaffe's senior test pilot, taking each prototype in turn, trying it out, improving it, putting it into production. The Ministry of Aviation was one big toy-cupboard full of planes, and Göring held the key to it.

'What other head of the Technical Division would try out every new aircraft himself? Twice, when you were testing a machine in its early development stage, you had to jump out with a parachute and you saved your valuable life for us', recalled Göring in his hypocritical eulogy. It was quite true that Udet made use of every free minute, and many that were not in fact free, to test new types of aircraft. He raced from factory to factory, from airfield to airfield, placing a contract here, suggesting a technical improvement there, without ever seriously checking that things were actually being done.

> The aeroplane will be the instrument of a fortunate human race; one which will bring its blessings to all peoples and nations, and will bring back theirs in return.
>
> *Professor Hugo Junkers*

Udet was happier when in search of new adventures. In 1937, while the cameras rolled, he docked an aircraft with the airship *Hindenburg* – a highly dangerous operation. Only a few days later the *Hindenburg* exploded in flames on arrival at Lakehurst, near New York. Thirty-five people lost their lives. Thanks to his talent as a pilot Udet had for many years been accustomed to climbing into any plane and taking off without a moment's thought. As long he was dealing with aircraft of a simple design, he got away with it. But the era was past when the cockpit controls consisted only of a throttle and a joystick. When testing an He-118, he had been given express instructions by the designer, Ernst Heinkel, to keep a close eye on the propeller pitch. As usual, Udet had not been listening. The propeller failed. Only at the last moment did he manage to climb out of the aircraft. One foot had been caught in the cabin and he was only able to free himself because he was wearing casual shoes instead of the regulation flying boots. Coming down by parachute, he made a hard landing, was knocked unconscious and had to be rushed to hospital. But the same evening he was already chipper enough to phone Heinkel: 'Come over right away. I'm dying of thirst!' A little later, the champagne bottles were being passed around at his bedside. The crash-landing had no effect on Udet. He kept on demanding more: more speed, more manoeuvrability, more risk.

In 1938, around Whitsun, he visited Ernst Heinkel in Warnemünde. He was curious to see the prototype of the He-100, a fighter which Heinkel had promised would achieve a speed of 420mph. He boarded the aircraft at 7.27 p.m., and in nine and a half minutes thundered along the measured distance between Müritz and Wustrow, reaching 634.32kph, or 380.59mph – a world record! As he climbed out, Udet remarked laconically: 'I didn't do anything special. Incidentally, what are those damfool red lights on the dashboard for? The buggers were on the whole time.' The 'buggers' were warning lights indicating that the cooling system was overheating.

These and other heroic deeds in the air made up the repertoire of Udet stories, which were well known throughout Germany and kept people amused. Yet every time Udet climbed into a cockpit, he gambled on a higher card. It was often a miracle that he clambered out alive, even from a total wreck, without ever suffering any serious injury. He certainly took tremendous risks, but he was also born under a lucky star. He was not infrequently drunk when he got into the cockpit. The Head of Flying Schools, General Mahnke, wanted to have Udet's book, *A Pilot's Life*, removed from all Luftwaffe libraries. It seems that the author, and the madcap flying escapades he described, were hardly suitable as a model for budding pilots.

After Udet broke the world air speed record, Hitler laid down the law. The crazy airman was banned from flying. Only with great difficulty did he manage to get the ban restricted to display flying. But even this he was to ignore completely.

Udet sought adventure as an escape from the daily grind of tedious office work he had got himself into in the Ministry of Aviation. For now his place of work was no longer the pilot's seat but behind a desk in room 201 of Hermann Göring's gigantic ministry. The building in Leipziger Strasse was megalomania built in stone: an empire of over 3,000 rooms, in which the emperor himself was seldom glimpsed. Since his promotion to 'Reich Commissioner for the Four-Year Plan', Göring's interest in the minutiae of building up the Luftwaffe, which had been moderate at the best of times, was now scaled down to a minimum. He left it to his staff to find their way through the jungle of administrative work, conferences and mountains of paper.

Ernst Udet was the poacher who had turned gamekeeper. Like Göring, he too was almost incapable of concentrating on work for any length of time. All he had ever wanted was to fly, and now he felt robbed of his wings. Udet, 'the bright young spark', now drew pictures of himself hunched over a desk piled high with papers, fettered to his chair by a gigantic chain. In a 'thought-bubble' above his head the smiling air ace is flying happily around the sky, with the mountains below him.

> I tell you frankly, my wings have been clipped, my job here is a prison. The amount that's expected of me is crazy. I let Göring talk me into taking over the Technical Division. I now know very well that my erstwhile squadron comrade had no intention of furthering my career; he just used me to secure his own position. The job is killing me. All around me are intrigues, falsity and the Gestapo – so ends my free and happy life as a pilot.
>
> *Ernst Udet*

The man taking care of things in the Leipziger Strasse was the industrious Erhard Milch. The son of a pharmacist from Wilhelmshaven, he could already look back on a notable career, when Göring brought him into the ministry in 1933. Back in 1926, aged just 33, he had been appointed to the management board of the newly created national airline, Deutsche Lufthansa AG. After the Nazis seized power, Göring urged him to take up the post of Permanent Secretary in his planned Ministry of Aviation. As a fervent admirer of Hitler, Milch did not have to be asked twice. He ruled with a grim harshness, which he applied not least to himself. It was one of his senior colleagues, Paul Körner, who originated the saying: 'That man Milch pisses ice.' When rumours about his Jewish ancestry came to the surface, Milch got his parents to produce written confirmation to the effect that he was in fact illegitimate.

His natural father, they claimed, had been his mother's uncle, an 'unexceptionable' Aryan. Hermann Göring cared little about such canards. 'I decide who's a Jew', he once pronounced.

Göring needed men like Milch. In common with most of the staff in the aviation ministry, the 'Reich Commissioner' had scant knowledge of aircraft technology and still less interest in organisational matters. But Erhard Milch was hewn from different timber. He was well versed in everything to do with air armaments, had a grip on his job and a thirst for hard work. Yet he was also possessed of a dogged ambition, which worried Göring. He needed Milch's undisputed technical expertise, provided it was kept within the bounds of the authority he was willing to grant him.

Divide and rule: that was the principle on which Göring played his subordinates off against each other. In Ernst Udet he found the trump card he could always play against Milch, whenever he liked. So began a game which Udet, unhappy and out of his depth, was eventually to lose.

> Whenever anything goes wrong, Milch says: 'I saw that coming ages ago.' He's constantly on the look-out for a chance to trip me up.
>
> *Ernst Udet*

In June 1936 the Chief-of-Staff of the Luftwaffe, General Wevers, died and Göring used the opportunity to rearrange the players on his Leipziger Strasse field. In Wevers' job he placed Albert Kesselring, later to play a major role in the war in the Mediterrannean and Italy. Ernst Udet replaced General Wimmer, who had long been a thorn in Göring's ample flesh. Thus Secretary Milch suddenly found himself excluded from most of the technical and tactical decisions.

The following year Göring once again restructured his department. And once again the result was a downgrading for Milch. The head of the Luftwaffe reported directly to the Wehrmacht General Staff, which meant that Milch found himself stripped of most of his duties as Göring's deputy. Only during 'unforeseeable absences' might he assume the role of deputy. It was an unparalleled reprimand for the man who believed he had Hitler's backing. He had, after all, been awarded the Nazi Party's coveted Gold Medal. What is more, in June he had been given the task of 'ensuring uniform ideological indoctrination for the Luftwaffe forces'.

On 1 February 1939 Udet was promoted to 'Air Armourer-General', a fantasy title in typical Göring style. For Udet, as a ministerial department head, there was in theory no further scope for promotion beyond the rank of lieutenant-general – unless a new rung in the career ladder was invented especially for him. Harking back to the *Generalfeldzeugmeister*, or Field Amourer-General, of the First World War, they had thought up the title of '*Generalluftzeugmeister*'. To explain Udet's sudden fit of vanity, his biographers also draw attention to his permanent state of financial crisis. Yet the new position scarcely did anything to improve his income. It is more likely that Udet was by now infected by the competition for titles and honours between himself and his rivals, expecially Erhard Milch, who was always a step ahead of him. The award of the title of *Generalluftzeugmeister* to Udet was a slap in the face for Milch. The power over all rearmament matters was not vested in him, the assiduous organiser, but in the lightweight Udet. Many historians today see Udet's preferment as the turning point, the moment when Milch made up his mind to abandon his rival to his fate. Oddly enough, the two men had once been bound by a friendship in private life. Udet had given Milch flying lessons, and during one of his first outings had shouted to him that he now had full confidence in the new pilot. So saying he threw the joystick out of the cockpit. Milch had feigned total terror – but he knew that on these occasions the fun-loving flyer always carried a dummy joystick with him. Udet had been highly amused; he loved jokes like that. At the time Erhard Milch had laughed along with him.

For Udet the reverse of the coin was a massive enlargement of his sphere of responsibility, which even at its previous extent he had been unable to keep on top of. In addition to the development and trialling of new aircraft he was now responsible for the procurement and supply of equipment, fuel and provisions. By the end he had 26 departments reporting to him, making up an impenetrable labyrinth of 4,000 officers, bureaucrats and engineers, who were nominally responsible for everything, but in practice accountable for nothing. Even Milch, who was not afraid of desk work, had never had to manage more than four departments simultaneously. 'In Udet's hands everything turns to dust', groaned the Permanent Secretary. The man to whom money was handed out in large-denomination notes, so that he would not get through it all in one night, was now administering an armaments budget that ran into millions. The man who was obsessed with new types of aircraft was expected to force the industry to optimise its existing models. The man who made repeated crash-landings because he ignored the most elementary safety precautions held the highest technological post in the Luftwaffe. He was absurdly miscast.

And for some time the storm-warnings had been hoisted. While Göring's men were sharpening their knives in readiness, the 'emergency' – feared and hoped for in equal measure – drew ever nearer. Outwardly the protagonists seemed to be keeping up a united front. Udet and Milch visited London and Paris to get a first-hand impression of the status of the opposition's air defences. In the shadow of the Tower of London and the Eiffel Tower they made a perfect team: the sober expert and the charming conversationalist, of whom old flying comrades everywhere still had happy memories. After each trip they showed up dutifully at Hitler's Berghof retreat and delivered their report, not least on Britain's very considerable activities on the air combat front. There would be no war with Britain, the Führer blithely assured them. And his eager listeners were only too happy to believe him.

Udet is a jovial, friendly man. He only became reticent when I asked him about the future of German military aviation. He described as nonsense the rumours that German bombers could destroy Paris overnight. Looking at him and listening to him, one is convinced of his goodwill.

Article in Les Ailes, *a French flying magazine*

The return visits were not long in coming. In August 1938 Göring generously invited Joseph Vuillemin, the head of the French air force, to inspect German aircraft production. On the Döberitz airfield, row upon row of Me-109 fighters glittered in the sun, and at the very moment when Vuillemin stopped to look at them, a Focke-Wulf Condor landed, supposedly straight from New York. At the Heinkel factory in Oranienburg, near Berlin, the Frenchman marvelled at the He-111 bomber, and Udet, who was enjoying the little game no end, invited him for a quick flight over the complex. As they landed again a He-100 fighter thundered overhead at breathtaking speed. Udet and Milch reeled off the lines they had learnt by heart. How were production plans progressing, Milch asked casually. 'The second production line has just gone on stream, and the third is starting in three weeks time', Udet brazenly assured him. And it did the trick. Vuillemin reported to Paris on the 'truly devastating strike-power of the German Luftwaffe'. Round One to Germany in the shadow-boxing contest.

But an air force that would be effective over the longer term did not exist, even though by 1939 the German aircraft industry had probably achieved a unique position in the world. At the outbreak of war it is thought that the Luftwaffe had 4,000 combat aircraft and more than 8,000 training, transport and other non-combat planes at its disposal. Nevertheless, the Luftwaffe giant stood on feet of clay. It was short of fuel and other supplies. Furthermore, numerous aircraft for which the designers had held out impressive prospects were still years away from volume production. Most importantly, medium- and long-range bombers only existed on the drawing board. As early as 1936 their manufacture had been put on ice. 'The Führer's not asking me how big my bombers are, but how many I've got', was how Göring defiantly justified his decision. With the arrogance of a commander who considers himself unbeatable, he equipped the Luftwaffe for short invasion campaigns, without developing a more comprehensive air-war strategy. Both he and his cohorts lacked the vision for that.

One solution to the dilemma that even the top Luftwaffe brass were gradually becoming aware of was to be provided by the building of Junkers Ju-88s. The contract and also the supervision of its completion was put in the hands of Heinrich Koppenberg, the chief executive of the Junkers aircraft company. 'And now clear the decks and create for me in the shortest time possible a massive bomber fleet of Ju-88s', Göring wrote to Koppenberg. The aircraft was to have the same dive-bombing capabilities as its predecessor, the Ju-87. The 'Stuka' principle had 'proved its worth' in the Spanish Civil War. Now it was elevated to a panacea, regardless of the fact that a dive-bombing capability made the machine considerably heavier and less manoeuvrable. During the interminable pre-production phase, in which, as Koppenberg later claimed, the Ju-88 underwent no less than 25,000 design changes, the weight of the aircraft increased from its original 6 to *13* tons. At the same time its speed decreased from 300mph to just 210mph. Milch later described it contemptuously as a 'flying barn-door'. The story of the Ju-88 would be repeated with the He-177 heavy bomber which, because of the dive-bombing capability imposed on it, came into service considerably later than expected and, to make matters worse, in a technically undeveloped state. It was not until the autumn of 1942 that Göring would realise the 'idiocy' of trying to make an aircraft like that operate as a dive-bomber. Udet was among the many senior Luftwaffe figures who stood firmly behind the 'Stuka' principle. It was his own idea that the aircraft should plummet out of the sky emitting an ear-splitting howl from their sirens. When first used, the so-called 'trumpets of Jericho' caused fear and horror among those under attack. Germany's rapid early victories in the Second World War appeared to prove the advocates of dive-bombing right.

> What matters now is that Germany has parity in the air. I will carry on this battle with all the fervour and tenacity that people expect from us old National Socialists, until I know that the safety of the German nation is assured.
>
> *Hermann Göring*

On 26 September 1938 Hitler ordered a fivefold increase in the size of the Luftwaffe. A total of 31,300 aircraft, including 3,500 fighters and 7,700 bombers, were to be conjured up out of nowhere in short order. As far as bombers were concerned, not a single functioning prototype existed. Everyone knew how unrealistic this programme was, and also that the man who had put his name to it would have to bear the responsibility for carrying it through. That man was Ernst Udet. The more clearly the war began to loom in the months that followed, the worse the problem looked to those running the Luftwaffe. They were not adequately prepared for a war, and certainly not for a conflict with Britain. A demonstration of the Luftwaffe's strength was planned, which was intended to show the Führer the difficulties they faced, without actually 'leaving him with a negative impression'. After that he would be certain to allocate bigger quotas of raw materials to the Luftwaffe. On 3 July 1939 the airmen showed their Führer what they had achieved. Hitler was impressed – and considered that the Luftwaffe was sufficiently well equipped.

Udet seems not have seen the dark clouds that were gathering over him. If anything, he had become even more insouciant. His journal, a collection of witty caricatures, which he used to give to friends at the turn of the year, is evidence of his cheerful mood on New Year's Eve 1938. During the year he had drawn the 'Dream of a Department-Head'. This time it showed Göring looking up at gigantic fleets of aircraft, the magician 'Koppenbergini' pulling an armada of Ju-88s out of a top hat and himself – in what was probably his most telling self-portrait – standing on a ladder and reaching for a star in the sky.

In the early hours of 1 September 1939, as German troops crossed the Polish frontier, Ernst Udet was enjoying a wild party with his woman-friend Inge Bleyle, and Ernst Heinkel and his wife. Wearing a Red Indian headdress Udet was blasting away with a pistol at the target on his wall. Heinkel later recalled the riotous atmosphere. Someone happened to turn on the radio: '. . . Since 5.45 a.m. there has been a return of fire.' Udet removed his headdress and said in a toneless voice: 'So . . . he's really done it.'

German forces overran the Polish opposition like a steamroller. Göring was jubilant: 'And what the Luftwaffe has promised in Poland, the Luftwaffe will deliver in Britain and France', he boasted in the heady euphoria of victory.

On 10 May 1940 the German armies stormed into western Europe. And once again they 'proved their worth'. On 22 June, at Göring's invitation, Udet attended the signing of the French surrender in the historic railway carriage at Compiègne. As Göring had prophesied in 1918, their 'hour' had come.

Arm in arm, Udet and Milch sauntered down the Champs Elysées, with red flying scarves slung around their necks, and drank a toast to victory. Again Hitler showered his warriors with decorations and honours. For 'outstanding services in building up the Luftwaffe' Udet was promoted to *Generaloberst*, full general. His mentor Göring now wore the insignia of the highest of all fantasy ranks: *Reichsmarschall*.

Now, 'all' they had to do was wrestle Britain to the ground. This would turn out to reveal the true weakness of the German Luftwaffe. It had been equipped for the *Blitzkrieg*, not for a battle against the Royal Air Force. At Dunkirk on 4 June 1940 the Luftwaffe experienced its first débâcle. The British Expeditionary Force escaped across the Channel almost intact. Yet Göring still gloated: 'We've done it. The Luftwaffe is wiping out the British on the beaches.' In company with Udet and Bruno Loerzer, the Reich Marshal flew off to raid the art and antique treasures of The Hague and Amsterdam. 'There are nothing but fishing-smacks coming over. I hope those Tommies are good swimmers', he crowed while on a flying visit to the Führer's military HQ. By the end of the evacuation on 4 June, over 338,000 British and French troops had left Dunkirk by sea.

Six weeks later, from his country estate, Karinhall, the Reich Marshal announced the intensification of attacks on Britain and the total destruction of the RAF. Five weeks, he prophesied, was all the Luftwaffe needed to achieve 'aerial supremacy' over Britain, in order to make possible 'Operation Sea-lion', the invasion of the British Isles. When one of those present hesitantly drew attention to the considerable strength of the RAF, Göring cut him off brusquely: 'Even if the British aircraft are as good and as numerous as they say, if I were Churchill I would have my air-force chief shot for incompetence.' Udet, who was standing near by with a drink or two inside him, was enjoying himself hugely and emphasised his boss's tub-thumping with a throat-cutting gesture.

On 13 May 1940, the so-called *Adlertag*, or 'Day of the Eagle', there began a decisive baptism of fire for the Luftwaffe, which up to that date had had things pretty easy. But Britain's Fighter Command gave as good as they got. In the breathing space allowed them, they had grown into an opponent that was fully a match for the Germans. The dream of an invincible Luftwaffe was shattered by the shells of Britain's air defences.

Even the massive bombing raids on London failed to produce the desired result. Though devastating in their effect, the principal aim of demoralising the enemy was never achieved. Quite the reverse – for when, in August 1940, the first British bombers appeared in the skies above Berlin, Göring suffered a painful loss of prestige. His name would be 'Meier', he had boasted, if a single enemy plane were sighted over Germany. From now on he was dubbed 'Hermann Meier' by a sardonic population. The damage inflicted by British air raids was as yet slight, but it gave a foretaste of the devastating saturation bombing that was to come.

The Luftwaffe's losses over Britain were catastrophic. By October 1940 it had lost 1,700 aircraft, more than twice the losses sustained by the RAF. Putting 'Operation Sea-lion' (the planned invasion of Britain) into effect was no longer thinkable. In May 1941 Göring's bombers took off for their last major raid on London. Hitler put 'Sea-lion' on ice. He had long since turned his attention to new objectives: the 'conquest of living space in the east' – a manic dream whose horrifying reality Ernst Udet would not live to see.

Being hunted out of Britain's skies was the first blot on the escutcheon of Göring's Luftwaffe. For the preening Reich Marshal it was more than just a defeat in battle. It also meant the loss of Hitler's confidence in him. But Göring did not intend to be burdened with this disgrace himself; he needed a scapegoat. And Udet knew full well what that meant. He stayed away from Göring's meetings and hid behind sarcastic jibes. When a test-pilot named Warsitz urged further development work on Heinkel's newly invented jet propulsion, Udet's ironic riposte was: 'Warsitz, when will your lot grasp the fact that the war will be won in a year, and we won't need any more fighters!'

Indeed, it was not particularly difficult to present the Air Armourer-General with an array of his own erroneous decisions, especially those in the technical field. The Ju-88, which a year earlier he had seen as his salvation, was now under heavy criticism from the men who had to fly it. And this was grist to Milch's mill. 'The crews aren't afraid of the enemy, they're afraid of the Ju-88', he whispered to the Reich Marshal, who was now ever more willing to listen to criticism of his protégé Udet, and kept him on a tighter rein. In autumn 1940, from his grandiose fantasy-domain Karinhall, Göring ordered Udet to give up his bachelor pad in Berlin's Pommersche Strasse and move into a residence that befitted his status. This was a house in the Stallupöner Allee, part of a top people's enclave in Grunewald – clearly visible and kept under surveillance by Göring's 'Research Department', the bugging-centre of the Third Reich. The house was to be Udet's last home. He never liked it. On first arriving, he noticed a small crucifix in the iron grille of the front door, and announced loudly: 'I'm not going in *there*, there's a cross on the door!'

Two days after moving in he collapsed, and on being taken to hospital he was found to have suffered a haemorrhage. Udet's state of health had deteriorated hugely. Outwardly, he was scarcely recognisable. The once dashing pilot was now pale and puffy in the face, his hair unkempt. His eyes, which could once locate an enemy in a split second, now looked restless and vague. Udet's consumption of alcohol – already far beyond the capacity of a normal man – had increased sharply. To make matters worse, for some time now he had sought salvation in a new drug called Pervitin. The medication was a pure 'upper', which was increasingly being used as an all-purpose stimulant for exhausted front-line troops, since it reduced their natural sleep requirements to an absolute minimum.

Udet needed it for his personal battle – with his rivals and with himself. Under the influence of Pervitin he was cheerful, talkative and self-confident. People who saw him at the time say he took the drug by the handful, even though the normal dosage was only 3 milligrams. In the light of today's medical knowledge, we know that Pervitin abuse leads to persecution mania and to rapid swings between extreme euphoria and depression. Addicts report hearing voices and seeing mysterious, menacing figures. Ernst Udet was affected in this way. He told people he had seen dark figures with black hats. To him Erhard Milch appeared the incarnation of evil. As he muttered to Ernst Heinkel: 'They're all against me. "Ironsides" [Göring] has simply gone off on leave and left me alone with Milch. It's Milch who speaks for him in dealings with the Führer. And he'll make sure that every mistake I've ever made is put under the Führer's nose. I can't cope with all that. I can't stand this persecution.'

On a subsequent visit, Heinkel scarcely recognised his friend. Udet looked wan and jittery. 'Ironsides wants to shove me off to a sanatorium, but I'm not going.' Nevertheless, and obviously against his will, he was checked into the famous Bühler Höhe sanatorium in the Black Forest. On the journey down there, he stacked the back seat of his car with cartons of cigarettes and crate-loads of alcohol. The doctors could only keep him there a few days. Göring had sent him a telegram, which to Udet seemed like pure cynicism: 'Absolutely no need to worry about your job. Your excellent staff, especially General Ploch, will do whatever is necessary. In any case, have asked Milch to look after things as well.'

Milch, of all people! Udet got the message: 'Ironsides' was freezing him out and no longer made any secret of it.

Once more he pulled himself together and took on some of his office duties. At the end of the year he sketched his last journal, which was more eloquent than words: one of his drawings shows Erhard Milch, floating with little wings over a burning city. We see Udet's own figure trudging sadly through pouring rain to the Bühler Höhe sanatorium.

The year 1941 would offer no more than the chronicle of his downfall. His friends were concerned. In March, when Udet visited Bruno Loerzer in Amsterdam, he murmured resignedly: 'Bruno, I'm the wrong man for this job. They'll get me in the end. They'll need a scapegoat. But don't worry, I haven't given up yet. It's just that I sometimes get tired of playing games.'

A bomber-pilot, Werner Baumbach, recalled a discussion in Göring's office in March 1941: 'Towards the end of the meeting someone tapped me on the shoulder. It was *Generaloberst* Udet. . . . He told me jokingly that whatever the Reich Marshal was saying wasn't important. Wouldn't I and a few friends like to go round the corner and sit down with him? He then produced a bottle of brandy.'

Udet could now hardly bear to be alone. After trailing endlessly from one smoke-laden bar to the next, he implored his companions to come back home with him for a nightcap. And while his friends sat slumped, drunk and tired out, in armchairs, Udet would invoke the 'good old days' in rambling monologues. From time to time the guests would leap to their feet in terror, as their host fired wildly at a target on the wall. What was really happening to him was seldom discussed. As it was, his numerous 'best friends' knew little about him. Even the woman pilot, Elly Beinhorn, with whom he had flown for many years, was amazed when once, while playing with her small son, he suddenly confessed: 'I have a little daughter, you know. It's high time I made friends with her.'

'I'm nothing but a ghost in uniform', he sighed to his long-time mistress, Inge Bleyle. She was the one person able to lend a little stability to his life in those final months. Several times he had announced he would marry her, but he never kept his promises. She attempted to halt his accelerating decline, and reproached him for his heavy drinking. 'Inge, my love, people with worries drink. And I have worries.' It was then that he first talked about ending his life.

The intervals during which he could summon up the will to work became ever shorter. In April he handed Erhard Milch a study in which he used exaggerated arguments to prove that the war had to be ended by September – due to a shortage of aviation fuel. Milch filed the document in his waste-paper basket without further ado, and ordered Udet to pull himself together. It is true that in the spring months Udet's appointment diary shows frequent meetings with Göring, for instance regarding the 'delivery situation', but the fact was that he tried to divert the Reich Marshal on to other topics as rapidly as possible. The Advocate-General, Christian von Hammerstein, recalled later in an investigation by a military court: 'When he and Göring got together, they talked about old times. . . . Any discussion of service matters was scrupulous avoided.'

The newsreels were now showing, without censorship, what the former sunshine boy had turned into. At Emmy Göring's birthday party he just stared apathetically into space. His *Heil Hitler* salute went askew. That was how the hero was seen by the public. He was made to look a fool. During a situation conference in the summer of 1941, as the newsreel cameras were rolling, all his papers fell on the floor. He did not even notice.

Even the self-important aircraft designers, who were subject to increasing criticism for the endless delays in delivery, now abandoned him to his fate. On 13 March 1941 Messerschmitt wrote an angry letter to the planning department in the Air Armourer-General's division: 'I have gradually gained the impression that the greatest problems concerning the timely procurement of aircraft and equipment are due to the unplanned way the Ministry of Aviation works. I well remember the enormous number of times the programmes have been rescheduled. I would welcome it if you would try, once and for all, to remedy this absence of Ministry planning, to introduce a modicum of planning at least, and not to go on blaming the suppliers for things which the Ministry is solely responsible for.'

Yet Udet went on fighting his corner. Was it his fault that the Me-210 had not been technically developed even as a prototype? Or that the range of the Ju-88 was inadequate? Or that the engines of the He-177 kept bursting into flames?

In the end he adopted the tone of voice that he should have used long ago to discipline the aircraft manufacturers: 'There is one thing, my dear Messerschmitt, that we must be quite clear about. There can be no more losses of aircraft in normal landings, as a result of faulty undercarriages. These hardly rate as an innovation in aircraft design.' But who would now accept his authority? The reins had long since been in other hands.

> You now have to manufacture bombers. The war will continue.
> *Hitler to Göring, Milch and Udet*

After the launch of the Russian campaign in the summer of 1941, Göring demanded an immediate fourfold increase in the size of the Luftwaffe. The industrious Milch submitted a plan to the Reich Marshal, which, being well aware of his boss's vanity, he named the 'Göring Programme'. The plan vested sole authority for its execution in one person: Erhard Milch himself. This meant that Milch inherited the mantle of the Air Armourer-General even while Udet was still alive.

Ernst Udet was a broken man. One last time Inge Bleyle managed to persuade him to take a health cure. While he was away, Göring and Milch rearranged the furniture in the Reich Ministry of Aviation. Milch fired the head of the Technical Planning department, Tschersich, and replaced him by Carl August von Gablenz. Udet's friend of many years, *Generalmajor* Ploch, was forced to accept a posting to the Russian front.

The Air Armourer-General was left with nothing but his title. And even that he only held by Milch's good grace. He had been a puppet in Göring's hands, and Göring now cut the strings.

It was in October 1941 that the last crucial session at the Reich Ministry of Aviation took place with Ernst Udet present as Air Armourer-General. Fifty ministry staff sat in judgement on him. Fritz Seiler, the Finance Director of the Messerschmitt company, who had been wrong-footed by a rescheduling of production authorised by Udet, presented documents that proved Udet had taken his decision on the basis of falsified figures. Udet was horrified. He had not expected a frontal attack of this kind. He sensed with foreboding the real reason behind this formal meeting. In fact, Messerschmitt had telephoned Milch and provided him with the ammunition he needed in order to blow Udet out of the water at last. Messerschmitt, Milch and Göring had staged this final 'tribunal' together: 'It would have been more decent of you to warn me about it in advance', Udet stammered helplessly. 'It's like a game of chess, Herr Udet. I am merely making the second move', Seiler retorted coldly. Milch suggested that he and Udet should fly to Paris together 'for a few days' recuperation', in order, as he put it, to 'restore our amicable relations'. The smiling enemy was still keeping up the pretence. However, by the date fixed for the trip Ernst Udet was already dead.

On 16 November 1941 Erich Baier, Udet's mechanic from a happier era, telephoned him at home in the Stallupöner Allee. Wouldn't it be nice to meet up and talk about the old days? Ernst said he'd like that and asked his friend to fetch him in a taxi straight away. 'Strange that you should show up today of all days', he murmured pensively as he opened the door to Baier. As they lunched together it was almost like old times. Udet was calmer than he had been in recent days; he talked about Africa, about Greenland, about flying. After Baier had said goodbye, Udet turned to Inge Bleyle and said gloomily: 'He won't be back. I'll never see him again.' Then he broke down in a fit of sobbing. 'Today is our last day together. Tomorrow you'll be a widow.' Inge tried to calm him. The evening meal was served: roast duck, red cabbage and *Apfelstrudel*. 'Yesterday that poor duck was alive. That's what happens to a lot of people. One day they're alive, the next they're dead.' Udet was not to be deterred. 'I don't want to go on. I don't want to test another bomber and I don't want to see another newsreel.' Frau Bleyle persuaded him to accept an invitation to friends. 'Tomorrow you won't see Uncle any more', he sang to the children. He drove Inge to her house, and then headed for Tempelhof airfield. There Kurt Schnittke, whom Udet employed as a mechanic, was working on a new type of aircraft. To this day he can remember seeing Udet climb into his old Fh-104, his favourite aircraft. He took a bottle of brandy from the bar installed in it, and drank. As he said goodbye to Schnittke he pulled a piece of red chalk from the mechanic's breast pocket and took it with him.

The next morning Inge Bleyle woke with a start when she heard the phone ring. She picked it up. It was Udet. They must have breakfast together, she insisted. 'No, don't come. It's too late. My dearest Inge, there's no one I've loved more than you. Tell Pilli

Körner [a colleague at the Ministry] he'll find my will in the cupboard.' Then Inge heard the shot.

In the Stallupöner Allee, the housekeepers, Herr Peters and his wife, leapt up from the breakfast table. They dashed upstairs to Udet's bedroom and found the door locked. 'What were we to do?' Herr Peters recalls. '"Open the door! Open the door!", we shouted. Then we forced our way in and he was lying there . . .' Ernst Udet lay on the bed in his dressing gown, covered in blood. In his hand he still held the Mexican Colt revolver with which he had shot himself in the head. All around him was a shambles of brandy bottles and papers.

Soon Inge Bleyle arrived. Frau Peters shook her head. 'He wasn't alive; we just heard the death rattle.' Things now began to happen very fast. Udet's adjutant, *Oberst* Pendele, appeared with a doctor. A Permanent Secretary from the ministry, Paul ('Pilli') Körner, burst in, and it was probably he who first noticed the words written in red chalk above the bedhead. 'Ironsides, you betrayed me!' The men frantically wiped the writing off the wall and collected the pieces of paper scattered all over the room. They swore to say nothing.

The meaning of Ernst Udet's last words could never really be explained, which was why they gave rise to so much speculation. There was talk of Milch and Gablenz being 'Jews'; and he is said to have accused his mistress: 'Inge, why did you forsake me?' Obscene insults, scribbled on the bed and the walls, had to be hastily removed. Udet had ended his life in a state of confusion and left those closest to him with feelings of guilt. But, the fact was that he had been destroyed by himself and by his times.

Unlike Harras, the pilot hero of *The Devil's General*, Udet played no part in the anti-Hitler resistance. His aversion to the criminal regime went no further than corny jokes told at dinner in the officers' mess. But behind the comedian's mask he concealed a revulsion against discipline and conformity. The military historian Horst Boog calls Udet 'Hermann Göring's most famous failure in appointing men to jobs'. Udet was the wrong man in the wrong place. And yet Göring had taken him on – voluntarily – and defended him to the last. Udet was Hitler's warrior in building up and equipping the Luftwaffe, in the *Blitzkrieg* campaigns of 1939 and 1940, and in the Battle of Britain. However his most important role had been in the propaganda war. He was the carefree flyer, whose portrait was collected by children on cigarette-cards, whom their mothers swooned over and whose daredevil courage their fathers admired. His popularity had been his fortune, and it became his downfall. He had no noble or conscience-driven sentiments, as Harras had. If Udet saw the way the regime was heading, he certainly gave his friends no indication of it. He hid the failure of his personal and professional life, and perhaps his political doubts too, behind the mask of a genial drinker. But he became so physically and mentally raddled by liquor that he saw no other way out than this theatrical exit from a stage that he had chosen for himself.

He was no longer capable of defending himself against the flood of accusations which engulfed his name after his death. In Udet Hitler and Göring had found the perfect scapegoat, someone on whom they could unload any criticism about the shortcomings in the expansion of the Luftwaffe. A military tribunal placed the entire responsibility for the 'tragedy' of the Luftwaffe on his shoulders. The Führer shed few tears over the loss to his propaganda machine of this emblematic figure: 'He took such an easy way out', was the verdict, a year after Udet's death, from the man who committed suicide on 30 April 1945, and thus tried to abdicate all responsibility for the catastrophe which he himself had invoked.

'Never been anything but a pilot', Harras had said of himself. Ernst Udet did become more, through a willing allegiance to Nazism, even though he had wanted to remain just that: a pilot and nothing else.

And the man who succeeded him as Air Armourer-General was Erhard Milch.

While test-flying a new warplane. That's right. State funeral.
The last line of The Devil's General, *by Carl Zuckmayer*

CHAPTER SIX

The Conspirator – Wilhelm Canaris

The man who is a good soldier will also be – whether he admits it or not – a good National Socialist

Anyone who mistreats animals cannot be a good human being

I cannot be a part of this any longer. We will not let ourselves be used to circulate tales of horror

The hour has come to draw attention to the Abwehr by great new deeds

A war that is waged with total disregard of any kind of ethics, can never be won. There really is a divine justice on earth

Wilhelm Canaris

———————————— * ————————————

Canaris always took trouble to maintain a particularly good relationship with Himmler and Heydrich, so that they would not be suspicious of him.

Alfred Jodl

. . . during his time in the navy, he was an officer who inspired little trust. He was a very different kind of person to us. We used to say he had seven souls in his breast . . .

Karl Dönitz

On first meeting him, Canaris was a disappointment. He looked old, tired and war-weary. His hair was almost white, and he was shabbily dressed. Though little more than 5 ft 3 ins tall he nonetheless walked with a stoop.

Walter Huppenkothen, SS Standartenführer

In my view Canaris demonstrated, by the way he built up his organisation, that he was not – as legend often claims – an inscrutable secret service genius, but a typical German officer, who imposes military structures on everything, and furthermore was a typical German of his age, with an unmistakable leaning towards large-scale organisations. Under him, the Abwehr (military intelligence) became a gigantic bureaucracy, which employed more desk-bound officials than agents.

Werner Best, SS Obergruppenführer

He could be as childish as a schoolboy, though he often refrained from acting that way. He could pull faces, which made the smile freeze on the lips of ramrod-straight uniformed officers, and he would secretly derive great amusement from this kind of paralysing embarrassment. I can still see the crafty look in his blue eyes when the Devil was in him. But all this likeable mischief disappeared under the oppressive gravity of events, and often broke out in downright grotesque fits of caustic moodiness.

Otto Wagner

Canaris was a person of pure intellect, a man who in his fascinating, very strange and complicated nature hated violence in itself and therefore detested war, Hitler, his system and his methods.

Erwin Lahousen, head of the sabotage section of the Abwehr's foreign department

The whole Canaris stable laid themselves open to attack and really did not come up to the expectations that we had of them.

If the 'good men' are not as clever as snakes as well as being totally genuine, then nothing can be achieved.

Ulrich von Hassell, German ambassador in Rome and opponent of Hitler

Canaris kept on letting my husband know that he had gone to the limits of what was possible; that his political position was no longer strong enough for him to thump the table. To the very end my husband held a different view.

Christine von Dohnanyi, widow of anti-Nazi resister Hans von Dohnanyi

I have seldom met a man who had such a precise sense of the way things were heading. As a rule he was so stunned by the unreality of it all that he was unable to show any outward reaction.

Hans Bernd Gisevius, Abwehr foreign section

On one hand he was an ardent German patriot, willing to do anything for his country, but on the other he was also a self-centred man who said to himself: if I play along then I'll safeguard my position.

Wilhelm Höttl, SS Obersturmbannführer

I believe Canaris suffered appallingly, right through the war years. That's why he travelled so much. And grew so restless; he really never found any peace again. He would suddenly disappear. For a whole week. And then suddenly he was back again.

Reinhard Spitzy, on the staff of the Abwehr's foreign section

It was Canaris, in his position and with the activities of his department, who made the whole resistance to Hitler possible in the first place.

Prof. Dr Eberhard Bethge, Abwehr foreign section

———————————— * ————————————

In the grey light of dawn the prisoners were roused from their sleep by the barking of guard dogs. The courtyard of the Flossenbürg concentration camp was flooded with the glare of searchlights. The bark of orders and hurried tramp of boots echoed through the barracks. Colonel Hans Lunding, a former secret service officer from Denmark, heard the lock of Cell 22 being opened right next door to him. 'Out you come!' Handcuffs and ankle-irons fell to the floor with a clatter. Through a chink in the door he took a last look at the man from the neighbouring cell, who had been brought to the camp only two months previously. The diminutive man with the snow-white hair was deathly pale. He knew what was coming. The evening before, he had sent a last message to Lunding by tapping in Morse code on the wall between them: 'My time is up. Was never a traitor. Did my duty as a German.' A short time later the Dane heard someone give the order: 'Everyone undress!' As the first of five condemned men, the prisoner from Cell 22 was led into the courtyard – naked. Despite the humiliation he was calm and self-possessed. An SS man, who had been one of the eager spectators at the hideous ceremony, stated later that the death agony had 'gone on a very long time. He had to be hauled up and down several times.'

On that day, 9 April 1945, thousands more were to lose their lives. In the east the 'fortress' of Königsberg fell to the Russians, while in the west the battle for the industrial Ruhr district raged. American tanks had almost reached the Elbe. In Flossenbürg and many other death camps countless men and women were still dying on the gallows and in front of firing squads, through systematic malnutrition and in the gas chambers. The perpetrators were getting rid of witnesses. This was particularly true of the five killings that dawn in Flossenbürg. Hitler had ordered them in one of his fits of insane rage. In this way he dragged with him to destruction a man whom he had long admired. A man who applied as much ingenuity to waging war on behalf of the tyrant as he did to wresting himself and Germany free from the same tyrant: the secret service chief of the Third Reich – Wilhelm Canaris.

Scarcely any leading figure in Hitler's dictatorship has been the subject of such differing verdicts as the 'little admiral'. And after the war, none was so revered and at the same time so reviled as he was. Was he really the 'traitor', who 'sent many thousands of German servicemen to their death', as one of his early biographers believed? Or was he primarily Hitler's efficient henchman, as a more recent judgement has it, 'fettered to the regime by innumerable bonds'? Was he, as the CIA chief, Allen Dulles, considered, a 'brilliant manager' of his secret service network, or, a 'dilettante' - the derisive term applied to him by the former head of the postwar Federal German intelligence service, Reinhard Gehlen. (He also described the Abwehr as 'The Canaris Family Company Limited'.) Was he really the 'patron and leading mind of the anti-Nazi resistance', as the veterans' association of his former staff still like to see him, or did he always remain a ditherer, 'a man who never found a way to freedom of action'? Was he Hitler's henchman or his adversary? Or was he both at the same time?

What is beyond dispute is that Canaris and his colleague Hans von Dohnanyi used the resources of the secret service to enable Jews and other victims of persecution to escape to neutral countries. Many hundreds were rescued from certain death. A number of them petitioned the Israeli Holocaust memorial body, Yad Vashem, to honour their rescuer Dohnanyi as a representative of the 'just men among nations'. The petition was refused. Such figures as Dohnanyi seemed too ambivalent to merit such an honour. No military barracks in Germany bears the name of Admiral Canaris. He never rated as a hero, either at the peak of his fame as the Third Reich's secret service boss or in the postwar era of Chancellor Adenauer, when members of the anti-Nazi resistance were held up as paragons of virtue. Even in the celebrated feature film about Canaris, with the actor O.E. Hasse (who bore an uncanny physical resemblance to Canaris) in the leading role, the tragic element prevailed over the heroic. As his biographer Heinz Höhne summed it up: the path taken by this man was too tortuous; too much 'twilight' surrounded him for him ever to be a paragon of virtue.

When, on his 48th birthday, 1 January 1935, Wilhelm Canaris was appointed head of Germany's military intelligence, he had already served as an officer for three decades. He had sworn three oaths of allegiance: to the Kaiser, to the Republic and to the Führer. He had lived through the bright peaks and gloomy troughs of German military glory, had narrowly escaped death several times and believed that, with his posting as commander of the naval base in the small Baltic town of Swinemünde, he had reached the top of his particular career ladder. He was married, had two school-age daughters, and was known to be a dedicated horseman and talented amateur cook. Canaris had only a vague idea why he, of all people, should be taking over the boss's office in the annexe to the Reich Defence Ministry building, as head of that small department which, after the abstinence imposed by the Treaty of Versailles, was now to revive the tradition of a military intelligence service. The dark corridors of the building on the Tirpitzufer were very familiar to him. It was here that, as adjutant to the republic's first Army minister, Gustav Noske, he had cultivated contacts with the illegal *Freikorps* militia, at the end of the First World War. He still had warm memories of the 'good old days', fighting against the 'Reds'. As a former naval officer he also knew, of course, that it was in this building that the Kaiser's admiral, Alfred von Tirpitz, had pursued his master's dream of steel hulls and sea-power – that nationalistic obsession, which gripped the young Canaris too, and led him, against the will of his family, to don the uniform of the Imperial Navy.

It had all started with Tirpitz. The flood of pro-navy newspaper articles, leaflets and brochures, directed and paid for by the Navy Office, had attracted the attention of many young men, including the Duisburg high school student, Wilhelm Canaris. Soon, all he wanted was to serve the Fatherland at sea. However, his father, a well-to-do businessman in the steel industry of the booming Ruhr district, would have much preferred to see his youngest son join the cavalry. But then the paterfamilias died suddenly from a stroke and Wilhelm was free to go his own way. On 1 April 1905 he became a cadet in the Kaiser's navy. Despite a somewhat puny physique, he rapidly made a career for himself. In 1908 his first commanding officer said of him: 'He promises to become a good officer, as soon as he has gained more confidence and self-assurance.' When the First World War broke out Canaris was serving as a lieutenant on the cruiser *Dresden*, operating in the South Atlantic. On 31 August 1914 the ship received a radio message from the German admiralty: 'Wage a cruiser war in accordance with the requirements of mobilisation.' Everyone on board knew that this order was tantamount to certain destruction: they would be making war on merchant shipping in the face of the British Royal Navy, the most powerful fleet in the world – and, to make matters worse, Germany lacked any naval bases in the South Atlantic. Tirpitz's expansion of the German battle-fleet now brought devastating consequences: the Imperial Navy was too large to be Britannia's friend, yet still far too small to be able to defeat her. On 14 March 1915 the voyage of the *Dresden* ended in the harbour of the small Chilean island of Más a Tierra in the South Pacific. After a brief engagement with the British cruiser *Glasgow*, the ship had lost steerage way and caught fire. The navy's code of honour left only one choice: to scuttle the *Dresden*. To gain time, the German captain despatched his linguistically gifted lieutenant in a bid to hold spurious negotiations with the British. It was the first of many diplomatic missions in the career of Wilhelm Canaris.

Arriving on board HMS *Glasgow*, the envoy was given short shrift. There was nothing to negotiate about, he was told. When he protested that the *Dresden* was lying in the territorial waters of a neutral state, and that the British attack was thus an infringement of international law, the British captain replied coldly that he had orders to sink the *Dresden*. Any other matters 'can be settled by the diplomats afterwards'. Canaris had to leave the *Glasgow* again. But he had gained crucial time for the detonating squad on board his vessel. At 11.15 a.m. a massive explosion shattered the silence in the bay of Más a Tierra. The crew, who had gone ashore, saluted the *Dresden* for the last time; then the officers and men were interned by the Chilean authorities. Most of the crew members thought themselves very lucky to be able to sit out the rest of the war, well looked after and with their feet on terra firma. But not Canaris. Before the month was out, he seized the first available opportunity to escape from the lightly guarded camp. This was the first example of the restlessness that would drive him on for the rest of his life – an inward rebellion against the constraints of his situation. After all, he had not become a naval officer simply to sit on dry land, at the moment when his distant homeland was engaged in a titanic struggle. However, the greatest obstacle still lay ahead of him: in the depths of the South American winter he had to cross the Andes, from neutral Chile to the still pro-German country of Argentina. It was a daring enterprise. Countless other fugitives had simply disappeared in the high mountains. Yet Canaris made it. The young officer's slight frame seemed to contain an energy which at first sight was hidden from observers.

I would recommend employing him firstly on assignments requiring sharp powers of observation and diplomatic skill, but also in posts where his great intellectual abilities come to the fore, provided his sceptical nature, born of some far from ordinary experiences, does not influence too large a circle of people.

Assessment of Canaris by Konteradmiral *Bastian*

The German Admiralty rewarded this determination to succeed by promoting him to *Kapitänleutnant* (lieutenant-commander). Canaris was then posted to Spain. His assignment was to build up a supply network for German submarines in that neutral country. The naval officer now called himself 'Señor Kika' and began establishing contacts with all manner of trustworthy and not so trustworthy Spanish gentlemen, who all had one thing in common: an interest in the illegal funds provided by the German Admiralty. This may not have been exactly a mission on the 'battlefield of honour', yet the risky game appealed to Canaris. At the age of 28, a new world was opening up for him. Even as a child he had played with invisible ink and thought up code-names for himself. Now he was plunged into the 'dirty tricks' of the secret services. A delight in disguise and the double game would never leave him throughout his life.

'Señor Kika' did indeed manage to organise supplies for German U-boats off the coast of Spain. The 'sea-wolves' usually appeared at dusk in remote bays and took on board ammunition, provisions and fuel from supply-vessels disguised as fishing-boats. As a result of this, the murderous war on cargo and passenger shipping was extended – thanks mainly to Canaris – to the western reaches of the Mediterranean. Yet very soon he displayed that other trait in his character, which later, in times of the greatest danger, would become dominant. Now that his assignment had been completed, the talented secret service man began to get restless in Spain. To friends he seemed like an outcast, like someone always on his way to somewhere else.

Early in 1916 the German navy showed some understanding for his plight. Canaris received orders to join a torpedo-boat in Kiel; at last he would see real action again. But how was he to get home from Spain? The safe way, waiting for a U-boat to take him across the Mediterranean to the Adriatic, would have taken too long. Instead he slipped into a new disguise: as a Chilean named 'Reed Rosa', supposedly suffering from tuberculosis and on his way to a sanatorium in Switzerland. Canaris planned to travel through France and northern Italy, the heart of enemy territory, but this time his camouflage let him down. A few miles short of the Swiss frontier he was arrested by Italian police. Very soon Canaris was in prison in Genoa.

What happened next has become the stuff of legend. All that is certain is that, in the middle of March 1916, Wilhelm Canaris reappeared in Madrid, a free man. How did he manage it? One version of events in the Genoese jail maintains that Canaris was condemned to death; then, when a priest came to prepare him for execution, Canaris cold-bloodedly despatched him to eternity, donned his soutane and made his escape. Other biographers believe that the Italians simply released him for lack of evidence. Whatever the truth, Canaris later gave a naval doctor some clues about 'maltreatment' and 'escape', but that was the only light he shed on this murky episode in his career – another example of how carefully he cultivated the myth of his early years.

After failing to pass himself off as 'Reed Rosa', the young hothead finally succeeded in returning to Germany later in 1916, this time in a U-boat. During the last two years of the war he rapidly ascended the career ladder in the Imperial Navy, and by the end of hostilities was himself in command of a U-boat, with a considerable score of 'kills' to his credit: three enemy vessels sunk and another severely damaged. Even His Majesty the Kaiser had begun to notice him.

> He was known as 'the little Levantine'! Of course, it was only a nickname of the kind that often gets used in the officers' mess. But it wasn't so far off the mark. Wilhelm Canaris did have a generous dash of mischief in his many-sided nature.
>
> *Otto Wagner, a naval colleague of Canaris*
>
> He was small, looked at you with wide innocent eyes and enjoyed being able to catch people out.
>
> *Reinhard Spitzy, a member of Canaris' Abwehr staff*

But then defeat and revolution turned the war-hero into a politicised officer, who kept reappearing like a will-o'-the-wisp along the fault-lines between armed forces and government, and thus earned himself a certain notoriety. In 1928, left-wing newspapers like the *Weltbühne* published 'spicy revelations' about the murder in 1919 of the communist leaders Rosa Luxemburg and Karl Liebknecht, and about the trial that followed.* No very clear picture emerged from the jumble of accusations and denials, but the suspicion that Canaris had had something to do with the killings clung to him – not without justification. It is true that, on the night of 15 January

---

* In early January 1919 there had been violent demonstrations by workers in Berlin, the 'Spartacists', against the elected Social-Democrat government. The Marxist Rosa Luxemburg urged moderate reform but the more hotheaded Liebknecht called for armed revolution. However, by 11 January the army had quelled the riots and the murder of the two leaders four days later was quite gratuitous.

1919, when soldiers murdered the two communists, Canaris was not in Berlin, but the part he played in the judicial examination of the case revealed his unparalleled grasp of the legal detail.

In the weeks following the end of the war Canaris had found a new home in the *Freikorps*. Under the banner of a struggle against the supposed danger of communism, these units made up of disillusioned battle-front troops were covering Germany with a broad trail of blood. Men of the 'Cavalry Guard Rifle Division', a formation well known for their extremism, acting on the orders of their commanding officer *Hauptmann* Waldemar Pabst, had arrested Luxemburg and Liebknecht and then murdered them. The Army Minister, Noske, hesitated to take any action, but under pressure from Social-Democrat members of parliament he eventually opened court martial proceedings against the principal defendant, *Oberleutnant* Kurt Vogel. However, Pabst succeeded in sneaking Canaris in as an assessor on the tribunal. Thus the poacher had been made a gamekeeper, for, like most *Freikorps* fighters, Canaris considered the murder of 'Red Rosa' and her colleague a legitimate act of war, rather than a crime.

As one of the judges, he now did everything possible to conceal the true background, with striking success. In the end Vogel received a prison sentence of only two years and four months for 'abuse of force in the course of duty and disposal of bodies'. By contrast, the man really responsible, his superior officer Pabst, continued to enjoy his liberty; and even under the Federal Republic, forty years later, still remained unpunished, bombastically claiming that by issuing the murder order he had saved Germany from 'a communist victory' which would have 'brought down the entire Christian west'. However, 'Judge' Canaris was still not satisfied with the mild sentence on Vogel. On 17 May 1919 a certain *Oberleutnant* Lindemann appeared at Berlin's Moabit prison and presented a written order for the transfer of prisoner Vogel to another jail. Minutes later the murderer of Luxemburg and Liebknecht had disappeared with the sinister lieutenant. Not until the next day did it transpire that 'Lindemann' was none other than Canaris; his identity papers and the supposed transfer order were all forgeries.

The 'judge' had released from detention the very man he had sentenced! Such a degree of energy in bending the law quickly earned Canaris the reputation as a man for special situations.

> He was pleased that a bit of a myth had grown up around him . . . he liked to act a bit mysterious. I think he rather enjoyed that.
>
> *Wilhelm Höttl, SS* Obersturmbannführer
>
> The myth of the 'Levantine' who came from the Navy has certainly contributed, and will continue to reinforce the aura of mystery around Canaris.
>
> *Werner Best, SS* Obergruppenführer

He received no punishment for what he did; instead, Army Minister Noske recruited him to his personal staff for liaison duties – something which would come back to haunt the minister. In the spring of 1920 Noske put his faith in information from Canaris, to the effect that the army did not pose any acute threat to the government. As a result of this the coup led by an army officer, General von Lüttwitz, came as a complete surprise.* The coup failed within only a few days due to a general strike; yet the Army Minister was forced to resign, not realising that his adjutant had taken the side of the conspirators. In almost any other country in the world an officer who had made a fool of his boss would surely, at the very least, have been dismissed immediately. Yet Canaris was acquitted by a commission of enquiry and merely transferred from Berlin to Kiel. Later, one of his superior officers, Admiral von Gagern, even wrote approvingly of him that his 'objective and accurate judgement of political events' was 'worthy of special note'. The first democracy to take root in German soil had thus proved too weak to demand the army's genuine loyalty to the constitution.

---

* In March 1920, Wolfgang Kapp, a civil servant, and General Walther von Lüttwitz staged a *coup d'état* against the left-wing government, which fled from Berlin to Dresden, and then to Stuttgart. The workers supported the elected government by mounting a nationwide strike. The coup petered out, but not before forcing the appointment of a new and more right-wing cabinet.

In 1935, after the long, terminal sickness of Weimar democracy had come to an end, the former rendering of such 'services' was of course an excellent recommendation for any candidate for the post of head of the secret service. Furthermore, Canaris' demonstration of support for the new men in power had already attracted attention. Only two months before his appointment as head of the secret service, his commanding officer wrote glowingly: 'I must emphasise the tireless efforts of *Kapitän-zur-See* Canaris in giving personal lectures to familiarise his crew with the philosophy of the national movement, and the principles of the governmental structure of the new Reich. His work in this field has been exemplary.' Even though numerous biographers, benevolently concerned about his reputation, are unwilling to accept it, Canaris at least began his rise in the Third Reich as a Nazi sympathiser. 'Almost all of us went along with it', admits Otto Wagner, an old naval colleague of Canaris.

> If I want to explain the National Socialist attitude of the Wehrmacht officer, then I must focus principally on the wonderfully clear-cut development of the German army, which had its origins in a great deed of National Socialism and has recently seen its completion in a National Socialist revolution. . . . Just as before the First World War an officer was naturally a monarchist, and just as after the war he was naturally anxious to preserve the heritage of front-line experiences, so today, when all our front-line experience has been found in the realisation of the National Socialist state, it is natural to be a National Socialist. And as servicemen we are happy to be able to confess to its political ideology, which is a profoundly military one.
>
> *Canaris in a lecture given in Vienna on 22 April 1938*

As well as his secret service experience from the First World War and his requisite political 'attitude', there was in fact a third reason for selecting Canaris: his acquaintance with Reinhard Heydrich. In 1923 they had been in the navy together on the training-cruiser *Berlin*, and Heydrich, then junior to Canaris as a cadet, was now head of the 'Security Service of the *Reichsführer*-SS' (the SD), which made him one of the new strongmen of the Reich. Because of his ambition to build up an all-powerful surveillance apparatus, there had been frequent turf wars between him and Canaris' predecessor, *Fregattenkapitän* Conrad Patzig. Patzig had stubbornly defended the monopoly his office held in domestic counter-espionage; and to make matters worse had provoked Heydrich's hostility by describing the SS as a 'pigsty'. Department heads of this kind were of no use to the new Army Minister, Blomberg, whose motto was to 'lead the army into the new state' as silently as possible. Patzig had to go. Blomberg hoped that Canaris would finally achieve friction-free collaboration with 'the men in black', as the SS were known, and the shared naval past could only be useful here. When the new department chief paid a courtesy call on the departing Patzig, he made the required statement that he had no time for the endless bickering with Heydrich. Patzig replied by describing the dangers he perceived in the burgeoning 'Führer state'. Canaris countered coolly: 'Don't you worry, I'll soon deal with these lads.' Patzig took his leave with dark forebodings.

. . . craftier than Himmler and Heydrich put together.
Hans Bernd Gisevius, staff member of the Abwehr's foreign division

---

Canaris' first official acts at his headquarters on the Tirpitzufer certainly gave no reason to suppose that a leading figure in the resistance was in the making. 'Thoroughly old and worn out', was how the new boss appeared to one staff member. The shabby naval jacket, the stooping walk and 'sloppy style' came as a disappointment. Added to this were the Nazi slogans, which Canaris, unlike the combative Patzig, was able to recite like mantras. 'The officer must exemplify National Socialism in his life', he lectured his group heads, and warned that 'non-political conduct in the National Socialist state is sabotage and a crime'. In his dealings with the SD and Gestapo he demanded, as a matter of duty, 'comradely co-operation'.

He himself set a good example by seeking to get close to Heydrich. Soon the two men renewed their acquaintance in private life. The two families relaxed together playing croquet in the Heydrichs' garden. Canaris' wife Erika, an excellent violinist, found an enthusiastic second fiddle in the SD chief. From time to time the totally unmusical Canaris donned his chef's hat and prepared culinary delights for the musicians. His speciality was herring salad with caviar and brandy, and his stuffed pork fillets were said to be particularly good. Even later on, when relations between the Abwehr and the SS were becoming increasingly strained, the two chiefs continued to cultivate their friendship. When the Canaris family moved to the leafy Berlin suburb of Schlachtensee, the Heydrichs took a property that could be reached through the garden of the Abwehr boss. The two neighbours regularly went riding together, which gave them the opportunity to discuss sensitive subjects on an unofficial basis.

> It was usual for breakfast meetings between Heydrich and Canaris to take place every few weeks.
>
> *Walter Huppenkothen, SS* Standartenführer
>
> Each knew what the other thought of him, and so both behaved in a very, very friendly manner. That's to say, they were putting on a show of friendship.
>
> *Wilhelm Höttl, SS* Obersturmbannführer

Canaris soon sensed that the ambitious Heydrich would have preferred to incorporate the whole Abwehr into the rampantly expanding structure of the SD, and he guessed that the balance of power in Germany would shift more and more in favour of the 'men in black'. Head-on resistance of the kind practised by Patzig seemed to hold out little promise in the long run. The new Abwehr chief banked on a *rapprochement*. He struck a deal with the competition and encouraged his staff to work actively with their 'comrades'. In this way he gradually succeeded in securing space in which to expand his Abwehr undisturbed. For that was his only objective in the early years of his office: the establishment of an effectively functioning military intelligence service. As Werner Best, for a long time the SD chief's right-hand man, recalls: 'His duel with Heydrich was a battle *for* the National Socialist state, not against it.'

It was a strange relationship that linked two men who were outwardly so completely different – a sort of mutual love-hate. In his diary Canaris noted, after his first encounter with his erstwhile shipmate, that he would probably never be able to co-operate on a frank and open basis with Heydrich, since the latter had become a 'brutal fanatic'. Heydrich, for his part, warned his staff insistently that his Schlachtensee neighbour was an 'old fox, whom you have to be wary of'. In contrast to this, though, we have the recollection of Heydrich's wife Lina, who claimed that Canaris often remarked to her that he regarded her husband 'almost as something like a son'.

Is it possible that all the hours spent together were no more than a cunning double game by the Abwehr boss, in order to eavesdrop on Heydrich in private – as the guardians of the Canaris legend believe? No, Canaris probably did have a 'weakness' for this tall, blond man with a Mongolian slant to his eyes. Perhaps he recognised something of himself in Heydrich's razor-sharp intelligence, which always distanced him from others. Occasionally, both men revealed a soft, sensitive side, which contrasted oddly with the demands of their professional work. Both shared a passion for deception, tricks and feints: it is no coincidence that the SD chief's favourite sport was fencing, with its subtle interplay of action and reaction, of attack and parry. If the two secret service gentlemen discussed business on their early morning rides, then this no doubt sometimes came close to a verbal swordfight.

> They played music together, they saw a lot of each other and each one was eavesdropping on the other.
>
> *Reinhard Spitzy, member of the Abwehr's foreign division*

Furthermore, according to Walter Schellenberg, who in the war years became the new strongman in Himmler's secret service,

Canaris and Heydrich both held such mutually incriminating evidence that neither could make a move against the other without putting himself at risk. According to Schellenberg, the Abwehr boss possessed documents about his rival's 'non-Aryan' grandmother, while Heydrich assiduously gathered material evidence on resistance members in his adversary's department. Thus the hours they spent together were now tinged with fear. Even when Canaris had long since turned into a bitter opponent of the regime and knew in detail that Heydrich was personally responsible for mass murder, the old affection did not fade completely. Canaris spent New Year's Eve 1941 at Heydrich's Stolpshof hunting estate, and at Heydrich's funeral in 1942 – he had been assassinated by Czech resistance fighters – the tears in Canaris' eyes were probably genuine.

The first stocktaking proved disappointing for the new chief. When he took up the job in the 'fox-earth', as the Abwehr building on the Tirpitzufer was called, in an allusion to its many corridors and dark corners, Canaris found a disorganised and ineffective 'heap'. Division I, under *Oberst* Piekenbrock, responsible for obtaining intelligence abroad and thus in effect the core of the espionage organisation, consisted of only a handful of agents, who were anything but fruitful sources. Canaris put things right and upgraded the Abwehr: within a short time the department had sufficient financial resources to recruit an army of contacts and agents, who were able to keep Berlin informed about foreign defence projects or troop movements. The boss involved himself personally in everything. Canaris made his contribution when the guarding of German armaments plants was discussed; he handed out advice on recruiting agents abroad and displayed a keen interest in the latest developments in radio technology and microphotography. The officers at headquarters soon had to revise their initial verdict and now grudgingly admitted that Canaris had 'plenty between the ears'. His Abwehr was admittedly still far from being a match for an organisation such as Britain's MI6, but was nonetheless effective enough for Hitler to notice the man running it.

The fact was, the dictator urgently needed information with which to plan his risky game of 'week-end' *coups de main*. Would France mobilise if he reintroduced compulsory military service, or marched into the de-militarised Rhineland? Canaris had to supply the answers, and he did so to Hitler's satisfaction. Between December 1935 and March 1936 alone, the Abwehr chief was summoned to the Reich Chancellery no less then seventeen times. His unruffled way of presenting things appealed to Hitler. What is more, as one who had read Karl May's blood-and-thunder novels in a men's hostel, the Führer was delighted when the secret service chief told him tales of his agents' adventures. Canaris was able to secure Hitler's lasting trust, to such an extent that, almost to the end, the latter was unwilling to believe the Abwehr chief had been involved in the conspiracy to assassinate him. Yet Canaris equally misjudged Hitler. He told confidants in all seriousness: 'He is approachable, and grasps anything as long as it is presented to him properly.' He was so thrilled to be close to Hitler and thus to the levers of power that at times he became a genuine workaholic. His daughter Brigitte recalls 'how seldom he came home in those days'. He had already abolished Saturdays off for his closest staff, and even on Sundays the divisional heads, the so-called 'chain-gang', had to turn up for meetings. Whenever important foreign policy decisions were imminent, Canaris appeared 'as though galvanised'.

In the early summer of 1936 things were coming to a head again: civil war was breaking out in Spain. The champion of the right-wing rebels, General Franco, was stuck in Spanish Morocco with his crack troops and had neither ships nor aircraft at his disposal with which to throw his forces into the battle for their country. The General turned simultaneously to Hitler and Mussolini for help. But the two dictators hesitated. Now it was the turn of Canaris, who had got to know and respect Franco at a meeting in Madrid, to come to his of assistance. At a 'Führer conference' he beat the drum on behalf of the rebel Spanish general. He adumbrated the growing threat of a communist bridgehead in south-west Europe, and held out the attractive prospect of Germany gaining political influence in the Mediterranean. The decision was reached on the night of 25 July 1936 in Bayreuth, after a performance of Wagner's *The Valkyrie*, with Wilhelm Furtwängler conducting. Hitler had gone into a huddle with Göring, Blomberg (the Reich Minister of War) and Canaris. Whether encouraged by the euphoric strains of the opera, or by the advice of his secret service chief – the dictator was now willing to risk the Spanish adventure.

> He dedicated himself wholeheartedly to rearmament, in other words to building up the Wehrmacht. He played a thoroughly enthusiastic part in a number of Hitler's particular enterprises, e.g. his involvement in the Spanish Civil war.
>
> *Werner Best, SS Obergruppenführer*

Only two days later the first Junkers Ju-52 transport aircraft took off to provide an air-bridge for Franco's troops. A few months after that German servicemen, the 'Legion Condor', were actually fighting in Spain. In this proxy war between conflicting ideologies, Canaris played a central role: his Abwehr spied assiduously on the 'Reds' and kept Franco informed about the offensives planned by his Republican opponents. He stayed, incognito, in Spain for weeks on end, ignoring the business that was piling up on his desk in Berlin. He was in his element once again, just as he had been in 1919, fighting with the *Freikorps* and busily pulling strings behind the scenes. Radio specialists from Canaris' department were even entrusted with providing intelligence links between the different divisions of Franco's army. The civil war made the Spanish general and the German secret service chief friends for life. After Franco's victory in 1939, whenever Canaris turned up in Madrid, the Generalissimo had time for him. The Abwehr chief kept a portrait of Franco on his desk in Berlin, and told a colleague he was planning one day to enjoy his pension in Spain.

For the moment, however, there was no question of retirement. The Abwehr was expanding, and despite all the friction with Heydrich's SD, Canaris' position within the Wehrmacht seemed unchallengeable. At the beginning of 1938, his promotion to vice-admiral was in prospect. In fact all should have been well in the world of Wilhelm Canaris, in that era of national delusion when most Germans were still happy to belong to Hitler's *Volksgemeinschaft*, or 'National Community'. Yet this was precisely the moment when something in Canaris began to change. His departmental staff first noticed it from the increasingly strange behaviour he displayed. His fondness for his two rough-haired dachshunds, Seppel and Sabine, intensified from a quirk to an obsession. When travelling he would sometimes make hour-long telephone calls to enquire about the mood and digestion of his darlings. As one senior staffer recalled, anyone who did not pay due respect to the dogs was quickly 'out on his ear'. Even in his legendary diary, which disappeared without trace after the war, Canaris devoted much attention to his 'Dackels'. One Abwehr officer describes how, in his diary, he 'often in witty phrases rated dogs above women'.

> Put your faith in the goodness of animals – look, my dachshunds stay silent and will never betray me.
>
> No one who mistreats animals can be a good person.
>
> *Canaris*

It was very clear that Canaris was becoming more and more of a loner. Notoriously anxious about his health, he gulped down huge quantities of different medications. If any staff member had a cold, he would be given panicky orders to go home immediately. One subordinate called him 'the most difficult superior in my thirty-year career with the military'. It was not unusual for Canaris, when travelling by train, as once happened on a journey from Wiesbaden to Berlin, to send his adjutant up to the engine driver and tell him to kindly drive faster.

However, only a very few of his close associates recognised that his behaviour was the expression of an inner crisis. When, in the spring of 1937, Canaris' predecessor, Conrad Patzig, visited him once more, he was more than a little surprised to find that the same man who, two years earlier, had said he would 'deal with' Heydrich and Himmler, now groaned dejectedly: 'From top to bottom, they're all criminals, and they're ruining Germany.' When Patzig then advised him to resign, Canaris replied: 'If I go, Heydrich will come in, and that'll be the finish.' What had happened in the two years that he had been running the secret service? There is no question that Canaris continued to regard himself as a loyal servant of the Führer. During lectures, when he told his audience that for an officer it was 'a matter of course, today, to be a National Socialist', his words still rang with deep conviction. Yet the initial doubts were beginning to emerge. The totalitarian power he saw taking shape before his eyes in Himmler's SS empire, the persecution of Jews and nonconformists, the tangible climate of terror – for a Christian, as Canaris was, all these things were symptoms of moral degeneration. Yet he still believed a reformation was possible. He still had not abandoned hope of halting the landslide, by his own efforts if necessary. A civilised human being could 'not make decisions based purely on expediency', he told a friend at this time, but must also 'preserve an ethical foundation'.

As his doubts grew, he became more and more aware of a man with whom his destiny would be linked to the bitter end: Hans Oster, a colonel in Division III (counter-espionage) of his department. Like Canaris, Oster belonged to the generation of officers from the First World War, who had only with reluctance worn the uniform of the Republic. At first glance the two men had little in common: Oster, the high-spirited pastor's son from Saxony, a typical daredevil and man-about-town; and the rather introverted, sometimes diffident Canaris. Whereas the wall of Oster's office boasted the motto 'An eagle does not eat flies', his chief's desk was adorned by a bronze of the three oriental monkeys, with hands covering ears, eyes and mouth respectively: 'Hear no evil, see no evil, speak no evil.' In fact, however, the two dissimilar men soon formed a close liaison, and exchanged information freely. In this, Oster always took the more radical part. He began criticising the regime sooner than Canaris; as early as June 1934 and the slaying of Ernst Röhm and the SA leadership. He wanted to take more decisive action than his chief.

Unlike Canaris, Oster was never heard to mouth fanatical Nazi slogans. Instead he used to make statements, both at work and at home, which – had they reached the wrong ears – would have 'landed him in a concentration camp' as one of his staff put it.

For the two friends 1938 would be the year of decision. It began with Hitler's totally unpredicted attack on the army leadership, which historians rather dismissively refer to as the 'Blomberg-Fritsch' affair. Within a few weeks the Reich Army Minister, Blomberg, and the army's Chief-of-Staff, Fritsch, had been forced to resign: the former because he had married a prostitute, the latter following a sleazy frame-up involving a rent-boy, which had been staged by the Gestapo. Hitler then appointed himself commander-in-chief of the Wehrmacht (the combined armed forces) and replaced Fritsch with the compliant Brauchitsch. Excitement over the spurious 'matters of honour', given as reasons for these dismissals, preoccupied the officer-corps of the Wehrmacht to such an extent that, at first, few of them recognised the strategic significance of these changes of personnel. It was the final act in the 'seizure of power', and only now did the dictator hold totalitarian powers.

However, Canaris, who had for a long time been one of the best-informed men in the Reich, quickly saw the way things were going. He could still recall well the minutes taken by one of Hitler's adjutants, Hossbach, during the secret speech by the Führer on 5 November 1937. To a select audience of service chiefs, Hitler had announced unambiguously his wish to go to war as soon as possible. 'For the solution of the German question, force can now be the only route', the minute read. The objective was a swift 'assault on Czechoslovakia'. Hossbach had also noted that violent objections had then been raised by Blomberg and Fritsch, and that a discussion ensued in 'very sharp terms'. The Admiral put two and two together: Hitler realised that with such irresolution on the part of the two army chiefs, no victory could be won and certainly no 'living space' acquired by conquest. Their removal meant nothing less than that the scene was now set for war.

Canaris was devastated. He too considered Hitler's course of action suicidal. 'The very first shots of the war', he predicted darkly, 'will be the end of Germany.' Furthermore, the underhand manner in which Fritsch and Blomberg had been dismissed deeply offended his sense of decency. If Hitler could mess about like that with his most senior generals, what values still counted for anything at all in Germany – other than the will of the dictator? A close friend of the Abwehr chief from his days as a cadet in the Imperial Navy, Richard Protze, saw this experience as the turning point for Canaris: 'If you are seeking any one event which made Canaris' loyalty to Hitler start to wobble, then here you have it.' Within six months the doubting intelligence boss had metamorphosed into an active opponent – and this was despite the wave of nationalist enthusiasm following the *Anschluss* of Austria, which left him still on the side of those who believed in Hitler. As he stated with enthusiasm in a speech to officers in Vienna on 22 April 1938, 'Today we all stand in admiration of an event that uplifts the hearts of all Germans – one that we have longed for, worked for and fought for, with the words on our lips: *ein Reich, ein Volk, ein Führer.*' On 14 September the same Canaris gave an order to one of his section heads, Georg Groscurth, to issue arms, live ammunition and explosives to a task force commanded by Major Heinz of the Abwehr. Heinz's mission was nothing less than to arrest the Führer.

It was the climax of a 'peace plot', which had come close to fruition in that fateful summer of 1938. The driving force and communicator behind it was Hans Oster. The army's Chief-of-Staff, Halder, was part of it, as was his predecessor, Beck, as well as the Permanent Secretary at the Foreign Ministry, Ernst von Weizsäcker, and the former Mayor of Leipzig, Carl Goerdeler. They all wanted to prevent Hitler from dragging to destruction the new German Reich, which he had, in the eyes of most of them, done great service in rebuilding. The Abwehr's foreign section, with its contacts and sources of information, had proved to be the ideal apparatus for camouflaging and co-ordinating the many strands of opposition. Canaris had even gone as far as creating a new office for Oster – Section Z – precisely so that he could carry on his activities undisturbed. Officially set up to handle tasks of 'central administration', its purpose was in fact wholly political. Reinhard

Spitzy, then a member of the Abwehr staff, with an office only two doors away from Oster's, remembers that '"Section Z" was really "Section Coup d'Etat"'.

The plot had begun with the sobering realisation that the resisters were in the minority. An attempt to persuade the top military brass to stage a kind of general strike, in the event of war against Czechoslovakia breaking out, was a miserable failure. Most of them certainly shared the view of their former chief-of-staff, Beck, that Germany's strategic position made a war unfeasible, but the senior generals were not prepared to mutiny against their supreme commander. This would remain the case for an overwhelming number of them until 1945 – the tragic paradigm and historic guilt of a generation of senior officers, who lacked the courage to place justice and morality above obedience to orders.

The second great disappointment to the conspirators was the attitude of the Western Powers: envoys of the resistance made pilgrimages to Paris and London, pleaded for a tough stance against Hitler's lust for expansion, and begged for support for the opposition. Yet all attempts were in vain: in the west the threat posed by Hitler was apparently still not recognised, and in London an opposition made up of 'Junkers and generals' scarcely seemed an attractive alternative to the Nazis. The lack of understanding of the precarious position of the 'rebels' was so great that Lord Vansittart, the chief foreign affairs adviser to the British government, announced to an astonished Goerdeler that what he was doing was 'treason'.

For Canaris, these were two lessons that he was never to forget. Chastened, he withdrew from the front rank of the conspirators, though without losing sight of the larger goal. 'You chaps just get on with it', he instructed the dynamic Oster. From now on he only took a mild interest in the detailed preparations. Did he doubt the chances of success, or did he want to cover himself in the event of failure? Halder, Beck's successor as chief-of-staff, found Canaris hard to fathom during those weeks: 'It was often really difficult to guess what he was trying to say to one.' Yet Hitler's policy of putting ever-increasing pressure on Prague forced the plotters to take action. The Wehrmacht Supreme Command had already been given objectives and a date for the attack.

Canaris urged: 'Act at once!' By now Oster had managed to win over one army commander, Erwin von Witzleben, for the attempt to overthrow Hitler. As commander of the Berlin military district, he had powerful units of the 23rd Division at his disposal. A plan was drawn up; offices and barracks of the SS and Gestapo had to be occupied. There were even two men from the Nazi side involved in the plot: Berlin's police chief and SA veteran Wolf-Heinrich von Helldorf, and the Gestapo chief in the capital, Arthur Nebe. This meant that, for the time being, no intervention by the police need be expected. It was a plan that had excellent prospects of succeeding.

Major Heinz's force was to arrest Hitler. What should then be done with 'Emil', as the plotters contemptuously called their chief adversary, was something over which opinions were divided. Canaris and Halder wanted him either to be declared insane by a medical committee, or else put on trial. There was no shortage of evidence against him. A government lawyer, Hans von Dohnanyi, whom Canaris would bring into the Abwehr a year later, had since 1933 been building up a thick file on breaches of the law by the dictator. Assassination, on the other hand, which was what Heinz secretly planned, was rejected by Canaris 'on account of his fundamentally religious position', as Franz Liedig, a comrade-in-arms from *Freikorps* days, recalled.

But then all the plans collapsed like a house of cards. Out of a proverbially clear blue sky, Britain's prime minister, Neville Chamberlain, floated into Germany to grant crucial concessions to Hitler on the question of Sudetenland. This put an abrupt end to any prospects of a *coup d'état*. In his hour of triumph as a saviour of peace, Hitler could not be toppled. The one thing that Canaris and the other plotters never expected, had happened: the Western Powers had sacrificed their Czech ally. Chamberlain hoped that, in doing so, he had satisfied Hitler's demands permanently, and backed his fatal error with the pathetically optimistic slogan: 'Peace in our time.' Canaris took a more realistic view. Fate appeared to have sided with Hitler. With the historic visit by the British premier, the dictator had, without knowing it, escaped two dangers: the war he had wanted, which would, in the view of military historians, have ended in Germany's defeat; and the internal overthrow of his regime, which was on the brink of succeeding. 'It would have been the end of Hitler', as Goerdeler, one of the frustrated rebels, remarked with sad resignation.

Thus it was that German soldiers marched into Czechoslovakia's Sudeten region without firing a shot. Just as after the annexation of Austria, a wave of enthusiasm swept over the country, and belief in the 'genius of the Führer' received new nourishment. With no apparent inhibition even Canaris added his voice to the chorus of congratulations. He instructed Oster to lose no time in destroying all documents relating to the coup. The circle of conspirators had in any case begun to break up: Witzleben was annoyed by the incorrect analysis of foreign intentions supplied by Canaris and Weizsäcker, while the Abwehr boss once again shook his head over the amateurishness and 'irresponsible carelessness' of the men around Oster. Canaris distanced himself and for the moment wanted to hear no more about plans to overthrow Hitler.

He now slipped back into the role of a department head toeing the party line, a loyal vassal of the Führer. He enjoined staff in the Hamburg office of the Abwehr always to give the Nazi salute when reporting to him. The morning rides with Heydrich, who appeared to have no inkling about the failed *putsch*, became more frequent, and nothing seemed more important to Canaris than the increased expansion of his intelligence service. The first successes of his new espionage network came just in time to make everyone forget about the series of misinformed Abwehr reports during the Sudeten crisis. From the USA his spies 'procured' designs of a new bomb-aiming device for combat aircraft, which was far superior to German equipment. From Paris his headquarters received the secret codes used by the French Navy. Soon the Abwehr boss was again *persona grata* with Hitler, and was permitted to accompany the dictator to official events such as the launching of the battleship *Tirpitz* and the triumphant homecoming of the 'Legion Condor' from Spain.

> Hitler felt that Canaris was an incomparable espionage chief. And no one could convince him otherwise.
>
> *Reinhard Spitzy, on the staff of the Abwehr's foreign division*

Was all this no more than brilliant deception by a member of the resistance, who was waiting for his next opportunity – as proclaimed after the war by the guardians of Canaris' reputation? Hardly. The truth is probably that the Admiral did not need to dissemble. His greatest anxiety, that Hitler might drive Germany into a war that could only end in the nation's destruction, had, after all, proved unfounded. Neither the incorporation of the Sudentenland into the Reich, nor the 'Grab for Prague' had cost any blood. He, Canaris, had been wrong – the Führer had been right all along. In the face of such successes, the Abwehr chief was not alone in being susceptible to a fatal belief in miracles. Had Hitler been deposed or assassinated at that moment, then, as his biographer Joachim Fest maintains, the Germans would probably have regarded him as one of the greatest statesmen in the country's history. There were sadly all too few who refused to be deceived, but one of them was the dismissed army chief, Werner von Fritsch, who prophesied at the time: 'This man is Germany's destiny, for good or ill, and this destiny will take its course to the end; if it leads to the abyss, he will drag us all down with him – there is nothing anyone can do about it.' But this time Canaris was not one of the far-sighted ones; his volte-face from rebel to loyalist was prompted by the illusion, albeit short-lived, that war had been avoided, and we can understand his inner relief at not having to plot against a form of government which, next to monarchy, he always considered the best that could be devised for Germany.

> There is a typical Austrian expression: an 'official mollifier', which suits Canaris perfectly. He had to placate both sides, and that wasn't easy.
>
> *Wilhelm Höttl, SS Obersturmbannführer*

It is also significant that he continued to believe it possible to keep terror in check, in the course of his duties, so to speak. After the anti-Semitic atrocities of *Kristallnacht* on 9 November 1938, he submitted a detailed report on the repulsive behaviour of the brown-

shirted rabble to the Wehrmacht chief, Wilhelm Keitel, in the hope
that, in doing so, he would at least provoke a protest from the
military leadership. However, Keitel dismissed the report with the
irritated comment that events on the domestic front did not lie
within his competence – which did nothing to deter Canaris from
sending further catalogues of crimes for the attention of his superior
officer. The Abwehr chief, for whom the rule of law in the Kaiser's
day represented the norm that was to be aspired to, clung to his
concept of law and order as a drowning man clutches at a straw. Yet
a storm was brewing on the horizon, which was to sweep all
Canaris' hopes away.

On the morning of 26 August 1939, at 3.55 a.m. exactly, thirteen
men in civilian clothes and one in uniform opened fire on the
railway station at Mosty, in the strategically important Jablunka Pass
in southern Poland. The soldiers guarding it were rudely awoken
from their sleep. Minutes later the station building was in the hands
of the attackers. The section leader radioed to his command-post:
'Mosty station taken. Losses: one wounded.' What this laconic
message announced was the first skirmish of the Second World War,
six days before the outbreak that has been recorded in the history
books. The commanding officer, *Oberleutnant* Herzner, was under
orders from Division II of the Abwehr's foreign department,
responsible for sabotage and commando operations. The first shots of
that war, which Canaris had predicted would be '*finis Germaniae*', the
end of Germany, had been fired by men of his own Abwehr –
without a declaration of war and in breach of all international law.

The weeks leading up to this had cruelly exposed the dilemma in
which the Admiral found himself. Hitler's policy of aggression
towards Poland and his pact with Stalin, which ran counter to all
his ideological principles, had shattered any illusions that the
occupation of Prague would bring calm to international politics. As
the head of the secret service Canaris obeyed orders and, using
considerable ingenuity, set about the task of preparing to sabotage
important bridges, mountain passes and industrial installations,
supplying information about the strength and disposition of the

Polish forces, and concealing German preparations for invasion. But as a secret opponent of the imminent war he simultaneously disseminated intelligence about the inevitability of a war on two fronts and tried, once again in vain, to recruit allies in the General Staff. This time, admittedly, there were no serious plans for a *coup d'état*. Disappointment at the previous year's failure ran too deep. However, for a brief moment hopes were raised once more. On 25 August two reports, arriving almost simultaneously from Rome and London, threw the Reich Chancellery into a turmoil. Mussolini had announced that, in the event of war, Italy could not offer any support, and from London came news of a pact between Britain and Poland. Hitler lost his nerve. He hastily cancelled the assault scheduled for the next morning, even though most of the troops were already on the march. It verged on a miracle that every unit, except *Oberleutnant* Herzner's detachment, could still be halted.

A huge weight was lifted from Canaris' mind. Had the dictator not made a complete fool of himself? 'It's one thing one minute, and another the next', joked the adjutants in the Abwehr headquarters. In his office the chief made no attempt to conceal his delight: 'He'll never recover from this blow. Peace is guaranteed for twenty years.' His only headache was the commando unit in the Jablunka Pass. Supposing *Oberleutnant* Herzner triggered off an international crisis, and after all launched the war that Hitler had only just called off? It was true that Herzner's men were already under fire from Polish units when they finally received the radio message with the order to withdraw. Since the force had suffered no casualties and none of them was taken prisoner, the Poles were left with no proof of who had captured their railway station. The whole affair petered out without serious consequence.

At daybreak on 1 September, all trace of the dictator's previous discomfiture, which had given Canaris such satisfaction, had been erased. Without the slightest sign of disobedience to orders, the Wehrmacht overran Germany's Polish neighbour. The night before, when the order to launch the assault reached Canaris, he no longer had any illusions. Canaris was not a pacifist, but he was a realist: the logic of the international situation would inevitably lead in the end to Germany's defeat; he had been certain of that for a long time, just as he was well aware of the new and terrible power of modern weapon systems, which would bring with them far more death and suffering than in the First World War. In this too he would be proved right. A close colleague from Oster's circle, the one-time Gestapo man Hans Bernd Gisevius, had a meeting with the Admiral in the Abwehr building on the Tirpitzufer, late on 31 August, the very eve of the Second World War. Gisevius described Canaris as being in a kind of trance, and then, 'in a voice choking with tears' he said with dark foreboding: 'This is the end of Germany.'

At first, reports of early successes swept such gloomy thoughts aside. Much more swiftly than anticipated, the Wehrmacht smashed their Polish adversary, thanks in no small part to groundwork by the Abwehr's foreign division. For a brief time Canaris revelled in the success of his commando operations and sabotage exploits. For example, when the commander of the Eighth Army Corps, General Busch, singled out for praise 400 fighters recruited by the Abwehr station in Breslau, staff at headquarters basked in reflected glory. Soon, however, intelligence from the Abwehr outposts put the Admiral in a very different mood, for these reports revealed the true character of this war. Hitler's propaganda machine had hyped a 'Polish attack' on the German radio station at Gleiwitz, close to the Polish border, as the actual cause of the war. But Canaris learned the truth, which was that the attack had been 'acted out' by SD men in Polish uniforms. The dead bodies left after the attack, presented as casualties of war by the press, had in fact been taken from the mortuaries of German concentration camps. And the Polish uniforms had been acquired for this first German war crime by none other than his own Abwehr! A week after the war started, Heydrich revealed to him that reports of systematic shootings by SS *Einsatzgruppen* were not exaggerated. 'We intend to spare the ordinary people', his riding partner explained coldly, 'but the aristocrats, priests and Jews have to be killed.' Visits to the front line and car journeys through bomb-flattened Warsaw were the final straw. 'Our children's children will bear the guilt for this', he cried, appalled at the sight of long straggling columns of refugees and acres of ruins. 'God's judgement will descend on us.'

It is perhaps astonishing that a man who knew every secret about the impact and the targeting of German weaponry could have been so utterly stunned when faced with the destruction they wrought. It is certainly true that the continuous vacillation between loyalty and resistance had had a serious effect on the sensitive Admiral's nervous health. Yet the terror that shook him to the core amid the clamour of battle, was more than a failure of nerve – it was the dread knowledge that all the values which he, Wilhelm Canaris, had believed in all his life, were being set at nought. Hitler's Polish campaign was no longer a war to which Clausewitz's formula, 'the continuation of foreign policy by other means', was applicable. Here a murderous ideology was taking the battlefield, one whose objectives were not expressed in terms of victory or defeat, but of survival or annihilation. The Kaiser's cadet was staring into the abyss that his new warlord had opened up. 'A war that is waged with disregard of any kind of ethic can never be won', he said to his deputy, Bürkner. 'There really is divine justice on earth.'

Canaris did what he had to do – despite all his dire premonitions. On 12 September 1939, while on the Führer's personal train, the Abwehr chief made a report on crimes behind the front line. Once again the addressee was Keitel. The notes taken at this meeting were later used as evidence at the Nuremberg war crime trials. 'I drew *Generaloberst* Keitel's attention to the fact that I knew that large-scale shootings were planned in Poland', Canaris had noted. 'I said that ultimately the world would of course hold the Wehrmacht responsible for such methods, since these things were being done under their noses.' Keitel replied curtly that the Führer had already decided 'these things' and that 'if the Wehrmacht wished to have nothing to do with it', then they would just have to accept 'that the SS and Gestapo will make their appearance alongside them'. Once again Canaris had collided with the Wehrmacht's Chief-of-Staff, whose reply demonstrated the full extent of his guilty involvement.

At Canaris' behest, his organisation now began to subvert the regime of terror. The prominent Chief Rabbi of Warsaw,

Schneersohn, was smuggled out of the country with the help of the Abwehr, after the US Consulate-General had discreetly requested help. He also facilitated the escape to Switzerland of the widow of the former Polish Military Attaché, Szymanski, whom Canaris had got to know in Berlin. The woman and her children were maintained with generous financial support from the Abwehr. These are the first of Canaris' documented rescue operations, and many more were to follow. His motive was humanity towards the victims of persecution. There was a high risk that the Gestapo or the SD would get wind of such operations. Yet Canaris still possessed sufficient power to block investigations, or to camouflage his rescue missions as fictitious secret service manoeuvres. Whenever acquaintances, employees or even his wife Erika requested help for people suffering harassment, Canaris, Dohnanyi and Oster took action. Often the victims were simply 'drafted' into the Abwehr to protect them from persecution. The reason for their predicament was of no importance. Whether they were 'socialists, communists, freemasons, Jews or Bible-bashers', recalls a friend of Canaris, Franz Josef Furtwängler, they all found protection under the Abwehr's roof.

However, the daring with which the Admiral and his assistants 'threw a spanner in the works' of the murder-machine (to use the phrase of Helmuth James von Moltke, who also took part in rescue operations), was not just an expression of humanity and a sense of justice. Canaris also had pangs of conscience caused by other divisions of the Abwehr. Working hand in glove with Heydrich's *Einsatzgruppen*, a unit of the Abwehr actually went on the hunt for Polish Jews, aristocrats and priests: it was called the Secret Field Police (*Geheime Feldpolizei* or GFP). Before the war, their commanding officer, Oberst Wilhelm Krichbaum from the Abwehr's Division III (Counter-espionage), held the rank of SS *Standartenführer* and worked at the SD's headquarters. Now his erstwhile contacts made it easy for him to arrange smoothly functioning collaboration with the *Einsatzgruppen*. Soon his force was so effective in carrying out its mission, which was to combat 'all movements that threaten the German nation and government', that on 15 September 1939 Heydrich asked the GFP to 'carry out the shootings yourselves'. By the time of the Russian campaign the unit, now numbering some 6,000 members, were only distinguishable by their Wehrmacht uniforms from the murder squads of the SS. They supervised mass shootings, co-ordinated the operations of their 'SS comrades' and were especially noted for tracking down Jewish minority populations who had hitherto been spared.

True, the GFP led a comparatively isolated and independent existence within the Abwehr organisation, but we can imagine what suffering Canaris was caused by the reports submitted by his Division III; how very uncomfortable he was to see that this steadily expanding unit had become the efficient instrument of a murderous tyrant. Those close to him tell of conversations in which the question of his resignation was debated back and forth. The most frequently deployed argument was that, in the hands of Himmler or Heydrich, the Abwehr would become a still more dangerous weapon in the reign of terror; and this indeed proved to be the case following the removal of Canaris. Was it permissible for him to accept responsibility himself for these crimes, in order to 'prevent worse things from happening'?

One look at his department was enough for Canaris to realise what a desperate situation he, Oster and a few loyal colleagues were caught in. During the war the staff of the Abwehr had increased to over 10,000. Of those, 50 at the most knew about the secret rescue operations, let alone being involved in plans to overthrow the Nazi regime. The great majority of the others were Hitler supporters and more or less line-toeing functionaries. It was Division III in particular which, because of its closeness to Himmler's 'Central Office of Reich Security' (RSHA), was seen as a stronghold of Nazi fanaticism. Then came a growing number of lower-ranking individuals who abused their positions with the Abwehr for purely personal ends, while convincingly mouthing Nazi slogans. Thus there was constantly mounting criticism aimed at Canaris by his black-uniformed SS rivals, to the effect that his department was full of 'corruption and shirking', as an RSHA officer, Wilhelm Höttl, phrased it. Höttl's boss, Walter Schellenberg, summed it up like this: 'Alongside some first-rate people, there were a lot of incompetents fooling around there, as well as a hotch-potch of very dubious individuals.'

Faced with the changes in his own 'shop', Canaris was more than ever overcome with a feeling of solitude and fatalism, which he tried to escape through ever more frequent official trips. Those with him often found him in the semi-darkness of Roman Catholic churches which he, a Protestant, preferred as places of silent meditation. The surprisingly swift victory over Poland could no longer distract him from the truth. 'The war is lost', he confided to an old *Freikorps* chum named Erhardt, 'no matter how many more victories we win.' On the very day that Warsaw surrendered, Hitler had informed the top military brass of his intention to strike against the west, if possible as early as that November. Canaris was not the only one to shake his head in disbelief at this. Most of the generals considered it suicidal to launch a new invasion in winter, with troops still weakened from the Polish campaign. The erstwhile putschists of 1938 scented a new dawn. Halder, the army chief-of-staff, even succeeded temporarily in winning the support of the commander-in-chief, Brauchitsch, for a new plan for a 'down-tools' by all the generals. Canaris applied pressure again. As Halder recounted later, the Admiral played the role of 'whipping people into action'. He personally paid visits to the generals commanding the army groups in the west. In his luggage he had files on German crimes in Poland and analyses of the prospects for a continuation of the war. Soon, however, Canaris had to accept with disappointment that the generals would prefer to carry out suicidal invasion orders than to mutiny in the middle of a war. He received one rebuff after another. Even though a number of army commanders agreed with his assessment, once again none had the courage to do what had to be done. At the headquarters of the pro-Nazi General Reichenau, when Canaris mentioned German crimes in Poland, he received the reply from Reichenau's chief-of-staff, Paulus – later the tragic figure of Stalingrad – that such bloodthirsty actions were simply 'the necessity of war'. Then Canaris discovered that Brauchitsch, rather than taking action, had sought an interview with Hitler, from which he returned empty-handed, though with a flea in his ear. At this point, Canaris finally abandoned hope of a united resistance with the Wehrmacht leadership. 'He wants nothing more to do with those spineless generals', noted the trusted Groscurth.

This second failure provoked the same reaction from Canaris as in 1938. Apparently unmoved, he hurled himself into working for the war that he actually wanted to prevent. In the invasion of Denmark and Norway in April 1940 and even in the preparations for the western offensive scheduled for the summer of that year, the Abwehr once again fought in the most advanced positions. On orders from Canaris, high-level Luftwaffe reconnaissance aircraft photographed Belgian and French fortifications, and once again agents of Division II 'got hold of' uniforms from the opposing armies. The head of the Abwehr was a regular guest at Hitler's 'war councils'. The minutes of one session in the Reich Chancellery reveal him as an expert, with a dazzling knowledge of the enemy's bunkers, and of detonation points for blowing up bridges. A special new Abwehr formation, the 'Brandenburg' battalion (later a division) was allotted a key role on the first day of the western campaign, which was to capture the bridges over the River Meuse. Canaris seems once again to have rejoined the 'Round Table', and even his close associates found it hard to judge whether he had merely swapped one mask for another, or had really changed sides. On 1 April 1940 he was promoted from vice-admiral to full admiral.

Now, the Abwehr chief did distance himself, inwardly as well as outwardly, from the revolutionaries under his roof. Oster and Dohnanyi now wanted to act without the support of the army. Their new watchword: first get rid of Hitler, then a solution to the other problems will be found. In their desperation they dropped the precautions that hitherto had been fundamental. Oster carried with him a list of all the potential conspirators when travelling from one rendezvous to the next, as though he were immune to the attentions of the Gestapo. General von Witzleben, who had actually been receptive to all plans for overthrowing the Nazis, threw Oster out of his headquarters without ceremony, after glancing at the explosive contents of his briefcase. Halder banned the 'eternal rebel' from talking to any member of the army general staff. Even the head of the Abwehr's Division II, Erwin Lahousen, was not a little astonished when Oster asked him one day, quite out of the blue, whether he could get hold of explosives and detonators for an attack on Hitler. When Lahousen enquired if Canaris knew about this, Oster replied: 'No, the old man is already screwed up enough as it is.'

It was the moment when Canaris and Oster came to a parting of the ways. The Admiral had returned to his role as Hitler's henchman, whereas his friend drew even greater determination from the fact that the second attempt to end Hitler's life had failed. Hans Oster chose the road that he knew would be a solitary one for him. If the army was incapable, from its own resources, of freeing itself from the demon at its head, then nothing but an annihilating defeat, he calculated, would open the generals' eyes. Oster was prepared to sacrifice the lives of German soldiers for the cause: this meant he now crossed a threshold that Canaris would never have overstepped. Oster would commit treason. From November 1939 onward, he used an acquaintance, the Dutch military attaché Gijsbertus Sas, as a conduit through which to supply the west with information about the Wehrmacht's invasion plans. At the same time, another Abwehr man, Josef Müller, a Bavarian Catholic who had been a lawyer in civilian life, informed trusted friends in the Vatican about German military preparations, though officially his mission was to monitor British peace terms.

Without Canaris' knowledge both sources began to pour out information, though without altering the course of history to the slightest degree. Because the launch dates for the invasion of Norway as well as for the offensive in the west had been postponed several times, the 'moles' in the Abwehr also kept on supplying different information. However, this 'inflation' in the number of launch dates made the recipients suspicious – as did the lack of authentication for the sources. Thus, in the event, the German invasion fleet that approached the Norwegian fjords was *not* met by a barrage from British warships, nor did the Dutch government put their army on the alert. Ultimately Hans Oster had put his life on the line for nothing. Once again Hitler celebrated *Blitzkrieg* victories that raised his aura of invincibility to absurd heights. Without a hint of irony, the Wehrmacht Chief-of-Staff, Keitel, now hailed him as 'the greatest military leader of all time'. For the military opposition, Germany's successes proved to be a severe blow. Among many of the generals, who might still have been considered as potential fellow-plotters, euphoria and a blind faith in the Führer were once again widespread. This is why the climax of Hitler's fame as a war leader also marked the weakest moment for those who would resist him.

Ironically, Oster's act of desperation did not have any impact until after the war. In the search for people to blame for Germany's defeat, the ex-Nazis and neo-Nazis made a big thing of the Colonel's 'treason' and even accused Canaris – wrongly – of being involved in it. For example, in 1955 a neo-Nazi publication, the *Heidebote*, ran the headline: 'Canaris unmasked as a traitor' and, under a photograph of marching German infantrymen, printed the caption: 'Their efforts were completely in vain.' The Admiral's daughter, Brigitte Canaris, can also bear witness to similar experiences ranging from problems with the German authorities to personal vilification. The Canaris family had chosen to spend the early postwar years in Spain. It is surely indicative of the historical priorities in the 1950s, that the search for reasons for the defeat of the Wehrmacht occupied more time than the enquiry into why it obeyed orders from the greatest criminals of the twentieth century.

It was in June 1940 that Canaris found out about the leaking of information on the western offensive. As was to be expected, Oster's telephone conversations with Sas had been bugged. Now a transcript of those conversations lay on his boss's desk. The only thing missing was the caller's name. The Admiral was shattered. 'Anyone who dares raise a hand against his Fatherland', he wrote in an instruction to his Division III, 'can expect only death.' That was no hollow slogan, but an expression of his deepest conviction. In 1937 he justified the death sentence against a German army captain, who had spied for Czechoslovakia, with orotund phrases. The traitor, Canaris said at the time, had 'forfeited his honour and his life, and plunged his own and other families into unspeakable misery'.

Now he stood with Heydrich in front of a furious Hitler, who ordered that the traitors be tracked down and neutralised. Canaris ordered his counter-espionage bloodhounds to fan out. But the investigators came back with results he would have preferred not to hear. One morning in the summer of 1941 Oster, and the group head of Division III F, Joachim Rohleder, came into the chief's office looking grim. Rohleder placed a file, whose cover bore the significant code-name 'Palm-Branch', on the desk. The seasoned spy-hunter then stated baldly that his investigations in Rome had shown that none other than *Oberleutnant* Josef Müller and *Oberst* Oster were responsible for giving away the launch date of the invasion in the west. Oster only put up a weak defence. Rohleder said later that Canaris had been 'visibly taken aback'. His friend Hans Oster a traitor! Certainly he had acted out of motives that Canaris shared with him. Yet, for the Admiral, crossing this Rubicon would have been unthinkable.

However, their long-standing friendship triumphed once more over his revulsion at Oster's deed. Rohleder was flabbergasted when Canaris informed him that investigations into the 'Palm-Branch' affair were to be wound up due to a lack of conclusive evidence. The ambitious group head, who had never been part of the inner circle of initiates, protested vehemently. He knew how good his evidence was. He then took the liberty of pointing out, with a certain smugness, that the Gestapo could have carried out 'the same investigations with equal success'. Indeed, the Admiral's greatest anxiety was caused by his rivals in the RSHA. What did Heydrich know about Oster's blunder? Much to Canaris' relief, it seemed that again Heydrich was aware of nothing. Neither on their morning rides together, nor from informal soundings in the offices of the opposition, was there any hint of suspicion. In the SD, people were still really groping in the dark, even though the Abwehr's persistent efforts to find out about the progress of their investigations was 'noticeable', as one of Heydrich's officials recalled later.

Once again, Oster seemed to have got away with it, though his boss and close colleagues did not want to hear any more about plans for a coup. A morose Canaris now gave orders that all documents relating to past plots were to be destroyed. For in Oster's and Dohnanyi's filing cabinets there were still draft cabinet lists and instructions for action on the big day which had never come. However, Dohnanyi had no intention of carrying out the order. The lawyer had, since his time as an official in the Ministry of Justice, gathered evidence against the Nazi regime and proof to posterity that there had been a spirit of resistance; he had not done all this work for it now to go up in flames. He later stated that his reason for not destroying the papers was 'so that one day it could be proved that we civilians did in fact do something'. Dohnanyi arranged for most of his papers to be deposited in a safe in the army headquarters at Zossen, near Berlin. It was a decision that was to cost him his life.

In the summer of 1940 the dictator once again summoned his secret service chief, whose double life he still did not in the least suspect. After his victory over France, he now had his sights on Spain. Hitler calculated that Franco would either repay Germany's assistance in the civil war by siding with her now, or would at least support an attack on Gibraltar, to which Spain had long laid claim. The Rock was seen as the Achilles heel of the troublesome British. Alfred Jodl, one of Hitler's favourite strategists, had coined the optimistic slogan, that by cutting off the sea-route into the Mediterranean 'the British will to resist will be broken'. The man with the diplomatic skills needed to convince Madrid of this was not Foreign Minister Ribbentrop, with his nationalistic blustering, but someone who knew the Spanish language and mentality. Hitler remembered Canaris' role in the Spanish Civil War and entrusted the mission to him.

Not long afterwards, on 23 July 1940, Canaris was facing his former comrade-in-arms, Franco. The *Caudillo* was clearly open to German approaches. With back-up from Spanish intelligence operatives, Canaris and an Abwehr team were able to reconnoitre the possibilities of an assault on Gibraltar. Soon the code-name 'Operation Felix' was dreamed up. From nearby Algeciras, he studied through binoculars the bunkers and gun-emplacements on Gibraltar. Canaris wore a grey flannel suit and a broad-brimmed felt hat. He spoke Spanish to the men with him. When he had to register at a hotel, he produced an Argentinian passport in the name of Guillermo – a masterpiece from the Abwehr's forgery workshop. Canaris was happy to be back in Spain and to have an assignment that had nothing to do with treason and conspiracy. He was soon batting plans for 'Felix' back and forth. One proposal called for his 'Brandenburg' force to march in civilian clothes, on little-used roads, right across Spain; another described in detail the air raids and massive artillery barrages need to soften up the British prior to storming the Rock. In Germany preparations were in full swing, but the deciding factor was still lacking – Franco's approval.

The Spanish dictator was, however, clearly hesitant, since he did not want to back the wrong horse. The fact that Hitler had abandoned preparations for an invasion of England, and the mounting figures of Luftwaffe losses, were signs that Hitler's star might already be in decline. Entry into the war on Germany's side was out of the question anyway, given the parlous state of the Spanish army; but even to allow German troops to march through his country could mean getting dragged into the maelstrom that was likely to bring an early end to the 'Thousand Year Reich'. Hitler reacted with disappointment to Franco's reluctance, but tried all the harder to win him over. The two dictators agreed to hold talks in October, on the Spanish-French frontier. Once again it was Canaris who was to prepare the ground for this meeting, and in mid-September he went to see the *Caudillo*.

But the emissary did not carry out his mission. By now Canaris knew not only of Franco's private change of heart, but also about plans for 'Operation Barbarossa', Germany's invasion of Russia; and he had no intention of doing Hitler's bidding. Instead, in his own convoluted way, he advised the Spanish dictator to steer clear of any commitment to the swastika. Enthusiasm for 'Operation Felix' was forgotten. Now Canaris wanted to contribute what he could to preserving the corner of Europe he loved most from the ravages of war. In a report to Berlin he painted such a gloomy picture of the situation in Spain that a 'No' from Madrid would scarcely come as a surprise. 'The internal political situation in Spain', the report stated in exaggerated terms, 'is very, very bad, and Franco's position is anything but secure.' The actor had switched scripts. Instead of beguiling the *Caudillo*, as required, he had cunningly acted as an advocate of Spanish neutrality. Franco was never to forget this service. When the Admiral's widow and her children settled in Madrid after the war, a spacious apartment and an assured income awaited her.

> Although he led a very harmonious family life with his wife and two daughters, who were still little girls at that time, he never really had any private life outside his job, and to my knowledge, in all the years we worked together, he never took a holiday.
>
> *Werner Best, SS* Obergruppenführer

In Berlin, Canaris was astonished to discover that Hitler had not seen through his double game, and did not take the failure of his Spanish assignment amiss. In fact the dictator rated the actions of his spy-master as 'particularly skilful', as Himmler's lieutenant, Karl Wolff, recalled after the war. But the Abwehr chief could not smile over this for long. From the beginning of 1941 more and more documents crossed his desk relating to the campaign against the Soviet Union, 'Operation Barbarossa'. Again Canaris was plunged into the same agonising dilemma as with every new act of aggression by Hitler. On one hand he was looking for partners who could be mobilised into opposing the dictator's intentions. He spoke to Halder, Weizsäcker, and even Keitel; all of them had doubts about the Russian adventure. Two of Hitler's most notorious yes-men, Keitel and Ribbentrop, even staged a kind of revolt in an attempt to dissuade Hitler from his project. In the end, though, they all followed the Führer's orders and remained in their posts – as did Canaris. All were trapped in the fetters of loyalty. And perhaps their warlord's prediction, that the Russian giant would collapse under the first blows from the Wehrmacht, would yet again prove true . . .

At the same time as he was conspiring with opponents of 'Barbarossa', Canaris tackled his secret service work with an energy that can only be explained by his all too versatile nature. At the outset the Abwehr was faced with the problem that it had no agents in the Soviet Union. Blame for this misfortune lay personally with Hitler, for after the conclusion of the Hitler–Stalin Pact in August 1939 all secret service activity against the new ally had been forbidden on his orders. In this self-inflicted predicament even old intelligence documents about the Soviet Union, which had been looted from Poland in 1939, were put into circulation. Once again, aerial reconnaissance planes were sent on mission after mission, which at least yielded a picture of Soviet troop dispositions. Nevertheless, as far as the capacity of Soviet armaments factories was concerned, the senior German military were completely in the dark. In a very few months this fatal gap in their knowledge would be revealed.

The second great difficulty was the task of camouflaging the Wehrmacht's advance. How do you hide three million soldiers and over 3,000 tanks from the eyes of the world? Canaris began by spreading extravagant reports through Europe's rumour-mills. Sometimes he would start a whispering campaign to the effect that the Wehrmacht's troop-transports eastward were in truth a cover for the imminent invasion of England; at other times the word was that Hitler would strike in the Mediterranean. A mass of misleading material was fed through the foreign military attachés in Berlin, and even Goebbels, the Minister of Propaganda, joined the game of blind man's buff, when on 13 June he dropped hints in the party newspaper, *Völkischer Beobachter*, about an assault on Britain. Canaris himself may have been surprised at how successful his shadow-boxing had been. In the early dawn of 22 June 1941, when the spearhead formations of the Wehrmacht plunged into Russia, they encountered a Red Army that was virtually unprepared. In many places the Germans roused the opposition from their beds. Nowhere did they find any effective defensive positions. The chief responsibility for this bloody débâcle certainly lay with Stalin himself. His stubborn refusal to take the numerous warnings seriously probably cost hundreds of thousands of Red Army lives. But the Abwehr must be given considerable credit for contributing to this fatal miscalculation. In historical terms the deception operations prior to 'Barbarossa' were perhaps its most effective 'achievement'.

Very soon after the launch of the Russian campaign, Dohnanyi's files began to fill with reports of new atrocities being committed in the name of Germany. Lahousen, the head of Division II, came back from a visit to the battlefront with a report that left no more room for illusion. Having personally witnessed the mass shooting of Jews, he wrote: 'The circumstances thus created are so distressing that they cannot be described. The effect on the German squads is inevitable. Generally speaking the executions can only be carried out by men who are numbed with alcohol.' Again units of the Secret Field Police were conspicuous in these manhunts. In the Belorussian town of Kodyma, for instance, a troop of the GFP proposed to the murderers in the *Einsatzgruppe* detailed for the task that they should jointly carry out the mass shooting.

Canaris learned of the start of the genocide through reports from his own Division III, to which the GFP belonged. For a long time he had been convinced that Germany would have to bear this un-speakable guilt for generations to come. 'The pessimism that was a basic element in his character', wrote the SS man Werner Best, another of Canaris' riding companions, 'became so much the dominant aspect of his personality, that being with him was downright depressing.' The few rescue operations by Dohnanyi and Oster did nothing to disguise the Admiral's helplessness. Yet with the second wave of mass murder, which began with 'Barbarossa', he believed there was something he could do about it. The three million and more Soviet prisoners-of-war were plainly being crammed together in conditions that were a threat to their lives. After his trip Lahousen reported numerous cases of 'cannibalism'. Faced with a 'Final Solution' that was set in ideological stone, official complaints made no impression, but in the case of prisoners, the direct interests of the Abwehr were affected. On 15 September 1941 Canaris signed a formal submission to Keitel, which had been compiled by the Abwehr's experts on international law, and by Count Helmuth James von Moltke, the leading figure in the resistance group known as the Kreisau Circle. In it the Admiral argued that the illegality of the treatment of prisoners was threatening 'the maintenance of discipline and the fighting capacity of our own troops'. In ponderous official language he warned of 'the certain eventuality of prejudicial consequences from a political and a military standpoint'.

> . . . the expressly approved measures are bound to lead to arbitrary maltreatment and killings. . . . The establishment of a camp police-force equipped with cudgels, whips and similar weapons is inconsistent with the military code . . .
>
> *From Canaris' submission to the Chief of the Wehrmacht Supreme Command, Wilhelm Keitel, concerning the treatment of Russian prisoners-of-war, 15 September 1941*

But the addressee remained unmoved. With a cynical disregard for humanity Keitel noted in the margin of the Canaris document: 'These anxieties belong to the concept of chivalrous warfare. Here we engaged in the destruction of an ideology. For this reason I approve of these measures and stand by them.' Subsequent approaches were similarly ineffectual. The sole success of this official offensive was to obtain the assurance of the Gestapo chief, Heinrich Müller, that executions of Soviet prisoners would in future, as far as possible, be carried out away from the eyes of fighting troops. Six months later, in the spring of 1942, the chief Nazi ideologue, Alfred Rosenberg, himself produced the terrible statistic that of over three million Red Army prisoners captured, only a million were still alive.

With the failure of the *Blitzkrieg* concept of warfare in Russia Canaris was visibly losing favour with his increasingly jittery war leader. As early as 20 July 1941, in Hitler's headquarters, Canaris heard that 'attempts were in progress to place the blame on the Abwehr'. Lahousen confided to his diary that the Führer 'stated that if he had known of the existence of the super-heavy Russian tanks and armoured vehicles, the war would not have been fought'. Canaris knew, of course, that his sources in the Soviet Union were inadequate, to say the least. Yet for a long time he had ceased to have any illusions about the prospects of 'Barbarossa' succeeding. No-one had wanted to listen to his warnings. And now Hitler wanted to make him, of all people, the scapegoat. As an officer he could not accept that. He gave orders to his divisional heads, 'to assemble all material providing evidence that for a long time we had been drawing attention to all those things [i.e. the strength of the Red Army]'.

But all attempts at self-justification were useless. Hardly had Canaris been summoned to the headquarters than his star began to sink. With a sure nose for opportunities in the Nazi jungle, Himmler and Heydrich now seized their chance to mount a frontal attack. According to one of Hitler's adjutants, Engel, at a meeting the *Reichsführer*-SS made so many snide remarks about Canaris' 'positive attitude' towards the Jews, which was reinforced by his numerous Jewish agents, that Hitler finally had one of his notorious fits of rage. He summoned Keitel and ordered him to suspend the Admiral from duty immediately. As Engels tells us, Canaris thereupon took a plane to the 'Wolf's Lair' and privately persuaded the dictator to reinstate him. What powers of rhetoric, what assurances of loyalty were necessary to achieve this, even the adjutant could only guess at. Yet even if old affections had once again prevented his downfall, for Canaris the affair was an alarming indicator. If a few remarks by the Grand Inquisitor of the SS were enough to trip him up, then the balance of power must have shifted drastically to his disadvantage.

> We ought to open a little coffee-stall by the harbour in Piraeus. I'd make the coffee and you'd serve it. It would be marvellous to live such a simple life.
>
> *Canaris to his friend Otto Wagner in 1942*

We may wonder, in any case, why the Admiral was so anxious to be reinstated. Unmistakeable signs that he was wearying of the job, but most of all his scruples over Nazi crimes, would have made his departure entirely understandable. He would have been able to move abroad with his family – various foreign currency deposits had, according to his secretary, been set up by the Abwehr, in case he decided to flee. But Canaris chose to stay. We will never know how much of a part his vanity played in this, the conviction that as an officer in time of war he had to remain at his post, or whether it was the desire to prevent something worse, namely the takeover of the Abwehr by Himmler. Whatever the truth, he let slip the last chance of separating his own fate from the already looming destruction of Hitler's Reich. Perhaps he was convinced deep down that he must personally share in the 'expiation', which in his view the German people could not avoid.

Discussion about the 'failings' of the Abwehr at the start of the Russian campaign raises the question of how good Admiral Canaris' espionage network really was. (Ammunition was eagerly supplied by the scarcely glorious 'Foreign Armies East' section of the general staff, run by Reinhard Gehlen, who later headed the postwar intelligence service of Federal Germany.) Here, the verdict of former members of the Abwehr is no more informative than the opinions of Germany's former adversaries. Both sides are notorious for embellishing the facts. What is, however, beyond dispute is that the war being fought out of sight on both sides was characterised by high losses and countless débâcles. Very, very few operations had any direct influence on the course of the war: one that did was 'Operation North Pole', in which the Abwehr succeeded in rolling up a complete British spy network and then operated it to Germany's advantage for more than a year, feeding it with carefully contrived disinformation. In this way hundreds of Allied air raids dropped their bombs on empty countryside. Then there was the legendary spy and businessman named 'Klatt', who through channels in the Balkans found out about the latest decisions of the Soviet general staff, and then radioed them to the Abwehr. True, Klatt was working simultaneously for the other side.

What is most surprising is the amount that the other side was *not* able to find out by espionage. For example, the Allies were completely surprised by the Ardennes offensive in the winter of 1944–5, just as they were by the size of the production facilities for the V2 'miracle weapon'. They had no idea about Manstein's 'sickle-cut' in the 1940 invasion of France, nor did they have any concrete information about Stauffenberg's attempt to kill Hitler in July 1944.

Yet the German intelligence services, the Abwehr and the SD, were all too often groping in the dark as well. Neither Canaris nor Himmler ever found out about British success in deciphering German radio signals, encoded with the 'Enigma' machine that was considered absolutely secure; nor did they know which stretches of beach in northern France would be selected for the Allied invasion. The US atomic bomb programme remained a complete secret, as did the arrival of the elite Siberian divisions, which halted the Wehrmacht's advance outside Moscow in the winter of 1941. The outcome of the Second World War was not decided by espionage, but by the industrial capacity and the number of troops available to each side. Against this background, the many high-risk activities by agents on both sides were principally combat operations with high losses and not much gained. Among these were the deployment of the 'Weather Force' in the permanent ice of the Arctic, or the desert expedition in North Africa of the Hungarian Count Almassy – the historical basis for the novel and film *The English Patient* – who, working for the Abwehr, was meant to find a route behind the British positions in Egypt.

Nevertheless, notable items in the Abwehr's balance sheet are the numerous political operations carried out by Lahousen's Division II. Money and explosives were supplied to IRA saboteurs, and rifles to anti-British freedom-fighters from Palestine to Afghanistan; agitation was fomented among the non-Russian peoples of the Soviet Union, and all this was aimed at weakening Germany's enemies in the areas they controlled. Thus bomb outrages from Belfast to Kabul were committed with German explosives. Yet even this Fifth Column was unable to turn the course of history decisively in favour of the Reich. After Hitler's declaration of war against the USA in December 1941, America was also targeted by German exporters of sabotage. Yet here Canaris faced the same problem as he had done six months earlier at the start of 'Barbarossa': the lack of agents on the ground. But Hitler would not listen. The dictator commented brusquely that there were masses of German-Americans who were just waiting to 'throw the bombs we send them', and so 'Operation Pastorius' was put into action. This provided for U-boats off the American east coast to land German agents who had previously lived in the States. Putting Hitler's orders into practice, these men would build up a sabotage network and in particular mount attacks on the US aircraft industry. Eight volunteers were quickly found, all of them ardent Nazis, who were only too keen to put their lives on the line. Lahousen who, like Canaris, was sceptical about the whole exercise, recalled that one of them had even been awarded the Gold Medal of the Nazi Party.

On 12 and 17 June 1942 two groups of agents were put ashore on beaches in Long Island and Florida respectively. A week later all eight would-be saboteurs were rounded up. 'Operation Pastorius' had been betrayed – not once but twice: first by an American spy who had been mixing with the U-boat crews, and then by the leader of the operation himself, one Georg Dasch who, when faced with the death penalty in New York, got cold feet and phoned the FBI. A wave of outrage swept across the United States. Americans volunteered in large numbers for the firing squads which would liquidate 'Hitler's agents'. In the event, six of the culprits were executed by electric chair, and the other two, including the turncoat Dasch, were sentenced to life imprisonment.

In Germany, too, news of the agents' arrest provoked anger and confusion – albeit only among a small circle. On 30 June Canaris and Lahousen were summoned to the 'Wolf's Lair' for a severe dressing-down. 'I demand an explanation from you', bellowed Hitler by way of welcome. 'Why on earth do I have a secret service, when unmitigated disasters like this happen?' The dictator was beside himself. Would another sacking follow? According to Lahousen's description, Canaris bowed his head. 'You are responsible for this', Hitler said menacingly. 'You should at least have taken a better look at those people.' Not until the minutes-long torrent of words had died down somewhat did the Abwehr boss reply. '*Mein Führer*', he said quietly, almost humbly, 'everyone who took part in the operation was a Party member. All of them were passed on to me by the Party's foreign organisation, as being convinced National Socialists. The organiser of the operation is a bearer of the *Blutorden* [the Order of Blood, a Nazi decoration].' His answer was probably intended as no more than damage limitation. But then Hitler reacted with an unexpected suggestion: 'If that's the way you work, then you should use criminals or Jews.' With that he terminated the interview and left the room without a word. However, Canaris remained behind, anything but downcast. According to Lahousen's recollection he kept repeating with obvious delight Hitler's parting words: 'Then use criminals or Jews.'

Inspired by these words from Hitler, certain things began to happen. Hans von Dohnanyi did now organise a large-scale operation to rescue Jews. Through perfectly legal channels, families from Berlin, predominantly Jewish, were issued with passports and then sent to neutral countries, ostensibly on secret intelligence missions. It was a rebellion of humanity, under the guise of following Hitler's supposed instructions. With the Abwehr code 'Operation Seven', for example, in late September 1942, long after the deportation trains had started rumbling into Auschwitz, twelve Jewish 'agents', including women and children, travelled on the night train to Basel, in Switzerland. The group, all equipped with the correct papers, included the family of a Jewish lawyer named Fliess. His daughter Dorothee Fliess remembers to this day the moment of their arrival in Basel, when a border official asked the travellers to remove their yellow Stars of David. 'He actually held out a pair of scissors. My mother did the necessary for my father and herself. In my case it was even easier; my star was not even sewn on, only fixed with press-studs.'

The agents of 'Operation Seven' were to be among the last human souls whom it was possible to save under the aegis of Canaris. As the Admiral's power began to evaporate, so did the opportunities to provide humanitarian aid under the cover of 'normal' Abwehr activities. Adolf Eichmann, the chief hunter and deporter of Jews, had turned up in person at his office to veto any further aid to refugees by the Abwehr. Keitel had intervened as well. When, early in 1943, the journalist Franz Josef Furtwängler came to see Canaris with another plea for help for a friend threatened with deportation, he remembers that 'we had a shattering experience. The head of the Abwehr confessed to us openly that he was pretty much "boxed in".

It was Himmler who was finally making the running, and he, the Admiral, no longer had the power to protect any individuals or to recruit them for his intelligence services.' It sounded like a declaration of bankruptcy. Apart from this, there were other signs of his terminal decline. The Admiral's uniform looked uncared-for, his eyes were sunken. To one of his adversaries from the RSHA he gave the impression of being 'old, tired and worn out'. Canaris' biographer Heinz Höhne is among those who conclude that in his final years in office, the Abwehr chief had simply given up, lost his grip on the job and tried to escape his predicament through unnecessarily frequent official trips.

In fact, however, out of his despair there grew a new strength for a last desperate battle against Hitler – a battle that had been given fresh impetus when the war finally turned against Germany at Stalingrad. Again the principal protagonists were Oster and Dohnanyi. Canaris was not *au fait* with all they were doing, and probably did not want to be, but he gave his tacit approval to most of it. The deteriorating military situation had shifted the conspirators' objectives. True, the removal of Hitler was still their chief priority, yet more and more emphasis was now placed on the plan to make a separate peace with the Western Powers, and then to continue fighting the Soviets side by side. Such visions naturally roused the last drop of energy in the notoriously anti-communist Canaris. Putting out several feelers simultaneously he now attempted to sound out the willingness of the West to switch fronts. Once again, of course, this was all done under the camouflage of 'normal' Abwehr operations. Moltke took soundings in Istanbul, contacts with the Vatican were revived, the Admiral's intermediaries turned up in Sweden, and the Abwehr chief himself had already set a date for a meeting in Santander, northern Spain, with his opposite numbers, Donovan of the US secret service and Menzies of the British.

Yet all peace-feelers produced the same result. The Western Allies insisted on their demand for an unconditional surrender and were not prepared to revoke their alliance with Stalin. Donovan and Menzies, who would probably both have been open to the idea of an alliance against the Soviets, were brought to heel by their governments. The deciding factors were the wretched state of the German resistance, which had been announcing since 1938 their intention to remove Hitler, as well as the erroneous predictions of the Allied secret services that Hitler's Reich would collapse as early as 1943.

The negative response from the Western Powers forced the conspirators in the Abwehr more and more on to the defensive. If not even the faintest prospect of a separate peace could be held out to the army, no field-marshal would lead his troops in a mutiny against Hitler. The only way out was an attempt on Hitler's life with no real guarantee that it would be followed by a successful *coup d'état*. Yet Oster and Dohnanyi were willing to risk even this step, in conjunction with a group of younger army officers headed by Count von Stauffenberg. Their watchword was the one coined by Henning von Tresckow: the German resistance must strike a blow that at least showed the world they existed. What now followed was a whole series of attempts to assassinate Hitler, which did not yield any result until 20 July 1944. There has been much puzzling over why Hitler remained unscathed for so long. Was it merely due to coincidence, to technical failure, or to Hitler's frequent last-minute changes of plan? Or did the conspirators lack the ultimate resolve? 'The fellow simply had an awful lot of luck', muses one of Stauffenberg's close confidants, Ewald von Kleist, today.

Canaris was personally involved in at least one assassination attempt that went wrong. The two time bombs placed in Hitler's aircraft on 13 March 1943, which failed to explode due to extreme cold, had previously arrived at the HQ of Army Group Centre in the Admiral's luggage. The head of the Abwehr's Division II, Lahousen, later described the events leading up to this attempt. It seems that in February 1943 he had been asked by Oster and Dohnanyi whether Army Group Centre had sufficient explosives with time fuses. 'I replied in the affirmative', says Lahousen. 'Nonetheless, Dr von Dohnanyi suggested supplying the Abwehr II commando with the latest type of explosives and detonators.' Lahousen realised this could only be construed as a pretext. On 7 March he, Canaris and

Dohnanyi flew to Smolensk and 'used the opportunity to take with us a crate of the said explosive materials'. So none other than the Admiral acted as courier for a bomb that was intended for Hitler! Biographers of Canaris have preferred to keep quiet about this episode, because it does not fit too well with the image of a man whose Christian principles are supposed to have led him steadfastly to resist tyrannicide. In fact however, it is highly improbable that Lahousen knew the use the explosives were to be put to, but that his boss did not – particularly since it was in any case highly unusual to carry explosives in an aircraft. Even Lahousen himself had 'the impression that Canaris was aware of the real purpose of the explosives we had with us'.

Soon, however, there was no time left to prepare a new assassination attempt. The Abwehr was in the greatest danger. It had all started with a harmless currency scam, involving Wilhelm Schmidhuber, a Bavarian brewery-owner and Honorary Portuguese Consul. Schmidhuber, who was an officer in the Munich Abwehr and a friend of Dohnanyi, had being making considerable sums on the side through illegal dollar transactions. When the customs investigators got on the trail of his finagling, the ingenious consul came up with the extravagant story that the currency smuggling was in fact an Abwehr operation of the highest importance. In spinning this yarn he gradually got so tangled in contradictions that the affair was brought to the notice of the Gestapo. Canaris and Oster stepped in and despatched him to Italy under the pretext of official business. But the intervention failed. Schmidhuber was arrested by the Carabinieri and handed over to the Gestapo.

In his desperation and convinced that the Abwehr was leaving him to sink or swim, Schmidhuber finally started talking. The brewery-owner told of Müller's Vatican discussions in 1940, of a 'highly treasonable agreement between *Generaloberst* Beck, Goerdeler and others as the leading figures', and of the Abwehr's rescue operations for German Jews, for whom a 'maintenance fund' of $100,000 had been set up in Switzerland. The Gestapo's chief interrogator, named Sonderegger, could not believe his ears. Finally, he had in his hands the evidence against the Abwehr that they had been after for so long. Finally, he had found the source of the intercepted telegrams from Rome, betraying the launch date for the western offensive. There was no doubt, Sonderegger believed, that Canaris' downfall was imminent. But then the Gestapo man received a shock that toppled his whole faith in the internal cohesion of the Third Reich. His report, which he had passed on to his boss, the notorious 'Gestapo-Müller', was returned with a handwritten comment by Himmler himself: 'Just leave old Canaris alone!' Sonderegger had no choice but to see the case being handed over, on the instructions of the *Reichsführer-SS*, to the Wehrmacht's legal department, with the Gestapo only appearing in an auxiliary role, since otherwise there would have been a risk 'that in a case like this Canaris would employ the resources of his department'.

> It is certain that for a long time, for many months indeed, he was still being backed at the very highest level.
>
> *Wilhelm Höttl, SS* Obersturmbannführer
>
> The feeling of security – I might almost say of being protected – never left those who were close to him.
>
> *Paul Leverkuehn, a member of the Abwehr's foreign division*

Was Himmler really acting as Canaris' protector? Indeed, this was not the first instance of Hitler's executioner shielding the Abwehr chief. At least three times already, as Sonderegger reported after the war, the SS chief had vetoed investigations into the Abwehr. As to the real reasons for this, one can only speculate. More than once the *Reichsführer* had cropped up on the periphery of the resistance, and had tried to establish contact with Oster and Dohnanyi. What lay behind this was probably his strategic calculation that Hitler's days were numbered and that the SS needed to keep its options open for the period that would follow. Josef Müller, Dohnanyi's confidant and after the war a minister in the Bavarian state government, gave an account of discussions within the anti-Hitler conspiracy about exploiting Himmler's powerful influence in the plans to overthrow the regime. Another reason may have been the sober realisation that the Abwehr would still have been just too large a chunk for the RSHA to bite off. Leaderless and broken up, Canaris' department would presumably have lost its effectiveness. On top of all this, Himmler probably still had an irrational weakness for a secret service 'pro' like Canaris who, in his personal encounters with the SS chief, had always been capable of arousing his admiration and goodwill. Even at the Nuremberg Trials, the defendant Alfred Jodl kept alluding to what he called 'the exceptional understanding' between Himmler and Canaris.

> I'm actually amazed that they still let the Old Man run around freely.
> *Colonel Piekenbrock, a section head in the Abwehr, to one of his staff*

Yet ultimately not even the protection of the *Reichsführer* could help, for once the proceedings were put in the hands of the Wehrmacht's legal department a man stepped on stage, who would perform his task with the tenacity of a terrier: the senior military prosecutor, *Oberkriegsgerichtsrat* Manfred Roeder. He was well known for being one of the toughest military lawyers in Hitler's Reich. Though not a dyed-in-the-wool Nazi, he was a jurist who knew how to use brute force in enforcing the letter of the law – regardless of whether that law was itself criminal. In March and April 1943 one warning after another was received by the Abwehr's foreign section. On the evening of 4 April, a former Abwehr expert, Reinhard Spitzy, slipped into the offices by a side entrance in order to warn of a move against Canaris, which he had heard about from an old acquaintance in the SD. In the 'fox-earth' of the Abwehr, the only man he could find was Karl Ludwig von Guttenberg, Oster's adviser. Spitzy made him promise to inform the Admiral and his close associates, and 'for God's sake once and for all, get rid of the disastrous collection of documents without delay'. Spitzy, who himself had once worked for Oster, knew that, contrary to his chief's orders, Dohnanyi's incriminating files still existed.

The next morning at 10 a.m. a short, stocky man in a Luftwaffe uniform and a nondescript-looking civilian stood in front of Canaris' desk: they were Roeder and Sonderegger. The military prosecutor announced to the Abwehr chief that he was authorised to arrest Dohnanyi and search his office. Canaris was too overcome to offer any resistance. Instead of playing for time and using his authority to have the investigator thrown out of the building, he stood up and led the way to Oster's room. When he explained to his old friend what the two men wanted, Oster blurted out: 'I must ask you to arrest me at the same time, since Herr von Dohnanyi has done nothing that I don't know about.' Soon afterwards, all four men appeared in Dohnanyi's office. Roeder announced that the Abwehr official was under arrest, and began searching his safe. Oster and Dohnanyi went white. They were not prepared for a lightning strike like this. Had Canaris not said, only a few days before, that there was no danger to fear for the time being? In a panic Oster now tried to save what he could – but to no avail. 'In the course of the investigations', Sonderegger later recalled, 'General Oster made for the desk on which lay the piece of paper mentioned earlier. He tried to pick up the paper behind his back with his left hand, which Dr Roeder and I noticed simultaneously.'

There was no longer any chance of repairing the damage. With one blow the Gestapo had first-class evidence of subversive activities in the Abwehr headquarters: Dohnanyi's files. Dohnanyi himself, his wife, Josef Müller and also the theologian Dietrich Bonhoeffer, who had been promoting the resistance cause abroad, were arrested, and Oster was suspended from duty. Canaris could do nothing more to help his colleagues. Worse, his own position was also in tatters, and it could only be a matter of time before the now alerted spooks would discover his involvement in the plans for a *coup d'état*. If Keitel and Himmler agreed provisionally to let him stay in post, it was only in order to keep the Abwehr machinery running. For the German resistance it was 'the severest blow that fate could ever have delivered', as Hans Bernd Gisevius, one of conspirators, put it. Yet among that circle, bitter regret was accompanied by mounting criticism of the carelessness shown by Oster and Dohnanyi. 'If the "good men" are not as clever as snakes as well as being totally genuine, then nothing can be achieved', Ulrich von Hassell wrote in his diary.

From now on Canaris was obliged to witness his own obliteration. New men were put into many of the Abwehr's top positions. It was obvious that the SS was gearing up for a final takeover of the military secret service. On his last official trips the Admiral seemed like someone saying his goodbyes. In Rome he surprised the Italian secret service chief, Amé, with an unusual request to visit St Peter's once more. 'In a side aisle of the vast cathedral', the Italian recalled, Canaris spoke from the heart. 'He talked about the blood and the tears caused by the merciless Hitler regime, and about the consequences that would now be visited on his Fatherland.' He was equally frank with an army general, Köstring, whom he accompanied on a trip to the Ukraine. The general was utterly taken aback to hear 'with what profound hate and disgust' Canaris had spoken of Hitler.

Soon the Abwehr chief realised that Roeder was now only keeping him superficially informed of the progress of his investigations. It was clear that Canaris himself was under suspicion. Obeying his old instinct for imminent danger, he distanced himself from his former colleagues when attending official interrogations as a witness. At the same time, through discreet channels he kept on sending messages of solidarity to the men now imprisoned at the Gestapo headquarters in Prinz-Albrecht-Strasse. But the time was past when a few words from Canaris could get anyone out of a secret police cell.

He is a typical example of the over-refined, highly intelligent drawing-room conspirator.
Otto Nelte, Keitel's defence lawyer at Nuremberg, on Canaris

By 11 February it was all over. Relatively minor hitches in the work of the Abwehr had provoked another of Hitler's fits of rage. He had 'had enough of Herr Canaris and his whole Abwehr', the dictator fumed. With a few strokes of his pen he transferred the entire department to the *Reichsführer*-SS. At last the Third Reich had the 'super secret-service' that the spooks within the Black Order has always dreamed of. In the gathering twilight of Nazism Himmler was thus closer than ever before to absolute power. 'Well, have you got everything you want now?' Hitler mockingly enquired of Ernst Kaltenbrunner, the Number Two in the SS empire. Keitel and Jodl, the two most senior officers in the Wehrmacht Supreme Command, went to see Canaris to present him with the silver German Cross for 'outstanding services in the military conduct of the war' and to pass on a few cordial words of farewell from Hitler. Then he had to clear his desk. Hitler had given orders that he should be placed in a kind of honorary detention in the Burg Lauenstein castle. With only a little luggage, but with his two dachshunds, Canaris allowed himself to be driven off in a service car in the direction of Upper Franconia. Earlier he had moved his family to a house in Ammersee, deep in Bavaria, where they would be safe from Allied bombing.

To Canaris, his sojourn in the remote Lauenstein castle was like an exile. True, Hitler had not actually had him arrested, which was a good sign. But, cut off from news from Berlin, he could only guess at how close the Gestapo sleuths were to discovering the truth about him. As to the resurrection of the resistance movement in 1944 under Stauffenberg's leadership, Canaris only picked up a few vague pieces of information. The attempt to kill Hitler on 20 July came as a surprise to him; and when he heard that the Führer had survived, he hurriedly despatched a telegram of congratulations to the 'Wolf's Lair'. But the days of deception were over. Only three days later, on 23 July, Canaris was arrested by a member of the dictator's vengeance squad. It was one of his erstwhile riding companions, SD chief Walter Schellenberg, who came in person to fetch him. Schellenberg recounted later that he told his old rival he would give him an hour. 'During that time', the SS man claims to have said, 'you can do whatever you want.' But Canaris replied: 'No, Schellenberg. For me, escaping is out of the question; and I won't kill myself either. I am certain of my cause.' Then he went off to change and came back with a small travelling-bag – and with tears in his eyes.

For Canaris, the last stage of his life was beginning. Despite the use of unparalleled brutality, the head of the investigation, Walter Huppenkothen, only gradually succeeded in shedding light on the conspiracy. The Abwehr chief himself proved the hardest nut to crack. Once more the old enthusiasm for shadow-boxing flared up. No matter how much his gaolers harassed him, whether they used a bright light to keep him awake all night long, or made him scrub the prison corridors – the Admiral maintained a sphinx-like inscrutability. On Oster's plans he is on record as saying that 'in all those matters I never imagined they could be serious considerations. I was never in doubt that any change of government during the war would be seen as a stab in the back and would shatter internal solidarity.' The documents discovered in Dohnanyi's filing cabinet were, as far as he was concerned, no more than material for secret-service 'game-playing'. With the ex-chief of the Abwehr making statements like that, the case against him would not stand up in court. Thanks to this lack of evidence he remained spared from prosecution before the People's Court.

On 3 February 1945 a heavy American air raid on Berlin hit the SS prison in Prinz-Albrecht-Strasse. Among other things, parts of the cell-wing were destroyed. Müller, the Gestapo boss, immediately ordered the transfer of his prominent prisoner to a region that was safe from bombs. This gave Canaris new hope: if the SS were now sparing him from the danger of air raids, then obviously they wanted to keep him alive, perhaps as a bargaining-counter in negotiations with the victorious Allies. The prisoners were taken to Flossenbürg concentration camp. There, Canaris was allowed to wear a light-coloured suit instead of prison garb. His neighbour in the next-door cell, a Danish secret-service officer named Hans Lunding, became the chronicler of the Admiral's final days. By tapping out signals he exchanged information with Canaris. At first the signals from Cell 22 sounded optimistic, since the inmates of Flossenbürg were well aware of the approach of the Allied armies.

But then disaster struck. Early in April 1945, in a deep bunker at the Zossen army headquarters, south of Berlin, officers came across a safe containing some unusual documents. They were volumes of the legendary Canaris diaries. A short time later the SS vice-chief, Kaltenbrunner, was standing in front of Hitler and pointing out to him passages marked in the notes of the erstwhile Abwehr chief. In a moment the dictator pictured the whole scenario. In the fantasy world of his bunker under the Reich Chancellery in Berlin, he imagined a vast plot against him and against Germany's ultimate victory. Beside himself with fury he ordered the 'liquidation of the conspirators'.

On 8 April, just one month before the German surrender, a court martial assembled in the commandant's office at Flossenbürg camp. Its task was to carry out the murder ordered by Hitler, under a threadbare cloak of legality. The presiding judge was an SS man named Otto Thorbeck, the prosecutor was Huppenkothen, who had headed the investigation. At 8 o'clock in the evening, Canaris was led before this 'court', to which even the laws of the illegal Nazi regime no longer gave any credence. Yet even when faced with the certainty of a guilty verdict, he would not give up. Huppenkothen described later how Canaris had 'talked every one of the prosecution's points to a standstill, in order to save his neck. We had a lot of trouble with him.' But then Thorbeck called for Oster, who had already been sentenced to death. Canaris' old friend argued passionately that of course his boss had been involved in the plans to overthrow the regime; they had, after all, acted jointly. The Admiral remained obdurate: 'You know very well it was all a pretence on my part'. Oster: 'No, that's not true. I can only state what I know. I'm not a crook.' When the judge asked Canaris once more whether the charges against him were unjust, he replied with a quiet 'No'.

It was his final confession to being a member of the resistance. Since his appointment as head of the secret service he had avoided ever having to commit himself. Now he did so and finally helped himself achieve redemption. He had attempted to play both sides against the middle, and had thus become hopelessly caught up between obedience and morality, between patriotism and humanity. Serving both good and evil simultaneously – this was the trap in which Canaris destroyed himself. Without his help many people would not have been rescued; under his orders far too many died.

What alternatives might have been open to him? More heroic courage, such as his friend Oster possessed, would have meant an earlier end. Then even less time would have remained for the luckless resisters as well as for the courageous rescuers. Canaris remained stubbornly in his job, even at the cost of bending morality beyond all limits. He and many other conservatives from the Kaiser's era considered they were serving the Fatherland, rather than aiding Hitler. To the very end he held on to this mistaken belief.

The sentence was death by hanging. That night Lunding, the Dane in the next-door cell, heard another message tapped out by Canaris: 'Nose broken in the last interrogation. . . . Was not a traitor. Did my duty as a German. If you survive, give my love to my wife.' In the grey dawn of the following day the sentences were carried out on Canaris, Oster, Bonhoeffer and two other victims. Hans von Dohnanyi had already been murdered in Sachsenhausen concentration camp. A few days later US troops rolled into Flossenbürg.

> It was noticeable how unusually long those executions took. As far as I could make out, in terms of time, only Canaris and Oster were executed in this horrible, protracted manner – by strangulation, in fact. The next ones were hanged in the normal way. That's to say, it may have taken eight to ten minutes.
>
> *Jörgen Mogensen, prisoner in Flossenbürg*
>
> With the little admiral it took a very long time – he was hauled up and down several times.
>
> *Statement by a witness to the executions*

In 1956 the Federal German Supreme Court declared the Flossenbürg verdicts to be within the law. Thorbeck was acquitted. Huppenkothen only received a six-year prison sentence, because he had failed to have the executions confirmed by the court. Not until 1996 did the Provincial Court of Berlin rehabilitate the victims of 9 April 1945 and officially quash the verdicts of the SS judge Thorbeck.

Index

Note: major entries are in chronological order, where appropriate.